A·N·N·U·A·L E·D·I

Teaching English as a Second Language

99/00

Second Edition

EDITORS

Inez Avalos Heath, Ph.D.
Valdosta State University

Dr. Inez Avalos Heath is an associate professor in social science and multicultural education at Valdosta State University in Valdosta, Georgia. She received her Ph.D. in Curriculum and Instruction in Multilingual and Multicultural Education from Florida State University. She has been a bilingual and ESL resource teacher in the elementary and middle grades. As a Master Trainer and member of the State of Florida Multicultural Advisory Board, she helped to develop and implement the ESL multicultural curriculum. She has been an ESL consultant in New York, Boston, California, Florida, and the southeast. In addition to teaching graduate and undergraduate courses, she has published several articles that focus on integrating technology in the social studies to enhance language development.

Cheryl J. Serrano, Ph.D.
Lynn University

Dr. Cheryl Serrano, associate professor and assistant to the dean of the College of Education at Lynn University in Boca Raton, Florida, earned her B.S. degree in Secondary Spanish Education from the University of Wisconsin-LaCrosse, an M.A. in Curriculum and Instruction with major concentration in Bilingual-Bicultural Education at the University of Northern Colorado, and was awarded a Ph.D. from Florida State University in Multilingual-Multicultural Education. As a training associate at the Multifuntional Resource Center, she served on the TESOL Advisory Board for the Florida Department of Education in the development of ESOL teacher training curricula, Training of Trainers Institutes, and a distance learning course.

Dushkin/McGraw-Hill
Sluice Dock, Guilford, Connecticut 06437

Visit us on the Internet
http://www.dushkin.com/annualeditions/

Credits

1. Introduction: The Process of Acquiring English as a Second Language for School
Facing overview—© 1998 by PhotoDisc, Inc.
2. The Sociocultural Aspects of Acquiring a Second Language
Facing overview—© 1998 by Cleo Photography.
3. Literacy: A Critical Factor for Developing English Language and Academic Skills
Facing overview—Suzanne DeChillo/New York Times Pictures
4. The Integrative Classroom: Organizing Instruction to Enhance the Acquisition of Language and Content
Facing overview—© 1998 by PhotoDisc, Inc.
5. Assessment Issues and Practices
Facing overview—Dushkin/McGraw-Hill photo.
6. Building Partnerships with Linguistically Diverse Families, Schools, and Communities
Facing overview—© 1998 by PhotoDisc, Inc.
7. Exemplary Program Models for Linguistically and Culturally Diverse Students
Facing overview—© 1998 by Cleo Photography.
8. Special Topics Affecting English-Language Learners
Facing overview—© by PhotoDisc, Inc.

Cataloging in Publication Data
Main entry under title: Annual Editions: Teaching English as a second language. 1999/2000.
    1. English language—Study and teaching—Foreign students. I. Heath, Inez Avalos; *comp.*
II. Serrano, Cheryl J., *comp.* III. Title: Teaching English as a second language.
ISBN 0-07-033140-5   657'.05   ISSN 1096-4266

Second Edition

Cover image © 1999 PhotoDisc, Inc.

Printed in the United States of America.   1234567890BAHBAH54321098   Printed on Recycled Paper

Copyright

In publishing ANNUAL EDITIONS we recognize the enormous role played by the magazines, newspapers, and journals of the public press in providing current, first-rate educational information in a broad spectrum of interest areas. Many of these articles are appropriate for students, researchers, and professionals seeking accurate, current material to help bridge the gap between principles and theories and the real world. These articles, however, become more useful for study when those of lasting value are carefully collected, organized, indexed, and reproduced in a low-cost format, which provides easy and permanent access when the material is needed. That is the role played by ANNUAL EDITIONS.

New to ANNUAL EDITIONS is the inclusion of related World Wide Web sites. These sites have been selected by our editorial staff to represent some of the best resources found on the World Wide Web today. Through our carefully developed topic guide, we have linked these Web resources to the articles covered in this ANNUAL EDITIONS reader. We think that you will find this volume useful, and we hope that you will take a moment to visit us on the Web at *http://www.dushkin.com* to tell us what you think.

The continuous increases in English-language learners entering our nation's public schools over the past two decades has placed a tremendous strain on our educational system. Educators at all levels have been challenged to develop and implement a variety of new and different approaches to address the many and complex problems that have become evident.

Efforts to integrate strategies that effectively teach English as a second language (ESL) across the curriculum have been compounded by the fact that many ESL students are lacking in linguistic/literacy skills in their native language and also have limited academic preparation as well. Additionally, the diversity of sociocultural variables among many of these ethnolinguistic groups has contributed to difficulties in school.

The response to these challenges in education over the past 20 years has led to rigorous research in the field of applied linguistics, which has provided new understanding on how to deal with the complex experience of acquiring a second language. Such insights have also led to closer collaboration between educators and researchers in the process of assessing program models, such as two-way bilingual and ESL pull-out programs, and working to develop more effective strategies to deal with these students' unique needs.

Awareness of the important correlation between linguistic proficiency in the second language and cognitive academic development, which is essential for success in the school, has also prompted a move to emphasize ESL strategies in teacher education programs. This relationship has many implications, especially as we consider America's transition to an information society. The changing demands of the workplace and global accessibility will require highly literate individuals who can process and organize large amounts of information within a multicultural environment. The need to prepare teachers who have the pedagogical knowledge to teach oral and written communication skills effectively across disciplines, regardless of their students' native linguistic origins, will also be reflected in the curriculum.

The articles selected for *Annual Editions: Teaching English as a Second Language 99/00* present various perspectives on research, theory, sociocultural issues, pedagogical practices, school and program reform, and language policy concerns. The eight units complement ESL courses in methods, curriculum and materials development, applied linguistics, cross-cultural communication, and assessment. The perspectives presented in the articles are intended to provide interesting information that is meaningful and relevant for pre- and inservice teachers, grades PK–12, as well as for other professionals who are involved in working with ESL students and their families.

It is our hope that this volume of *Annual Editions: Teaching English as a Second Language 99/00* will stimulate interest in this complex and fascinating field. As we move toward global economic interdependence, increasing debate regarding linguistic and cultural diversity policies and educational program reforms seems inevitable. Subsequently, the growing demand for teachers who can address the more complex issues related to teaching English as a second language in various contexts will also become apparent.

We are especially grateful to the members of our Advisory Board. Their support and interest in this project as evidenced by their promptness in providing constructive comments, as well as their expert recommendations in the development of this year's edition, has been invaluable. We appreciate their efforts in providing additional articles to expand the scope of this publication. They share our vision of developing a resource that can be used to enhance knowledge and understanding of the issues involved in working with ESL students.

We hope that you, the reader, will take the time to provide input regarding the article selection and to recommend other articles that you feel would be appropriate for the next edition. Please use the postage-paid article review form found at the end of the book for your comments.

Inez A. Health, Ph.D.

Cheryl Serrano, Ph.D.
Editors

Contents

To the Reader   iv
Topic Guide   2
◎ Selected World Wide Web Sites   4

Overview   6

1. **Bilingual Education and the Politics of Teacher**   8
Preparation, Hermán S. García, *Cultural Circles*, Spring
1998.
Hermán García addresses **the preparation of bilingual education teachers** and the critical issues related to the traditional
educational philosophy underlying the approach to preservice training that is implemented in most universities. As a result, educators
remain socially and intellectually unengaged. He provides an important rationale for considering a change in teacher education
programs that would result in school improvement for both teachers
and students in multilingual classrooms.

2. **Acquiring a Second Language for School,** Virginia   16
P. Collier, *Directions in Language & Education*, Fall 1995.
Virginia Collier presents a conceptual model that explores the length
of time needed for students learning English to compete with native
speakers in academic areas. This model attempts to explain the
complex interactions that ESL (English as a Second Language) students experience while **acquiring English for school.**

3. **NAEYC Position Statement: Responding to Lin-**   22
guistic and Cultural Diversity—Recommendations
for Effective Early Childhood Education, *Young Children*, January 1996.
The goal of this position statement by the **National Association
for the Education of Young Children** is to build support for
equal access to high-quality educational programs that promote
children's development and learning regardless of **linguistic and
cultural background.** The paper provides recommendations for
involving parents in the learning process, teacher preparation, and
effective programs and practices.

4. **Factors Affecting Language Development from**   30
the Perspectives of Four Bilingual Teachers,
Nancy Lemberger, *The Journal of Educational Issues of Language Minority Students*, Winter 1996.
Nancy Lemberger describes the classroom practices that four primary bilingual education teachers implement in order to develop
language and academic skills in English and Spanish. In addition
to the internal factors affecting **dual language development,**
she shares the external factors inhibiting the process.

UNIT 1

Introduction: The Process of Acquiring English as a Second Language for School

Four articles discuss current thinking
on second language acquisition,
emphasizing the work of leading
educators, researchers, and linguists
who have influenced the field
of second language teaching.

The concepts in bold italics are developed in the article. For further expansion please refer to the Topic Guide and the Index.

UNIT 2

The Sociocultural Aspects of Acquiring a Second Language

Four articles consider the important connection between sociocultural status and success in the classroom. The articles focus on Hispanics, Asians, and Native Americans living in the United States and the problems, due to cultural differences, that affect these students' relationships with family and peers, as well as their performance in school.

UNIT 3

Literacy: A Critical Factor for Developing English Language and Academic Skills

Five articles address the importance of developing literacy as integral to the process of second language acquisition. Various ways to enhance literacy development in the classroom are examined.

Overview   **38**

5. The Disappearance of American Indian Languages, Barbara J. Boseker, *Journal of Multilingual and Multicultural Development,* Volume 15, Numbers 2 & 3, 1994.   **40**

Barbara Boseker reports on the tragic loss of two-thirds (100) of the Native American languages and the near extinction of the remaining third. She raises the educational implications for Native American children and provides a linguistic and *sociocultural rationale for supporting the preservation* and protection of their languages.

6. Between Two Worlds: Refugee Youth, Donald A. Ranard, *In America: Perspectives on Refugee Resettlement,* January 1989.   **48**

This article describes a study of the array of difficulties that Asian students encounter when enrolled in U.S. schools. Donald Ranard discusses the underlying causes for the problems and successes that were found to distinguish different ethnic groups. A key finding, he reports, is the link between *cultural values and academic performance.*

7. An Indian Father's Plea, Robert Lake, *Literacy Harvest,* Winter 1993.   **53**

Robert Lake shares a refreshing perspective from a Native American father in a letter to his son's classroom teacher. His letter establishes support for developing a *culturally sensitive learning environment* for all children whose language, literacy, and socialization practices are distinct from the mainstream.

8. Mexican Immigrants from El Rincón: A Case Study of Resilience and Empowerment, Enrique (Henry) T. Trueba, *TESOL Journal,* Spring 1998.   **56**

Enrique Trueba offers a brief description of the lifestyle of Mexican migrant workers and their strong educational commitment for their children. Included in this article are three very moving perspectives from former migrant students who share their stories of true empowerment. Trueba makes recommendations for *developing appropriate pedagogies* to meet the educational needs of Spanish-speaking immigrant children.

Overview   **62**

9. Reading and Writing Pathways to Conversation in the ESL Classroom, Gisela Ernst and Kerri J. Richard, *The Reading Teacher,* December 1994/January 1995.   **64**

The authors provide a rich description of an elementary ESL (English as a Second Language) teacher's *integrated language classroom,* composed of students from numerous linguistic backgrounds. The philosophy supported by applied linguistics and *literacy development* is evident in the physical design of the classroom and the recommended strategies for engaging ESL students in language activities.

10. Buddy Journals for ESL and Native-English-Speaking Students, Karen Bromley, *TESOL Journal,* Spring 1995.   **71**

The buddy journal, as described by Karen Bromley, is a diary in which two students write to each other over an extended period of time. Bromley offers a sound rationale for establishing a writing program that includes ESL students and native English speakers. She shares specific guidelines for implementation, authentic journal entries, and a description of a *cross-cultural* friendship that evolved.

The concepts in bold italics are developed in the article. For further expansion please refer to the Topic Guide and the Index.

11. **Entering the Fictive World: Enhancing the Reading Experience,** Karen L. Ogulnick, Sharon Shelton-
Colangelo, and Cheryl N. Williams, Cultural Circles, Summer 1998.
The authors discuss an approach called hotseating, which enriches
the literacy experiences for *second language learners* by making reading a more active, interactive, and empowering experience. This approach, which combines reading and drama, asks a
participant to take on the role of a character in a text and to
respond to questions as that character. The implications for ESOL
students are shared.

76

12. **Literacy Instruction for Students Acquiring English: Moving beyond the Immersion Debate,**
James Flood, Diane Lapp, Josefina Villamil Tinajero, and
Sandra Rollins Hurley, *The Reading Teacher,* December
1996/January 1997.
The authors provide a review and discussion of *the myths related to second language education.* They also include recommendations related to program, methods, materials, and parental
involvement for students who are acquiring language and literacy
skills in English in order to participate fully, in school and out.

81

13. **Multicultural Children's Literature: Canon of the
Future,** Suzanne S. Monroe, *Language Arts Journal of
Michigan,* Spring 1996.
Suzanne Monroe considers exploring children's literature through
their culture by using a variety of *approaches* that include *genre,
theme,* and author-illustrator studies. She emphasizes the importance of integrating students' culture through literature not only on
special holidays but throughout the year.

84

Overview

90

14. **Effective Math and Science Instruction—The Project Approach for LEP Students,** Joseph Vigil, *IDRA
Newsletter,* March 1998.
This article presents *strategies for enhancing language
learning in math and science* through a hands-on "project
approach" that can motivate all students to communicate, using
math and science language, with the goal of producing a final
product.

92

15. **Below the Tip of the Iceberg: Teaching Language-
Minority Students,** Vivian Fueyo, *Teaching Exceptional
Children,* September/October 1997.
Language-minority students are often diagnosed as having speech
and language disabilities that can be attributed to lack of cognitive
academic language instruction. In this article the "tip of the iceberg"
represents the superficial approach taken by many teachers *working with language minority* students, often disregarding the
importance of developing critical-thinking skills and cognitive academic language.

94

UNIT 4

The Integrative Classroom: Organizing Instruction to Enhance the Acquisition of Language and Content

Five articles review strategies that
are especially effective in the
English as a second language
(ESL) classroom. Whole
language, content-based ESL
instruction, learning styles, and
cooperative learning are
highlighted in this section.

16. **Learning Strategy Instruction in the Bilingual/ESL Classroom,** Robin Stergis and Jeanne Perrin, *NABE News*, March 15, 1997.   **99**

Learning-strategy instruction is especially effective with language learners at the middle- and high-school level. This article provides a sampling of activities and effective strategies that have been used with Haitian and Vietnamese students to promote *metacognitive, cognitive, and social-affective development.*

17. **Teaching and Learning Languages through Multiple Intelligences,** Mary Ann Christison, *TESOL Journal*, Autumn 1996.   **103**

Mary Ann Christison presents a paradigm shift in the ESL community that includes an increased recognition of the diversity of learners and the enormous *range of human skills and capacities* as illuminated in Howard Gardner's theory of multiple intelligences. Christison analyzes classroom activities and the kinds of intelligences they promote, and she discusses using this theory in problem-solving activities.

18. **The Social Studies Video Project: A Holistic Approach for Teaching Linguistically and Culturally Diverse Students,** Inez A. Heath, *The Social Studies*, May/June 1996.   **108**

Inez Heath presents a video project in social studies that uses *technology in a student-centered* and focused *manner* while developing interpersonal and linguistic proficiency among English-language learners. Heath includes a survey of student responses to the video project.

Overview   **114**

19. **Alternative Assessment: Responses to Commonly Asked Questions,** Ana Huerta-Macías, *TESOL Journal*, Autumn 1995.   **116**

Ana Huerta-Macías discusses *the value of alternative assessment with language learners.* Contrary to traditional assessment practices, which are based on discrete points of knowledge, alternative assessment has the "power to tell a story" about the learner. Through alternative assessment, teachers can reflect and discuss their students' development on a more holistic level, which includes language acquisition within the context of academic content.

20. **Moving toward Authentic Assessment,** J. Michael O'Malley and Lorraine Valdez Pierce, from *Authentic Assessment for English Language Learners: Practical Approaches for Teachers*, Addison–Wesley Publishing Company, 1996.   **119**

This article concerns the attempt to provide *alternative assessment* that more closely resembles instructional activities in classrooms. The authors review the purposes of assessment, which include screening and identification, placement, reclassification or exit, monitoring student progress, program evaluation, and accountability.

UNIT 5

Assessment Issues and Practices

Various issues related to the assessment of limited English proficient (LEP) students are addressed in this unit. Authentic assessment, portfolios at the elementary and secondary level, and assessing integrated language and content instruction are reviewed.

The concepts in bold italics are developed in the article. For further expansion please refer to the Topic Guide and the Index.

21. **Portfolio Assessment in Second Language Teacher Education,** Karen E. Johnson, *TESOL Journal,* Winter 1996.   125

Three critical components of **portfolio design and development** in second language teacher education are discussed in this article. These are: the purposes of portfolio assessment, the evidence gathered, and the assessment criteria. Karen Johnson provides examples.

22. **Assessing Integrated Language and Content Instruction,** Deborah J. Short, *TESOL Quarterly,* Winter 1993.   129

Deborah Short discusses the difficulty of isolating language features from content objectives. She provides a framework for organizing assessment objectives, with recommendations for using **checklist, portfolios, interviews, and performance-based tasks** in the assessment process.

Overview   142

23. **Low Income Does Not Cause Low School Achievement: Creating a Sense of Family and Respect in the School Environment,** Anita Tijerina Revilla and Yvette De La Gorza Sweeney, *IDRA Newsletter,* June/July 1997.   144

In this article, three studies highlighting five major factors that contribute to success for students are summarized. The research discussed in this article helps to dispel **the myth that low income equals low academic achievement.**

24. **Parents as First Teachers: Creating an Enriched Home Learning Environment,** Abelardo Villarreal, *NABE News,* February 1, 1996.   148

The role of the parent as a child's first teacher is emphasized by Abelardo Villarreal, along with recommendations and examples of strategies for early childhood personnel to provide meaningful workshops for parents of 3- to 5-year-olds whose native language is not English.

25. **The Education of Hispanics in Early Childhood: Of Roots and Wings,** Eugene E. Garcia, *Young Children,* March 1997.   153

Eugene Garcia addresses early childhood education from three personal perspectives: Eugene is the intellectual and scholar; Gene is the citizen, involved in the daily challenges of the community at large; and Gino is associated with **cultural values and beliefs** that tie the author to his youth and family.

26. **Attending to New Voices,** Chris Liska Carger, *Educational Leadership,* April 1997.   163

Using a case-study approach, Chris Carger visited homes to observe Mexican American families. Her findings support the need for involving families in their children's education, especially in the early years, and the importance of understanding diverse **cultural values.**

UNIT 6

Building Partnerships with Linguistically Diverse Families, Schools, and Communities

Four selections consider the importance of the family, the home language, and cultural attitudes and perceptions as critical factors contributing to the child's overall success in the academic setting.

UNIT 7

Exemplary Program Models for Linguistically and Culturally Diverse Students

Four selections review current public educational program reforms (K–12) that examine the needs of culturally and linguistically diverse students. Support for programs such as two-way bilingual, which place value on the student's native language and culture based on long-term research, is especially evident throughout the articles.

Overview   **168**

27. Language-Minority Student Achievement and Program Effectiveness, Wayne P. Thomas and Virginia P. Collier, *NABE News,* May 1, 1996.   **170**
The authors' 12-year longitudinal study examines the **length of time needed for academic success in a second language.** Three areas identified for success are cognitive complexity in instruction in students' native language, encouraging higher-level thinking in both languages, and changes in the sociocultural context of schooling.

28. Two Languages Are Better than One, Wayne P. Thomas and Virginia P. Collier, *Educational Leadership,* December 1997/January 1998.   **173**
Wayne Thomas and Virginia Collier discuss the **two-way bilingual language model,** emphasizing its value as a cost-effective method of teaching that leads to high academic achievement for all students involved. Citing Berliner and Biddle's 1995 predictions of a 40 percent linguistically diverse student population by 2030, they emphasize that it is in our pragmatic self-interest to ensure that these students are successful, realizing their value in helping to maintain a robust economy for the future.

29. School Reform and Student Diversity, Catherine Minicucci et al., *Phi Delta Kappan,* September 1995.   **177**
The authors present **exemplary models** in which students with limited English proficiency learn the same curriculum in language arts, science, and math as native English speakers, while also becoming literate in the second language. The importance of national reforms that address the needs of minority-language students is emphasized.

30. A Gradual Exit, Variable Threshold Model for Limited English Proficient Children, Stephen Krashen, *NABE News,* June 15, 1996.   **181**
Stephen Krashen discusses the "input hypothesis," which states that we acquire language when we understand it. The author stresses the importance of developing **comprehensible input** in the native language, which will **transfer** to the second language.

The concepts in bold italics are developed in the article. For further expansion please refer to the Topic Guide and the Index.

Overview   **186**

31. Cruising the Web with English Language Learners, Laura Chris Green, *IDRA Newsletter*, May 1997.   **188**
Laura Green presents several descriptions of how she uses technology, specifically, the **World Wide Web, to introduce or enhance units** of instruction that are especially appropriate for the ESL student at the elementary level.

32. Confronting an Embarrassment of Riches: Internet Search Tools, Dennis Sayers, *NABE News*, February 1, 1997.   **193**
An overview of Internet tools and resources that are especially useful for second language and bilingual education teachers and students is presented. As coauthor of *Brave New Schools* with Jim Commins, Dennis Sayers reflects on technology and the vastness of the Internet, calling it **"a very special library."**

33. The Case for Bilingual Education, Stephen D. Krashen, from *Under Attack: The Case against Bilingual Education*, Language Education Associates, 1996.   **196**
Developing subject matter knowledge using the language most familiar to the learner enhances the transition from first language to second. Stephen Krashen presents real-world examples of the language-transfer process that results in the **acquisition of the second language.**

34. What's New in Ebonics? Jacqueline Brice-Finch, A. Duku Anokye, and Bob Reising, *The Clearing House*, May/June 1997.   **199**
The authors provide their **perspectives on dialect and language policy in America.** Brice-Finch introduces the idea of International English versus Standard English. A. Duku Anokye presents a case for teachers to adopt strategies that maintain African American learning. Bob Reising proposes a three-language national policy on language.

35. Beyond Adversarial Discourse: Searching for Common Ground in the Education of Bilingual Students, Jim Cummins, *Dushkin/McGraw-Hill*, 1998.   **204**
In an address that was to be presented to the California Board of Education, Jim Cummins elaborates on misconceptions and distortions used to interpret **the research that supports bilingual education.** He points to these misleading reviews as politically motivated and used to influence educational policies that neglect the educational and linguistic needs of language-minority students, who in many areas constitute the majority student population.

Index   **225**
Article Review Form   **228**
Article Rating Form   **229**

UNIT 8

Special Topics Affecting English-Language Learners

Current issues that relate to the teaching of English as a second language are addressed in this section. Topics include effective use of technology, problems in identifying gifted and talented limited-English-proficient (LEP) students, and language policy concerns that are related to effective program models and dialect issues.

This topic guide suggests how the selections and World Wide Web sites found in the next section of this book relate to topics of traditional concern to teaching English as a second language students and professionals. It is useful for locating interrelated articles and Web sites for reading and research. The guide is arranged alphabetically according to topic.

The relevant Web sites, which are numbered and annotated on pages 4 and 5, are easily identified by the Web icon (◉) under the topic articles. By linking the articles and the Web sites by topic, this ANNUAL EDITIONS reader becomes a powerful learning and research tool.

TOPIC AREA	TREATED IN	TOPIC AREA	TREATED IN
Asian Students	3. NAEYC Position Statement 4. Factors Affecting Language Development from the Perspectives of Four Bilingual Teachers 6. Between Two Worlds: Refugee Youth 10. Buddy Journals for ESL and Native-English-Speaking Students 19. Alternative Assessment 27. Language-Minority Student Achievement and Program Effectiveness 29. School Reform and Student Diversity ◉ *4, 7, 8, 14, 15, 20, 30, 33, 35, 36*	**Dialects/ Vernacular English**	17. Teaching and Learning Languages through Multiple Intelligences 34. What's New in Ebonics? ◉ *6, 15, 16, 20, 30*
		Early Childhood/ Elementary Education	3. NAEYC Position Statement 23. Low Income Does Not Cause Low School Achievement 25. Education of Hispanics in Early Childhood 26. Attending to New Voices 29. School Reform and Student Diversity 30. Gradual Exit, Variable Threshold Model for Limited English Proficient Children ◉ *3, 7, 8, 9, 11, 12, 26, 28, 29, 31, 32, 33*
Assessment	19. Alternative Assessment 20. Moving toward Authentic Assessment 21. Portfolio Assessment in Second Language Teacher Education 22. Assessing Integrated Language and Content Instruction 24. Parents as First Teachers 25. Education of Hispanics in Early Childhood 26. Attending to New Voices ◉ *23, 24, 25, 34*		
		Exceptionality, Gifted and Talented	15. Below the Tip of the Iceberg: Teaching Language-Minority Students
Bilingual Education	1. Bilingual Education and the Politics of Teacher Preparation 2. Acquiring a Second Language for School 4. Factors Affecting Language Development from the Perspectives of Four Bilingual Teachers 16. Learning Strategy Instruction in the Bilingual/ESL Classroom 19. Alternative Assessment 28. Two Languages Are Better than One 33. Case for Bilingual Education 35. Beyond Adversarial Discourse ◉ *4, 6, 7, 18, 20, 21, 29, 33, 35*	**Family Issues**	3. NAEYC Position Statement 7. Indian Father's Plea 8. Mexican Immigrants from El Rincón 23. Low Income Does Not Cause Low School Achievement 24. Parents as First Teachers 26. Attending to New Voices 27. Language-Minority Student Achievement and Program Effectiveness 29. School Reform and Student Diversity ◉ *2, 3, 9, 11, 12, 13, 14, 26*
		Hispanics	1. Bilingual Education and the Politics of Teacher Preparation 7. Indian Father's Plea 8. Mexican Immigrants from El Rincón 15. Below the Tip of the Iceberg: Teaching Language-Minority Students 23. Low Income Does Not Cause Low School Achievement ◉ *9, 11, 31, 34*
Culture and Language	4. Factors Affecting Language Development from the Perspectives of Four Bilingual Teachers 6. Between Two Worlds: Refugee Youth 8. Mexican Immigrants from El Rincón 13. Multicultural Children's Literature 27. Language-Minority Student Achievement and Program Effectiveness ◉ *5, 9, 11, 14, 15, 16, 17, 29, 30, 31, 33*	**Immigrants**	6. Between Two Worlds: Refugee Youth 8. Mexican Immigrants from El Rincón 12. Literacy Instruction for Students Acquiring English 13. Multicultural Children's Literature 28. Two Languages Are Better than One ◉ *11, 14, 17, 31, 34*

TOPIC AREA	TREATED IN	TOPIC AREA	TREATED IN
Integrating Content in ESL	14. Effective Math and Science Instruction 22. Assessing Integrated Language and Content Instruction ○ *4, 8, 18, 19, 20, 21*	**Program Models**	1. Bilingual Education and the Politics of Teacher Preparation 2. Acquiring a Second Language for School 12. Literacy Instruction for Students Acquiring English 19. Alternative Assessment 28. Two Languages Are Better than One 35. Beyond Adversarial Discourse ○ *5, 7, 8, 17, 23, 24, 25, 28, 32*
Language Acquisition Theory	17. Teaching and Learning Languages through Multiple Intelligences 19. Alternative Assessment 20. Moving toward Authentic Assessment 30. Gradual Exit, Variable Threshold Model for Limited English Proficient Children ○ *6, 17, 23, 24, 25*	**Program Reforms**	1. Bilingual Education and the Politics of Teacher Preparation 28. Two Languages Are Better than One 35. Beyond Adversarial Discourse ○ *5, 7, 28, 32*
Language Immersion Models	1. Bilingual Education and the Politics of Teacher Preparation 12. Literacy Instruction for Students Acquiring English 35. Beyond Adversarial Discourse ○ *4, 7, 17, 18, 29*	**Second Language Acquisition**	1. Bilingual Education and the Politics of Teacher Preparation 4. Factors Affecting Language Development from the Perspectives of Four Bilingual Teachers 20. Moving toward Authentic Assessment 21. Portfolio Assessment in Second Language Teacher Education ○ *5, 7, 23, 24, 25*
Literacy	9. Reading and Writing Pathways to Conversation in the ESL Classroom 10. Buddy Journals for ESL and Native-English-Speaking Students 11. Entering the Fictive World: Enhancing the Reading Experience 12. Literacy Instruction for Students Acquiring English 13. Multicultural Children's Literature 15. Below the Tip of the Iceberg: Teaching Language-Minority Students 20. Moving toward Authentic Assessment 34. What's New in Ebonics? ○ *15, 16, 17, 18, 23, 24, 25*	**Social Skills in ESL**	9. Reading and Writing Pathways to Conversation in the ESL Classroom ○ *15, 16, 20*
Middle and Secondary Language Learners	11. Entering the Fictive World: Enhancing the Reading Experience ○ *9, 10, 16, 18, 22*	**Teaching Methods and Strategies**	4. Factors Affecting Language Development from the Perspectives of Four Bilingual Teachers 7. Indian Father's Plea 9. Reading and Writing Pathways to Conversation in the ESL Classroom 10. Buddy Journals for ESL and Native-English-Speaking Students 11. Entering the Fictive World: Enhancing the Reading Experience 12. Literacy Instruction for Students Acquiring English 14. Effective Math and Science Instruction 20. Moving toward Authentic Assessment ○ *1, 3, 8, 9, 10, 12, 13, 14, 16, 17, 18, 21, 23, 24, 25*
Migrant Students	8. Mexican Immigrants from El Rincón ○ *11, 12, 31, 34*		
Multiple Intelligence	17. Teaching and Learning Languages through Multiple Intelligences ○ *6, 15, 16, 20, 30*		
Native Americans	5. Disappearance of American Indian Languages 7. Indian Father's Plea ○ *11, 12, 13*	**Technology**	18. Social Studies Video Project 21. Portfolio Assessment in Second Language Teacher Education 31. Cruising the Web with English Language Learners 32. Confronting an Embarrassment of Riches: Internet Search Tools ○ *15, 18, 19, 22, 26*
Over-Age Language Learners	16. Learning Strategy Instruction in the Bilingual/ESL Classroom ○ *4, 7*		

3

● AE: Teaching English as a Second Language

The following World Wide Web sites have been carefully researched and selected to support the articles found in this reader. If you are interested in learning more about specific topics found in this book, these Web sites are a good place to start. The sites are cross-referenced by number and appear in the topic guide on the previous two pages. Also, you can link to these Web sites through our DUSHKIN ONLINE support site at *http://www.dushkin.com/online/.*

The following sites were available at the time of publication. Visit our Web site—we update DUSHKIN ONLINE regularly to reflect any changes.

General Sites

1. Educational Resources Information Center
http://www.accesseric.org:81/
Links to all ERIC sites: clearinghouses, support components, publishers of ERIC material.

2. National Regional Educational Laboratories
http://www.nwrel.org/national/
The Regional Educational Laboratories are organizations across the country that provide research on resources for education.

3. Teachers Guide to the Department of Education
http://www.ed.gov/pubs/TeachersGuide/
Government goals, projects, grants, and educational programs and links to services and resources are listed here.

Introduction

4. Bilingual ESL Network (BEN)
http://www.redmundial.com/ben.htm
Dedicated to building a global community of bilingual/ESL educators, BEN has created school sites and hyperlinks to existing Web pages. Click on the bar at the bottom of the page for school sites, news, and more.

5. Center for Applied Linguistics
http://www.cal.org
CAL, a contract and grant firm, has as a primary objective the improvement of the teaching of English as a second or foreign language.

6. ERIC Clearinghouse on Languages and Linguistics
http://www.cal.org/ericcll/
This ERIC clearinghouse leads to sources on English as a second or foreign language, bilingualism and bilingual education, intercultural communication, and cultural education in publications, newsletters, and digests.

7. National Association for Bilingual Education
http://www.nabe.org
NABE is exclusively concerned with the education of language-minority students in American schools. A professional and advocacy group, its members work at all levels from preschool through postgraduate education.

8. The Internet TESL Journal
http://www.aitech.ac.jp/~iteslj/
This monthly Web magazine for Teachers of English as a Second Language contains articles, research papers, lesson plans, classroom handouts, teaching ideas, and links.

Sociocultural Aspects

9. Center for the Study of Books in Spanish for Children and Adolescents
http://www.csusm.edu/cwis/campus_centers/csb/index.html
This book source for Spanish-speaking readers includes I. Schon's recommended bibliographies of books on culture and heritage, and other book links.

10. Longman Dictionaries Web Site
http://www.awl-elt.com/dictionaries/
This home page is for English language students, teachers, and researchers and contains word games, study exercises, lesson plans, and information about linguistic research. Fifteen top related Web sites are linked here.

11. Mexican Heritage Almanac
http://www.ironhorse.com/~nagual/alma.html
This page is a daily file on everything Mexican. It also provides an "On This Day" history that relates to Mexico's past.

12. Migrant Education Program
http://jeffco.k12.co.us/edcenter/migrant/migrant.html
This Migrant Education Program in Jefferson County, Colorado, is funded by the Office of Migrant Education of the U.S. Department of Education.

13. National Institute on the Education of At-Risk Students
http://www.ed.gov/offices/OERI/At-Risk/
The At-Risk Institute, created by OERI (Office of Educational Research and Improvement) supports a range of research and development activities designed to improve the education of students at risk of educational failure due to limited English proficiency, poverty, race, geographic location, or economic disadvantage. Access their work at this site.

14. Newcomer Program: Helping Immigrant Students
http://www.ncbe.gwu.edu/ncbepubs/pigs/pig8.htm
Monica Friedlander's article, "Helping Immigrant Students Succeed in U.S. Schools" is part of the NCBE Program Information Guide Series.

Literacy

15. Intercultural E-Mail Classroom Connections
http://www.stolaf.edu/network/iecc/
The mailing lists at this site are provided by St. Olaf College to help teachers and classes link with partners in other countries and cultures for e-mail classroom exchanges.

16. Multicultural Book Review Home Page
http://www.isomedia.com/homes/jmele/homepage.html
From this page access Multicultural Links and Book Reviews.

17. National Clearinghouse for ESL Literacy Education (NCLE)
http://www.cal.org/ncle/
This is the only national clearinghouse focusing on literacy education. It offers online access to articles, books, newsletters, and bibliographies on literacy.

Integrative Classroom

18. Computer Enhanced Language Instruction Archive (CELIA)
http://www.latrobe.edu.au/www/education/celia/celia.html
This archive of software for Computer Assisted Language Learning of English as a Second Language. It is maintained at LaTrobe University in Melbourne, Australia.

19. Cutting Edge CALL Demos
http://www-writing.berkeley.edu/chorus/call/cuttingedge.html
Computer Assisted Language Learning (CALL) demonstrations for ESL students include Interactive Animation on Prepositions, Grammar and Listening Quizzes, and Interactive Listening Practice.

20. Dave's ESL Café on the Web
http://www.pacificnet.net/~sperling/
Dave Sperling's site for ESL/EFL students and teachers around the world is subtitled "Where Learning English Is Fun!" The "menu" includes ESL Discussion Center, ESL Idiom Page, ESL Quiz Center, and many other tasty selections.

21. ESL Student Page
http://www2.wgbh.org/mbcweis/ltc/telecom/esl.html
This page contains a list of links, for example, The Virtual English Language Center, and Fluency through Fables for ESOL Learners.

22. Interactive Internet Language Learning
http://babel.uoregon.edu/yamada/interact.html
This page will help students find places on the Internet to interact with others for the purpose of language learning.

Assessment Issues and Practices

23. Dr. Helen Barrett's Bookmarks
http://transition.alaska.edu/www/Portfolios/bookmarks.html
Here is a long list of sites on Alternative Assessment and Electronic Portfolios compiled and used by Dr. Helen Barrett, principal investigator for the National Transition Study in the Anchorage School District in Alaska.

24. Performance and Portfolio Assessment for Language Minority Students
http://www.ncbe.gwu.edu/ncbepubs/pigs/pig9.htm
Lorraine Valdez Pierce and J. Michael O'Malley introduce their subject in the NCBE Program Information Guide Series.

25. Portfolio Assessment
http://www.eduplace.com/rdg/res/literacy/assess6.html
This description of portfolio assessment on literacy also contains bibliographic references. It links to Effects on Instruction and Classroom Management.

Building Partnerships

26. Internet Resources
http://ericps.ed.uiuc.edu/clas/links.html
Collected by an Early Childhood Research Institute, many of these resources relate to early childhood educational resources for various cultural and linguistic groups.

27. Prospects: The Congressionally Mandated Study of Educational Growth and Opportunity
http://www.ed.gov/pubs/Prospects/index.html
This report analyzes cross-sectional data on minority and LEP students in the United States and outlines what actions are needed to improve the educational situation.

28. The Rice School/La Escuela Rice
http://riceinfo.rice.edu/armadillo/Rice/dev.html
Part of the mission of this experimental school is to see that the schoolchildren develop proficiency in communication in English and another language.

Exemplary Program Models

29. For All Students: Limited English Proficient Students and Goals 2000
http://www.ncbe.gwu.edu/ncbepubs/focus/focus10.htm
Diane August has prepared this NCBE Focus paper on bilingual education in which she offers recommendations to ensure that LEP children are included in the proposals embodied in the *Goals 2000: Educate America Act.*

30. Multicultural Education
http://www.ceousa.org/multic.html
An article by Rosalie Pedalino Porter, "The Politics of Bilingual Education Revisited," is reprinted here by the Center for Equal Opportunity.

31. Mundo Latino—Rincon Literario
http://www.mundolatino.org/cultura/litera/
This Web site is a rich mine of cultural and literary information in Spanish and Portuguese.

32. School Reform and Student Diversity
http://www.ncbe.gwu.edu/ncbepubs/resource/schref.htm
This is a full reprint of an article by Beverly McLeod, "Exemplary Schooling for Language Minority Students." Includes an Appendix with case examples from several schools, including the Linda Vista Elementary School in California.

33. Schools on the Web: Sites of Interest to Bilingual/Multicultural Educators
http://www.ncbe.gwu.edu/classroom/bilschool.htm
Link to Web sites of schools that share information, ideas, and resources related to the education of diverse students. Summaries of the schools' activities are available here.

Special Topics

34. Hispanic Online: Latino Links
http://www.hisp.com/links.html
This is an excellent resource in English for teachers to use with Spanish-speaking students.

35. National Clearinghouse for Bilingual Education (NCBE)
http://www.ncbe.gwu.edu
The NCBE home page leads to language and education links, technical assistance, data bases, success stories, classroom activity, and an online library.

36. TESOL Online
http://www.tesol.edu/index.html
The home page of Teachers of English to Speakers of Other Languages contains basic information about the association and its mission.

We highly recommend that you review our Web site for expanded information and our other product lines. We are continually updating and adding links to our Web site in order to offer you the most usable and useful information that will support and expand the value of your Annual Editions. You can reach us at: *http://www.dushkin.com/annualeditions/*.

www.dushkin.com/online/

Unit Selections

1. **Bilingual Education and the Politics of Teacher Preparation,** Hermán S. García
2. **Acquiring a Second Language for School,** Virginia P. Collier
3. **NAEYC Position Statement: Responding to Linguistic and Cultural Diversity—Recommendations for Effective Early Childhood Education,** *Young Children*
4. **Factors Affecting Language Development from the Perspectives of Four Bilingual Teachers,** Nancy Lemberger

Key Points to Consider

❖ How can classroom teachers become more involved with decision making for educational policies and practices affecting English-language learners?

❖ How can teachers address the four interrelated components of the conceptual model in their classrooms?

❖ What is the role of ESL in the broader curriculum?

 **Links** **www.dushkin.com/online/**

4. **Bilingual ESL Network (BEN)**
   http://www.redmundial.com/ben.htm
5. **Center for Applied Linguistics**
   http://www.cal.org
6. **ERIC Clearinghouse on Languages and Linguistics**
   http://www.cal.org/ericcll/
7. **National Association for Bilingual Education**
   http://www.nabe.org
8. **The Internet TESL Journal**
   http://www.aitech.ac.jp/~iteslj/

These sites are annotated on pages 4 and 5.

Introduction: The Process of Acquiring English as a Second Language for School

Ever-increasing concern with the inconsistent academic performance of students at all grade levels who are learning English in our classrooms has had an enormous effect on educators and policymakers across the United States in recent years. Positive outcomes of this concern include rigorous collaborative research, an abundance of articles and conference presentations related to all aspects of the education of linguistic minority youth, the integration of English for speakers of other languages (ESOL) performance standards in preservice teacher education courses, university faculty training, inservice teacher training through local school district staff development, and the development of ESOL instructional materials by state departments of education in response to school districts' training needs. It is evident that the many needs of our second-language learners must be addressed with expediency, or large numbers of these students will continue to fail to meet grade-level and graduation requirements as defined by local educational agencies and state departments of education. The lack of meaningful education will lead to decreased career and decision-making opportunities over a lifetime. ESL content standards have been designed to help educators develop student competency in the areas of social language, academic language, and sociocultural knowledge. The standards reflect three curricular trends affecting the implementation of ESL instruction: process-oriented approaches to instruction, more cooperative, integrative classroom settings, and the natural and holistic development of ESL.

The current reform movement in American education represents a major transition in thinking about the formal education of all students, especially of children arriving in school who have not yet become proficient in English—the medium for instruction in the vast majority of classrooms. In the recent past, the thinking of most educators and U.S. policymakers involved with English-language learners and program development was that the key to success for these students was to become proficient speakers of English without making the distinction between social language and academic language.

This one-dimensional picture of language learning assumes that it is possible to isolate language from other crucial issues that need to be considered when planning instructional programs. A conceptual model has recently emerged that provides greater understanding of the interrelationships among these components of acquiring of a second language: sociocultural, linguistic, academic, and cognitive processes. The process of acquiring English for school success is more complex than previously believed, and each component deserves equal attention as educational personnel develop programs.

The ESL services provided to these learners must not be limited in scope. Regular classroom teachers and all educational personnel must assume responsibility for the education of ESOL students. Mainstream teachers can no longer depend on ESOL teachers or paraprofessionals alone, but should recognize the critical role they must play in the linguistic development of ESOL students enrolled in their classes. According to demographics, approximately half of all American teachers will teach a speaker of limited English at some time during their careers. A major trend in teaching ESL, which is strongly supported by the research, is the integration of content area and second-language instruction. Current research indicates that there are three key predictors of academic success that are more important than any other set of variables this unit addresses. The first predictor is the provision of cognitively complex on-grade-level instruction through the students' first and second languages. The second is the use of current approaches to teaching the academic curriculum through two languages. The third predictor is a supportive learning environment.

The articles in this unit address key variables that have a major impact on the acquisition of English as a second language for school contexts. In addition, they provide educators with a strong rationale for programmatic reform that affects English-language learners.

Bilingual Education and the Politics of Teacher Preparation

Hermán S. García

The history of bilingual education is rooted in a struggle of resistance politics similar to the oppositional struggles of other pedagogical themes such as special education and multicultural education. That history of struggle emanates from an even longer history of resistance within and among the various multilingual communities in the United States to change their identity along monolithic canons and narratives that serve to divide and conquer their cultural and linguistic legacy of diversity. The primary intention of those mainstream discourses addressing linguistic diversity have striven to truncate bilingual education from its cultural and pedagogical legacy and to infantilize it as a fatuous formulae for supposedly wounding the academic performance of linguistically diverse students. Linda Chávez (Denver Post, 1997), for example, frequently attempts in almost everything she writes concerning bilingual education to smudge it as an impediment to bilingual children's academic progress. In some cases it may well do that. It, however, does that not because the concept of educating children in two languages is debauched, but because bilingual education has been envenomed by mainstream edification. In other words, educating children in two languages is more about indoctrinating children through the traditional methodological processes of instruction than it is about using a dual language approach. As such, bilingual education as it is being practiced in schools today has

Hermán S. García, EdD, is department head and professor of curriculum and instruction at New Mexico State University, Las Cruces, New Mexico. He is a nationally recognized critical bilingual educator and has authored and coauthored numerous articles, chapters, and books in critical bilingual education.

become a pedagogical insurance for schools to secure minority children's grasp of mainstream schooling skills and society's rules and procedures for proper allegiance to American citizenship. Bilingual education has become, in a sense, a mainstream sociocultural practice for maintaining the proper transmission of dominant cultural codes.

Educating children can occur in any language or in any number of languages. What remains vacant for most children is whether in a monolingual or bilingual classroom the engagement of ideas and information occurs more often than the challenge of learning a second language. There is little difference in what children learn in monolingual English classrooms from what they learn in bilingual classrooms regarding content and that should be a leading concern of educators. What are children learning in classrooms? Pat Buchanan and other social conservatives are concerned about losing America to a "tide" of illegal immigrants who fail to assimilate. They should be more worried about completely losing America to a host of militia groups whose benign intent is to destroy America rather than share and reinvent her with new groups whom they (militias) deem menacing to their monopolous values. The content of dominant ideologically constructed curriculum which children receive in monolingual and bilingual classrooms all offer assimilationists' views so that children who come from other countries and who don't speak English are able to contiguously gain the same reproductive influence that American-born children have. Once they have acquired and learned English, the brainwashing mission of the curriculum and its caretakers becomes quite easy for the schools to inject its ideology. The cultural content and context of school curricula by nature

 From *Cultural Circles*, Vol. 2, Spring 1998, pp. 75-90. Published by Boise State University. Reprinted by permission.

does not intellectually challenge students of any background. Yet, by the time bilingual children learn English, they have been socially and culturally reproduced in the image of the dominant culture and thus naturally and assuredly, reject their cultural and linguistic identity. The symbolic violence (Bourdieu, 1991) inherent in the cultural politics of traditional curricula destroy any remnant of who they really are.

Teacher Education

Approaching the debate of how to educate bilingual children must be conducted within a dialectical format which allows a variety of critical views and strategies to be considered. The approach of the last twenty plus years among most bilingual educators has been to use the traditional educational philosophies albeit using bilingual students' native languages to impart knowledge. Little debate, if any, has transpired at the intellectual level in relation to what is informing the educational constructs of bilingual teachers, and as a result, how bilingual students are socially produced via the curriculum. Most bilingual educators follow school district curricula and guidelines with minimal regard for how bilingual children are emotionally and culturally impacted by the curriculum. As well, most bilingual teachers have not been provided with an alternative language for referencing their teaching which commonly results in unproblematized locations of their work. In other words, educators remain socially and intellectually unengaged just as most of their training calls for. The discussion of intellectual engagement is void in most materials and narratives regarding the formation of bilingual teachers in most colleges and schools of education. There has been little opportunity for bilingual teachers at any level to connect with critical perspectives and discourses in their preparation programs.

The primary logic invoked in the preparation of bilingual teachers remains monolithic and traditional except for the provision of native language instruction in a language other than English. More importantly, the philosophical formation of bilingual teachers remains positivistic and non-analytical. It is within this formational context that bilingual teachers are denuded of any opportunity to understand their roles more broadly as public intellectuals and cultural workers than just

simply as classroom mechanics whose roles are reduced to technicians or clerks (Giroux, 1983). The call for teachers as public and critically engaged intellectuals and cultural workers places teacher work as the forefront of a pedagogical politics that raises questions, subjectifies knowledge with which they labor, and pushes classrooms toward a democratizing notion concerning schooling.

The life of a society projects itself into the life of a school. School policy plays out much of what is practiced in the larger society with regard to democracy or an autocracy and the power of its cultural politics. What is seriously needed in the United States is a new way of thinking about schooling, or as Renato Rosaldo (1989) so aptly puts it, a remaking of social analyses. Transformation and improvement of schools is not likely to occur with the utilization of a colonial language which refuses to acknowledge change as a natural and healthy phenomenon. Instead, schools insist on drawing their operational language from the standardized knowledge industry and reject any new discourses for remapping schools as sites of on-going provocation regarding human agency, social, and political dynamics.

Human agency among bilingual teachers is largely limited to the extent that most of them use few theoretical and philosophical groupings for situating their practice. Most bilingual educators mistakenly place experience as the primary condition for justifying what they do and don't do as teachers. Much of the success students apperceive is to their own credit as they struggle against an educational arrangement that perceives them as deficient in a number of ways. The diverse identities of poor and working-class children work against them in standardized learning school settings. Those school settings are socioculturally constructed and positioned for dominant-class children and youth whose gender, ethnicity, race, and everyday life are reflected in the school curricula more closely. Invoking Pierre Bourdieu's (1991) notion of symbolic violence which is constituted in school curricula, it correspondingly attacks the identities of children who are not represented by conservative, conceptions of knowing and being.

In ideological terms, bilingual education has stood boldly against the European American conception of schooling. It has denounced a false American spirit of forgetting one's roots in order to become a full-fledged member of society. History is rarely discussed or used to inform various sociocultural positions regarding native-to-America multilingual populations. Also, any discussion of a peoples' history is not included because its role usually serves to promote awareness of longtime injustices which, of course, we can't have in America. American history is not about the suffering of people. Instead, it is about the celebration of great events originated by great white people, invariably men. But bilingual education's original impetus for rupturing colonial hegemony has been, in a sense, swallowed up by the predatory cultural and pedagogical politics located in ideologically traditional educational discourses and narratives (McLaren, 1997). In a slow but calculated move, the established discourses of conservative theories and philosophies have devoured bilingual education's distinct features for educating children. In its initial stages at least, some of those distinct features included a close correlation between language, culture, history, class, sociolinguistics, and multiethnic and racial commemoration. The empowering assets which bilingual education constituted at the outset promoted cultural and linguistic pride, avenues of hope for bilingual children to perform and complete school, and a determined sense that dreams can be realized. Bilingual education at one time contained within it an agency for empowering bilingual teachers and for children to take pride in their identities and histories which naturally befitted the multicultural terrain inherent to America.

Over the last twenty years, however, the relentless assault of bilingual education by traditional canons and conservative narratives has diminished the supportive stance of bilingual teachers and generally sympathetic school administrators. The asymmetrical relations of power between bilingual education and the established discourses to name the practice of bilingual education has increased. Bilingual education increasingly is associated with remedial education and special education in the disability sense of the term. The epistemology of bilingual education is associated with assisting bilingual children to join and participate in mainstream schooling activities. It is also associated with making bilingual education a comprehensive education for all children. Bilingual education's most vicious and vile attacks came and continue to come from English-only advocates. According to English-only proponents, bilingual education is un-American, divisive, damaging to bilingual children's academic development, and

fosters welfare-type native language dependency. Never is it mentioned by English-only advocates that research on properly supported and implemented bilingual education renders bilingual children increased sociocultural fulfillment, improved intellectual aptness, broader appreciation of their cultural and historical heritage, and numerous other advantages. Unfortunately, the focus of today's bilingual education programs is English language development, mostly speaking and reading with a strong push for improving standardized test performance. According to that view, the faster bilingual children learn English and become monolingual English speakers, the more success is attributed to bilingual education. In other words, the more bilingual education becomes like mainstream and traditional education, the more it is accepted as a transitioning practice for bilingual children. In its original design, bilingual education supported a dual language education for all children over a twelve-year period of education. Shortly after the inception of bilingual education as an educational practice for all children, the federal government moved swiftly to require it only for children who needed it according to the measurements of a variety of linguistic needs assessments. Of course, these were politically motivated actions imposed by federal policy although they were never regarded as cultural politics.

For traditional educators, bilingual education today represents a passive revolution, menacing in sound, but ineffective in action. For bilingual educators it represents a hegemonic position because it is forced to consent to a second-class pedagogical stratum. Antonio Gramci's (1920) counter-hegemony calls for taking a position against the ruling social bloc. In Gramcian terms, bilingual education at one point in its history constituted a counter-hegemonic form of education when it contained sociocultural political content and context. This counter-hegemony moves against the "common sense" of established notions of knowing and allows for the formation of opportunities for disenfranchised groups to negotiate their plight in life. That is now a more difficult construct to pursue as bilingual education has been reduced to a mechanistic pedagogy that refrains from challenging dominant discourses and narratives.

Few educators have written or talked about bilingual education as a pedagogy of resistance, or a pedagogy of everyday life and struggle for agency. Antonia Darder's (1991) *Culture and Power in the Classroom* and Maracia Moraes's (1996) *Bilingual Education: A Dialogue with the Bakhtin Circle,* are some of the critical views one can find on bilingual education. That is not to suggest in any manner there are not others, only that critical views regarding bilingual education are limited at this current juncture in its history. The language of critical theory and pedagogy offer an exciting new trek for rerouting and reinventing bilingual education as a viable and resistant pedagogy. Authoritarianism has long characterized the roles of teachers and schools (Pinar, et al., 1995). Bilingual education has the potential to offer, by virtue of its multidiglossic negotiating position, a broader democratic promise for engaging in sociopolitical, cultural, and pedagogical dialogues. That cannot and will not happen automatically. That space has to be created, exercised, and negotiated by various groups. The promise of such a possibility, however, deserves pursuit and struggle.

Language and Bilingual Education

The narrow and almost strict boundaries in which bilingual education has been constructed and defined has reduced the notion of educating bilingual children to mostly linguistic treatises. Culture, everyday life, history, and other pedagogical categories were addressed in dominant cultural terms which provided little opportunity to politicize those concepts against dominant cultural politics. Bilingual children's learning was reduced to language acquisition and learning with little regard for how cultural power and politics played a controlling role on pedagogical themes aside from language, as if language was the principle category for promoting academic achievement among bilingual children. Although bicultural concepts were initially introduced, bicultural themes and topics were introduced as cultural commodities or artifactual items rather than political entities through which cultural power and curricular issues were negotiated.

At the risk of sounding pessimistic and unable to move beyond a political and pedagogical paralysis, this text offers an analysis for a transformative pedagogy in which bilingual and monolingual teachers can work collectively through an agency of emancipation. Without a critique, however narrow and limited it may appear, it provides an opportunity

for all educators, but especially bilingual educators to rethink where and how bilingual education might be reconstituted as part of a broader pedagogical knowledge base where bilingual education can be considered a viable pedagogical theory and practice. The ideology from which the education of bilingual students needs to be considered must be open to critique and analyses. It is in this spirit of critique and possibility that I address the themes and issues found in this text. To not employ a critiquing discourse would make little difference to the ways in which we now understand and practice bilingual education.

An issue which weakened bilingual education as a viable pedagogy for educating bilingual children was its promotional understanding through a series of mainstream methods, strategies, and approaches reproduced from the standardized knowledge industry in which lock-step, time-on-task, and back-to-basics assumptions are utilized to distribute, implement, and measure the learning abilities of *all* children regardless of their class, gender, ethnic, racial and physical ability surroundings. Teaching and learning are commonly practiced using transmission packages in which all children are viewed as having no need to be culturally and linguistically acknowledged as diverse from what the official school curriculum offers. Teachers, even though they are educated as bilingual educators, are reduced to technocrats whose role is to carry out their educator tasks which are congenitally born from accountability and management schemes and theories. In the overall picture of things, little difference is attributed to how children perceive and experience the world inasmuch as they will all be provided the same pedagogical prescription for learning in the classroom. It is really more of a recipe for proper socialization and assimilation into mainstream American life and service than it is about language learning, academic and conceptual development, and cultivating democratic values and constructs. It is also a great deal about ideologically indoctrinating children and youth to understand the world in traditional, dominant terms with regard to its history, culture, and politics.

The struggle against this powerful ideology becomes a major challenge since most teachers are not aware of its presence or underpinnings (Freire, 1970). Most teachers who understand traditional schooling ideology rarely engage it in ways to contest its operative dogma. In bilingual education theory and practice this has especially been the case although one would think the opposite effect might be true since the birth of bilingual education came from civil rights and equality of educational opportunity struggles. In the initial stages of the inception of the Bilingual Education Act, federal and state laws and guidelines forced school districts to comply with meeting the diverse needs of learners. On the other side of that coin, however, many sociocultural principles necessary for ensuring effective bilingual and multicultural curriculum and instruction were negotiated out of the ensuing bilingual education acts. For example, in its original configuration, bilingual instruction offered children's social, economic, historical, and cultural content to be utilized and implemented via the bilingual education program. The spirit of creating culturally democratic educational environments (Ramírez and Castañeda, 1974; Darder, 1991) was quickly smothered after the focus of the act became to learn English as quickly as possible. Unfortunately, that is still very much with us today. Little regard for academic development, cultural diversity, and a sociohistorical framework is provided given the strong emphasis on learning English in as little time as possible.

The time spent learning English has always been a controversial issue in bilingual education programs. Most educators attribute learning English to academic success or academic achievement and mastery. Many educators do not distinguish between learning English and being academically successful. There is a common public belief, including among traditional educators, that once children learn English, learning curriculum content will become an automatic procedure for bilingual children. When this doesn't happen, bilingual children are pathologized as slow or non-learners. Too many educators, including bilingual educators, do not comprehend that one does not necessarily need know a language to understand a concept in that language. The real concern here is that language learning becomes a prerequisite for learning concepts, which, of course, is not the case. Learning occurs in a variety of ways, some of which do not require one to understand the language in which the concept is being presented or used. The psychogized versions of learning have provided educators, and the public at large, a one dimensional view of learning as something that happens somewhere within the brain only.

Language and Learning

The ideological constructions of learning have fastened many educators' beliefs to the notion that learning is exclusively an enterprise of brain activity. One of the broader views of learning is offered by Howard Gardner (1983) in which he presents the exciting verisimilitude of *multiple intelligences,* all of which contribute in varying degrees to learning. Although little has been written to connect this theory of multiple intelligences to ethnic and language issues, it seems to hold much promise for diffusing learning myths regarding language minority populations. As such, bilingual education has continuously been running from mainstream concoctions of what it is, should be, and isn't. It has also been running from itself in that its definitions among bilingual educators and non-bilingual educators convey a variety of pedagogical views and practices regarding learning. For some, bilingual education connotes a model for mainstream education conducted temporarily in two languages until English is acquired, while for others it represents a process of always utilizing two languages to pursue learning and living. In any event, the identity of bilingual children and adults is imbued in the painstaking struggle to know and perplex about who one is given various dominant renditions of who one should be. Many bilingual populations and individuals unknowingly embrace an outlaw status accorded them by dominant social construction and perception. Bilingualism in school settings has completely tarnished the immaculate notion for which America ideologically stands. That stance systematically rejected the use of two languages by ideologically censuring it as un-American. What one knows vis-à-vis one's ethnic culture and experience is commonly regarded or dismissed as fugitive because it was not borne of European or European American canon or experience. Ethnic cultures and languages are frequently constructed by mainstream society as artifactual items to be nostalgically talked about or referred to as relics rather than real life agencies which contain within them a problematics to contend with and to study.

The status of outlawry (bell hooks, 1994) for diverse school children and youth extends beyond the perception of what schools deem as un-American. Children whose culture, language, gender, able bodiedness, ethnicity, and race and class are diverse from the mainstream canon definitions of those categories, befall an outlaw status bestowed on them by traditional narratives from the pages of Americana culture à la John Wayne and Ozzie and Harriet. Many bilingual children in America have for generations given up their native languages and cultural identities associated with their heritage and history only to be inevitably denied access to full participation in America's social, cultural, and institutional spheres. But for America, it is not enough for diverse groups to give up their identities. They must reject their diverse identities to prove their "loyalty" to America, displaying an incisive measure of patriotism which in the long run conditionally accepts them as hyphenated-Americans. Bilingual children are constantly imperiled with forms of symbolic violence when they have to deny their native social, cultural, and linguistic identities as part of their academic success and development in the schooling process. Americanization is by nature a predatory process for severing culturally and linguistically diverse populations from their natural identities.

Identity

The denial of self identity is related to low academic performance among a wide range of ethnic and diverse cultural and linguistic populations. It is precisely the way in which difference is not appreciated that children are made to feel as players outside the social and economic boundaries of society and are inadvertently ascribed a fugitive status (Giroux, 1996). bell hooks (1994) speaks of outlaw culture in which various diverse populations fall outside the traditional and mainstream social order and are treated as social, cultural and linguistic outlaws. Bilingual children naturally fall into this category given their socially constructed outlaw culture.

Across this identity crisis, there has been a strong backlash against bilingual education in recent years which has come in the form of an authoritative cultural politics that speaks with an uncontested power. In an effort to locate and name a cultural politics that provides a voice for bilingual education, there must first be a working delineation that places bilingual education in a milieu of identity and cultural politics that allows for diversity and multiculturalism to play a pivotal role. There is strong need for an historical understanding of how bilingual education originated. Bilingual Education was naïvely borne out of a survival form of cultural politics. The initiators of bilingual education launched what they thought was a politically instinctive pedagogy to help non-English and bilingual students access learning via dual language pedagogical constructs. Broadly unaware of their cultural political location, pioneer bilingual educators worked from a virtuous viewpoint that bilingual education would genuinely assist bilingual children through the schooling process by providing them linguistic tools for mastering learning in schools. Although bilingual educators were generally aware that mainstream educators were uncomfortable and that some were desperately concerned about a dual language approach to educating bilingual children, little did bilingual educators realize at that point the vehement attacks bilingual education would undergo in the ensuing twenty-five years.

Traditional American models of learning psychology cogently reject the notion that learning in two languages is helpful or useful and, in fact, pungently allege that it damages children socially, academically, and emotionally. Learning is rarely presented as a problematized sphere in teacher education programs. Most of the time, learning theory and practice are presented as linear, uncomplicated commodities to be acquired and applied rather than questioned and negotiated. They are presented as part of a repository of cultural goods to be attained and implemented in classrooms regardless of children's needs and backgrounds (Giroux, 1988a). Traditional learning theory impels a reproductive agenda of learning and knowing in traditional educational domains where it is presented as predetermined status quo and is not negotiable. The socialization process students experience is emitted from the curriculum which marginalizes them in society even though students frequently do not engage it. The dominant cultural codes etched into the minds of all children are not negotiated between giver (schools) and receiver (children) but rather, are inserted into children's repertoires without their conscious consent. It is a matter of dominant discourse objectification of children from which the organized practice of teaching emanates and remains highly reproductive. The view of the world with which children are provided is already named and constructed for them. There is little opportunity for students to engage the knowledge base offered by schools through the curriculum (Macedo, 1994).

Bilingual educators, who with all their hearts and best intentions, try to make an advantageous difference for bilingual children in classrooms, yet are not aware of what informs their pedagogy, will most likely fall prey to the predatory cultural politics located within dominant curriculum discourses and narratives. What is presented as legitimate knowledge is always constructed inside a dominant cultural politics which has the power to name, substantiate, and consider what students will study and how teachers will present it. Bilingual education in this view is situated as a subordinate pedagogy whose agency to empower bilingual children is diminished in its description by mainstream discourses and narratives. Although bilingual education comes to us by way of various civil rights initiatives and struggles, today's bilingual educators have little, if any, awareness of its original commitment to equality of educational opportunity. Also, the history of bilingual education has been eroded to the point of suggesting it never had an oppositional posture toward mainstream educational constructs. The political anesthetization of bilingual education, through a predatory cultural politics, has in many cases turned bilingual educators against it, hence intellectually defeating its very advocates.

Providing an historical background postulated on an empowering cultural politics will assist bilingual education's struggle for dual language forms of instruction. Bilingual education has utilized forms of border pedagogy (Giroux, 1990) to locate itself inside and outside traditional discourses of educational theory and practice. Bilingual education initially combined border crossing efforts accented by history, sociology, economics, and cultural politics to present a comprehensive view of bilingual children and their learning. Bilingual education initially considered within it issues of culture, language, pedagogical politics, and other challenges facing the education of bilingual students and populations. For many educators working with bilingual children year in and year out, they remain ready to be visited by pedagogical formulae that will lighten and enlighten their daily struggle of educating bilingual children. What is missing for the majority of bilingual educators is a basic understanding that their work in teacher education is informed by unproblematic, apolitical educational constructs. These constructs address student learning as a unitary process bereft of transformative, emancipatory, and

intellectual imaginations. The survival of bilingual education is dependent on several factors including the role of educators and the public at large. If educator groups and key public and private assemblies are willing to move outside the dominant circles of power and knowing, there is a greater possibility that bilingual education could develop its own identity regarding the education of culturally and linguistically diverse populations whom bilingual education was intended to empower. Bilingual educators in North America are losing the battle over bilingual education as a pedagogical practice that has remained limited to language development. Learning to speak English has been the primary if not the only emphasis bilingual educators have argued for in the debate over bilingual education as a pedagogical approach to educating children.

Testing

Bilingual communities in the United States represent a life-long pedagogical struggle against European American constructions of academic achievement vis-à-vis the notion of intelligence quotients (IQ) à-la-Stanford-Binet and later, other combinations of knowledge standardization. Under the guise of the melting pot theory, and with the predilectory call of *liberty and justice for all*, standardized tests have been and continue to be misused to stratify the social order by using a supposedly harmless and disarmed (neutral) academic foundationalism to select, sort, label, and place the student population. In his early works, Alfred Binet (Binet test) argued that high intelligence was tied to cerebral volume. In his later research, however, Binet discredited this claim and turned to other forms of measurements but remained cautious that measurements of the brain could be misused quite easily and admitted of his trepidation regarding how someone could move in adverse directions with his findings (Gould, 1981). And so his fear came to pass time and again as European American educationists fell captive to the ideologies of academic superiority.

The single number notion of IQ played a major role in the academic emplacement of multiethnic children in American schools. The use of physical science research placed an overemphasis on positivistic and reductionistic assumptions about achievement that strongly remains with us today even as we realize how social science research has a cogent influence on curriculum and instruction (social undertakings). Numbers alone cannot be used to consign children to the lower academic strata and the social and economic margins. Numbers alone cannot interpret diverse cultural and linguistic meanings or be used to decide the academic performance of multiethnic children whose scholarly abilities are also woven into the edification of their everyday life. The power of numbers to industrialize the mind cannot be overlooked. Numbers are callous and cannot take into consideration the feelings, beliefs, and personal desires of humans. Numbers have so often misrepresented the desires of humans in areas such as sheer will power, desire of the heart, a vision of the future, and thought and imagination. And numbers cannot express passion, love, resistance, and the qualities of human aspirations. The point here is that numbers have misguided many educators who, in turn, have used them to undermine the basic human elements which move people to overcome their subordination and despair. Numbers cannot measure these human attributes. Why then, is there so much value placed on the numbers game? Stephen Jay Gould (1981) eloquently responded to this topic stating "the urge to classify people, to rank them according to their supposed gifts and limits, is strong in us. It has been so, from prescientific times when the tools of classification were said to be divine, to our day when numbers are king" (book flap). This bold announcement (or denouncement) by Gould assisted in alerting a broad audience of social scientists though his claim remained silent among most educators. In fact, most educators went blissfully about their employment of standardized tests and in various ways the practice of standardization has increased.

For bilingual communities who do not and cannot fall into standardized ways of knowing and being, we must continue to struggle against them. We need a language that allows diversity in its broadest sense to fulfill the lives of all children without standardizing their lives and identities.

References

Bourdieu, P. (1991) *Language and symbolic power*, John B. Thompson, (Ed.), Cambridge: Harvard University Press.

Chávez, L. (July 30, 1997). End the bilingual stranglehold. *The Denver Post*, p. 11B.

Darder, A. (1991). *Culture and power in the classroom: A critical foundation for bicultural education*. Westport, Conn: Bergin & Garvey.

Freire, P. (1970). *Pedagogia do oprimido*. Rio de Janeiro: Paz e Terra.

Gardner, H. (1983). *Frames of mind: The theory of multiple intelligences*. New York: Basic Books.

Giroux, H. A. (1983). *Theory and resistance in education: A pedagogy for the opposition*. New York: State University of New York.

Giroux, H. A. (1988a). *Teachers as intellectuals: Towards a critical pedagogy of learning*. South Hadley, MA: Bergin & Garvey.

Giroux, H. A. (1990). *Curriculum discourse as postmodernist critical practice*. Geelong, Victoria, Australia: A Deakin University Publication.

Giroux, H. A. (1996). *Fugitive cultures: Race, violence & youth*. New York: Routledge Publishers.

Gould, S. J. (1981). *The mismeasure of man*. New York: Norton and Company.

Gramci, A. (1990). *Selections from political writings: 1910–1920, 1921–1926*. Minneapolis, University of Minnesota Press.

hooks, b. (1994). *Outlaw culture: Resisting representation*. New York: Routledge Publishers.

Macedo, D. (1994). *Literacies of power: What Americans are not allowed to know*. Boulder, CO: Westview Press.

McLaren, P. (1997). *Revolutionary multiculturalism: Pedagogy of dissent for the new millennium*. Boulder, CO: Westview Press.

Moraes, M. (1996). *Bilingual education: A dialogue with the Bakhtin circle*. New York: State University of New York Press.

Pinar, W. F. (1995). *Understanding curriculum*. New York: Peter Lang, Inc.

Ramírez M. & Catañeda A. (1974). *Cultural democracy, bicognitive development and education*. New York: Academic Press.

Renato, R. (1989). *Culture and truth: The remaking of social analysis*. Boston, MA: Beacon Press.

ACQUIRING A SECOND LANGUAGE FOR SCHOOL

Virginia P. Collier,
George Mason University

During the past two decades, rapidly increasing language minority demographics have had a major impact on U.S. schools. Yet even with all the varied instructional approaches that U.S. educators have undertaken to address the concern for providing a "meaningful education" for language minority students (Lau v. Nichols, 1974), we are still struggling to identify the most effective education practices. When newcomers arrive, a school district's first response is usually to provide additional staff development training. To provide current information, trainers work hard to keep up with the latest research, but the issues are complex and difficult to present in a short training session. Given the misinformation that persists about second language acquisition among both educators and the public, this short publication is written to guide the reader through the substantial research knowledge base that our field has developed over the past 25 years.

Much misunderstanding occurs because many U.S. policy makers and educators assume that language learning can be isolated from other issues and that the first thing students must do is to learn English. To understand the reasons why this oversimplistic perception does not work, a conceptual model that explains the process that students are going through when acquiring a second language during the school years was developed. This conceptual model is based on the work of many researchers in linguistics, education, and the social sciences, as well as my own work with co-researcher Wayne Thomas. For the past ten years we have been exploring the length of time needed for students attending school where instruction is provided in their second language to reach deep enough levels of proficiency in the second language to compete on an equal footing with native speakers of that language. In this research, we have also worked on identifying key variables that have major impact on the acquisition of a second language for school contexts.

We believe that the conceptual model that has emerged from our research helps to explain many complex interacting factors that the school child experiences when acquiring a second language during the school years, especially when that second language is used in school for instructional purposes across the curriculum. This process of acquiring a second language through the school curriculum is very different from foreign language learning taught as a subject in school. The examples in this paper will focus on the language minority student, who comes from a home where a language other than the dominant language of the society is spoken, and is being schooled in a second language for at least part or perhaps all of the school day. The conceptual model may also be applied to the language majority student who speaks the dominant language and is being schooled in a bilingual classroom.

Acquiring a Second Language for School: A Conceptual Model

The model has four major components: sociocultural, linguistic, academic, and cognitive processes. To understand the interrelationships among these four components, figure one illustrates the developmental second language acquisition process that occurs in the school context. While this figure looks simple on paper, it is important to imagine that this is a multifaceted prism with many dimensions. The four major components—sociocultural, linguistic, academic, and cognitive processes—are interdependent and complex.

Sociocultural processes. At the heart of the figure is the individual student going through the process of acquiring a second language in school. Central to that student's acquisition of language are all of the surrounding social and cultural processes occurring through everyday life within the student's past, present, and future, in all contexts—home, school, community, and the broader society. For example, sociocultural processes at work in second language acquisition may include individual student variables such as self-esteem or anxiety or other affective factors. At school the instructional environment in a

 Reprinted from *Directions in Language & Education,* Fall 1995, pp. 1-12. Published by the National Clearinghouse for Bilingual Education (NCBE).

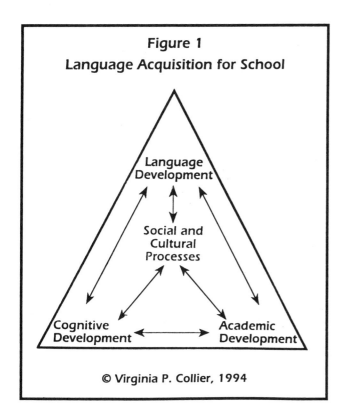

Figure 1
Language Acquisition for School

Language Development

Social and Cultural Processes

Cognitive Development

Academic Development

© Virginia P. Collier, 1994

classroom or administrative program structure may create social and psychological distance between groups. Community or regional social patterns such as prejudice and discrimination expressed towards groups or individuals in personal and professional contexts can influence students' achievement in school, as well as societal patterns such as subordinate status of a minority group or acculturation vs. assimilation forces at work. These factors can strongly influence the student's response to the new language, affecting the process positively only when the student is in a socioculturally supportive environment.

Language development. Linguistic processes, a second component of the model, consist of the subconscious aspects of language development (an innate ability all humans possess for acquisition of oral language), as well as the metalinguistic, conscious, formal teaching of language in school, and acquisition of the written system of language. This includes the acquisition of the oral and written systems of the student's first and second languages across all language domains, such as phonology (the pronunciation system), vocabulary, morphology and syntax (the grammar system), semantics (meaning), pragmatics (the context of language use), paralinguistics (nonverbal and other extralinguistic features), and discourse (formal thought patterns). To assure cognitive and academic success in a second language, a student's first language system, oral and written, must be developed to a high cognitive level at least through the elementary-school years.

Academic development. A third component of the model, academic development, includes all school work in language arts, mathematics, the sciences, and social studies for each grade level, Grades K–12 and beyond. With each succeeding

grade, academic work dramatically expands the vocabulary, sociolinguistic, and discourse dimensions of language to higher cognitive levels. Academic knowledge and conceptual development transfer from the first language to the second language; thus it is most efficient to develop academic work through students' first language, while teaching the second language during other periods of the school day through meaningful academic content. In earlier decades in the United States, we emphasized teaching the second language as the first step, and postponed the teaching of academics. Research has shown us that postponing or interrupting academic development is likely to promote academic failure. In an information driven society that demands more knowledge processing with each succeeding year, students cannot afford the lost time.

Cognitive development. The fourth component of this model, the cognitive dimension, has been mostly neglected by second language educators in the U.S. until the past decade. In language teaching, we simplified, structured, and sequenced language curricula during the 1970s, and when we added academic content into our language lessons in the 1980s, we watered down academics into cognitively simple tasks. We also too often neglected the crucial role of cognitive development in the first language. Now we know from our growing research base that we must address all of these components equally if we are to succeed in developing deep academic proficiency in a second language.

Interdependence of the four components. All of these four components—sociocultural, academic, cognitive, and linguistic—are interdependent. If one is developed to the neglect of another, this may be detrimental to a student's overall growth and future success. The academic, cognitive, and linguistic components must be viewed as developmental, and for the child, adolescent, and young adult still going through the process of formal schooling, development of any one of these three components depends critically on simultaneous development of the other two, through both first and second languages. Sociocultural processes strongly influence, in both positive and negative ways, students' access to cognitive, academic, and language development. It is crucial that educators provide a socioculturally supportive school environment that allows natural language, academic, and cognitive development to flourish.

Research Evidence to Support the Model

First and second language acquisition: A lifelong process. To understand the processes occurring in language acquisition during the school years, it is important to recognize the complex, lifelong process that we go through in acquiring our first language and the parallel processes that occur in second language acquisition. Development of a complex oral language system from birth to age five is universal, given no physical disabilities and no isolation from humans. But the most gifted five-year-old entering kindergarten is not yet half-way through the process of first language development. Children from ages 6 to 12 continue to acquire subtle phonological distinctions, vocabulary, semantics, syntax, formal discourse patterns, and complex aspects of pragmatics in the oral system of their first language (Berko Gleason, 1993). In addition, children being formally schooled during these years add reading and writing to the language skills of listening and speaking, across all the domains of language, with each age and grade level increasing the cognitive level of language use within each academic subject. An adolescent entering college must acquire enormous amounts of vocabulary in every discipline of study and continue the acquisition of complex writing skills, processes that continue through our adult life as we add new contexts of language use to our life experience. As adults we acquire new subtleties in pragmatics, as well as the constantly changing patterns in language use that affect our everyday oral and written communication with others. Thus first language acquisition is an unending process throughout our lifetime (Berko Gleason, 1993; Collier, 1992a). Second language acquisition is an equally complex phenomenon. We use some of the same innate processes that are used to acquire our first language, going through developmental stages and relying on native speakers to provide modified speech that we can at least partially comprehend (Ellis, 1985; Hakuta, 1986). However, second language acquisition is more subject to influence from other factors than was oral development in our first language. When the context of second language use is school, a very deep level of proficiency is required.

Academic second language proficiency: How long? Cummins (1989) popularized for educators the concept of different levels of language proficiency needed depending on the context of language use, basing his theories on the work of many other researchers before him. Given the level of language development needed to succeed in an academic context, my coresearcher, Wayne Thomas, and I have been exploring the "how long" question for the past ten years, following Cummins' initial examination (1981) of long-term academic achievement of immigrants in Canada. In the Thomas and Collier series of studies (Collier, 1987, 1989, 1992b; Collier & Thomas, 1989; Thomas & Collier, 1995), we have carefully controlled for a wide variety of student background variables and instructional treatments, to examine student performance on many different types of outcome measures across time. The measures we are using are the academic achievement measures used by school systems to monitor students' progress in school, including standardized tests and performance assessment measures in language arts, reading, mathematics, science, and social studies. In contrast to a typical language proficiency test, these are not static measures. Instead, they change with each succeeding grade level, because the academic and cognitive work expected with each additional year of schooling becomes increasingly more complex. Therefore, results on these tests are very different from the results on a language proficiency instrument that uses the same form each time it is administered. We choose to use these tests because they are the ultimate measures of academic proficiency

in a second language. When students being schooled in a second language reach deep enough proficiency levels in a second language to compete at the typical level of native speaker performance (expressed on a standardized test as 50th percentile or normal curve equivalent [NCE]), this is a major achievement, because native speakers are not sitting around waiting for non-native speakers to catch up with them. During the school years, native speakers' first language development is continuing at a rapid rate. For non-native speakers, the goal of proficiency equal to a native speaker is a moving target (Thomas, 1992).

In our studies we have found that in U.S. schools where all instruction is given through the second language (English), non-native speakers of English with no schooling in their first language take 7–10 years or more to reach age and grade-level norms of their native English-speaking peers. Immigrant students who have had 2–3 years of first language schooling in their home country before they come to the U.S. take at least 5–7 years to reach typical native-speaker performance (similar to what Cummins [1981] found). This pattern exists across many student groups, regardless of the particular home language that students speak, country of origin, socioeconomic status, and other student background variables. In our examination of large data sets across many different research sites, we have found that the most significant student background variable is the amount of formal schooling students have received in their first language. Across all program treatments, we have found that non-native speakers being schooled in a second language for part or all of the school day typically do reasonably well in the early years of schooling (kindergarten through second or third grade). But from fourth grade on through middle school and high school, when the academic and cognitive demands of the curriculum increase rapidly with each succeeding year, students with little or no academic and cognitive development in their first language do less and less well as they move into the upper grades.

What about students schooled bilingually in the U.S.? It still takes a long time to demonstrate academic proficiency in a second language comparable to a native speaker. But the difference in student performance in a bilingual program, in contrast to an all-English program, is that students typically score at or above grade level in their first language in all subject areas, while they are building academic development in the second language. When students are tested in their second language, they typically reach and surpass native speakers' performance across all subject areas after 4–7 years in a quality bilingual program. Because they have not fallen behind in cognitive and academic growth during the 4–7 years that it takes to build academic proficiency in a second language, bilingually schooled students typically sustain this level of academic achievement and outperform monolingually schooled students in the upper grades (Collier, 1992b; Thomas & Collier, 1995). Remarkably, these findings apply to students of many different backgrounds, including language majority students in a bilingual program. For example, in Canada, English-speaking students who receive all their schooling bilingually, typically begin to reach native-speaker norms on academic tests given in their second language (French) around fifth or sixth grade, and when tested in their first language, they outperform monolingually schooled students (Collier, 1992a; Genesee, 1987).

Role of first language.   Many studies have found that cognitive and academic development in the first language has an extremely important and positive effect on second language schooling (e.g. Bialystok, 1991; Collier, 1989, 1992b; Garcia, 1994; Genesee, 1987, 1994; Thomas & Collier, 1995). Academic skills, literacy development, concept formation, subject knowledge, and learning strategies developed in the first language will all transfer to the second language. As students expand their vocabulary and their oral and written communication skills in the second language, they can increasingly demonstrate their knowledge base developed in the first language.

Furthermore, some studies indicate that if students do not reach a certain threshold in their first language, including literacy, they may experience cognitive difficulties in the second language (Collier, 1987; Collier & Thomas, 1989; Cummins, 1981, 1991; Thomas & Collier, 1995). The key to understanding the role of the first language in the academic development of the second language is to understand the function of uninterrupted cognitive development. When students switch to second language use at school and teachers encourage parents to speak in the second language at home, both students and parents are functioning at a level cognitively far below their age. Whereas, when parents and children speak the language that they know best, they are working at their actual level of cognitive maturity. Cognitive development can occur at home even with non-formally-schooled parents through, for example, asking questions, solving problems together, building or fixing something, cooking together, and talking about life experiences.

Role of input and interaction in language development. In our current research (Thomas & Collier, 1995), we have also found that classes in school that are highly interactive, emphasizing student problem-solving and discovery learning through thematic experiences across the curriculum are likely to provide the kind of social setting for natural language acquisition to take place, simultaneously with academic and cognitive development. Collaborative interaction in which meaning is negotiated with peers is central to the language acquisition process, both for oral and written language development (Ellis, 1985; Enright & McCloskey, 1988; Freeman & Freeman, 1992; Goodman & Wilde, 1992; Swain, 1985; Wong Fillmore, 1991).

Sociocultural context of schooling.   Research from anthropology, sociology, sociolinguistics, psycholinguistics, and education has provided insights into the powerful and complex influence that sociocultural processes have on language acquisition. Just a few examples are provided here. Among our new arrivals to the U.S. are undocumented as well as legal refugees seeking refuge from war, political oppression, or severe economic conditions. These students bring to our classes special social, emotional, and academic needs, often having experienced interrupted schooling in their home countries. Students escaping war may exhibit symptoms of post-traumatic stress disorder, such as depression, withdrawal, hyperactivity, aggression, and intense anxiety in response to situations that recall traumatic events in their lives (Coelho, 1994). Studies of these refugees' adaptation to life in the U.S. and success in school have emphasized the importance of a bicultural schooling context, integrating first language, culture, and community knowledge into the curriculum, as well as the importance of parents' maintenance of home language and cultural traditions (Caplan, Choy & Whitmore, 1992; Tharp & Gallimore, 1988; Trueba, Jacobs & Kirton, 1990).

External societal factors in the U.S. may have major influence on language acquisition for school. Examples are the social and psychological distance often created between first and second language speakers, perceptions of each group in inter-ethnic comparisons, cultural stereotyping, intergroup hostility, subordinate status of a minority group, or societal patterns of acculturation vs. assimilation forces at work. Majority-minority and inter-ethnic relations, as well as social class differences are at the heart of these factors influencing second language acquisition and success in school. Researchers such as Ogbu (1993), Oakes (1985), and Minicucci and Olsen (1992) have found extensive evidence of institutionalized structures in U.S. schools that deny access to the core curriculum through tracking, ability grouping, and special programs that segregate language minority students. Segregated transitional bilingual classes and English as a second language (ESL) classes can sometimes heighten the social inequities and subconsciously maintain the status quo in majority-minority relations (Hernández-Chávez, 1984; Spener, 1988).

The negative social perception of these classes that both English-speaking and language minority students have often developed in U.S. schools has led to second-language students' social isolation, denying them the critical conditions that Wong Fillmore (1991) says must be present for second language acquisition to take place. To break the cycle of special classes being perceived as remedial in nature, they must be a permanent, desired, integral part of the curriculum, taught through quality instruction that encourages interactive, problem-solving, experiential learning, through a multicultural, global perspective (Frederickson, 1995). Schools can serve as agents of change or places where teachers, students, and staff of many varied backgrounds join together and transform tensions between groups that currently exist in the broader society.

Research-based Recommendations for Educators

In our current research (Thomas & Collier, 1995), when examining interactions among student background variables and instructional treatments and their influence on student outcomes, we have found that two-way bilingual education at the elementary school level is the most promising program model for the long-term academic success of language minority students. As a group, students in this program maintain grade-level skills in their first language at least through sixth grade and reach the 50th percentile or NCE in their second language generally after 4–5 years of schooling in both languages. They also generally sustain the gains they made when they reach secondary education, unlike the students in programs that provide little or no academic support in the first language. Program characteristics include: (1) integrated schooling, with English speakers and language minority students learning academically through each others' languages; (2) perceptions among staff, students, and parents that it is a "gifted and talented" program, leading to high expectations for student performance; (3) equal status of the two languages achieved, to a large extent, creating self-confidence among language minority students; (4) healthy parent involvement among both language minority and language majority parents for closer home-school cooperation; and (5) continuous support for staff development, emphasizing whole language approaches, natural language acquisition through all content areas, cooperative learning, interactive and discovery learning, and cognitive complexity of the curriculum for all proficiency levels.

In our research, we have also found significant differences between "traditional vs. current" approaches to language teaching for students schooled in the U.S. for kindergarten through twelfth grade. In the long term, students do less well in programs that focus on discrete units of language taught in a structured, sequenced curriculum with the learner treated as a passive recipient of knowledge. Students achieve significantly better in programs that teach language through cognitively complex content, taught through problem-solving, discovery learning in highly interactive classroom activities. ESL pullout in the early grades, when taught traditionally, is the least successful program model for students' long-term academic success. During Grades K–3, there is little difference between programs, but significant differences appear as students continue in the mainstream at the secondary-level.

When first language instructional support cannot be provided, the following program characteristics can make a significant difference in academic achievement for English language learners entering U.S. schools at the secondary level: (1) second language taught through academic content; (2) conscious focus on teaching learning strategies needed to develop thinking skills and problem-solving abilities; and (3) continuous support for staff development emphasizing activation of students' prior knowledge, respect for students' home language and culture, cooperative learning, interactive and discovery learning, intense and meaningful cognitive/academic development, and ongoing assessment using multiple measures.

We have found that for young children and adolescents in Grades K–12, uninterrupted cognitive, academic, and linguistic development is essential to school success, and neglect or overemphasis of one of these three components may affect students' long-term growth. Our data show that extensive cognitive and academic development in students' first language is crucial to second language academic success. Furthermore, the sociocultural context in which students are schooled is equally important to students' long-term success in second lan-guage schooling. Contrary to the popular idea that it takes a motivated student a short time to acquire a second language, our studies examining immigrants and language minority students in many different regions of the U.S. and with many different background characteristics have found that 4–12 years of second language development are needed for the most advantaged students to reach deep academic proficiency and compete successfully with native speakers. Given the extensive length of time, educators must understand the complex variables influencing the second language process and provide a sociocultural context that is supportive while academically and cognitively challenging.

References

Berko Gleason, J. (1993). *The development of language* (3rd ed.). New York: Macmillan.

Bialystok, E. (Ed.). (1991). *Language processing in bilingual children.* Cambridge: Cambridge University Press.

Caplan, N., Choy, M. H., & Whitmore, J. K. (1992). Indochinese refugee families and academic achievement. *Scientific American, 266* (2), 36–42.

Coelho, E. (1994). Social integration of immigrant and refugee children. In F. Genesee (Ed.), *Educating second language children* (pp. 301–327). Cambridge: Cambridge University Press.

Collier, V. P. (1987). "Age and rate of acquisition of second language for academic purposes." *TESOL Quarterly, 21,* 617–641.

Collier, V. P. (1989). "How long? A synthesis of research on academic achievement in second language." *TESOL Quarterly, 23,* 509–531.

Collier, V. P. (1992a). "The Canadian bilingual immersion debate: A synthesis of research findings." *Studies in Second Language Acquisition, 14,* 87–97.

Collier, V. P. (1992b). A synthesis of studies examining long-term language minority student data on academic achievement. *Bilingual Research Journal, 16* (1–2), 187–212.

Collier, V. P., & Thomas, W. P. (1989). How quickly can immigrants become proficient in school English? *Journal of Educational Issues of Language Minority Students, 5,* 26–38.

Cummins, J. (1981). The role of primary language development in promoting educational success for language minority students. In *Schooling and language minority students* (pp. 3–49). Sacramento, CA: California Department of Education.

Cummins, J. (1989). *Empowering minority students.* Sacramento, CA: California Association for Bilingual Education.

Cummins, J. (1991). Interdependence of first- and second-language proficiency in bilingual children. In E. Bialystok (Ed.), *Language processing in bilingual children* (pp. 70–89). Cambridge: Cambridge University Press.

Ellis, R. (1985). *Understanding second language acquisition.* Oxford: Oxford University Press.

Enright, D. S., & McCloskey, M. L. (1988). *Integrating English: Developing English language and literacy in the multilingual classroom.* Reading, MA: Addison-Wesley.

Frederickson, J. (Ed.). (1995). *Reclaiming our voices: Bilingual education critical pedagogy and praxis.* Ontario, CA: California Association for Bilingual Education.

Freeman, Y. S., & Freeman, D. E. (1992). *Whole language for second language learner.* Portsmouth, NH: Heinemann.

Garcia, E. (1994). *Understanding and meeting the challenge of student cultural diversity.* Boston: Houghton Mifflin.

Genesee, F. (1987). *Learning through two languages: Studies of immersion and bilingual education.* Cambridge, MA: Newbury House.

Genesee, F. (Ed.). (1994). *Educating second language children: The whole child, the whole curriculum, the whole community.* Cambridge: Cambridge University Press.

Goodman, Y. M., & Wilde, S. (Eds.). (1992). *Literacy events in a community of young writers.* New York: Teachers College Press.

Hakuta, K. (1986). *Mirror of language: The debate on bilingualism.* New York: Basic Books.

Hernández-Chávez, E. (1984). The inadequacy of English immersion education as an educational approach for language minority students in the

United States. In *Studies on immersion education: A collection for United States educators* (pp. 144–183). Sacramento, CA: California Department of Education.

Minicucci, C., & Olsen, L. (1992). *Programs for secondary limited English proficient students: A California study* Washington, DC: NCBE.

Oakes, J. (1985). *Keeping track: How schools structure inequality.* New Haven: Yale University Press.

Ogbu, J. (1993). Variability in minority school performance: A problem in search of an explanation. In E. Jacob & C. Jordan (Eds.), *Minority education: Anthropological perspectives* (pp. 83–111). Norwood, NJ: Ablex.

Spener, D. (1988). "Transitional bilingual education and the socialization of immigrants." *Harvard Educational Review,* 58, 133–153.

Swain, M. (1985). Communicative competence: Some roles of comprehensible input and comprehensible output in its development. In S. Gass & C. Madden (Eds.), *Input in second language acquisition* (pp. 235–253). Cambridge, MA: Newbury House.

Tharp, R. G., & Gallimore, R. (1988). *Rousing minds to life: Teaching, learning, and schooling in social context.* Cambridge: Cambridge University Press.

Thomas, W. P. (1992). "An analysis of the research methodology of the Ramírez study." *Bilingual Research Journal,* 16 (1–2), 213–245.

Thomas, W. P., & Collier, V. P. (1995). *Language minority student achievement and program effectiveness.* Manuscript in preparation.

Trueba, H. T., Jacobs, L., & Kirton, E. (1990). *Cultural conflict and adaptation: The case of Hmong children in American society.* New York: Falmer Press.

Wong Fillmore, L. (1991). Second language learning in children: A model of language learning in social context. In E. Bialystok (Ed.), *Language processing in bilingual children* (pp. 49–69). Cambridge: Cambridge University Press.

Author's Note

This publication has been adapted by the author from a paper presented at the 1995 Georgetown University Roundtable, to be published by Georgetown University Press. For a more detailed discussion of the extensive research base presented in short form here, see Collier, V. P. (1995) *Promoting academic success for ESL students: Understanding second language acquisition for school.* Elizabeth, NJ: New Jersey Teachers of English to Speakers of Other Languages–Bilingual Educators.

NAEYC Position Statement: Responding to Linguistic and Cultural Diversity—Recommendations for Effective Early Childhood Education

Adopted November 1995

Linguistically and culturally diverse *is an educational term used by the U.S. Department of Education to define children enrolled in educational programs who are either non-English-proficient (NEP) or limited-English-proficient (LEP). Educators use this phrase,* linguistically and culturally diverse, *to identify children from homes and communities where English* is not *the primary language of communication (Garciá 1991). For the purposes of this statement, the phrase will be used in a similar manner.*

This document primarily describes linguistically and culturally diverse children who speak languages other than English. However, the recommendations of this position statement can also apply to children who, although they speak only English, are also linguistically and culturally diverse.

Introduction

The children and families served in early childhood programs reflect the ethnic, cultural, and linguistic diversity of the nation. The nation's children all deserve an early childhood education that is responsive to their families, communities, and racial, ethnic, and cultural backgrounds. For young children to develop and learn optimally, the early childhood professional must be prepared to meet their diverse developmental, cultural, linguistic, and educational needs. Early childhood educators face the challenge of how best to respond to these needs.

The acquisition of language is essential to children's cognitive and social development. Regardless of what language children speak, they still develop and learn. Educators recognize that linguistically and culturally diverse children come to early childhood programs with previously acquired knowledge and learning based upon the language used in their home. For young children, the language of the home is the language they have used since birth, the language they use to make and establish meaningful communicative relationships, and the language they use to begin to construct their knowledge and test their learning. The home language is tied to children's culture, and culture and language communicate traditions, values, and attitudes (Chang 1993). Parents should be encouraged to use and develop children's home language; early childhood educators should respect children's linguistic and cultural backgrounds and their diverse learning styles. In so doing, adults will enhance children's learning and development.

Just as children learn and develop at different rates, individual differences exist in how children whose home language is not English acquire English. For example, some children may experience a silent period (of six or more months)

From *Young Children*, January 1996, pp. 4-12. © 1996 by the National Association for the Education of Young Children. Reprinted by permission.

while they acquire English; other children may practice their knowledge by mixing or combining languages (for example, "Mi mamá me put on mi coat"); still other children may seem to have acquired English-language skills (appropriate accent, use of vernacular, vocabulary, and grammatical rules) but are not truly proficient; yet some children will quickly acquire English-language proficiency. Each child's way of learning a new language should be viewed as acceptable, logical, and part of the ongoing development and learning of any new language.

Defining the problem

At younger and younger ages, children are negotiating difficult transitions between their home and educational settings, requiring an adaptation to two or more diverse sets of rules, values, expectations, and behaviors. Educational programs and families must *respect* and *reinforce* each other as they work together to achieve the greatest benefit for all children. For some young children, entering any new environment—including early childhood programs—can be intimidating. The lives of many young children today are further complicated by having to communicate and learn in a language that may be unfamiliar. In the past, children entering U.S. schools from families whose home language is not English were expected to immerse themselves in the mainstream of schools, primarily through the use of English (Soto 1991; Wong Fillmore 1991). Sometimes the negative attitudes conveyed or expressed toward certain languages lead children to "give up" their home language. Early childhood professionals must recognize the feeling of loneliness, fear, and abandonment children may feel when they are thrust into settings that isolate them from their home community and language. The loss of children's home language may result in

the disruption of family communication patterns, which may lead to the loss of intergenerational wisdom; damage to individual and community esteem; and children's potential nonmastery of their home language or English.

NAEYC's position

NAEYC's goal is to build support for equal access to high-quality educational programs that recognize and promote all aspects of children's development and learning, enabling all children to become competent, successful, and socially responsible adults. Children's educational experiences should afford them the opportunity to learn and to become effective, functioning members of society. Language development is essential for learning, and the development of children's home language does not interfere with their ability to learn English. Because knowing more than one language is a cognitive asset (Hakuta & García 1989), early education programs should encourage the development of children's home language while fostering the acquisition of English.

*For the optimal development and learning of all children, educators must **accept** the legitimacy of children's home language, **respect** (hold in high regard) and **value** (esteem, appreciate) the home culture, and **promote** and **encourage** the active involvement and support of all families, including extended and nontraditional family units.*

When early childhood educators acknowledge and respect children's home language and culture, ties between the family and programs are strengthened. This atmosphere provides increased opportunity for learning because young children feel supported, nurtured, and connected not only to their home communities and families but also to teachers and the educational setting.

The challenges

The United States is a nation of great cultural diversity, and our diversity creates opportunities to learn and share both similar and different experiences. There are opportunities to learn about people from different backgrounds; the opportunity to foster a bilingual citizenry with skills necessary to succeed in a global economy; and opportunities to share one's own cherished heritage and traditions with others.

Historically, our nation has tended to regard differences, especially language differences, as cultural handicaps rather than cultural resources (Meier & Cazden 1982). "Although most Americans are reluctant to say it publicly, many are anxious about the changing racial and ethnic composition of the country" (Sharry 1994). As the early childhood profession transforms its thinking,

the challenge for early childhood educators is to become more knowledgeable about how to relate to children and families whose linguistic or cultural background is different from their own.

Between 1979 and 1989 the number of children in the United States from culturally and linguistically diverse backgrounds increased considerably (NCES 1993), and, according to a report released by the Center for the Study of Social Policy (1992), that diversity is even more pronounced among children younger than age 6. Contrary to popular belief, many of these children are neither foreign born nor immigrants but were born in the United States (Waggoner 1993). Approximately 9.9 million of the estimated 45 million school-age children, more than one in five, live in households in which languages other than English are spoken (Waggoner 1994). In some communities, however, the number of children living in a family in which a language other than English is spoken is likely to be much larger. Head Start reports that the largest

23

number of linguistically and culturally diverse children served through Head Start are Spanish speakers, with other language groups representing smaller but growing percentages (Head Start Bureau 1995).

The challenge for teachers is to provide high-quality care and education for the increasing number of children who are likely to be linguistically and culturally diverse.

Families and communities are faced with increasingly complex responsibilities. Children used to be cared for by parents and family members who typically spoke the home language of their family, be it English or another language. With the increasing need of family members to work, even while children are very young, more and more children are placed in care and educational settings with adults who may not speak the child's home language or share their cultural background. Even so, children will spend an ever-increasing amount of their waking lives with these teachers. What happens in care will have a tremendous impact on the child's social, emotional, and cognitive development. These interactions will influence the child's values, view of the world, perspectives on family, and connections to community. This places a tremendous responsibility in the hands of the early childhood community.

Responding to linguistic and cultural diversity can be challenging. At times the challenges can be complicated further by the specific needs or issues of the child, the family, or the educational program. Solutions may not be evident. Individual circumstances can affect each situation differently. There are no easy answers, and often myths and misinformation may flourish. The challenges may even seem to be too numerous for any one teacher or provider to manage. Nonetheless, despite the complexity, it is the responsibility of all educators to assume the tasks and meet the challenges. Once a situation occurs, the early childhood educator should enter into a dialogue with colleagues, parents, and others in an effort to arrive at a negotiated agreement that will meet the best interest of the child. For example,

• A mother, father, and primary caregiver each have different cultural and linguistic backgrounds and do not speak English. Should the language of one of these persons be affirmed or respected above the others? How can the teacher affirm and respect the backgrounds of each of these individuals?

• The principal is concerned that all children learn English and, therefore, does not want any language other than English spoken in the early childhood setting. In the interest of the child, how should the educator respond?

• An educator questions whether a child will ever learn English if the home language is used as the primary language in the early childhood setting. How is this concern best addressed?

Solutions exist for each of these linguistic and cultural challenges, just as they do for the many other issues that early childhood educators confront within the early childhood setting. These challenges must be viewed as opportunities for the early childhood educator to reflect, question, and effectively respond to the needs of linguistically and culturally diverse children. Although appropriate responses to every linguistically and culturally diverse situation cannot be addressed through this document, early childhood educators should consider the following recommendations.

Recommendations for a responsive learning environment

Early childhood educators should stop and reflect on the best ways to ensure appropriate educational and developmental experiences for all young children. The unique qualities and characteristics of each individual child must be acknowledged. Just as each child is different, methods and strategies to work with young children must vary.

The issue of home language and its importance to young children is also relevant for children who speak English but come from different cultural backgrounds, for example, speakers of English who have dialects, such as people from Appalachia or other regions having distinct patterns of speech, speakers of Black English, or second- and third-generation speakers of English who maintain the dominant accent of their heritage language. While this position statement basically responds to children who are from homes in which English is not the dominant language, the recommendations provided may be helpful when working with children who come from diverse cultural backgrounds, even when they only speak English. The overall goal for early childhood professionals, however, is to provide every child, including children who are linguistically and culturally diverse, with a responsive learning environment. The following recommendations help achieve this goal.

A. Recommendations for working with children

Recognize that all children are cognitively, linguistically, and emotionally connected to the language and culture of their home.

When program settings acknowledge and support children's home language and culture, ties between the family and school are strengthened. In a supportive atmosphere young children's home language is less likely to atrophy (Chang 1993), a situation that could threaten the children's important ties to family and community.

Acknowledge that children can demonstrate their knowledge and capabilities in many ways.

In response to linguistic and cultural diversity, the goal for early childhood educators should be to make the most of children's potential, strengthening and building upon the skills they bring when they enter programs. Education, as Cummins states, implies "drawing out children's potential and making them more than they were" (1989, vii). Educational programs and practices must recognize the strengths that children possess. Whatever language children speak, they should be able to demonstrate their capabilities and also feel the success of being appreciated and valued. Teachers must build upon children's diversity of gifts and skills and provide young children opportunities to exhibit these skills in early childhood programs.

The learning environment must focus on the learner and allow opportunities for children to express themselves across the curriculum, including art, music, dramatization, and even block building. By using a nondeficit approach (tapping and recognizing children's strengths rather than focusing the child's home environment on skills yet unlearned) in their teaching, teachers should take the time to observe and engage children in a variety of learning activities. Children's strengths should be celebrated, and they should be given numerous ways to express their interests and talents. In doing this, teachers will provide children an opportunity to display their intellect and knowledge that may far exceed the boundaries of language.

Understand that without comprehensible input, second-language learning can be difficult.

It takes time to become linguistically proficient and competent in any language. Linguistically and culturally diverse children may be able to master basic communication skills; however, mastery of the more cognitively complex language skills needed for academic learning (Cummins 1989) is more dependent on the learning environment. Academic learning relies on significant amounts of information presented in decontextualized learning situations. Success in school becomes more and more difficult as children are required to learn, to be tested and evaluated based on ever-increasing amounts of information, consistently presented in a decontextualized manner. Children learn best when they are given a context in which to learn, and the knowledge that children acquire in "their first language can make second-language input much more comprehensible" (Krashen 1992, 37). Young children can gain knowledge more easily when they obtain quality instruction through their first language. Children can acquire the necessary language and cognitive skills required to succeed in school when given an appropriate learning environment, one that is tailored to meet their needs (NAEYC & NAECS/SDE 1991; Bredekamp & Rosegrant 1992).

Although verbal proficiency in a second language can be accomplished within two to three years, the skills necessary to achieve the higher level educational skills of understanding academic content through reading and writing may require four or more years (Cummins 1981; Collier 1989). Young children may seem to be fluent and at ease with English but may not be capable of understanding or expressing themselves as competently as their English-speaking peers. Although children seem to be speaking a second language with ease, *speaking* a language does not equate to being *proficient* in that language. Full proficiency in the first language, including complex uses of the language, contributes to the development of the second language. Children who do not become proficient in their second language after two or three years of regular use probably are not proficient in their first language either.

Young children may seem to be fluent and at ease speaking a second language, but they may not be fully capable of understanding or expressing themselves in the more complex aspects of language and may demonstrate weaknesses in language-learning skills, including vocabulary skills, auditory memory and discrimination skills, simple problem-solving tasks, and the ability to follow sequenced directions. Language difficulties such as these often can result in the linguistically and culturally diverse child being overreferred to special education, classified as learning disabled, or perceived as developmentally delayed.

B. Recommendations for working with families

Actively involve parents and families in the early learning program and setting.

Parents and families should be actively involved in the learning and development of their children. Teachers should actively seek parental involvement and pursue establishing a partnership with children's families. When possible, teachers should visit the child's community (for example, shops, churches, and playgrounds); read and learn about the community through the use of books, pictures, observations, and conversations with community members; and visit the home and meet with other family members.

Parents and families should be invited to share, participate, and engage in activities with their children. Parent involvement can be accomplished in a number of ways, including asking parents to share stories, songs, drawings, and experiences of their linguistic and cultural background and asking parents to serve as monitors or field trip organizers. Families and parents should be invited to share activities that are developmentally appropriate and meaningful within their culture. These opportunities demonstrate to the parent what their child is learning; increase the knowledge, information, and understanding of all children regarding people of different cultures and linguistic backgrounds; and establish a meaningful relationship with the parent. The early childhood educator should ensure that parents are informed and engaged with their child in meaningful activities that promote linkages between the home and the early care setting.

Encourage and assist all parents in becoming knowledgeable about the cognitive value for children of knowing more than one language, and provide them with strategies to support, maintain, and preserve home-language learning.

In an early childhood setting and atmosphere in which home language is preserved, acknowledged, and respected, all parents can learn the value of home-language development and the strength it provides children as they add to their existing knowledge and understanding. Parents and teachers can learn how to become advocates regarding the long-term benefits that result from bilingualism.

Parents and teachers recognize the acquisition of English as an intellectual accomplishment, an opportunity for economic growth and development, and a means for achieving academic success. There are even times when parents may wish for the ability, or have been mistakenly encouraged, to speak to their children only in English, a language of which the parents themselves may not have command. The educator should understand the effects that speaking only in English can have upon the child, the family, and the child's learning. The

teacher must be able to explain that speaking to the child only in English can often result in communications being significantly hindered and verbal interactions being limited and unnatural between the parent and the child. In using limited English, parents may communicate to children using simple phrases and commands (for example, "Sit down" or "Stop"); modeling grammatically incorrect phrases (for example, "We no go store"); or demonstrating other incorrect usages of language that are common when persons acquire a second language. From these limited and incorrect verbal interactions, the amount of language the child is hearing is reduced, and the child's vocabulary growth is restricted, contributing to an overall decrease in verbal expression. When parents do not master the second language yet use the second language to communicate with their child, there is an increased likelihood that the child will not hear complex ideas or abstract thoughts—important skills needed for cognitive and language development. The teacher must explain that language is developed through natural language interactions. These natural interactions occur within the day-to-day setting, through radio and television, when using public transportation, and in play with children whose dominant language is English. The parent and the teacher must work collaboratively to achieve the goal of children's learning English.

Through the home language and culture, families transmit to their children a sense of identity, an understanding of how to relate to other people, and a sense of belonging. When parents and children cannot communicate with one another, family and community destabilization can occur. Children who are proficient in their home language are able to maintain a connectedness to their histories, their stories, and the day-to-day events shared by parents, grandparents, and other family members who may speak only the home language. Without the ability to com-

municate, parents are not able to socialize their children, share beliefs and value systems, and directly influence, coach, and model with their children.

Recognize that parents and families must rely on caregivers and educators to honor and support their children in the cultural values and norms of the home.

Parents depend on high-quality early childhood programs to assist them with their children's development and learning. Early childhood programs should make provisions to communicate with families in their home language and to provide parent–teacher encounters that both welcome and accommodate families. Partnerships between the home and the early childhood setting must be developed to ensure that practices of the home and expectations of the program are complementary. Linguistic and cultural continuity between the home and the early childhood program supports children's social and emotional development. By working together, parents and teachers have the opportunity to influence the understanding of language and culture and to encourage multicultural learning and acceptance in a positive way.

C. Recommendations for professional preparation

Provide early childhood educators with professional preparation and development in the areas of culture, language, and diversity.

Efforts to understand the languages and cultural backgrounds of young children are essential in helping children to learn. Uncertainty can exist when educators are unsure of how to relate to children and families of linguistic and cultural backgrounds different from their own. Early childhood educators need to understand and appreciate their own cultural and linguistic backgrounds. Adults' cultural background affects how they interact with and/or teach young children. The educator's background influences how children are taught, reinforced, and disciplined. The child's background influences how the child constructs knowledge, responds to discipline and praise, and interacts in the early childhood setting.

Preservice and inservice training opportunities in early childhood education programs assist educators in overcoming some of the linguistic and cultural challenges they may face in working with young children. Training institutions and programs can consider providing specific courses in the following topic areas or include these issues in current courses: language acquisition; second-language learning; use of translators; working with diverse families; sociolinguistics; cross-cultural communication; issues pertaining to the politics of race, language, and culture; and community involvement.

Recruit and support early childhood educators who are trained in languages other than English.

Within the field of early childhood education, there is a need for knowledgeable, trained, competent, and sensitive multilingual/multicultural early childhood educators. Early childhood educators who speak more than one language and are culturally knowledgeable are an invaluable resource in the early childhood setting. In some instances the educator may speak multiple languages or may be able to communicate using various linguistic regionalisms or dialects

spoken by the child or the family. The educator may have an understanding of sociocultural and economic issues relevant within the local linguistically and culturally diverse community and can help support the family in the use and development of the child's home language and in the acquisition of English. The early childhood teacher who is trained in linguistic and cultural diversity can be a much-needed resource for information about the community and can assist in the inservice cultural orientation and awareness training for the early childhood program. The bilingual educator also can be a strong advocate for family and community members.

Too often, however, bilingual early childhood professionals are called upon to provide numerous other services, some of which they may not be equipped to provide. For example, the bilingual professional, although a fluent speaker, may not have the vocabulary needed to effectively communicate with other adults or, in some instances, may be able to read and write only in English, not in the second language. In addition, bilingual teachers should not be expected to meet the needs of *all* linguistically and culturally diverse children and families in the program, especially those whose language they do not speak. Bilingual providers should not be asked to translate forms, particularly at a moment's notice, nor should they be required to stop their work in order to serve as interpreters. Bilingual teachers should not serve in roles, such as advising or counseling, in which they may lack professional training. These assignments may seem simple but often can be burdensome and must be viewed as added duties placed upon the bilingual teacher.

Preservice and inservice training programs are needed to support bilingual early childhood educators in furthering educators' knowledge and mastery of the language(s) other than English that they speak, and training should also credit content-based courses offered in lan-

guages other than English. Professional preparation instructors must urge all teachers to support multilingual/multicultural professionals in their role as advocates for linguistically and culturally diverse children. Early childhood professionals should be trained to work collaboratively with the bilingual early childhood teacher and should be informed of the vital role of the bilingual educator. Additionally, there is a need for continued research in the area of linguistic and cultural diversity of young children.

D. Recommendations for programs and practice

Recognize that children can and will acquire the use of English even when their home language is used and respected.

Children should build upon their current skills as they acquire new skills. While children maintain and build upon their home language skills and culture, children can organize and develop proficiency and knowledge in English. Bilingualism has been associated with higher levels of cognitive attainment (Hakuta & García 1989) and does not interfere with either language proficiency or cognitive development. Consistent learning opportunities to read, be read to, and see print messages should be given to linguistically and culturally diverse children. Literacy developed in the home language will transfer to the second language (Krashen 1992). Bilingualism should be viewed as an asset and an educational achievement.

Support and preserve home language usage.

If the early childhood teacher *speaks* the child's home language, then the teacher can comfortably use this language around the child, thereby providing the child with opportunities to hear and use the home language within the early childhood setting. Use of the language should be clearly evident throughout the learning environment (e.g., in meeting charts, tape recordings, the library corner). Educators should develop a parent information board, using a language and reading level appropriate for the parents. Teachers should involve parents and community members in the early childhood program. Parents and community members can assist children in hearing the home language from many different adults, in addition to the teacher who speaks the home language. Parents and community members can assist other parents who may be unable to read, or they can assist the teacher in communicating with families whose home language may not have a written form.

If the early childhood educator *does not speak* the language, he or she should make efforts to provide visible signs of the home language throughout the learning environment through books and other relevant reading material in the child's language and with a parent bulletin board (get a bilingual colleague to help review for accuracy of written messages). The teacher can learn a few selected words in the child's language, thus demonstrating a willingness to take risks similar to the risks asked of children as they learn a second language. This effort by the teacher also helps to validate and affirm the child's language and culture, further demonstrating the teacher's esteem and respect for the child's linguistic and cultural background. The teacher should model appropriate use of English and provide the child with opportunities to use newly acquired vocabulary and language. The teacher also must actively involve the parent and the community in the program.

If the teacher is *faced with many different languages* in the program or classroom, the suggestions listed above are still relevant. Often teachers feel overwhelmed if more than one language is spoken in the program; however, they should remember that the goal is for children to learn, and that learning is made easier when children can build on knowledge in their home language. The teacher should consider grouping together at specific times during the day children who speak the same or similar languages so that the children can construct knowledge with others who speak their home language. The early childhood educator should ensure that these children do not become socially isolated as efforts are made to optimize their learning. Care should be taken to continually create an environment that provides for high learning expectations.

Develop and provide alternative and creative strategies for young children's learning.

Early childhood educators are encouraged to rely on their creative skills in working with children to infuse cultural and linguistic diversity in their programs. They should provide children with multiple opportunities to learn and ways for them to demonstrate their learning, participate in program activities, and work interactively with other children.

To learn more about working with linguistically and culturally diverse children, early childhood educators should collaborate with each other and with colleagues from other professions. To guide the implementation of a developmentally, linguistically, and culturally appropriate program, collaborative parent and teacher workgroups should be developed. These committees should discuss activities and strategies that would be effective for use with linguistically and culturally diverse children. Such committees promote good practices for children and shared learning between teachers and parents.

Summary

Early childhood educators can best help linguistic and culturally diverse children and their families by acknowledging and responding to the importance of the child's home language and culture. Administrative support for bilingualism as a goal is necessary within the educational setting. Educational practices should focus on educating children toward the "school culture" while preserving and respecting the diversity of the home language and culture that each child brings to the early learning setting. Early childhood professionals and families must work together to achieve high-quality care and education for *all* children.

References

Bredekamp, S., & T. Rosegrant, eds. 1992. *Reaching potentials: Appropriate curriculum and assessment for young children.* Vol. 1. Washington, DC: NAEYC.

Center for the Study of Social Policy. 1992. *The challenge of change: What the 1990 census tells us about children.* Washington, DC: Author.

Chang, H.N.-L. 1993. *Affirming children's roots: Cultural and linguistic diversity in early care and education.* San Francisco: California Tomorrow.

Collier, V. 1989. How long: A synthesis of research on academic achievement in second language. *TESOL Quarterly* 23: 509–31.

Cummins, J. 1981. The role of primary language development in promoting educational success for language minority students. In *Schooling and language minority students: A theoretical framework,* eds. M. Ortiz, D. Parker, & F. Tempes. Office of Bilingual Bicultural Education, California State Department of Education. Los Angeles: Evaluation, Dissemination, and Assessment Center, California State University.

Cummins, J. 1989. *Empowering minority students.* Sacramento: California Association for Bilingual Education.

García, E. 1991. *The education of linguistically and culturally diverse students: Effective instructional practices.* Santa Cruz: National Center for Research on Cultural Diversity and Second Language Learning, University of California.

Hakuta, K., & E. García. 1989. Bilingualism and education. *American Psychologist* 44 (2): 374–79.

Head Start Bureau, Administration on Children, Youth, and Families, Department of Health and Human Services. 1995. *Program information report.* Washington, DC: Author.

Krashen, S. 1992. *Fundamentals of language education.* Torrance, CA: Laredo Publishing.

Meier, T.R., & C.B. Cazden. 1982. A focus on oral language and writing from a multicultural perspective. *Language Arts* 59: 504–12.

National Association for the Education of Young Children (NAEYC) and National Association of Early Childhood Specialists in State Departments of Education (NAECS/

SDE). 1991. Guidelines for appropriate curriculum content and assessment in programs serving children ages 3 through 8. *Young Children* 46 (3): 21–38.

National Center for Education Statistics (NCES). 1993. *Language characteristics and schooling in the United States, a changing picture: 1979 and 1989.* NCES 93-699. Washington, DC: U.S. Department of Education, Office of Educational Research and Improvement.

Sharry, F. 1994. *The rise of nativism in the United States and how to respond to it.* Washington, DC: National Education Forum.

Soto, L.D. 1991. Understanding bilingual/ bicultural children. *Young Children* 46 (2): 30–36.

Waggoner, D., ed. 1993. *Numbers and needs: Ethnic and linguistic minorities in the United States* 3 (6).

Waggoner, D. 1994. Language minority school age population now totals 9.9 million. *NABE News* 18 (1): 1, 24–26.

Wong Fillmore, L. 1991. When learning a second language means losing the first. *Early Childhood Research Quarterly* 6: 323–46.

Resources

Banks, J. 1993. Multicultural education for young children: Racial and ethnic attitudes and their modification. In *Handbook of research on the education of young children,* ed. B. Spodek, 236–51. New York: Macmillan.

Collier, V. 1989. How long: A synthesis of research on academic achievement in second language. *TESOL Quarterly* 23: 509–31.

Collier, V., & C. Twyford. 1988. The effect of age on acquisition of a second language for school. *National Clearinghouse for Bilingual Education* 2 (Winter): 1–12.

Derman-Sparks, L., & the A.B.C. Task Force. 1989. *Anti-bias curriculum: Tools for empowering young children.* Washington, DC: NAEYC.

McLaughlin, B. 1992. *Myths and misconceptions about second language learning: What every teacher needs to unlearn.* Santa Cruz: National Center for Research on Cultural Diversity and Second Language Learning, University of California.

Neugebauer, B., ed. 1992. *Alike and different: Exploring our humanity with young children.* Redmond, WA: Exchange Press, 1987. Reprint, Washington, DC: NAEYC.

Ogbu, J.U. 1978. *Minority education and caste: The American system in cross cultural perspective.* New York: Academic.

Phillips, C.B. 1988. Nurturing diversity for today's children and tomorrow's leaders. *Young Children* 43 (2): 42–47.

Tharp, R.G. 1989. Psychocultural variables and constants: Effects on teaching and learning in schools. *American Psychologist* 44: 349–59.

Factors Affecting Language Development from the Perspectives of Four Bilingual Teachers

Nancy Lemberger

Nancy Lemberger, EdD, is an assistant professor of bilingual teacher education at Long Island University in Brooklyn, New York.

How do bilingual teachers affect their students' dual language development? What can help them better develop students' language strengths? Bilingual education literature rarely describes bilingual teachers' practices. In a prior study (Lemberger, 1990), I provided some teachers' voices about their experiences in bilingual programs. This paper, drawn from oral history interviews and classroom observation data from that study, examines four veteran New York City Spanish/English bilingual primary teachers' efforts to develop their students' dual language abilities. These teachers were selected through recommendations because of their excellence and long-term commitment to bilingual teaching.

Assisting students in dual language development is a major task of bilingual teachers. Factors inside and outside the classroom that encourage and constrain teachers in accomplishing this task are (a) teachers' background and second language learning experiences, (b) the school composition, (c) bilingual program and testing policies, and (d) assimilation forces. After a brief case description of the four teachers' backgrounds and school contexts, I will show how these and other factors affect the language development process.

The Teachers and Their Schools

These cases are presented along a continuum from English dominant to Spanish dominant in terms of how much each language was used in each teacher's class and program.

Norma

Norma, born in New York City, moved to Puerto Rico with her family when she was four. When she was in sixth grade they returned to New York City. Her school success in Puerto Rico helped her succeed here. This success, however, alienated her from her Latino peers, making her feel as if she was "two people." Though she enjoyed doing well and pleasing her teachers, her peers became jealous and picked on her. Because of these experiences, Norma greatly values being sensitive to children's feelings and encourages respect among students.

Norma has taught in her New York City bilingual program for 14 years and teaches a second grade class. Though not initially trained as a bilingual teacher, she was expected to know how to teach bilingually because she was a bilingual person. The school population is primarily Puerto Rican but includes some African Americans and Italian Americans. The Puerto Rican parents, mostly second and third generation New Yorkers, speak primarily English. Many younger parents, for whom Spanish is their second language, speak a mixture of English and Spanish.

Because of the community's English dominance, the bilingual program has emphasized English. Most children opt into the program because they score above the minimal cutoff score on the English language proficiency tests.

The bilingual program has about 300 students. Since there is usually one class per grade level, there have never been enough limited English proficient (LEP) students to divide classes by language dominance, so the teachers must handle the two languages within each self-contained class. Because of the English emphasis, the school purchases mostly English materials.

Reprinted from *The Journal of Educational Issues of Language Minority Students,* Vol. 18, Winter 1996, pp. 17-31. Published by The Bilingual Education Teacher Preparation Program, Boise State University. © 1996.

Although the district espouses a maintenance bilingual education philosophy, Norma says,

No one really has followed through on [it]. . . . Spanish has become almost like learning a second language to them. What we're really trying to do, even more than the language, is maintain the culture: the music and the arts.

Spanish reading has not been required. Norma uses Spanish mostly to scold or to compliment children and to facilitate learning:

I always try to bring Spanish in . . . as a means of reaching kids. . . . If they don't understand something, . . . I'll explain it in Spanish, just to help the kids see how much they already know.

For the few LEP students, a stronger English as a Second Language (ESL) program is greatly needed. Norma explains,

I feel very bad for . . . the Spanish dominant children who weren't really given any ESL. . . . They were taught the alphabet in English and supposedly to read in English. . . . You are pulling teeth, because they don't know what's going on.

English testing is a priority in the school, and considerable time is spent on standardized test preparation. Norma states,

Because children were scoring very low [in reading], we started to teach them how to take the tests: . . . following directions, eliminating answers, . . . and guessing. . . . We've become too obsessed with test preparation, schedules, . . . and kits. . . . You start . . . in February, and by April [when they take the test], they're sick of it. The scores in the past couple of years have still gone down.

The bilingual teachers make great efforts to form relationships with students' families. Norma elaborates:

Parents feel that we're more here for them, than for the kids. Because [we're] bilingual, they are not asking, "Why isn't my child reading in Spanish?" They understand that we use Spanish to facilitate learning and to explain . . . what we're doing.

At Norma's school, the Spanish dominant student population was so small that they were never consistently instructed bilingually. Rather, she used Spanish for clarification and to relate to students and parents in culturally congruent ways.

Jennifer

Jennifer was born in Puerto Rico and migrated to New York City after first grade. Because she had already learned to read in Spanish, she easily transferred her skills to her English-only classroom in New York. She owed her school success to her father, who supported her with nightly homework assistance, and to a bilingual girl friend who interpreted her class work for her. Like the caring help she received, she encourages parents to help their children and uses in-class pairing and small group interaction.

Jennifer was hired to teach in a new bilingual program at a New York City elementary school, where she has been teaching for 17 years and presently has a K/1 class. Most of her students stay with her for both kindergarten and first grades.

The community's changing demographics have affected the program organization and priorities. In the first years, sizable numbers of LEP students created an urgent need to implement a bilingual program. Many children had such poor expressive skills that "it was just a question of getting them to speak, never mind to learn a second language." The large numbers of students allowed for one English and one Spanish dominant class per grade.

Over the years as the neighborhood has become more genteel, LEP students' families can no longer afford to settle there. With fewer LEP students, classes are no longer organized by language dominance. Entitled LEP children are dispersed in four bilingual classes where an enrichment model is the focus. English-speaking parents place their children in these bilingual classes to learn Spanish. LEP students receive Spanish literacy and content instruction along with ESL, while English-speaking students receive English literacy, content, and Spanish as a second language (SSL) instruction. Dealing with two languages frustrates Jennifer:

This . . . is wearing me down. . . . It's not fair to the Spanish dominant child. . . . There's a lot of nurturing that I'd like to give that I don't . . . get a chance to. . . . [Of the] eight [LEP] kids, only four don't understand [any] English. . . . They . . . get lost when we're having a really good group [English] discussion. [When] I stop in the middle to translate, then I'm losing the others. . . . I don't want to leave any of them out. . . . I don't know if they're getting anything out of it. That's my concern.

One strategy Jennifer uses is pairing a non-English-speaking student with a bilingual student to ensure that all children understand the content. As a child, she recalls how successful this was for her when she was paired with a "bilingual buddy" who translated the content and procedures in the new language. This pairing allows students to serve as language role models for one another.

The changes in Jennifer's community have affected the bilingual program. When there were more LEP students to divide classes by language dominance, she was able to devote more time and concerted effort to native language development.

Maria

Maria, a Mexican-American, was born in New York City, where she attended the public schools. Though her home language was Spanish, her parents emphasized the importance of speaking English outside the home.

In the only Mexican family in her neighborhood, she felt isolated because her parents did not allow her to play with other Caribbean Latino neighborhood children. Since Maria had few opportunities to connect with Mexican culture outside her home, she felt that she did not fit in anywhere. Over the years, through her education and experiences, she assimilated into the mainstream culture. Becoming a bilingual teacher, however, allowed her to reconnect with her language and background and to try to ease the painful transition for young children.

Maria has taught in two New York City bilingual schools for seven years each. Her present school is the focus of this discussion. The community is ethnically mixed with a high concentration of Latinos (mostly Puerto Ricans). The degree of bilingual language ability varies among the parents and children because, as Maria describes,

> a lot of them were Spanish dominant. But . . . some who were native born [in the U.S.] . . . spoke what they call 'Spanglish.' They neither dominated English nor Spanish. . . . Those children were in pretty bad shape because they would start a sentence in one language and finish it in another. Or they'd use the sentence structure of Spanish and they'd put in English words. . . . The children . . . don't even know that they are speaking a mixture of two languages.

Her approach to address this language mixing came from her own language learning experience. Maria wanted to separate and clarify the two languages,

> by . . . being a strong role model. I'd stick to one language at a time within a subject area, correct [students] as they spoke, and make them repeat. . . . I learned this from my father who wanted us to maintain our Spanish. . . . He'd correct us and made us repeat after him. It's not . . . enough to listen to . . . the correct way, but [you must] internalize it more by repeating it to yourself.

The school's transitional bilingual program is one where, as Maria explains, bilingual education is seen as a means . . . of mainstreaming children into the English school system. By law teachers are required to teach children in their native language so that the children will not lose out on their education. English is the language of this country, so eventually teachers want the children to be able to function in English.

The program is divided into Spanish or English dominant classes. Children are expected to make the transition to English instruction by the third grade. Maria has taught both English and Spanish dominant classes and is teaching a Spanish dominant second grade class.

Maria presents new content bilingually, giving students as many concepts as possible without losing them in the second language:

> Building concepts upon concepts better prepares the students for third grade. I . . . introduce concepts in the native language and then . . . I start explaining them in English. Sometimes when . . . I find that the majority of children are not ready for it, . . . I go back to Spanish, . . . so that I don't lose them in changing to the English. When they are stronger, then I go back to English.

District and school policies toward rapid transition to English were a driving force in reading instruction and testing priorities. New York City begins giving children the standardized reading tests in second grade if they have been in the system since kindergarten. (Children in the country fewer than two years are exempted from these tests.) Maria recounts,

> My principal must get the pressure down from the district. . . . They push us with English even though sometimes we feel the children aren't ready for all the English that they want them to have. They say, . . . "They aren't showing enough success. We've got to get the scores up. You've got to spend more time in English and with the reading." You don't want to frustrate the children or . . . yourself. Then we have all this test preparation, a lot of competition with that too. Sometimes I feel like I'm talking to the wall, it's just beyond their capabilities.

Maria draws on her own language learning experience by modeling and separating the two languages and developing concepts bilingually. The expectation of testing children in English before they were ready frustrated both her and her students.

Celia

Celia immigrated to the U.S. from Cuba in the late 1960s. As an adult Celia had a completely different transition experience than the other three teachers. Since she did not have to acquire English and assimilate to the American culture as a child, her identity as a Cuban woman was firmly intact. Unlike the others, she never had to straddle two cultures or decide to which she belonged. Aiding her transition was the support of her husband, children, and the tightly-knit Cuban community. Even though learning English was difficult, her life experiences and natural cognitive strategies helped her. Unlike the others who closely related to the children's painful transition experiences, Celia's adjustment was more congruent with the experiences of her students' parents.

Celia, formerly a teacher in Cuba, brought with her years of successful teaching approaches which included teacher-centered whole group instruction and rote learning techniques. These traditional approaches have facilitated her work with the predominantly Dominican school population because they fit the parents' views of what education should be.

After securing her teaching credentials, Celia got a bilingual teaching position at a New York City school where she has taught for 18 years. The bilingual program has grown from 8 to 30 teachers. The school is now almost completely bilingual with classes divided by language dominance. Celia has a Spanish dominant first grade class.

The school is located in an almost exclusively Dominican neighborhood. Celia's students' families are,

> [mostly] lower class... people... who come here to improve their economic situations. [They]... come... from places where there were no schools... and often have very low levels of education.

The school and district bilingual education philosophy has always been transitional. The goal is for children to make the transition to the English dominant classes by third grade. In the past, the district had a stronger English emphasis than now. Because of that emphasis, neither Spanish materials nor bilingual inservice training was provided. The overly strong English emphasis detrimentally affected children. As Celia explains,

> the children learned neither language well because they were very confused. They pushed us to give... the most English possible. [Even so] the reading levels... were very low. They have gone down so much that the district changed its philosophy. Now they give more Spanish... especially in the primary grades, so the children can overcome these difficulties in their own language.

Although the new district policy encourages teachers to emphasize native language development,

> ... the bilingual teacher [still] has to do double the work of other teachers... to cover all the subjects in two languages and [help students] pass the tests in both languages to show that the bilingual program has not been a failure.... The bilingual teacher must give extraordinary effort [to provide]... children all the background knowledge that they don't bring with them from their countries. One must develop the vocabulary in their first language in order to begin to teach... in the second language.

Celia's first graders have limited native language vocabulary which needs continual development:

> I don't know if it is because there is little communication at home or that children just watch too much television. They refer to everything as 'cosa' [thing].... They have sufficient Spanish oral language to... talk or to answer a question.... But, they often don't... know the names of objects,... their birthdays, or their addresses. They don't [even] know their parents' names, it's 'mami' or 'papi....' Until they have the vocabulary, learning is difficult even in their own language.

Celia develops vocabulary and background knowledge through stories, songs, movement, science demonstrations, learning center activities, and dramatizations.

In her holistic approach, she sees family contact as an integral part of connecting with her students. In seeking out this parent contact, she has had to play various roles:

> One has to do everything for them: fill out [forms], [interpret] immigration papers, write letters, and help them with welfare, housing, or health problems.

Her own immigration experience has made her empathetic to parents, which has enabled her to develop good relationships with them. When the program started, the bilingual teachers had to convince parents to enroll their children. Celia recalls,

> The parents had the idea that children should only learn English to be able to get along in this country. It took a lot of work to explain the need to develop the child's abilities and skills in his own language at the same time while he assimilated English.

Through her caring efforts, Celia has gradually eroded parents' misconceptions about English-only. She has won their support and convinced them of the value of native language development which strongly supports the English learning process.

Celia teaches almost exclusively in Spanish using eclectic approaches. Her major frustration is that immigrant children do not have highly developed native language skills when they come to her. Celia's connections with parents enriches both children's school experiences and the parents' lives.

Language Development in the Four Classrooms

The teachers holistically developed the four language skills of reading, writing, speaking, and listening in two languages. This discussion, based on what emerged from the data, focuses mainly on their efforts to develop oral language and reading. Topics included in this discussion are: (a) the caring classroom, (b) strategies to develop oral language, (c) reading instruction, and (d) external factors which influence language development.

The Caring Classroom: A Context for Learning

In the four classrooms, teachers created caring environments, a vital factor in successful early childhood and dual language classes. Teachers expressed care and respect [cariño y respeto] (Carrasco 1984; Montero-Seiburth & Perez, 1987) for students in a variety of ways. They openly communicated acceptance of students and were accessible to them. In class discussions and in private, they encouraged students to talk about their lives and feelings, including the sometimes tragic details. Teachers were keenly sensitive to home conditions and tried to make students' class experiences positive. The teachers welcomed and respected parents in the classrooms and understood that being a bilingual teacher meant not only helping the students academically but also helping the families in their adjustment processes. This trusting environment created a comfortable "nest" (Igoa, 1995) that fostered students' learning and parent support.

The teachers made lessons comprehensible (Krashen, 1981) through a variety of means: art projects, block play, science demonstrations, learning centers, collaborative and cooperative activities, songs, gestures, role plays, and field trips. The classrooms were print-rich, visually stimulating, and full of real objects and colorful pictures, so children could make referential connections in either language. Their approaches reflect current theories of cognition and learning where "learning is viewed as an *active* process that is enhanced through *interaction*" (Cummins, 1989, p. 65). They intuitively applied Vygotsky's "zone of proximal development" theory by socially constructing class activities and making information comprehensible and challenging through interaction with teachers and peers (Wink, Putney, Bravo-Lawerence, 1995). The buddy pairing that Jennifer used is an effective strategy for bilingual learners (Johnson, 1994; Williams & Snipper, 1990).

Strategies to Develop Oral Language

Teachers felt that oral language development was the key to students' academic success. Because many students had limited exposure to school-related vocabulary and broader experiences, the teachers felt compelled to provide these for students. As Celia put it, she first had to give them the language to name the things which surrounded them before she could begin to teach them English and other academic skills. For this reason, she used Spanish for most of her teaching.

In addition to helping children to "name their worlds" (Freire, 1970) in their own language, students learned to name their worlds in English. Simultaneously developing two languages frustrated the teachers because they were rarely able to give adequate time or emphasis to first language development, even though they know it is fundamental to learning English.

All the teachers modeled and respected the two languages. The teachers accepted and encouraged student communication in either language. The teachers responded in the language in which the student was most comfortable. Maria fought against the push for English and tried to let her children "come to English on their own" when they were ready and could value it.

For these teachers, language instruction was not a linear process of providing instruction in one language first and then in the other. The teachers fluidly used the two languages as they constantly gauged the children's readiness for English by discerning areas that needed clarification. In presenting concepts bilingually, Maria relied on linguistic summaries to shelter the English instruction by using the native language as comprehensible information (Freeman & Freeman, 1992; Williams & Snipper, 1990).

The dual language context facilitated the transfer of information and skills from English to Spanish and vice versa. In Norma and Jennifer's classes, through interaction with peers and teachers, children used their knowledge of English to discover and learn Spanish as well as to develop a positive attitude about Spanish.

Because of the mix of students in Jennifer's class, she used "quick translations" for Spanish dominant children during discussions. Using concurrent translation made her question whether she was reaching those children. Researchers support the notion that concurrent translation is not effective in dual language development (Legarreta-Marcaida, 1981; Wong-Fillmore & Valadez, 1986). In addition, this "linguistic gear switching" (Legarreta-Marcaida, 1981, p. 95) had tiring effects on her.

Reading Instruction

All teachers read many stories aloud to their students in both languages. In this way, they modeled reading skills as well as developed a joy for reading. They complained about the lack of appropriate reading materials in both Spanish and English for Spanish dominant students.

Spanish Reading

Available texts, personal preferences, and training experiences influenced the teachers' reading approaches. They all felt that Spanish reading texts were of inferior quality and less plentiful than English books. Maria felt comfortable using a phonetic approach. Celia's approach, derived from her Cuban training, embraced both phonetic decoding and sight reading. She motivated students by reading each story aloud to the whole class and then followed with small group work and individualized instruction. Because she wanted each child to regularly read to her, she asked parents to bring in their children before school for individual reading instruction.

Norma's limited formal bilingual teacher education made her less secure in teaching reading in Spanish than in English. She found the phonetic approach boring and felt it did not make sense to students. Instead, she adapted successful English reading methods to Spanish by asking students comprehension questions, and encouraging students to look for picture and context clues and to predict outcomes. Many of her students automatically transferred their English reading skills to Spanish reading.

For both Spanish and English dominant kindergartners, Jennifer used a language experience approach (Williams & Snipper, 1990) that incorporated drawing with student-dictated stories. She was unable to group the handful of Spanish dominant first graders because their levels and needs varied. Instead she individualized reading instruction by listening to them read stories from tradebooks rather than from basal readers. She was using a whole-language literature-based approach, a currently popular practice (Curtain & Pesola, 1994; Freeman & Freeman, 1992). Because there was no Spanish reading series, she often felt guilty that her Spanish reading program was less systematic and of lower quality than her English one. Like Norma's students, some of her bilingual children learned to read Spanish on their own from already knowing how to read in English.

English Reading

Overt and covert policies about reading instruction influenced the teachers' practices. The strong focus on English reading achievement pressured teachers to prepare LEP students for standardized reading tests. All the teachers found that more materials and time were devoted to English reading and testing than to Spanish.

The teachers' approaches to English reading varied. Celia did not teach English reading to her Spanish dominant first graders because they still needed to build their native language skills. Norma's excellent English reading preparation equipped her with many strategies and materials. She had her students respond to and interact with a variety of texts (literature, basals, and content texts) through oral discussion, creative writing, and projects. Jennifer liked the security of using a basal reader which she frequently augmented with children's literature. She also used language experience stories to connect spoken language to written symbols in both languages. Maria was successful in teaching English phonics to LEP children who transferred their phonetic decoding skills from Spanish.

External Factors Which Influence Language Development

Assimilation Forces

Even young children feel the pressure to learn English. According to Pease-Alvarez and Hakuta (1992), as LEP children learn English, the loss of the native language is possible. The pressure to assimilate stems from society, the media, and parents. Parents naturally want their children to succeed in school and society, but assimilation often means loss of the native language. What many parents do not realize is that when their children lose the native language, they lose their ability to communicate with family members (Rimer, 1992; Wong-Fillmore, 1991). To counter this, the teachers had to convince parents and students of the value of the native language. In doing so, they were fighting against "subtractive bilingualism" (i.e., replacing one language with another) (Lambert, 1984, cited in Ovando & Collier, 1985).

Despite the teachers' efforts to give Spanish and English equal prestige, some Spanish dominant students did not value Spanish as much as English. Norma's class often protested when it was time for Spanish reading. While some of Jennifer's students did not like Spanish, over the two years students were with her, the students became less resistant and felt pride in speaking Spanish because of the positive climate she created.

Classroom Language Use

Language use is influenced by an array of complex factors such as student composition, school and district policies, grade level, and teacher language dominance. Each teacher varied her dual language use depending on each class's linguistic make-up. In past years, Jennifer and Norma used more Spanish than they do now. Jennifer uses Spanish to clarify procedures and content for her few Spanish dominant children. As Norma realized her children's English capabilities, she increased her use of English. She mostly uses Spanish for noninstructional purposes such as complimenting or scolding students, because it produces a "quicker response" than English does. Use of Spanish also provides a cultural link similar to the way parents speak to their children. Noninstructional use of Spanish may have a positive effect on students, but not using it for instruction may communicate its lesser value to students. Children need to see the value of the native language through watching adults model it in a variety of interactions and literacy tasks (Legarreta-Marcaida, 1981).

In schools where there were sufficient numbers of LEP students for classes to be organized by language dominance, daily Spanish reading and language arts periods allowed teachers to build the native language, as in Celia and Maria's classes. Jennifer and Norma, however, had fewer LEP students and taught Spanish reading individually as time permitted. Without structures in place, time for the native language was more difficult to fit into daily activities.

Teacher language dominance also affects language use. As Jennifer states, regardless of a program's designated language preference, when the classroom door is closed, the teacher will use the language in which she feels most comfortable. Even though these teachers were bilingual, they, like their students, had different bilingual abilities. The age at which they learned English (and stopped learning Spanish) may have influenced their feelings about their language competence. Teachers who have gone through sink or swim schooling in the U.S. have been subject to the same assimilative forces as their students (Ada, 1986). Jennifer and Maria, who began learning English as young children, were more comfortable in English. They both felt their Spanish had not advanced comparably because they had not studied it as intensively as English. Because Norma had more exposure to Spanish, she felt equally competent in both. Celia, who learned English as an adult, was competent in English but felt more at ease in Spanish.

Even if bilingual teachers consciously try to model their less dominant language, bilingual students' sociolinguistic knowledge usually allows them to quickly assess the teacher's dominant language and respond in it. The implication emerges for having balanced bilingual teachers who have ease and linguistic competence to teach in either language. Though this may not always be possible, teachers can be encouraged to strengthen their weaker language through study, travel, or both (Ada, 1986). In developing their language skills, teachers can become stronger language role models and show themselves as learners to children.

Grade level may also influence the amount of each language a teacher uses. In many transitional bilingual programs, the higher the grade, the more English is emphasized. In these teachers' programs, by third grade children are expected to make the transition into English-only classrooms. Celia felt less pressure to push English with her first graders than did Norma and Maria with their second graders.

The Impact of Testing on Language Development

Testing priorities have increasingly affected teachers' practices. Consistent with Haney and Madaus' (1986) finding that testing often underlies what teachers teach, these teachers were acutely aware of the importance of the tests and prepared their students for them.

In some school systems, such as New York City, immigrant children who speak other languages have to take standardized English tests after being in the country for two years. Exempting students from testing for two years only gives them minimal time and exposure to build a firm cognitive and linguistic foundation in either language (Cummins, 1989; Thomas & Collier, 1995). Preparing students for tests in a language in which they have little proficiency frustrated teachers and students. Furthermore, the teachers felt that these tests did not evaluate the many language skills, concepts, cultures, and background knowledge that their students had learned. The tests seemed better suited to mainstream than to LEP children.

Spanish assessment measures, though mandated in New York City since 1974 by the Aspira Consent Decree (Santiago-Santiago, 1986), have been slow to be developed and were not consistently used. When used, the teachers found the Spanish language in the tests inappropriate to students' Caribbean dialects because the tests were normed on other Spanish-speaking populations.

These complaints echo those of Haney and Madaus (1986), who state that standardized tests "are biased against certain kinds of students and do not match what students have been taught" (p. 9). The teachers all felt that testing and its preparation took away valuable time that could have been better spent on more meaningful language development activities.

Conclusions

Let's return to the initial questions: How do bilingual teachers affect dual language development and what can help them better develop their students' language strengths. These teachers' practices, which were influenced by their language learning, schooling, and immigration experiences, clearly show their concerted efforts to create caring, interactive, language-rich learning environments which promote considerable dual language expression and literacy development in their students. They continually adapted their practices, not without frustration, to the changing student populations.

Their work, however, could be better supported if they did not have to fight against the external factors of transitional programs, testing policies, and assimilative forces. Administrators and policy makers can do much to help reduce the effects of these external factors. They can create language-sensitive programs where the native language is given equal status by allocating adequate time, purchasing quality materials, and providing staff development. Programs, such as two-way developmental or dual language, have been most effective in positively promoting long-term student linguistic and academic achievement (Morison, 1990; Thomas & Collier, 1995) as well as in promoting positive attitudes toward bilingualism. Testing priorities can be better aligned with instruction to more effectively use instructional time and more accurately reflect students' actual accomplishments (Genesee & Hamayan, 1994; Freeman & Freeman, 1992). Without administrative and policy support, bilingual teachers will continue to struggle to develop students' languages and to overcome the external factors.

References

Ada, A. F. (1986). Creative education for bilingual teachers. *Harvard Educational Review,* 56(4), 386–394.

Carrasco, R. L. (1984). Collective engagement in the segundo hogar: A microethnography of engagement in a bilingual first grade. *Dissertation Abstracts International,* 46, 348A. (University Microfilms No. 8507834).

Cummins, J. (1989). *Empowering minority students.* Sacramento, CA: California Association for Bilingual Education.

Curtain, H., & Pescola, C. A. B. (1994). *Languages and children: Making the match.* New York: Longman.

Freeman, Y. S., & Freeman, D. (1992). *Whole language for second language learners.* Portsmouth, NH: Heinemann.

Freire, P. (1970). *Pedagogy of the oppressed.* New York: Continuum.

Genesee, F., & Hamayan, E. V. (1994). Classroom-based assessment. In Fred Genesee, (Ed.), *Educating second language children: The whole child, the whole curriculum, the whole community* (pp. 214–240). New York: Cambridge University Press.

Haney, W., & Madaus, G. (1986). *Effects of standardized testing and the future of the national assessment of educational progress.* Chestnut Hill, MA: Center for the Study of Testing, Evaluation and Educational Policy.

Igoa, C. (1995). *The inner world of the immigrant child.* New York: St. Martin's Press.

Johnson, D. (1994). Grouping strategies for second language learners. In Fred Genesee, (Ed.), *Educating second language children: The whole child, the whole curriculum, the whole community* (pp. 181–211). New York: Cambridge University Press.

Krashen, S. (1981). Bilingual education and second language acquisition theory. In *Schooling and language minority students: A theoretical framework* (pp. 51–82). California State Department of Education. Los Angeles: Evaluation, Dissemination and Assessment Center, California State University.

Legarreta-Marcaida, D. (1981). Effective use of primary language in the classroom. In *Schooling and language minority students: A theoretical framework* (pp. 83–116). California State Department of Education. Los Angeles: Evaluation, Dissemination and Assessment Center, California State University.

Lemberger, N. (1990). *Bilingual education: Teachers' voices.* Unpublished dissertation. New York: Teachers College, Columbia University.

Montero-Seiburth, M., & Perez, M. (1987). Echar pa'lante, moving onward: The dilemmas and strategies of a bilingual teacher. *Anthropology & Education Quarterly, 18*(3), 180–189.

Morison, S. H. (1990). A Spanish-English dual language program in New York City. *The Annals of the American Academy of Political and Social Science, 508*, 160–169.

Ovando, C. J., & Collier, V. P. (1985). *Bilingual and ESL classrooms.* New York: McGraw-Hill.

Pease-Alvarez, L., & Hakuta, K. (1992). Enriching our views of bilingualism and bilingual education. *Educational Researcher, 21*(2), 4–6.

Rimer, S. (1992, January 17). Racing to learn to speak English: Parents worry their children will leave them behind. *The New York Times,* p. B1.

Santiago-Santiago, I. (1986). Aspira v. Board of Education Revised. *American Journal of Education, 95*(1), 149–199.

Thomas, W. P., & Collier, V. P. (1995). Language-minority student achievement and program effectiveness studies support native language development. *NABE NEWS, 18*(8), 5, 12.

Williams, J. D., & Snipper, G. C. (1990). *Literacy and bilingualism.* New York: Longman.

Wink, J., Putney, L., & Bravo-Lawerence, I. (1995). The zone of proximal development: How in the world do we create it? *CABE Newsletter, 17*(5), 12, 13, 24.

Wong-Fillmore, L. (1991). Language and cultural issues in early education. In Kagan, S. L. (Ed.), *The ninety-first year book of the national society for the study of education.* Chicago, IL: University of Chicago Press.

Wong-Fillmore, L., & Valadez, C. (1986). Teaching bilingual learners. In M. C. Wittrock. (Ed.), *Third handbook of research on teaching* (pp. 648–684). New York: Macmillan & Company.

Unit Selections

5. **The Disappearance of American Indian Languages,** Barbara J. Boseker
6. **Between Two Worlds: Refugee Youth,** Donald A. Ranard
7. **An Indian Father's Plea,** Robert Lake
8. **Mexican Immigrants from El Rincón: A Case Study of Resilience and Empowerment,** Enrique (Henry) T. Trueba

Key Points to Consider

❖ What are some of the factors that put English-language learners at risk when they arrive in the new language community?

❖ How can classroom teachers provide social and cultural support for immigrant and linguistic-minority students in their classrooms?

❖ How can classroom teachers and other educational personnel become culturally skilled providers for non-English-speaking newcomers in school?

 **Links**   **www.dushkin.com/online/**

9. **Center for the Study of Books in Spanish for Children and Adolescents**
   http://www.csusm.edu/cwis/campus_centers/csb/index.html
10. **Longman Dictionaries Web Site**
    http://www.awl-elt.com/dictionaries/
11. **Mexican Heritage Almanac**
    http://www.ironhorse.com/~nagual/alma.html
12. **Migrant Education Program**
    http://jeffco.k12.co.us/edcenter/migrant/migrant.html
13. **National Institute on the Education of At-Risk Students**
    http://www.ed.gov/offices/OERI/At-Risk/
14. **Newcomer Program: Helping Immigrant Students**
    http://www.ncbe.gwu.edu/ncbepubs/pigs/pig8.htm

These sites are annotated on pages 4 and 5.

A socioculturally supportive environment for English-language learners within both the classroom and the school is a crucial factor that cannot be ignored when planning instructional programs and activities. This environment is best described as one where the home language and culture are validated in a warm, caring context while students acquire the new language and culture of the larger community. In this type of environment, students' language and academic and cognitive development flourish. There is strong evidence from research that the social and cultural processes are integral to students' overall growth and success in school.

One of the most significant roles that school personnel perform with second-language learners is as a mediating agent in the socialization and acculturation processes of the newcomers into the mainstream school community. Anyone who teaches English as a second language or academic content using English as the medium for instruction simultaneously teaches the dominant culture, because language and culture are inseparable.

Numerous classroom and school routines and policies may be unfamiliar to the newcomer, which can cause anxiety. One example of difficulty for a second-language learner is cultural miscues in language and nonverbal behavior, such as the distance that speakers maintain from one another while conversing or when and with whom it is appropriate to make eye contact, which sends unintended messages. Nonverbal communication is not as universally similar as some might assume. A substantial amount of time in the new culture may be needed to adjust these behaviors.

Different cultures develop and reward different learning styles. Second-language learners may be accustomed to teacher-centered instruction that is unlike the student-centered approaches being advocated and implemented across the grade levels in U.S. classrooms. Native English-speaking students in such classrooms are often engaged in cooperative learning activities while the teacher facilitates the process. As a result, the second-language learner may be reluctant to participate.

In these and other experiences, school personnel, especially classroom teachers and bilingual para-professionals, can assist students by maintaining the social and cultural bridges between the students' home culture and that of the school. There are many effective strategies in the literature for promoting academic and social integration that can be implemented to bring the invisible school culture to a conscious level for second-language learners.

We emphasize that the adoption of mainstream school and social culture need not occur at the expense of the students' native culture and language, but should be additive. In other words, English-language learners will become bilingual and bicultural. The learner's culture can be an integral part of the

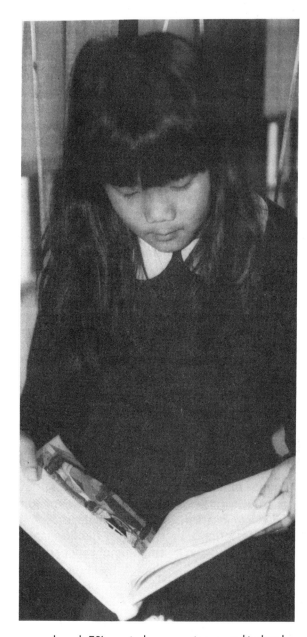

general and ESL curriculum, creating a multicultural environment in the school. The images and events that are celebrated in the school send strong messages about the relevance or importance of the various cultural groups in the school. A supportive environment may lead to a heightened cross-cultural understanding and mutual respect among all students and teachers. As a result, English-language learners may have increased motivation to integrate with their native-English-speaking peers, which will enhance their opportunities to become proficient speakers of the new language.

The articles in this unit provide opportunities for discussion on the approaches and strategies that educational personnel can implement to meet the sociocultural needs of English-language learners and their families.

THE DISAPPEARANCE OF AMERICAN INDIAN LANGUAGES

Abstract It has been reported that only 206 Native American languages remain; this is a third of the original number, and of these approximately 50 are near extinction. Why are these languages disappearing? What are the various issues involved in ensuring that Native American languages are sustained and nurtured? What are the socio-cultural factors which make it so difficult for Native American cultures as well as languages to exist? Are there some success stories of language maintenance instead of shift? Possible solutions are offered to the question of the disappearance of these minority languages.

Barbara J. Boseker

Barbara Boseker has a joint appointment as Professor of Special Education and Education at Winona State University, Winona, Minnesota. She was formerly Program Development Specialist for the Wisconsin Native American Teacher Corps on the Menominee Reservation. She also served as the evaluator for the Fargo Public Schools' Title IV Indian Education grant for 5 years.

The Problem

It has been estimated that there are perhaps 6,000 languages in the world of which as many as 90% are being lost (Diamond, 1993) with up to half no longer being learned by children. By some time in the next century all but a few hundred languages could be dead or dying (Diamond, 1993: 81). Although the vast majority of people use the so-called 'major' languages, sometimes called 'world' languages, such as Mandarin, Hindi, English, Spanish, Portu-guese, or Russian, most of the world's language diversity is in the so-called 'minor' languages with small numbers of speakers. The median number of speakers of these 'smaller' languages may only be some 5,000.

Languages with the most secure futures are the official languages of the world's sovereign states, which now number 170 or so. However, most states have officially adopted English, French, Spanish, Arabic, or Portuguese, leaving only about 70 states opting for other languages (Diamond, 1993); languages with over a million speakers might be secure as well, whether or not they are the official languages of a sovereign state. Official languages of sovereign states plus languages spoken by large numbers of people might number 200 out of the world's 6,000 languages. Are we to lose the other 5,800?

It has been estimated that at the time of their 'discovery' by Columbus the Americas had more than 1,000 languages. Of the 187 Indian languages surviving in North America outside Alaska, 149 are already moribund (Diamond, 1993) and even Navajo, with the largest number of speakers (approximately 100,000) and with its own Navajo language radio station, has a doubtful future because most Navajo children now speak only English (Diamond, 1993).

Case Studies

Let us examine some case studies of indigenous American languages which are disappearing. The last speaker of Cupeno, a southern California language, Roscinda Nolasquez of Pala, California, died in 1987 at the age of 94 (Diamond, 1993). Alaska has 20 Eskimo and Indian languages. Eyak, spoken by a

From *Journal of Multilingual and Multicultural Development*, Vol. 15, Nos. 2 & 3, 1994. © 1994 by Barbara J. Boseker. Reprinted by permission.

Table 1 Alaskan languages

Language	N speakers	Age of youngest speaker	Estimated date of loss
Eyak	3 (now 1)	Seventies	2000
Han	20	Thirties	2030
Holikachuk	25	Fifties	2015
Haida	100	Fifties	2015
Tanana	100	Fifties	2015
Ingalik	100	Thirties	2030
Tanacross	100	Teens	2055
Upper Kuskokwim	140	Children	2055
Tsimshian	200	Fifties	2015
Ahtna	200	Thirties	2030
Tanaina	250	Teens	2055
Upper Tanana	250	Teens	2055
Koyukon	700	Thirties	2035
Kutchin	700	Teens	2055
Aleut	700	Twenties	indefinite
Alutiiq	1,000	Teens	2055
Siberian Yupik	1,000	Children	indefinite
Tlingit	2,000	Forties	2030
Inupiaq	5,000	Teens	2055
Central Yupik	14,000	Children	indefinite

(*Source*: Senate Select Committee 1991: 19)

few hundred people on Alaska's south coast, had declined by 1982 to two native speakers, Marie Smith (age 72) and her sister Sophie Borodkin (Diamond, 1993). Sophie Borodkin died last year at the age of 80. The Eyak children speak only English. Seventeen other native Alaskan languages are dying, in that not a single child is learning them and that they have fewer than 1,000 speakers each. Of the original 20 indigenous Alaskan languages, only two are being learned by children: St Lawrence Island (Siberian) Yupik, with 1,000 speakers, and Central Yupik, with 10,000 speakers (Diamond, 1993; Senate Select Committee on Indian Affairs, 1991).

Table 1 is a list compiled by Michael Krauss, the Director of the Alaska Native Language Center, in 1980 and presented to the US Senate Select Committee considering a bill supporting indigenous languages in 1991. The list consists of Alaskan languages which are being lost, their current number of speakers, and the estimated date of their extinction.

The worst thing about this loss is that it was totally unnecessary: Alaskan mother tongues could have been supplemented instead of replaced by English. All Alaskan indigenous languages are now written, with excellent writing systems, but 'there is *not one* Alaskan school district ... which has a program of bilingual education that is designed realistically to reinforce the home language, or to allow the children to become speakers of an Alaska Native language' (Senate Select Committee, 1991:113).

Indigenous languages have disappeared not only in the United States, but also in Canada. In November 1990, 'the Standing Committee on Aboriginal Affairs of the Canadian Parliament published a report stating that of the fifty-three native languages still spoken in Canada, only three appeared to have a secure future and more than forty were in danger of prompt extinction' (Abley, 1992: 4).

A case in point is the Huron language, which was not even on the Canadian Parliament list. By the

early twentieth century the Huron language was all but extinct since the Hurons collapsed as a nation more than three hundred years ago. The Huron people divided into three fragments in the mid-seventeenth century. One fragment lived outside Quebec City, another was assimilated by the Iroquois, who were victorious over the Huron, and a third fragment settled near Detroit. In the nineteenth century the US government shipped the Detroit group out of Michigan to 'Indian Territory', soon to become Oklahoma. On the Oklahoma reservation Huron continued to be spoken into the 1960s or even later. It is strongly suspected that the language is now dead in the United States (Abley, 1992).

The Canadian branch of the Huron, however, are attempting to revive their language. The 1,500 survivors who speak French as a mother tongue plan to resurrect Huron, using the revivals of Hebrew and Cornish as models (Abley, 1992). Huron is fortunately well documented, thanks to the efforts of early Jesuits. The Huron adults hope to establish an informal club and relearn the language together. They then intend setting up an immersion school for their children modelled on that of the Mohawk several hundred miles away. The Mohawk language, too, was in the process of extinction and its future is also still uncertain.

In another area of Canada, Snowdrift, Northwest Territories, the Chipewyan language is also in danger of extinction. Snowdrift is situated on the eastern side of Great Slave Lake, accessible only by air and water. It is a community of three hundred people, over 90% of whom are Native Indian, or Dene. Due to its isolation, the Chipewyan language survives here relatively fluently in comparison to other Athapaskan or Chipewyan communities (Rodriguez & Sawyer, 1990). However, even in Snowdrift where the language is heard to a much greater extent than in most other

Dene communities, the actual knowledge of the language is much less than expected. The youth use not the language of the elders but a more contracted and changed form. Because of a lack of 'modern' vocabulary in Chipewyan, English was substituted for 'important' transactions such as giving directions (Rodriguez & Sawyer, 1990). Thus English has changed the mother tongue language to a greater degree than hoped for by those interested in language retention. Complicating the situation is employment in the Northwest Territories. Although there is employment for people who are fluent in both English and Chipewyan, most positions require literacy in English. Thus there is a conflict between those who want to teach mother tongue literacy, which has limited use for employment, and English, which assures a job.

The Bureau of Indian Affairs (BIA) faced the same policy decision in the Arctic in the 1930s and 1940s. At that time those who wanted the indigenous cultures preserved encouraged mother tongue usage only without encouraging learning English as well. But it was the Arctic people who spoke English who obtained the jobs in Anchorage, Vancouver and Seattle. Thus those [who] wanted strict 'preservation' of the Arctic cultures 'as is' actually did a disservice (Jenness, 1962, 1968). We should learn from this sad era that preservation does not mean fossilisation. Some communities have difficulty deciding which language they want used in the early grades because they see a conflict between learning English for jobs and learning the mother tongue for retention of the culture. The solution lies in a truly bilingual school system, offering competent instruction in both, but there 'is little evidence that serious bilingual policies are being attempted in the NWT' (Rodriguez & Sawyer, 1990:112). It is doubtful if either oral or literate mother tongue language will survive for any practical use through the next few generations, and the languages may be lost by default.

I was on the Stockbridge-Munsee Reservation in Wisconsin when the last native speaker of Munsee, a 90-year-old tribal elder, died. The Munsee had been moved from Massachusetts in a previous century by the expansion of white settlement from east to west and acquired the name of the Stockbridge-Munsee from the fort in Massachusetts where they had been housed in an earlier era. Since the Stockbridge-Munsee had no reservation, the Menominee of northern Wisconsin generously offered them a corner of their reservation, where the remaining Stockbridge-Munsee live today. It may be argued that when the last Munsee speaker died, the Munsee culture died with him.

How Did Native American Languages Disappear?

What happened to the language diversity of the Americas? Certainly many languages died when their speakers died. Columbus killed the Arawak Indians of the Caribbean and with them their language. Similarly, white Californians killed the Yahi Indians between 1853 and 1870 (Diamond, 1993). When Native Americans were not slaughtered, they often died from disease; indeed, it has been estimated that Native Americans died in greater numbers from diseases such as smallpox, measles and whooping cough than from outright slaughter. It is now known that even when Native Americans surrendered and came into the forts and agencies, they were purposely issued blankets with the smallpox virus on them so that they would hopefully acquire the disease and die.

For those Native Americans who were not slaughtered or who did not die from disease, there was the US government forced policy of assimilation. Indian children were forced into boarding schools where they would be 'civilised' by separation from their parents and through the use of English. This English-only policy was resisted strongly by the missionary schools which had operated bilingually. President Ulysses S. Grant condemned the missionaries for teaching in native languages, and the federal government threatened to cut off their funding. It was at this point in 1879 that the US BIA school system originated with coercive English instruction (Crawford 1990); Indian children were placed in boarding schools often far from their reservations and certainly away from their parents' influence.

When I was working on the Menominee reservation, several Menominee women told stories of how the boarding school teachers washed out their mouths with soap if they dared utter a word of Menominee. Indeed, Crawford (1990) reports that this practice was so common that the word 'soap' was often the first word Native American children learned in English. (The same thing happened in my own high school in Milwaukee, Wisconsin, where at South Division High School I myself observed my classmates, Mexican-American students, being dragged by teachers into the bathrooms if they dared speak Spanish. This same high school now takes pride in its bilingual programmes!) The BIA boarding schools soon became notorious for escape attempts, corporal discipline, and gender segregation.

The usual sequence of events of a language minority facing the onslaught of a majority language is that the minority young adults tend to become bilingual and their children monolingual in the majority language. 'Eventually the minority language is spoken only by older people, until the last of them dies' (Diamond, 1993: 82). Even before the death of the language, the minority language has degenerated through loss of grammatical complexities, loss of vocabulary, and incorporation of foreign vocabulary and grammar (Diamond, 1993).

Success Stories

One of the most well-known stories is the Rock Point Community School in the middle of the Navajo Nation in Northeast Arizona (see Spolsky, cited in Reyhner, 1990). The school is completely bilingual and operated through local community control under Public Law 638, the Indian Self-determination and Assistance Act. In 1988, 43% of the Rock Point students were dominant Navajo speakers while only 5% were dominant English speakers (Reyhner, 1990). When students begin kindergarten, two-thirds of their instruction is in Navajo while the remainder of their time is spent learning oral English. By second grade students are receiving half their instruction in English and half in Navajo. By the time students reach the intermediate level (grades 4, 5 and 6), 15–30% of their instruction is in Navajo with the rest in English. By seventh and eighth grade, students have one period of Navajo studies plus a quarter of Navajo writing each year. In ninth to twelfth grades, students have a half-year of Navajo studies plus a quarter of Navajo writing each year. 'Eighth graders and seniors must give graduation speeches in Navajo and/or English' (Reyhner, 1990: 105).

The bilingual programme at Rock Point can be described as being both a co-ordinate and a maintenance bilingual programme (Reyhner, 1990): instruction in the two languages is kept separate but complementary. Concepts introduced in Navajo are reviewed in English, but not repeated in each language and some teachers teach only in English, others only in Navajo.

The Rock Point curriculum is an example of what Cummins (cited in Reyhner, 1990) has called an additive rather than a subtractive educational programme. A subtractive programme is one that seeks to replace native language and culture with the English language and culture causing minority students to fail; an additive programme seeks to teach English language and culture in addition to the native language and culture creating the conditions for success. What Cummins advocates is consistent with the 'both/and' curriculum, currently considered the most appropriate for Native American students, which advocates teaching both modern aspects of the curriculum (such as computer science) and the traditional (such as incorporating traditional Indian beadwork in art classes), thus preparing Native American students for jobs in the next century as well as honouring and preserving their cultures of the past.

To obtain enough Navajo language teachers, most of the Rock Point elementary teachers were hired locally without college degrees; by now, however, many have earned degrees through on-site college programmes. Teachers without four-year college degrees are required to take 12 semester credits each year leading to appropriate education degrees. In my opinion, this is the only way to achieve language maintenance in isolated areas.

Teaching materials in the mother tongue are another problem. Bernard Spolsky found from his detailed study of Rock Point school in 1973 that there was a 'good bit' of Navajo language material around, but not enough 'to fill out a first grade year of reading' (Spolsky, cited in Reyhner, 1990: 108). Materials in Navajo are more available now, but teachers and students must still rely on their own efforts in materials production. Students learn to type both Navajo and English in the computer class and then use the Macintosh computers at both the elementary and secondary levels to publish school newspapers. The newspapers and booklets so developed are then used as reading material by other students.

Another key to success at Rock Point is strong parental involvement. There is a parent advisory committee that observes the school several times per year, sponsors cultural events, and serves community dinners. Students also participate during clanship week every year wearing slips of paper showing the clans of their mother, father, grandmothers and grandfathers, greeting each other with traditional kinship greetings in Navajo. As a result of parental support, student attendance rates are above 94% of school days attended, and parent conference attendance rates are above 80% (Reyhner, 1990). This is an extraordinary achievement when many other schools are finding parental participation a formidable task.

I can speak with experience of the importance of parental and community involvement. In my evaluation of the Title IV Indian Education Program in Fargo, North Dakota, Public Schools, a strong parental support group has been one of the factors in the excellent attendance of Indian children in Fargo schools (a 92% rate of school days attended) and an exceedingly low drop-out rate (zero drop-outs of Indian students by 1989) (Boseker, 1991).

The Isleta Headstart Computer Program is another success story. Isleta Pueblo is 12 miles south of Albuquerque, New Mexico, and Isletan is a dialect of Tiwa, a language spoken by only four New Mexican tribes (Donahue, 1990). In the 1950s and 1960s Isletan was threatened by technology and urbanisation as Isletans bought cars and took jobs in nearby Albuquerque. Many left their pueblos and took residence in government-subsidised housing tracts on the outskirts of Albuquerque. By the early 1980s Isletan had become a language almost solely reserved for rituals (Donahue, 1990).

Ted Jojola, a University of New Mexico professor who is Isletan and who chairs the UNM's Native American studies department, applied for a grant from Apple Corporation. Through Jojola's efforts, Apple Computer's Wheels for the Mind Foundation granted the Isleta Headstart Program three Macs and two printers. One difficult problem was that Isletan, an almost solely oral language, had never really been written, and the sounds can only be approximated by the English alphabet. A technical problem which emerged was to create programs that integrated sound and video, which became difficult because of the amount of memory needed. None the less, the computer program at the pueblo's Headstart school for four and five year olds began in 1985 and was one of the first of its kind in the United States (Donahue, 1990). Isletan children feed disks into their Macintosh computers that teach them Isletan words for various body parts as well as displays and names of animals (rabbits, pigs, and cows) that roam on Isleta's many farms. The computers helped the Isletan children develop self-esteem (a very serious educational concern for children in the United States today, especially Native American children) before they entered the Albuquerque Public Schools, which are filled with Anglo children whose parents work at high tech jobs such as Sandia labs. Pepper (1976) found that Native American children have some of the lowest self-images in the United States and that their anxiety level is the highest. Indian children used to be intimidated by the Anglo children, but now the Isletan children have technical skills and confidence as a side benefit of working with computers.

Having worked with Native American communities for many years, I can vouch for the grave difficulties which some Native American children have with the competitiveness of American schools. Co-operation, not competition, is a traditional Native American ethic still stressed in Native American childrearing. When I worked in Teacher Corps on the Menominee reservation in Wisconsin, Menominee teachers and teacher aides would constantly ask for ideas and activities which emphasised the ethic of cooperation. The Menominee felt that their children flourished in the spirit of co-operation. If the usage of computers provides the self-esteem Native American children need to face the immense competitiveness of Anglo schools, then this is an added benefit in addition to preserving their language.

The Zuni of New Mexico have followed the Isleta with a similar programme. Through a grant again from Apple, the Zuni have bought Macs, printers and modems which have been used to develop a written version of Zuni, which was until quite recently solely an oral language (Donahue, 1990). The Zuni Literacy Project has been compiling a Zuni/English dictionary and creating a series of filmstrip-like 'storybooks', which use sound and static visual images to tell stories in Zuni (Donahue, 1990). The Zuni have written five storybooks and English definitions for 700 Zuni words and the dictionary has been put to use in a middle school Zuni language class. Like the Isleta, the Zuni hope to create audible videos of Zuni folk tales, a much more technical challenge. The Acoma and San Juan pueblos of New Mexico have also developed Macintosh computer programs that help teach their mother tongues to youngsters.

Another road to success is the development of instructional programs such as the Ogwehowe:ka? Program for second language instruction using the languages of the eight Native American nations located in New York State: Mohawk, Onondaga, Seneca, Oneida, Cayuga, Tuscarora, Shinnecock and Unkechaug (New York State Education Department, 1988). 'Ogwe'o:weh' means 'the real people/the original beings' in Seneca, and 'ogweho:weh' means 'the real people/the original beings' in Onondaga, Oneida, Cayuga, and Mohawk. 'Ogwehowe:ka?' and 'Ongwehonwe:neha:' include all the characteristics pertaining to the way of life of 'the real people/the original beings'. In the syllabus for the program, 'Ogwehowe:ka?' refers specifically to the languages of the eight nations. The purpose of the syllabus is to encourage functional communication in the listening and speaking skills.

The emphasis of the Ogwehowe:ka? Program is not just on linguistics but on a holistic way of life stressing the creator, mother earth, community, nature, and values. The program has three goals: (1) functional communication in Ogwehowe:ka? languages with emphasis on listening and speaking, (2) sharing and understanding the holistic way of life, and (3) an appreciation of the heritage of the Ogweho:weh people. The Ogwehowe:ka? languages have been oral traditions until recent times. The program also shifts second language instruction from an approach which stresses the linguistic aspects of language to one that stresses the skills of functional communication.

Literacy is perceived by the eight nations using this syllabus in a way different from that encapsulated by the dominant society culture definition of 'ability to read and write'. These nations consider 'literate' to mean the ability to 'speak the native language(s), be totally knowledgeable of the "way of life", read all elements comprising the natural environment and the universe, read the lunar cycles, live within cycles and natural laws of nature, recognise purpose of everything comprising natural environment and universe, (and) respecting and being grateful for all of the Creator's gifts' (New York State Education Department, 1988: 54). This refocusing of what is a literate person truly acknowledges the need for linguists and educators to heed the cultural aspects of language learning, not merely the linguistic.

By no means are these success stories the only achievements of Native American language preservation. They do represent, however, solid bilingual programmes (Rock Point), newly innovative programmes (use of computers on Isleta and Zuni reservations), and the incorporation of cultural values (Ogwehowe:ka? Program).

The Future

The future in terms of preserving and protecting Native American languages lies beyond merely linguistics. From my work with Native American people, it would appear to me that the future of their languages is intertwined with the future of Native American cultures as a whole. The cultures as a whole are endangered, perhaps never more so than today with what traditional Indians see as an assault on their values. This assault is accompanied by the English language onslaught and influences such as Las Vegas style gambling on reservations, which as a result of the Indian Gaming Regulatory Act of 1988 pose new threats to cultural and linguistic heritage.

The Indian Gaming Regulatory Act basically states that if gambling is allowed in any form in a state, even bingo in a church basement, Native Americans in that state are allowed to set up gambling casinos of their own. Some traditional Indians view the Las Vegas style gambling on reservations today as antithetical to everything that is Indian. For example, Erma Vizenor, a colleague of mine who is a member of the White Earth band of the Ojibwe of Minnesota and who practices traditional Ojibwe values, feels that Indian reservation gambling is a scourge because when a person gambles, someone else has to lose in order for the gambler to win. That violates the fundamental Native American principle of sharing. On the other hand, the dependent relationship between Native American peoples and the US government is ceasing as a result of the revenue from the casinos. In my own state of Minnesota, Indian people are getting off welfare roles and increasing their own self-esteem through the jobs they have created for themselves in the gambling industry. Future developments in this area are anticipated.

According to some sources (Devenish, 1970; Pepper, 1976) Native American children actually perform as well as or better than whites in the early grades in school. Young Indian children often find school intriguing but it is when they reach the pre-adolescent level that they often fall behind. In terms of school achievement, between 64% and 74% of Native American students score below the national norm on standard achievement tests. Some Arizona data indicate that Indian students lag two to four grade levels behind the national norm (Boseker, 1991). It is at the pre-adolescent level that all children are discovering who they are. Native American children, too, are learning their identities and with those identities their estimate of themselves. And in America that means learning that the dominant society denigrates everything that Indian cultures stand for, including language. I believe that incorporating Native American values in one's teaching is paramount (see Boseker & Gordon, 1983; Gordon & Boseker, 1984). Some Native Americans feel that by incorporating Native American language and culture in the public schools, absenteeism of Indian children is reduced and academic achievement improves. 'That ties heavily into the self-esteem and the feeling of comfort in the schools, as the students realise that their languages and cultures are just as important as the English language and culture', said one Native Alaskan educator, testifying at US Senate hearings on indigenous language preservation (Senate Select Committee, 1991: 60).

Once Indian children fall behind they may never catch up; the ultimate result can be school drop-outs. The national drop-out rate for Native Americans is 60%; in some parts of the United States it is as high as 85% (Boseker, 1991). Currently, in the state of Minnesota, which has the highest high school graduation rate in the United States, 88% of ninth graders will receive a high school diploma in four years compared with only 52% of Native American ninth graders; Minnesota Native American students thus have a 48% drop-out rate, and this is in a state in which some glimmers of hope occasionally appear. For example, a recent advertisement asked for a part-time Ojibwe language teacher in one of Minnesota's school districts (District #317, Deer River), and in summer 1993 Moorhead State University is offering a course in beginning Ojibwe.

Possible Answers

The 1990 Native American Languages Act, signed into law by former President Bush on 10 October 1990, is at least a start in that it actually encourages the use of Native American languages. Furthermore, Senate Bill 2044, signed by former President Bush in October 1992, allocates $2 million a year for Native American language studies (Diamond, 1993); although this is not a large sum of money, it is a beginning.

There are other feasible developments. According to the report which accompanied Senate Joint Resolution 379 to establish a US policy for the preservation, protection, and promotion of indigenous languages, academic credit should be granted to Indian children for proficiency in an indigenous Native American language in the same way that it is granted for foreign languages (Senate Select Committee on Indian Affairs, 1988). For example, students in the remote villages of Alaska currently have the choice of Russian, Spanish or Japanese, all taught via the satellite system. One Native Alaskan student reported to the US Senate that she was in her second year of taking Spanish via satellite from Spokane, Washington (Senate Select Committee, 1991). Why not offer Yupik as the fourth 'foreign' language? A 1988 Senate Select Committee report also recommended that indigenous languages may be used as a medium of instruction as well as an official language in their traditional territories.

Increased usage of radio and television as modes of indigenous language transmission is also feasible. For example, in Bethel, Alaska, KYUK public radio and television has been on the air for 20 years. The station serves some 56 villages and transmits for 18 hours a day, three hours of which is in the Yupik language. KYUK offers two newscasts in Yupik, 30 minutes at noon and fifteen minutes at 6.30 p.m. One Native American broadcaster from the Yupik news department, John Active, envisions a Yupik 'classroom of the air' for 20 minutes on the radio after the news at noon and again at 6.30 p.m., teaching the Yupik language to both speakers and non-speakers (Senate Select Committee, 1991). Such efforts need to be supported, not cut back as John Active fears will happen.

Teaching materials will need to be produced, such as the many materials which have been developed in Yupik for kindergarten through twelfth grade in Alaska, and those available for Cree, which were developed in Canada. Much can be said about the use of videotape formats for the storage of and access to materials. For example, in the 1970s when I was a member of Teacher Corps on the Menominee Reservation, I established a videotape library which contained, among other things, videotapes of Menominee elders telling legends in Menominee accompanied by an English translation; cultural aspects, such as childrearing practices, were also recorded. (That videotape library is today located on the Menominee Reservation in Keshena, Wisconsin).

Fluent mother tongue speakers need to be hired as language teachers, then paid and treated as professionals by the school districts. I had experience of this particular problem in Teacher Corps. Often the people who knew most about how to teach the Indian children on the Menominee Reservation were the Native American teacher aides who were not certified. I personally witnessed experienced Menominee teacher aides being supplanted by inexperienced certified personnel, simply because the certified personnel held teaching licences and the aides did not. Thus career ladders need to be established so that experienced Native American teacher aides can achieve their licensures and 'legitimise' themselves. (One of the major components of Teacher Corps was the establishment and development of career ladders.)

Teaching methods must also be modified. From study after study (Pepper, 1976; Collier, 1979; Rodriguez & Sawyer, 1990) and from my own experience, Native Americans prefer a 'watch then do' approach. This means that teachers must help, wait, watch, help again, and wait some more, rather than the shorter, quicker, 'in and out' or 'cover the curriculum rapidly' modes used by non-Native American teachers. I have elsewhere (Boseker & Gordon, 1983; Gordon & Boseker, 1984) emphasised the importance of 'wait-time'—the time a teacher pauses after asking a question and also after a student's response. Increased wait-time is actually thinking time, giving both the speaker and the listener time to think or engage in speculative thinking; it has been shown that extended wait-time encourages higher-level thinking rather than simple recall (Rowe, 1978). Winterton (1976) found that extended wait-time results in: (1) significantly longer student responses, (2) significant increase in number of student-student comparisons of data, (3) more active verbal participation of usually low-verbal students, (4) decrease of students failing to respond, and (5) students tending to contribute unsolicited but appropriate responses and to initiate appropriate questions.

Finally, computer-assisted multimedia interactive programs could be developed because most schools, even in the most remote villages of Alaska, have access to computers. Indeed, the use of computers is perhaps the most important recent leap in language preservation.

The above are just some possibilities which could be instituted immediately. Other ideas, such as videodiscs, need to be pursued.

Conclusion

The tragic loss of Native American languages must stop. As linguists and educators we must support Native American people in every way possible in their efforts to preserve their cultural and linguistic heritage. As linguists and educators we have all learned that children do not suffer in any way from bilingualism: study after study has shown that when children continue to develop both languages, they are linguistically and cognitively enhanced (Cummins, 1990). Finally, language maintenance rather than language shift is also a human right guaranteed by United Nations Resolution 2200, Article 27, of the International Covenant on Civil and Political Rights. As one North Carolina Native American woman, Janice Jones Schroeder, whose tribe has lost all semblance of its native language after 500 years of white contact, said in testimony before the US Senate:

> I view the speaking of our language as a human right, given to us by the Creator. He chose what group and what individuals should be in those groups to speak the languages, as he gave the birds the individual songs, the animals of the woods, he gives us our languages. No one has the right to take those away. (Senate Select Committee, 1991: 49)

References

Abley, M. (1992) The prospects for the Huron language. *Times Literary Supplement* no. 4662, 7 August.

Boseker, B. J. (1991) Successful solutions for preventing Native American dropouts. *International Third World Studies Journal and Review* 3, 33–40.

Boseker, B. J. and Gordon, S. L. (1983) What Native Americans have taught us as teacher educators. *Journal of American Indian Education 22*, 20–4.

Collier, M. (1979) *A Film Study of Classrooms in Western Alaska*. Fairbanks: Center for Cross Cultural Studies, University of Alaska.

Crawford, J. (1990) Language freedom and restriction: A historical approach to the official language controversy. *Proceedings of the Ninth Annual International Native American Language Issues (NALI) Institute*. Choctaw, Oklahoma: Native American Language Issues Institute.

Cummins, J. (1990) ESL in the 21st century: From demographics to methodology. Speech to the Seventh Midwest Regional TESOL Conference, St Paul, Minnesota.

Devenish, R. (1970) *The North American Indian, Part III: The Lament of the Reservation*. New York: McGraw-Hill (16 mm film produced for J. K. Hoffman Presentations).

Diamond, J. (1993) Speaking with a single tongue. *Discover 14*, 78–85.

Donahue, B. (1990) Computer program helps revive ancient language. *Winds of Change: A Magazine of American Indians 5*, 20–5.

Gordon, S. L. and Boseker, B. J. (1984) Enriching education for Indian and non-Indian students. *Journal of Thought 19*, 143–8.

Jenness, D. (1962) *Eskimo Administration: I. Alaska*. Montreal: Arctic Institute of North America.

—— (1968) *Eskimo Administration: V. Analysis and Reflections*. Montreal: Arctic Institute of North America.

New York State Education Department (1988) *Ogwehowe:ka? Native Languages for Communication, New York State Syllabus*. Albany, NY: New York State Education Department.

Pepper, F. C. (1976) Teaching the American Indian child in mainstream settings. In R. L. Jones (ed.) *Mainstreaming and the Minority Child* (pp. 133–58). Reston, VA: Council for Exceptional Children.

Reyhner, J. (1990) A description of the Rock Point Community School bilingual education program. *Proceedings of the Ninth Annual International Native American Language Issues (NALI) Institute*. Choctaw, OK: Native American Language Issues Institute.

Rodriguez, C. and Sawyer, D. (1990) *Native Literacy Research Report*. Salmon Arm, BC: Native Adult Education Resource Centre.

Rowe, M. B. (1978) *Teaching Science as Continuous Inquiry*. New York: McGraw-Hill.

Senate Select Committee on Indian Affairs (1988) *Establishing as the Policy of the United States the Preservation, Protection, and Promotion of the Rights of Indigenous Americans To Use, Practice and Develop Native American Languages, and for Other Purposes (28 September)* Washington, DC: Congress of the United States, Senate Select Committee on Indian Affairs.

—— (1991) *Alaska Native Languages Preservation and Enhancement Act of 1991 (19 October)*. Washington, DC: Congress of the United States, Senate Select Committee on Indian Affairs.

Winterton, W. (1976) The effect of extended wait-time on selected verbal response characteristics of some Pueblo Indian children. PhD thesis, University of New Mexico.

Barbara Boseker has a joint appointment as Professor of Special Education and Education at Winona State University, Winona, Minnesota. She received her doctorate from the University of Wisconsin-Madison and was formerly Program Development Specialist for the Wisconsin Native American Teacher Corps on the Menominee Reservation. She also served as the evaluator for the Fargo Public Schools' Title IV Indian Education grant for five years.

Between Two Worlds: Refugee Youth

Refugees between the ages of 15 and 18 face a unique array of difficulties in the U.S. This issue of In America *examines how Vietnamese, Lao, Cambodian, and Hmong youth have adjusted to their new country, and looks at some of the reasons behind their problems as well as their successes at school, within their families, and in society.*

Donald A. Ranard

Study Documents Success and Problems

"Despite their many handicaps and in a remarkably short period of time, refugee youth have been able to make exceptional progress in American schools. . . ."

This is the conclusion of a recent study, *The Adaptation of Southeast Asian Refugee Youth,* by Rubén G. Rumbaut and Kenji Ima, sociologists at San Diego State University.

Funded by the U.S. office of Refugee Resettlement (ORR), the study examined the achievements, aspirations, and problems of Indochinese secondary school students in San Diego. It predicts a bright future for most refugee youth, but raises concerns about a significant minority of "at-risk" youth whose failures have been obscured by the achievements of their more successful peers.

Academic achievements

The study found that, except for a small number of East Asian groups, Indochinese students as a whole had higher grade point averages than all other ethnic groups, including white majority students.[1]

Their scores on standardized achievement tests were well above national norms in math, at about the average level in language mechanics and spelling, below the average in writing, and

[1] In fact, the data showed that all immigrants and refugee groups—whether from Asia, Europe, or Latin America—were doing better than native-born American students, "despite initial (or even persisting) English language handicaps."

well below the national average in reading comprehension.

The study revealed significant differences in educational achievement among the Indochinese groups. The first-ranking Vietnamese had a greater proportion of honor students and students with grade point averages (GPAs) above 3.0 than all other student groups. Almost one-half of the Vietnamese students ranked in the top 10% in math skills. The Vietnamese were followed in academic achievement by the Vietnamese-Chinese, the Hmong, the Cambodians, and the Lao.

Perhaps the study's most unexpected finding was the third-place rank of the Hmong students, who outperformed not only the Cambodians and the Lao, but almost all American-born groups, as well, including white majority students. The performance of the Hmong students was surprising, given the generally accepted link between children's performance in school and their parents' level of income and education. Hmong parents have one of the highest rates of unemployment and lowest levels of education in San Diego.

The performances of the Cambodians and Lao were also surprising: The Lao ranked last among Indochinese students, even though their parents had

Reprinted from *In America: Perspectives on Refugee Resettlement,* Number 2, January 1989, pp. 1-8. Published by the Center for Applied Linguistics, Washington, DC.

more education than Hmong parents and considerably higher rates of employment than both Cambodian and Hmong parents. The Cambodians averaged higher GPAs than American-born students, "despite the prevalence of emotional trauma in their community."

Cultural values linked to academic performance

Although parents' levels of education and income made a difference in how their children did in school, it was not the main factor, the study found. More important was the extent to which "cultural resources"—cultural values, attitudes, and coping strategies—helped or hindered the process of adaptation. The study attributed the superior achievements of the Vietnamese, Chinese, and Hmong to a combination of cultural resources which "work particularly well within the competitive American educational . . . system."[2] These resources include:

* a strong belief in the value of education, self-discipline, and hard work,
* a respect for the authority of parents and teachers,
* a strong sense of obligation between parent and child, in particular "the expectation of tremendous parental self-sacrifice to ensure . . . that the children will go as far as possible in pursuit of their education," and
* the ability of families to find collective solutions to problems—the tendency, for example, of Vietnamese families to function as "minischool systems, with older siblings serving as tutors to the younger ones and learning better themselves in the process of teaching."

In contrast to the Vietnamese, Chinese, and the Hmong, the Lao and Cambodians are described in the

[2] This analysis parallels a finding from a 1985 University of Michigan study by Caplan, Whitmore, Bui, and Trautman examining the academic achievements of Indochinese students, mostly children of the post-1978 Vietnamese and Chinese-Vietnamese "boat people." The study found that although "much of the past literature . . . has emphasized that successful resettlement comes about because refugees adopt the ways of the their nonrefugee neighbors," the Indochinese students "appear to have gotten along as well as they have because of what they have brought with them—in particular, their traditional cultural values, which are perceived as quite different from those attributed to their nonrefugee neighbors."

Youth in Trouble

The San Diego study analyzed data from an ongoing study of Indochinese delinquents being conducted by Kenji Ima, sociologist, and Jeanne Nidorf, psychologist. A profile of delinquent refugee youth emerged:

* Vietnamese and Lao youth are more likely to get into trouble with the law than Hmong or Cambodians.
* Delinquent refugees have a much lower level of English proficiency than their non-delinquent counterparts. Of those delinquent refugees who were given a language rating, only 7% had a good command of English and more than half needed translators. Among the serious offenders, none had a good command of English.
* Most have had school troubles, with the Vietnamese most likely to show a connection between school troubles and delinquency. Because their culture places such a high value on education, Vietnamese youth are more sensitive to failure and thus more likely to respond destructively to it.
* Delinquent refugee youth are more likely than whites and other minorities to live without one or both natural parents and much more likely to have unemployed fathers. Of 64 guardians whose language ability was assessed, 75% needed translators.
* Refugee youth are more likely than white or other minority students to be associated with gangs. The study notes "a striking 'compulsion' [among refugee youth] to associate with peers beyond what one expects of other youths."
* Refugee youth gangs lack the formal structure of gangs formed by other minority youth: there are, for example, no formal names, territory, or clothing markers. In contrast to white and minority gangs, which are "much more localized and territorial," refugee youth gang members often live together, wandering from town to town, living in motels. As a result, they are much more difficult to monitor and control than other gangs.
* For the most part, refugee delinquents are involved in minor crimes. They are more likely than other minority youth to commit property crimes rather than crimes against persons. They are less likely to get involved in crime for "kicks" and more likely to be motivated by financial gain. More interested in acquiring things than in destroying them, they are unlikely to get involved in vandalism.
* Delinquent refugee youth are more likely than white and other minority delinquents to respect authority. Police officers rated 65% of the delinquent refugees as having "good attitudes" toward authority, compared to only 45% of white delinquents and 35% of other minority delinquents. However, the study predicts that "respect and deference for authority is likely to decrease if the youth acculturates to American standards, especially within juvenile incarceration units, where they are likely to learn American anti-authority attitudes."

---

study as generally less competitive, more concerned with recreational activities, and more fatalistic—more likely to believe, for example, that success is a result of luck and merit earned from past lives, rather than hard work. In addition, Lao and Cambodians, who tend to be more individualistic, were less likely to find collective solutions to problems. In Lao and Cambodian parent-child relationships, the study found "looser social controls, less discipline (including less parental push and pressure to achieve) . . . and a weaker sense of obligation to parents. . . ."

Different ethnic groups face different problems

While most Indochinese refugees were doing well, a significant and often overlooked minority were experiencing serious problems adjusting to American schools, the study found.

The kinds of problems that Indochinese youth experience differed by ethnic group. Among Indochinese students, the Vietnamese and the Lao were more likely to get into trouble at school, the Cambodians had the highest dropout rate, and the Hmong had the most diffi-

Counseling and the Vietnamese Student

"Vietnamese are used to seeking help from only family members, and to a degree and scope that the professional helper cannot provide. First, the authority figure of the family counsels family members in every aspect of life; secondly, assistance includes economic and material help; thirdly, there is no specific time allocated for this counseling, any time of the day will be appropriate; and fourthly, there are no individual limits drawn in terms of the intimacy and the personal space between the head of the family and the member of the family who is seeking advice.

This creates a dilemma for the counselor who is advising immigrants in the U.S. If the counselor is successful, in the sense that the Vietnamese will treat him or her as a member of the family, then the counselor has to be open to be called any time of the day, asked for any type of help, and be expected to be personally involved in the situation. These are very unrealistic expectations from an American counselor. . . . [Vietnamese] students will expect a more personal involvement, and usually will end up feeling alienated because they feel they are being treated as a 'client,' rather than 'a special person.' "

—From *A Report on Needs Assessment of Vietnamese Students at California State University, Fullerton,* by Robert B. Ericksen & Dogan M. Cucelogu, 1987

culty in making the transition from high school to college. The Vietnamese and Lao were also more likely to get into trouble with the law. (See "Youth in Trouble.")

The study found that Vietnamese and Lao students were more likely than the Cambodians or the Hmong to be suspended from school. While the data showed that Vietnamese and Lao students were less likely than whites, blacks, or Hispanics to be suspended, they also indicated that suspensions for the Vietnamese and Lao had increased more rapidly than for any other group in San Diego.

Quoting from a San Diego County Schools report, the study attributed the increase in school suspensions among Indochinese students to "increasing prejudice towards all Asians, particularly the Indochinese" as well as "increased physical retaliation by Indochinese students in response to verbal and physical abuse from other students."

According to the study, Vietnamese and Lao youth had higher rates of suspension because they were more likely than the Hmong or Cambodians to respond to racial baiting.

"Some Vietnamese students . . . told us that they will not respond at the first insult from an American student, would take notice of a second insult from the same provocateur, and will 'blow up' and get into a fight in response to a third or subsequent provocation," the study reports.

One reason that confrontations between Vietnamese and American-born students often escalate to violence is that the two groups view conflict very differently. "Vietnamese culture treats conflict seriously and not as a casual affair—which is the way Americans view such confrontations," the study notes.

The Hmong, who had the one of the lowest suspension rates in the city, were less likely to respond to provocation. Unlike the Vietnamese and the Lao, who in their own countries were members of the ethnic majority, the Hmong seem to have developed strategies for coping with racism from their experiences as a subordinated minority in Laos.

While the Cambodians also had a low school suspension rate, they had one of the highest dropout rates in the city. The study relates this latter finding to a cultural tendency among Cambodians to withdraw from conflict—a characteristic that also explains their low suspension rate—as well as to the effects of the Pol Pot era.

The study documents the devastating effect that the Pol Pot era has had on both the physical and psychological stability of Cambodian families. Approximately 50% of Cambodian families in the study sample consisted of single-parent female households, and nearly 25% of Cambodian women were widows.

The Cambodians who had lived through the Pol Pot period—all but two of the respondents in the study—continued to suffer physically and emotionally: "[They] all mentioned their frequent nightmares, their inability to forget those terrible days, their breaking into a cold sweat whenever they hear unfamiliar

Struggling to Catch Up

Recent research documents what many educators have been saying for several years: A lack of previous education is a major obstacle to success in high school for many refugee youth—particularly those who arrive in the U.S. as teenagers and thus have less time than younger arrivals to catch up. "They withdraw from what seems to them an impossible task of simultaneously learning high school material while learning English," the San Diego study notes. "This is all the more difficult for older students who [are] illiterate in their own native language."

ORR-funded studies of refugee youth in Philadelphia and Minneapolis/St. Paul corroborate the San Diego finding. Less educated youth are "very likely to do relatively poorly in school and hence, likely to be at the lower end of the occupational ladder," the Minneapolis/St. Paul study noted.

One obstacle that this group faces is that their needs have not been publicized. "All we hear about are the valedictorians and the gang members," said a participant at a recent ORR-sponsored conference, Replanting Uprooted Refugee Youth. "A lot of kids are just quietly falling through the cracks."

Nevertheless, educators around the U.S. are increasingly aware that these less-educated students need more than just a few hours of ESL a day if they are to enter the academic mainstream. Rather, they need an entire school curriculum adapted to their levels of language and background knowledge—much like what the Preparation for American Secondary Schools (PASS) program provides. At the conference on refugee youth, for example, service providers from Philadelphia identified "appropriate curriculum for limited English proficient speakers" as one of that school system's most pressing needs.

The "1.5 Generation"

... they live in two worlds with two sets of languages, rules, and customs ...

"AT WORK I'm American, but at home I'm Cambodian," says Naroeun, a computer programmer in Arlington, Virginia. At work the outgoing 21-year-old college graduate speaks her mind, arguing a point, if necessary. Sometimes she enjoys a drink with colleagues after work, even though she knows her parents wouldn't approve.

But at home, Naroeun is a quiet, obedient daughter, especially in the presence of her father. "He's pretty conservative," she says, "and sometimes I don't agree with him, but I always say, 'Yes, yes, yes.' " Naroeun avoids conflict between her two worlds by keeping them separate. "I never invite my American friends home," she says.

Naroeun, who arrived in the US. at 16, is a member of what the San Diego study calls the "1.5 generation." Part of neither the first generation of their parents nor of the second generation of children born in the U.S., they occupy a place somewhere between the two. As a bridge between two cultures, they live in two worlds with two sets of languages, rules, and customs, a position that demands considerable tolerance for ambiguity and contradiction. And the challenge of bridging two cultures is complicated by a second challenge—making the transition from adolescence to adulthood. In contrast, their parents face only the first challenge, and the younger generation will have to contend mostly with the second.

But the 1.5 generation also enjoy a special advantage. They are in a better position than their parents to take advantage of opportunities in the new world, and in a better position than their American-born brothers and sisters to choose what is best from the old.

Van, a medical student at the University of California and a subject in the San Diego study, attributes his success to the Vietnamese work ethic. He is also traditionally Vietnamese in his attitudes toward dating, marriage, and family, he says. But when it comes to his ideas about professional work, Van describes himself as more American than Vietnamese. "Vietnamese tend to be a little more relaxed about working," he says. "Hard work in school is Vietnamese, but I think once you get out of the school system, Vietnamese are more relaxed in terms of working." He also sees himself as American in his punctuality. "I like to be right on time," he says. "Most of Vietnamese, they tend to stress 'rubberband time.' "

Van, who arrived in the U.S. at 15, has succeeded despite barriers of language and culture—barriers that his younger brothers and sisters don't face. Yet they seem to lack their older brother's single-minded determination to succeed.

"The younger ones see the easy life in America," says Van. "They don't know the value of money. They didn't have to go through the time that they starve to death and hungry and didn't have money." They even have "American" study habits, he says with dismay: They wait until the night before an exam to study and then study on their beds while listening to music—"instead of like [me], study for like a week in advance."

"I thought that they would do much better since they have no problem with English," Van says. But it turn out that they use that to just relax and study the night before the exam."

sounds which trigger thoughts of those traumatic days." According to a Cambodian service provider interviewed in the study, many Cambodian parents suffer "post-traumatic stress" so severe that they are unable to take care of their children, which in turn affects their children's school performance and increases the likelihood of their dropping out of school.[3]

Although the Hmong were found to have the lowest dropout rate in the city, they were among those least likely to continue their education beyond high school. One reason is economic. As members of one of the poorest groups in San Diego, where 94% of the Hmong live below the poverty level, Hmong parents are less able to support their children's education beyond high school. For refugee families on welfare—a majority of Hmong families in San Diego the loss of a child's benefits at 18 further increases pressure for the child to get a job in order to contribute to family income.

In addition, low levels of education and high rates of unemployment in the San Diego Hmong community mean that Hmong adults are less able to inform their children about educational and employment options after high school. This fact, coupled with an apparent reluctance among the Hmong to turn to "outsiders" for help, hinders their capacity to make clear and realistic plans for their future.

But early marriage emerges as the biggest obstacle to post-secondary education for the Hmong, especially among girls, for whom marriage seems to be a response to traditional pressures from parents and boyfriends as well as a means of escape from unhappy home lives.

Sources and Suggested Additional Reading

The articles in this issue of In America are based on interviews with service providers and refugees as well as the following publications:

Baizweman, Michael, Glenn Hendricks, Ruth Hammond, Norah Neale, & Phuc Nguyen. (1987). *A study of Southeast Asian refugee youth in the Twin Cities of Minneapolis and St. Paul, Minnesota.* Washington, DC: Government Printing Office.

---

[3] The psychological well-being of mothers is an important factor in the educational performance of their children, the study found, pointing to "the key role of Southeast Asian mothers in the socialization, supervision, and education of their children."

Friendship: The Cultural Factor

In a recent study, *A Report on Needs Assessment of Vietnamese Students at California State University, Fullerton,* 90% of the Vietnamese respondents agreed with the statement, "Vietnamese students do their best to establish friendly relationships with Americans students on this campus." This response surprised researchers Robert Ericksen and Dogan Cucelogu, given "the prevalent impression among American students and staff on campus that the Vietnamese show little interest in forming friendships with Americans."

One reason for the discrepancy may lie in the different ways the two groups view friendship, the study speculates. Vietnamese friends tend to get involved in every aspect of each other's lives—a level of involvement that most Americans don't want. Because of the commitment involved, Vietnamese are more cautious than Americans in starting friendships.

According to the study, Americans and Vietnamese are also different in how they "express friendly intentions." Americans are more explicit and direct in expressing their intentions than the Vietnamese and are thus unlikely to get the message when a Vietnamese smiles shyly or chooses to sit close to an American in the library. "The Vietnamese believe that by making themselves available for an interaction in the classroom, laboratory, or library, they have clearly expressed their intention of establishing friendly relationships," the study notes. The Vietnamese students also feel that since they are not in their own country, it is up to American-born students to make the first move. "Otherwise, the Vietnamese would be imposing themselves on the American."

Caplan, Nathan, John K. Whitmore, Quang L. Bui, & Marcella Trautman. (1987, October 11). Study shows boat refugees' children achieve academic success. *Refugee Reports, 6* (10), 1–6.

Ericksen, Robert B., & Dogan M. Cucelogu. (1987). *A report on needs assessment of Vietnamese students at California State University, Fullerton.* Fullerton, CA: California State University.

Peters, Heather. (1987). *A study of Southeast Asian youth in Philadelphia: A final report.* Washington, DC: Government Printing Office.

Rumbaut, Rubén G., & Kenji Ima. (1987). *The adaptation of Southeast Asian refugee youth: A comparative study.* Washington, DC: Government Printing Office.

Selected list of recent publications on refugee youth for additional reading

Arax, Marc (1987, December 13). Lost in LA. *Los Angeles Times Magazine,* pp. 10–14, 16, 42, 44, 46, 48.

Bell, David A. (1985, July 15 & 22). The triumph of Asian-Americans. *The New Republic,* pp. 24, 26, 28–31.

Bliatout, Bruce, Bruce T. Downing, Judy Lewis, & Dao Yang. (1988). *Handbook for teaching Hmong speaking students.* Folsom, CA: Folsom Cordova Unified School District.

Carlin, Jean E. (1986). Child and adolescent refugees: Psychiatric assessment and treatment. In Carolyn L. Williams & Joseph Westermeyer (Eds.), *Refugee mental health in resettlement countries.* Washington, DC: Hemisphere Publishing Corporation.

Goldstein, Beth Leah. (1985). *Schooling for cultural transitions: Hmong girls and boys in American high schools* (Doctoral dissertation, University of Wisconsin—Madison). Ann Arbor, MI: University Microfilms International (No. 8601538).

Hammond, Ruth. (1988, June 15–21). Young love—strangers in a strange land, part two. *Twin Cities Reader,* pp. 1, 12, 14–15.

Szymusiak, Molyda. (1986). *The stones cry out.* New York: Farrar, Straus and Giroux.

Vo, Thanh M. (1988). *Vietnamese runaways: A preliminary study of 57 cases in East Side Union High School District.* San Jose, CA: Education Center/East Side Union High School District.

Wehrly, Bea, & William Nelson. (1986). *The assimilation and acculturation of Indochinese refugees into Illinois schools.* Macomb, IL: Western Illinois University.

An Indian Father's Plea

by Robert Lake (Medicine Grizzlybear)

Wind-Wolf knows the names and migration patterns of more than 40 birds. He knows there are 13 tail feathers on a perfectly balanced eagle. What he needs is a teacher who knows his full measure.

Dear teacher,

I would like to introduce you to my son, Wind-Wolf. He is probably what you would consider a typical Indian kid. He was born and raised on the reservation. He has black hair, dark brown eyes, and an olive complexion. And like so many Indian children his age, he is shy and quiet in the classroom. He is 5 years old, in kindergarten, and I can't understand why you have already labeled him a "slow learner."

At the age of 5, he has already been through quite an education compared with his peers in Western society. As his first introduction into this world, he was bonded to his mother and to the Mother Earth in a traditional native childbirth ceremony. And he has been continuously cared for by his mother, father, sisters, cousins, aunts, uncles, grandparents, and extended tribal family since this ceremony.

From his mother's warm and loving arms, Wind-Wolf was placed in a secure and specially designed Indian baby basket. His father and the medicine elders conducted another ceremony with him that served to bond him with the essence of his genetic father, the Great Spirit, the Grandfather Sun, and the Grandmother Moon. This was all done in order to introduce him properly into the new and natural world, not the world of artificiality, and to protect his sensitive and delicate soul. It is our people's way of showing the newborn respect, ensuring that he starts his life on the path of spirituality.

The traditional Indian baby basket became his "turtle's shell" and served as the first seat for his classroom. He was strapped in for safety, protected from injury by the willow roots and hazel wood construction. The basket was made by a tribal elder who had gathered her materials with prayer and in a ceremonial way. It is the same kind of basket that people have used for thousands of years. It is specially designed to provide the child with the kind of knowledge and experience he will need in order to survive in his culture and environment.

Wind-Wolf was strapped in snuggly with a deliberate restriction upon his arms and legs. Although you in Western society may argue that such a method serves to hinder motor-skill development and abstract reasoning, we believe it forces the child to first develop his intuitive faculties, rational intellect, symbolic thinking, and five senses. Wind-Wolf was with his mother constantly, closely bonded physically, as she carried him on her back or held him in front while breast-feeding. She carried him everywhere she went, and every night he slept with both parents. Because of this, Wind-Wolf's educational setting was not only a "secure" environment but it was also very colorful, complicated, sensitive, and diverse. He has been with his mother at the ocean at daybreak when she made her prayers and gathered fresh seaweed from the rocks, he has sat with his uncles in a rowboat on the river while they fished with gill nets, and he has watched and listened to elders as they told creation stories and animal legends and sang songs around the campfires.

He has attended the sacred and ancient White Deerskin Dance of his people and is well acquainted with the cultures and languages of other tribes. He has been with his mother when she gathered herbs for healing and watched his tribal aunts and grandmothers gather and prepare traditional foods such as acorn, smoked salmon, eel, and deer meat. He has played with abalone shells, pine nuts, iris grass string, and leather while watching the women make beaded jewelry and traditional native regalia. He has had many opportunities to watch his father, uncles, and ceremonial leaders use different kinds of colorful feathers and sing different kinds of songs while preparing for the sacred dances and rituals.

As he grew older, Wind-Wolf began to crawl out of the baby basket, develop his motor skills, and explore the world around him. When frightened or sleepy, he could always return to the basket, as a turtle withdraws into its shell. Such an inward journey allows one to reflect in privacy on what he has learned and to carry the new knowledge deeply into the unconscious and the soul. Shapes, sizes, colors, texture, sound, smell, feeling, taste, and the learning process are therefore functionally integrated—the physical and spiritual, matter and energy, conscious and unconscious, individual and social.

This kind of learning goes beyond the basics of distinguishing the difference between rough and smooth, square and round, hard and soft, black and white, similarities and extremes.

For example, Wind-Wolf was with his mother

From *Literacy Harvest*, Vol. 2, No. 1, Winter 1993, pp. 18-20. Originally appeared in *Teacher* magazine, September 1990, pp. 48-53. © 1990 by Editorial Projects in Education, Inc., Washington, DC.

in South Dakota while she danced for seven days straight in the hot sun, fasting, and piercing herself in the sacred Sun Dance Ceremony of a distant tribe. He has been doctored in a number of different healing ceremonies by medicine men and women from diverse places ranging from Alaska and Arizona to New York and California. He has been in more than 20 different sacred sweat-lodge rituals — used by native tribes to purify mind, body, and soul — since he was 3 years old, and he has already been exposed to many different religions of his racial brothers: Protestant, Catholic, Asian Buddhist, and Tibetan Lamaist.

It takes a long time to absorb and reflect on these kinds of experiences, so maybe that is why you think my Indian child is a slow learner. His aunts and grandmothers taught him to count and know his numbers while they sorted out the complex materials used to make the abstract designs in the native baskets. He listened to his mother count each and every bead and sort out numerically according to color while she painstakingly made complex beaded belts and necklaces. He learned his basic numbers by helping his father count and sort the rocks to be used in the sweat lodge — 7 rocks for a medicine sweat, say, or 13 for the summer solstice ceremony. (The rocks are later heated and doused with water to create purifying steam). And he was taught to learn mathematics by counting the sticks we use in our traditional native hand game. So I realize he may be slow in grasping the methods and tools that you are now using in your classroom, ones quite familiar to his white peers, but I hope you will be patient with him. It takes time to adjust to a new cultural system and learn new things.

He is not culturally "disadvantaged," he is culturally "different." If you ask him how many months there are in a year, he will probably tell you 13. He will respond this way not because he doesn't know how to count properly, but because he has been taught by our traditional people that there are 13 full moons in a year according to the native tribal calendar and that there are really 13 planets in our solar system and 13 tail feathers on a perfectly balanced eagle, the most powerful kind of bird to use in ceremony and healing.

But he also knows that some eagles may only have 12 tail feathers, or 7, that they do not all have the same number. He knows that the flicker has exactly 10 tail feathers; that they are red and black, representing the directions of east and west, life and death - and that this bird is considered a "fire" bird, a power used in native doctoring and healing. He can probably count more than 40 different kinds of birds, tell you and his peers what kind of bird each is and where it lives, the season in which it appears, and how it is used in a sacred ceremony. He may

have trouble writing his name on a piece of paper, but he knows how to say it and many other things in several different Indian languages. He is not fluent yet because he is only 5 years old and required by law to attend your educational system, learn your language, your values, your ways of thinking, and your methods of teaching and learning.

So you see, all of these influences together make him somewhat shy and quiet — and perhaps "slow" according to your standards. But if Wind-Wolf was not prepared for his first tentative foray into your world, neither were you appreciative of his culture. On the first day of class, you had difficulty with his name. You wanted to call him "Wind" - insisting that Wolf somehow must be his middle name. The students in the class laughed at him, causing further embarrassment.

While you are trying to teach him your new methods, helping him learn new tools for self discovery and adapt to his new learning environment, he may be looking out the window as if daydreaming. Why? Because he has been taught to watch and study the changes in nature. It is hard for him to make the appropriate psychic switch from the right to the left hemisphere of the brain when he sees the leaves turning bright colors, the geese heading south, and the squirrels scurrying around for nuts to get ready for a harsh winter. In his heart, in his young mind, and almost by instinct, he knows that this is the time of year he is supposed to be with his people gathering and preparing fish, deer meat, and native plants and herbs, and learning his assigned tasks in this role. He is caught between two worlds torn by two distinct cultural systems.

Yesterday, for the third time in two weeks, he came home crying and said he wanted to have his hair cut. He said he doesn't have any friends at school because they make fun of his long hair. I tried to explain to him that in our culture, long hair is a sign of masculinity and balance and is a source of power. But he remained adamant in his position.

To make matters worse, he recently encountered his first harsh case of racism. Wind-Wolf had managed to adopt at least one good school friend. On the way home from school one day, he asked his new pal if he wanted to come home to play with him until supper. That was OK with Wind-Wolf's mother, who was walking with them. When they got to the little friend's house, the two boys ran inside to ask permission while Wind-Wolf's mother waited. But the other boy's mother lashed out "It is OK if you have to play with him at school, but we don't allow those kind of people in our house!" When my wife asked why not, the other boy's mother answered "Because you are Indians and we are white; and I don't want my kids growing up with your kind of people."

So now my young Indian child does not want to go to school anymore (even though his hair is cut). He feels that he does not belong. He is the only Indian child in your class, and he is well-aware of this fact. Instead of being proud of his race, heritage, and culture, he feels ashamed. When he watches television, he asks why the white people hate us so much and always kill our people in the movies and why they take everything away from us. He asks why the other kids in school are not taught about the power, beauty, and essence of nature or provided with an opportunity to experience the world around them first hand. He says he hates living in the city and that he misses his Indian cousins and friends. He asks why one young white girl at school who is his friend always tells him, "I like you Wind-Wolf, because you are a good Indian."

Now he refuses to sing his native songs, play with his Indian artifacts, learn his language, or participate in his sacred ceremonies. When I ask him to go to an urban powwow or help me with a sacred sweat-lodge ritual, he says no because "that's weird" and he doesn't want his friends at school to think he doesn't believe in God.

So, dear teacher, I want to introduce you to my son, Wind-Wolf, who is not really a "typical" little Indian kid after all. He stems from a long line of hereditary chiefs, medicine men and women, and ceremonial leaders whose accomplishments and unique forms of knowledge are still being studied and recorded in contemporary books. He has seven different tribal systems flowing through his blood; he is even part white. I want my child to succeed in school and in life. I don't want him to be a dropout or juvenile delinquent or to end up on drugs and alcohol because he is made to feel inferior or because of discrimination. I want him to be proud of his rich heritage and culture, and I would like him to develop the necessary capabilities to adapt to and succeed in both cultures. But I need your help.

What you say and what you do in the classroom, what you teach and how you teach it, and what you don't say and don't teach will have a significant effect on the potential success or failure of my child. Please remember that this is the primary year of his education and development. All I ask is that you work with me, not against me, to help educate my child in the best way. If you don't have the knowledge, preparation, experience, or training to effectively deal with culturally different children, I am willing to help you with the few resources I have available or direct you to such resources.

Millions of dollars have been appropriated by Congress and are being spent each year for "Indian Education." All you have to do is take advantage of it and encourage your school to make an effort to use it in the name of "equal education." My Indian child has a constitutional right to learn, retain, and maintain his heritage and culture. By the same token I strongly believe that non-Indian children also have a constitutional right to learn about our native American heritage and culture, because Indians play a significant part in the history of Western society. Until this reality is equally understood and applied in education as a whole, there will be a lot more schoolchildren in grades K-2 identified as "slow learners."

My son, Wind-Wolf, is not an empty glass coming into your class to be filled. He is a full basket coming into a different environment and society with something special to share. Please let him share his knowledge, heritage, and culture with you and his peers.

Lake reports that Wind-Wolf , now 8, is doing better in school, but the boy's struggle for cultural identity continues.

Robert Lake (Medicine Grizzlybear), a member of the Seneca and Cherokee Indian tribes, is an associate professor at Gonzaga University's School of Education in Spokane, Wash.

Mexican Immigrants From El Rincón: A Case Study of Resilience and Empowerment

Enrique (Henry) T. Trueba

At dawn, sometimes with temperatures in the mid 40s, old cars from El Rincón (a fictitious name for a rural town in central California) rush to the surrounding fields. Farm workers arrive carrying bags with food and drinks for their morning break and lunch. They wear jackets or sweaters, and many cover their face and head with a piece of cloth. During a few minutes of stretching exercises they receive last-minute instructions, prepare the bands and packing boxes on the tractor, and begin work, with the pickers on the ground and the packers on top of the tractors. The pickers pull out their little knives and start cutting broccoli—or lettuce, cauliflower, celery—as loud ranchero music from portable radios and cheerful conversation energize the group.

El Rincón is a small agricultural community of between 6,500 and 8,000 people, 95% of whom are Mexican immigrants. It is situated in the northwestern corner of Santa Barbara County, 75 miles (121 km) north of the city of Santa Barbara. It has 260 square miles (673 km^2) of rich farmland that yields amazingly vast volumes of vegetables and other specialized crops (e.g., lettuce, cauliflower, broccoli, celery, and strawberries). During the past 50 years, Mexican immigrants from the central Mexican states—particularly from Jalisco, Michoacán, Colima, and Guanajuato—have made their way to El Rincón in the central California valley of Santa Barbara County, 175 miles (282 km) north of Los Angeles. They began to come after World War II and have since worked in the fields as pickers, tractor drivers, and packers. For a number of historical and economic reasons they have developed a binational, bicultural existence, commuting between central Mexico and central California. As a very important survival strategy, they have developed extensive networks with Mexican families on both sides of the border, and they have provided their children with skills to function effectively in two very different cultures and languages. Consequently, they have maintained their home language and culture and their traditional family values through the annual civic and religious celebrations (e.g., baptism, confirmations, weddings, funerals, patron saints' days, fiestas) that reinforce the hierarchical structure of the family.

How and why would these immigrant families commit to educational excellence? Because they believe that the economic survival of the entire family will ultimately depend on the education of the children. A good education in the United States (so they think) will open up new cultural and linguistic panoramas in the near future. Thus, Mexican junior high school students talk about becoming engineers, doctors, computer technicians, journalists, and architects; their dream is to provide for their parents and make them feel proud. Their success in math, English, and science is carefully crafted by Chicano teachers and mentors (graduate students from California Polytechnic University at San Luis Obispo) via intensive efforts in class during the elementary school years through the use of both Spanish and English, and after-class working sessions for high school students who commute 46 miles (74 km) daily to attend school.

Mexican farm workers and their families began to reside permanently in town in the 1960s; from that time on, the increase in population has been dramatic. El Rincón's population grew from 3,225 in 1960 to 5,479 in 1990. In 1960, the Mexican-origin population constituted only 18% of the town's population, but by 1990 it constituted 83%. In 1996, the Mexican population made up an estimated 95% of the population of El Rincón.

The Process of Empowerment

The following narratives from Rita, a Mexican mother, Manuel Mora, a Grade 4 teacher, and Mario, a high school student, illustrate the process of empowerment from the perspective of the immigrants themselves. All of the names used in this article are pseudonyms.

Rita: A Mexican Immigrant Mother

Rita is the archetype of the many young women interviewed: although in poor health—with arthritis, ear infections, allergic reactions to pesticides, physical weakness,

From *TESOL Journal*, Spring 1998, pp. 12-17. © 1998 by Teachers of English to Speakers of Other Languages, Inc. Reprinted by permission.

and lack of access to medical care—she is committed to continue the struggle for a better life. She is decisive in her actions and passionate about her beliefs. She talks with great respect about her parents (both worked in California as farm workers) as role models in the fields, who taught her early in life the importance of working hard, never giving up, and never taking anything from others. She demands the respect of the Americans with her dignified behavior. She emphasizes to her four children, ages 6 to 16, the need to be responsible and persistent. The oldest and the two youngest are boys, and all three are considered gifted in school; their scores in mathematics are among the highest in their classes. The 12-year-old girl is mentally retarded and goes to special education classes. At times with a laugh and at times in tears, Rita described incidents of racial prejudice and hostility by U.S. schoolchildren. She is bitter about the insensitivity of some of her bosses; recent humiliations and insults suffered at work still bring to the surface deep feelings of anger and shame. Most of all, she

> When Rita came back from the cannery or the fields exhausted and muddy and tired, she still prepared a meal for her family, and she took the time to find out about schoolwork.

is deeply sorry that as a young mother she missed important intimate moments with her young children, such as not being able to hug them when they were asking for affection because she was always too busy or tired. In protest, she refused to speak English for many years. Only recently has she decided to use English and prepare for her citizenship examination in order to stay in this country. This is a major change in her life, but she thinks she will eventually have dual citizenship in Mexico and the United States. What follows is a summary of Rita's narrative.

Rita's family started coming to the United States together in 1961; prior to that, her father had been a farm worker for several years. Her father was not comfortable sending his children to the local schools in the United States because he knew they would not be treated well. Later on Rita was sent back to Michoacán, Mexico, to get some schooling. However, while there was sufficient work in Articia (near Los Angeles), Rita worked at home. "I was 8, my brother,

10, and my older sister, 12. Then the *patrón* (boss), who needed hands, hired them for half salary. I was helping drive the tractor. When I was 9 and 10, I became responsible for our house. I had to make corn tortillas in a machine, clean the house, prepare the meals for the family, and baby-sit younger children." People began to notice that Rita and her siblings did not attend school and put pressure on her father to send them to school. But her father instead sent them back to Mexico, where Rita finished elementary school and her older siblings only finished Grade 3. The youngest brother, 10 years younger than Rita, never did farm work and remained in Michoacán most of his life, where he became an accountant. Rita learned discipline as a very young child:

> Chona [Rita's younger sister] was very restless and was bothering all the other children and would not let me do my work. I would then tie her with a rope, but she knew how to untie herself; then she would say that she had the *diablo* (devil). One day my father showed up

to pick up his lunch, and I did not have it ready. I started to cry and explained that Chona did not let me work and said she had the *diablo*. My father says: "Oh, she does, eh! Come here Chona, I will take the *diablo* out of you. Then he hit her so hard with the rope that Chona was sick and had a high fever all day and night. She never bothered me any more, and I was responsible for the home.

Rita's father rarely spanked them (two or three times in the life of each child) and tried to persuade them to do the right thing in order not break their father's heart.

Rural Mexican children while in California had bitter experiences with their peers. Rita was supposed to attend Grade 4 in Articia, but the U.S. children made her life impossible, so she was sent back to Mexico. She just did not want to attend school in Articia:

> The kids were so bad! They would wait till the school bus got near to

throw water balloons and get me and my girlfriend all wet and without being able to go home and change. Other times they would kick us, pull our hair. I would tell them "Get off," but they continued. Then I began to insult them and they would call us names. One day they began to kick me, and I held this girl's foot and she fell down. They called and scolded me. During lunch they would grab us. The Americans did not like us.

As children, Rita and her siblings felt the oppression and abuse by the bosses, but they also learned from their parents to respond to abuse by defending their own rights. Rita was only 14 years old and was already picking strawberries at 6 a.m. At the end of the strawberry season, the entire family drove to Fresno to pick blueberries. The boss promised each member of the family (man, wife, and three children) $10 per box—a fairly large box. At the end of the day each had made about $30. The boss said: "Go to this address to pick up your money." When they showed up at the address, the boss threw a $10 bill at them and dismissed them. "My father was angry and said: 'You are cheating us.' The old man replied: 'If you don't shut up and leave, I will call the *Migra*.' Because we were legal, my father said: 'I should call the police on you because you are a thief'." Indeed, the next day the father went to the place where Mexican workers are hired and explained to the others that the man was dishonest and would cheat them. Most of them stayed, however, because they needed work.

Bad experiences with bosses is a central theme that provides women with a deep motivation to fight for their children and encourage them to learn in school so they will not be cheated. Rita was about 15 years old when she had a most humiliating experience:

> I remember one time we had this bad *patrón* who would not let us go to the bathroom all morning long [in the fields you had to take a long walk to get out of sight], and I could no longer hold it. Well, I held and held and could no longer hold it. So I urinated right there on my clothes and was so embarrassed that I began to cry. My mother, who was working nearby, came and covered me so the others would not notice, and I just cried and cried out of shame.

After 22 years of working in the fields, Rita finally "graduated" to one of the packing companies, but working conditions were just as inhuman there as they were in the fields. She soon found that there was pressure to work fast all the time, and the hours were long and often unpredictable; she ended up working the night shift. Any worker who refused to come to a shift was fired. So at the age of 37, after a long career of service in the worst of conditions, with arthritis, loss of hearing due to ear infections, allergic reactions from exposure to the chemicals used in the fields and packing companies, with four children (one of them mentally retarded) from Grade 1 to senior high school, and without medical insurance, Rita reflected on her life and found that the only reason for all

> Two things become clear to all students: that it is great to be in school, and that the use of either Spanish or English is equally acceptable as long as they know the subject.

these sacrifices was the education of her children.

Rita's personal life prepared her to socialize her children into hard work, self-respect—even when outsiders showed disdain and rejection for Mexicans—and a profound commitment to improve one's life at any cost. Rita was always on time at parents' meetings, spoke freely about the needs of students, and demanded attention when a student had been abused by a teacher. One time, word was that one of the high school teachers had manhandled by the neck a Mexican student and unfairly roughed him up for a minor fault (i.e., touching a tool he was not supposed to touch in auto mechanics class). El Rincón had only an elementary and a middle school; therefore, children had to travel 20 miles (32 km) to the larger city of Santa Maria in order to get an education, and Mexican students were not welcome. Rita organized parents to come to the city to speak to the principal and demand an explanation. In another instance, the buses taking students from El Rincón to the larger city were late, and on two occasions only one was sent, instead of two. Consequently the El Rincón students were crowded and uncomfortable. Rita called several parents and together they drove to the high school to remedy the situation. Advocacy for Mexican children was accompanied by a consistent policy of accountability and support. Rita wanted to know everything that was going on in school and was not happy if the children's grades went down.

Naturally, it was not enough to have parents like Rita. Teachers also played a pivotal role in the academic achievement of students. What is significant here is that, through similar types of assisted performance (to be discussed below), students acquired the skills to cope with school and the motivation to achieve (from interaction with their parents), as well as the knowledge and cognitive skills that translated into high achievement (from interaction with Mexican or Chicano teachers). Here is an example of the kinds of transaction that occurred between the children and their teacher.

Manuel Mora: The Grade 4 Teacher

The elementary school in El Rincón has 760 children, 98% of whom are Mexican—about half born in Mexico and half children of recent immigrants from Mexico. The Grade 4 teacher, Manuel Mora, is at least 6 ft (1.8 m) tall, with dark brown skin and black hair, and is perfectly fluent in Spanish and in English. His father, a tough guy, came from Mexico during the 1960s and became one of the most feared and respected Mexicans in the region. He was known to be fair and quiet, but always armed and dangerous if attacked. Mora is the second to last of five children, kind, and given to poetry, math, and music. He likes teaching and does it well. He has received a number of awards, has been featured in the local papers, and is the most popular teacher in the elementary school. He opens his class with loud *ranchero* (country music) or hip hop, inviting all children to sing loudly for a few minutes; then he makes them beg to start with math. Thus, the initial strategy is to involve all students in a group cultural activity, through rap music, banda, *ranchero*, hip hop, rhythm and blues, and other types of music. He creates a relaxed climate by using children's Mexican nicknames, such as *Pulga* (flea—given to small children in an affectionate way), *Mariposa* (butterfly), or by giving children English nicknames, such as Running Bear, Drama, White Fang, Pocahontas, and Wild Berry. Right after the music and initial greetings, he repeats as a mantra his daily "Nothing to it. But to do it" or "It's a piece of cake; all you have to do is eat it," or its equivalent in Spanish, "*Orale, a darle.*" On certain occasions when the class gets quiet, Mora uses his own poetry to inculcate in children the values of hard work, anti-drug and anti-gang attitudes, and notions of sacrifice for family and friends. In fact, if asked in an informal situation such as a social gathering what he does for a living, Mora may say half seriously, "*Soy po-e-taaa*" (I am a po-e-t).

Mora is always proud of teaching above the grade level of his students—and doing it in their language of preference. He often gives students a chance to go to the board and play with algebraic equations. The competition is tough, but he does not miss a single student and involves them all. The intensity of intellectual activity is the mark of his teaching. No one ever gets bored. His students not only excel in math but also in writing and most other subjects. Parents beg Mora to take their children, putting pressure on the principal if necessary. Mora lives to teach and share with his students. He retains control of the class at all times, although he gives the appearance of loud and free interaction. He calls it *controlled chaos*, or *abstract teaching*. Two things become clear to all students: that it is great to be in school, and that the use of either Spanish or English is equally acceptable as long as they know the subject.

During class, the intensity of the show and the strategically placed breaks to listen to music or to do other enjoyable activities cannot distract a systematic observer from the seriousness with which Mora teaches math, reading, and writing. Equally intensive is the socialization to be proud to be a Mexican. The theme in many of the songs is precisely this pride. The central topic in certain compositions is the pride in being Mexican, Chicano or Chicana, brown skinned, and able to use two languages. As a person, Mora is somewhat shy and distant. He is not close to his father, and he lives with his mother in a house for which he pays the mortgage. Although he loves to perform in class (e.g., teaching, singing, reciting poems, acting), he is a deeply sensitive person and often somewhat insecure and unsure of his talents. He is the best example I have ever found of a person who is able to engage with children in learning transactions with an absolute and profound knowledge of what the children know and how they function at every minute.

After an introduction to basic algebraic emotions, Mora wants to introduce negative and positive numbers as follows: "Bad, sad, and unpleasant feelings are negative, and happy, glad, smiling, pleasant feelings [are] for positive numbers." Then Mora transitions to difficult algebraic equations. He manages to select the students who are struggling with a concept, walk them through the concept, and set the stage for them to demonstrate their knowledge; indeed, he uses the Vygotskian (1972) concept of assisted performance with unique mastery. (See right)

Eventually, the students figure out the last algebraic problem and compete loudly to present the solution on the board. It is time for recreation, yet students do not want to leave. They are so involved with their work that would rather stay and share their progress with the teacher and friends. One leaves the classroom with a feeling that learning is a lot of fun, and that the penalties for making mistakes are rare, but the rewards for learning are many.

One of the basic cultural differences in the role of teachers among Mexicans, if compared with North American traditions, is that parents *entregan* (give away) their children to the teachers and clearly ask them to become surrogate parents. As a consequence, the relationship between a Mexican teacher and his or her students is of a different quality. For example, in addition to the enormous respect the students show Mora, and in contrast with collective behavior of submission on a personal level, the children hug Mora and playfully challenge him by breaking small rules regarding the use of space, leaving the classroom, not using the blackboard, becoming quiet, and so forth. There is a conspicuous demonstration of love and affection. The *maestro* is more than a regular teacher. In turn, Mora can become jokingly sarcastic or intimidating and say such things as *te voy a castigar* (I am going to punish you) or *le voy a decir a tu mamá* (I am going to tell your mother). The response on the part of the children is an affectionate hug, laugh, or a gesture of a pretend *I don't care*. What has happened, however, is that the teacher and children have created a bond that motivates children to learn. As we will see below, this is particularly congruent with a Vygotskian (1978) explanation of intellectual development.

Mario: "I want to become an engineer."

Mario is now a high school student commuting 46 miles (74 km) a day from El Rincón to the big city's high school. Twice a week he comes to his alma mater, the middle high school, for tutoring sessions in math, writing, and other subjects. He feels self-responsible and behaves like an adult. At home, he is the best informed about any matters that are discussed and the most trusted

Sample Text

Mora: *A ver, quién quiere pasar al pizarrón?* (Let's see, who is going to come to the blackboard?) [He scans the entire group as if looking for somebody in particular.] *A ver, a ver ... Un calladito como ... José, pasa al pizarrón.* (Let me see, let me see ... A quiet one like ... José, go to the blackboard). [José hesitantly gets up and goes to the blackboard.] *Escribe, 9x+7=61. Puedes resolver esa ecuación?* (Write 9x+7=61. Can you solve that equation?)

[José writes the equation and pauses.]

Mora [noticing some unrest among students who are anxious to go to the board, and in a loud voice]: *Callados todos! Espérate José* (Quiet all! Wait for José). [The students are instantly quiet and wait.] *Puedes resolver la ecuación? (Can you solve the equation?)*

José: *Pos, no sé, pero ... le haré la lucha.* (Well, I don't know ... but I will try).

Mora: *Andale pues, puedes explicarlo en español* (Do it, then, you can explain it in Spanish).

José: *9x+7=61. Entónces, 9x+7=61* (9x+7=61. Then, 9x+7=61). *OK, -7=-7. Le quito negativo 7 a los dos lados porque lo que le haga a un lado, lo tengo hacer al otro* (OK, -7=7. I take away negative 7 from both sides of the equation, because what I do on one side I have to do on the other). *Luego, cancelo los sietes y me queda, 9x+7-7=61-7, o sea 9x=54* (Then I cancel the sevens and I have 9x+7-7=61-7, that is, 9x=54).

Mora: Like Ricky Ricardo said, "Ssplain it to me." *Explícalo y redúcelo más* (Explain and reduce it further).

José: *Luego divido los dos lados de la ecuación entre 9, y me queda: 9x/9=54/9; eso es, x=6* (Then I divide both sides of the equation by 9, and I have: 9x/9=54/9, i.e., x=6).

Mora [smiling, proud of José's performance]: *Muy bien!* (Very good!). *Siéntate, Jose* (sit down, José). I have a very difficult problem for all of you. If any of you can resolve it, you will receive *un premio grande* (a big prize). This is a math problem that nobody even in Grade 7 can solve. But you are a very special class, and I know you will resolve it.

[Then he starts singing "*Cuarto año del 25, gana siempre y otra vez!*" (Fourth grade of room 25 always wins, and it will win once more!), and writes on the board the problem: 10x-3=97.]

Mora: You can work in teams. I will give you 5 minutes.

[Students pick their groups as they have done before, and start working individually within each group as Mora walks around].

Mora: Artemio, get to work. Help your group. *Alicia, qué haces mi'jita? Por qué no estás trabajando?* (Alicia, what are you doing, my child? Why are you not working?).

Alicia [touching her stomach and making a face intended to gain some sympathy from Mora, but in a whispering tone that will not call the attention of her classmates]: *Me duele el estómago, maestro, y la cabeza* (My stomach hurts, teacher, and my head).

Mora: *Vete con la enfermera a que te de algo, y no comas tantos chicharrones el domingo!* (Go the nurse so she can give you something, and don't eat so many *chicharrones*).

[The students laugh, continue their intensive work, and Alicia leaves class in the direction of the infirmary.]

person to make a judgment on serious economic and social affairs, family matters, and almost anything that requires a deep comprehension of English text and U.S. traditions. He was born in the United States, but was raised in El Rincón as a Mexican child. He is perfectly fluent in Spanish and English and prefers to read in Spanish, but can do well in English. His favorite subject is math. He wants to be an engineer to construct bridges, homes, factories and make a lot of money. One day, after returning from classes in the big city, he sat quietly on the back of the mentoring room. He was clearly upset. As we engaged in some conversation, he said:

> I almost got into a fight. The *gabachos* [Anglos] don't like us. They call us names; but the Chicanos don't like us either because we make good grades and study hard. *Quisiera partirle la madre a esos cabrones* ... [I wish I would break the neck of those bastards!]. But no, I will show them with my grades. They have to respect me! I will show them ...

As I asked if this kind of abuse occurred often, he said, "Too often. I am tired of it. But when I come back and I see my Mom working so hard, muddy from the field, tired and trying to help us, I realized that I have to be better than those *cabrones*." The frustration was evident, but the commitment to go on was strong. Mario went on studying and finished his homework. I noticed he was happy to talk to some of his peers being tutored in the same group. Among them there was Angela, a beautiful girl, very quiet, who also liked math a lot. Today, however, as Mario approached her, she seemed to avoid eye contact. She had obviously been crying. At the end of the session I walked home with Mario and asked him what was wrong with Angela. He said:

> Last week her parents lost their job. They have been unemployed frequently. They could not afford to pay the house rent, so the whole family is living in the garage of their cousins' home. To make things worse, Angela's parents are thinking about returning to Mexico. She is one of the best students and would like to stay in El Rincón, but they don't want to leave her behind. There are several high school students who have stayed alone, without their families, and the school knows nothing about it. Friends and relatives feed them and let them spend the night in their homes. It is so hard to finish school! Even for me. Both of my parents have work at least half of the year, but I feel so bad that I cannot help them. My Mom is young, and I

know she will die young. When she comes from the cannery at night, she cries because of the pain in her hands and joints. I would like to get out of

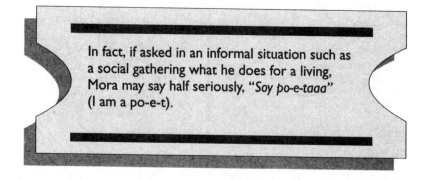

> In fact, if asked in an informal situation such as a social gathering what he does for a living, Mora may say half seriously, *"Soy po-e-taaa"* (I am a po-e-t).

my house. We are too crowded. My two younger brothers and I sleep in the garage, my parents in one of the two bedrooms and my sister in the other. I have not peace to work and study. But I have no place to go. I want to go to college but I may have to work and pay for my college, or perhaps go to the junior college around here. I have good grades but that is not enough ... And sometimes I just think that I should just marry and go away! I have a girlfriend and like her a lot ....

In the end, the will to continue is there, but the obstacles seem to be many—and very difficult. Still, the support of the family, the genuine joy of having relatives around, and the visit of the grandparents once in a while rekindles in Mario the commitment to become somebody and continue his studies.

Implications of Study

Primarily for economic reasons, there is a steady stream of immigrants from Mexico who, along with other Latino immigrants, have become the single largest continental proportion (nearly 38%) of legal immigrants and more than 80% of undocumented immigrants. In addition to the role of Mexico in modern migration movements into the United States, Mexico's economic and political importance was demonstrated by the U.S. government's role in pursuing the North American Free Trade Agreement (NAFTA) and the diligent response to Mexico's 1994 economic crisis. This flow of Mexican immigrants will continue at a rapid pace. According to the Harvard Project on Desegregation (Orfield, Bachmeier, James, & Eitle, 1997), between 1970 and 1994 Latino school enrollment rose significantly in California, Texas, New York, Florida, Illinois, Arizona, New Mexico and New Jersey—and the isolation of Latinos has

increased (Orfield & Eaton, 1996; Orfield et al., 1997). According to C. Suárez-Orozco and M. Suárez-Orozco (1995a, 1995b), and M. Suárez-Orozco (in press), immigrants must face at the same time problems of stress, housing, and racism. As C. Suárez-Orozco and M. Suárez-Orozco (1995b) write:

> The obvious difficulties that most migrants face include language inadequacies, a general unfamiliarity with the customs and expectations of the new country, limited economic opportunities, poor housing conditions, discrimination, and what psychologists term the 'stresses of acculturation' ... Despite these obstacles, many migrants often consider their lot as having improved from what it was in their country of origin. Because of a perception of relative improvement, many migrants may fail to internalize the negative attitudes of the host country toward them, maintaining their country of origin as a point of reference .... (p. 325)

Indeed, migrants hold to their belief of improvement by visiting their villages of origin and displaying wealth conspicuously (e.g., showing new trucks, good clothes, and spending money). C. Suárez-Orozco and M. Suárez-Orozco suggest that immigrants do not see their new life in terms of the ideals of the majority society but in terms of the old culture, thus holding to a "dual frame of reference" (1995b, p. 325).

Parents' naïve notions about the politics of employment, organization, and politics in schools, their perception of societal demands for cultural homogenization, and the acceptance of an inferior status are not shared by their children, who feel an ethical responsibility to react and fight back. Much of what happens in gang struggles and street violence is related to marginalization (Vigil, 1989, 1997). Many Mexican families reflect in their new lives a change not only from one country to another, but from a rural to an urban setting. Of course, the added dimension in this country is that in order to acquire the necessary sociopolitical knowledge of appropriate conduct in urban settings, immigrants must first acquire the communicative skills to do so in a second language. To compound the problem, immigrants often take jobs that are exhausting and leave them little time to acquire communicative skills in English. One of the consequences for the children of immigrants is that they are soon forced to play adult roles in making momentous decisions for their parents because the children know some English and understand the social system a bit better.

The Roots of Empowerment

True empowerment of Mexican immigrant children was not obtained by preaching to them the rhetoric of liberation from hegemonic structures and the need to resist oppression, or even the just and fair demand for respect of their rights that their parents had taught them. Beyond any abstract discourse on liberation, what made the difference was the teaching of the parents and teachers in very specific settings. When Rita came back from the cannery or the fields exhausted and muddy and tired, she still prepared a meal for her family, and she took the time to find out about schoolwork. That is a lesson never forgotten by her children. When Manuel Mora asked José to go to the board, and when he encouraged José to use his native language to explain difficult mathematical concepts, Mora pursued the assistance to give him feedback after each step of the operation.

The messages sent to the entire class by Mora are clear:

1. It is important to acquire knowledge.
2. You can use the language you know best and explain the concepts you have acquired.
3. You should be proud of who you are, and this pride should be reflected in your academic achievement.
4. The challenge is clearly above a Grade 4 level, but he is confident in his students' ability.

Modeling is not a task unique to the teacher. Often Mora would permit a bright student to model for the others, without necessarily creating a stratification system in terms of performance. Some children excel in some areas while their peers do well in others. In the end, the *esprit de corps* had priority over individual performance. The success of one student was the success of them all. Hence the importance of belonging, of feeling a part of the class regardless of one's cultural and linguistic characteristics. Imparting this message is what Mora accomplished best. In contrast, for a Mexican immigrant child who is struggling to acquire English as a second language, the inability to use Spanish in class means being automatically reduced to a handicapped student. That is precisely what happens to many immigrant children in regular classrooms.

Hegemonic classroom control must be denounced, but once that is done, the job of constructing appropriate pedagogies must start in earnest and must be based on three important principles:

1. Children should determine the level of learning, the type of reasoning, the taxonomies, and the cultural context of their own growth, as well as the pace of transition into the teacher's planned instruction.
2. Children need to participate fully and feel competent.
3. School activities and the role of teachers must be supported by the children's family and by the larger community.

How else can an immigrant child make sense of this new academic world and this new life; how else can a child have hope? And hope, as Freire (1995) often reminded us, is an ontological necessity; without hope we cannot exist.

References

Freire, P. (1995). *Pedagogy of hope: Reliving pedagogy of the oppressed.* (R.R. Barr, Trans.) New York: Continuum.

Orfield, G., Bachmeier, M., James, D., & Eitle, T. (1997). *Deepening segregation in American public schools.* Harvard Project on School Desegregation. Unpublished manuscript, Harvard University.

Orfield, G., & Eaton, S. E. (Eds.). (1996). *Dismantling desegregation: The quiet reversal of Brown v. Board of Education.* New York: New Press.

Suárez-Orozco, C., & Suárez-Orozco, M. (1995a). *Transformations: Immigration, family life and achievement motivation among Latino adolescents.* Stanford, CA: Stanford University Press.

Suárez-Orozco, C., & Suárez-Orozco, M. (1995b). Migration: Generational discontinuities and the making of Latino identities. In L. Romanucci-Ross & G. DeVos (Eds.), *Ethnic identity: Creation, conflict, and accommodation* (3rd ed., pp. 321-347). Walnut Creek, CA: AltaMira Press.

Suárez-Orozco, M. (in press). State terrors: Immigrants and refugees in the postnational space. In H. T. Trueba & Y. Zou (Eds.), *Ethnic identity and power: Cultural contexts of political action in school and society.* New York: State University of New York Press.

Vigil, D. (1989). *Barrio gangs.* Austin: University of Texas Press.

Vigil, D. (1997). Personas Mexicanas: Chicano high schoolers in a changing Los Angeles. In G. Spindler & L. Spindler (Series Eds.), *Case studies in cultural anthropology.* Fort Worth, TX: Harcourt Brace.

Vygotsky, L. S. (1972). *Thought and language.* Cambridge, MA: MIT Press.

Vygotsky, L. S. (1978). *Mind in society: The development of higher psychological processes* (M. Cole, V. John-Steiner, S. Scribner, & E. Souberman, Eds.). Cambridge, MA: Harvard University Press.

Author

Enrique (Henry) T. Trueba has a PhD in anthropology and has written a number of articles and books on minority children and ethnic identity. His most recent works are Ethnic Identity and Power: Cultural Contexts of Political Action in School and Society *(expected in April, 1998, SUNY Press, with Y. Zou), and* Latinos Unidos: Ethnic Solidarity in Linguistic, Cultural and Social Diversity *(expected in April, 1998, Rowman & Littlefield).*

Unit Selections

9. **Reading and Writing Pathways to Conversation in the ESL Classroom,** Gisela Ernst and Kerri J. Richard
10. **Buddy Journals for ESL and Native-English-Speaking Students,** Karen Bromley
11. **Entering the Fictive World: Enhancing the Reading Experience,** Karen L. Ogulnick, Sharon Shelton-Colangelo, and Cheryl N. Williams
12. **Literacy Instruction for Students Acquiring English: Moving beyond the Immersion Debate,** James Flood, Diane Lapp, Josefina Villamil Tinajero, and Sandra Rollins Hurley
13. **Multicultural Children's Literature: Canon of the Future,** Suzanne S. Monroe

Key Points to Consider

❖ How can reading and writing facilitate authentic classroom conversation?

❖ How do teachers' attitudes toward language have an impact on learning?

❖ How can teachers provide authentic reading and writing experiences for students?

❖ What is the research telling us about the importance of the native (first) language in developing literacy in the second language?

❖ What role does literacy have in social relationships?

❖ How are the four language bands (listening, speaking, reading, and writing) related? What can teachers do to strengthen this relationship?

 **Links**

www.dushkin.com/online/

15. **Intercultural E-Mail Classroom Connections**
    http://www.stolaf.edu/network/iecc/
16. **Multicultural Book Review Home Page**
    http://www.isomedia.com/homes/jmele/homepage.html
17. **National Clearinghouse for ESL Literacy Education (NCLE)**
    http://www.cal.org/ncle/

These sites are annotated on pages 4 and 5.

The number of linguistically diverse students in the United States will be approximately 3.5 million by the end of the century. Therefore, the need to ensure instruction that adequately prepares them to function successfully in school and beyond will be crucial. Since second-language learners bring unique strengths and needs to schools, it is essential to examine the one area that is probably the most important to their academic success—literacy.

In the past, second-language learners have had to fight a three-pronged attack. They have had to learn English, learn to read in English, and read to learn in English-speaking classes. Many of their monolingual counterparts have had the gift of time to learn to read before having to read to learn. In addition, second-language learners have had to read text that does not reflect their world view or experience. For these students, the focus on reading is outside in, instead of inside out.

Recent research in literacy strongly indicates that learning occurs when we begin with the known to teach the unknown. Since meaning is constructed by each reader and writer, it is important to have readers and writers discuss the processes they use as they attempt to make sense of their own text and that of others. This construction of meaning needs to occur in an environment that is social rather than isolated. In addition, literacy needs to be promoted in a context where students share ideas, struggles, and triumphs.

One approach, whole language, states that the true purpose of literacy is meaning-making. This meaning-making requires collaboration, sharing, and interaction. Whole language is an approach based on a set of beliefs about language and how children learn language. These beliefs include (a) that literacy learning involves all four language bands—listening, speaking, reading, and writing; (b) that language learning should be meaningful, purposeful, and relevant; (c) that literacy occurs with texts and writing; (d) that written language has a unique system that is somewhat different from oral language; (e) that language is learned in a social context; (f) that language learning is a process; and (g) that language is modeled by a teacher or more capable peer.

One way in which meaning-making may occur is when students are allowed to share and discuss their literacy experiences. Classroom discussion should reflect real life and facilitate language and vocabulary development. In addition, many of the skills that are necessary for oral language are also necessary for reading and writing. Some of these skills include planning, revising, setting purposes, creating predictions, applying background knowledge to the task, and interacting with others. Traditional classrooms that use imitate-response-evaluate patterns do not encourage students to discuss much beyond the expected answer already known by the teacher. This approach is a guessing game that allows for much discussion by the teacher, but not much by anyone else.

The more that language and literacy activities reflect authentic out-of-school experiences, the more likely it is that learning will be purposeful, meaningful, and relevant. Students who come from cultural backgrounds different from those found in the school may have different purposes and points of references. Sharing literacy experiences can validate these students' views of literacy and the world. Teachers who encourage this kind of interaction in their classrooms are giving the students the powerful message that their opinions and experiences are worth sharing.

In a whole-language classroom, students learn in a low-risk environment that allows them to learn written language the same way they learned oral language, through making meaningful approximations. For example, when a child says "I goed to the store yesterday," adults respond to the *message* of the utterance instead of reprimanding the child for its "incorrectness." The adults then model the accepted language form by stating, "Oh, you went to the store; I *went* to the dentist yesterday." Children learn that the purpose of language is meaning and that their language is no less important than that of adults. At the same time, they are hearing adults model adult-like language to them. Students learn literacy and language in the same manner in a whole-language environment; their language is accepted, and the standard form is modeled for them so that they may learn it.

Students also learn that their writing may be based on reading other people's writing. Just as adults model adult speech for children, more-capable authors may model writing for students. These authors may be adults writing published books or peers writing in journals that students share with one another. Students need to be exposed to a variety of writing in a variety of contexts. And, they need to respond in writing in a variety of contexts.

The articles in this unit address the issues pertinent to providing students with the skills, attitudes, and values that are associated with successful literacy learning. In addition, they provide teachers with the insight that may allow them to view literacy in a profoundly different way.

Gisela Ernst
Kerri J. Richard

Reading and writing pathways to conversation in the ESL classroom

Reading and writing provide springboards to conversation in this enriching ESL classroom.

...in my English as a second language classroom, writing is cool.... We can write what we want to write. And we talk and we read.... I wish I could be in ESL all day.

Ebele, Grade 2

To have elementary students think writing "is cool" is the aim of many language arts teachers. But when students who speak English as a second language (ESL) describe their love of reading and writing like Ebele, a second grader from Malawi, then the literacy component of her ESL classroom is truly something special.

Indeed, Ebele's conversational ESL classroom is quite different from second language programs that have traditionally emphasized mastery of oral language before the introduction of reading and writing and focused on separate language skills rather than on the integration of speaking, listening, reading, and writing processes (Freeman & Freeman, 1992; Hudelson, 1986). In her conversational ESL classroom, Ebele uses reading and writing to explore, share, enjoy, and think about topics that are of interest to her. The focus is on what second language learn-

ers *have* rather than on what they *lack* (Ernst, Castle, & Frostad, 1992). Although the shared language in this classroom is English, 20 other languages are respected and spoken, including Chichewa, Luvenda, Farsi, and Serbo-Croatian as well as the more common Spanish, Chinese, and Korean. In addition, students have varied educational backgrounds: with their parents some have fled their home countries as war refugees; some have immigrated in hopes of finding a better life; and some are experienced expatriates whose parents work in military or government positions. In short, Ebele's ESL program incorporates the multilingual wealth of students' languages and experiences into classroom life.

In this article, we outline how literacy can be a natural part of the ESL classroom, carving pathways to meaningful conversations between second language learners. We begin by describing the physical setting of a specific conversational ESL classroom and how the infusion of printed matter draws children into conversation. Then we take you through a typical day in an integrative language learning program that fosters first and second language and literacy development. Drawing on samples of students' writings, conversations, and narrative vignettes collected during a yearlong ethnographic study, we illustrate students' growth and enjoyment in relation to their oral and written language

From *The Reading Teacher*, December 1994/January 1995, pp. 320-326. © 1994 by the International Reading Association, Inc., 800 Barksdale Road, P.O. Box 8139, Newark, DE 19714-8139. Reprinted by permission.

development, resulting from their participation in the conversational ESL program.

Physical setting

The 75 children who enter this room each day meet a multitude of different faces, voices, and materials. The classroom is filled with attractive artifacts from diverse cultures, inviting bulletin boards, world maps, ample reading materials, and abundant environmental print.

As illustrated in the Figure, Terri, the classroom teacher, has arranged the chairs and tables to create three permanent learning centers for writing, computer, and listening activities and several floating centers for art projects and games. The floating centers operate for a limited time only—ranging from a week to a couple of months—depending on the type of activities required for a particular group of students or topic of study. This combination of centers allows students and teachers to be on the move, sharing books and conversations in one corner, working on art projects with the daily senior volunteer ("Grandma") in another, thinking and writing at the listening center with a parent or college student volunteer.

Words and print surround learners in this classroom, ranging from signs and labels on furniture and objects to books of all levels and dictionaries in a variety of languages. There are also plenty of world maps, pictures, posters, photographs of children from different cultures, paper flags—made by Grandma —representing students' countries, and all sorts of labeled displays of students' work. There is an abundance of realia and paper scraps that Terri calls "useful junk." Headphones, tape recorders, a record player, and a magnetic card reader are easily accessible. Even when children are not present, it is easy to envision who the students in this classroom are, to hear different languages in the richness of their words, and to see what they do as they work and play together.

An integrated language program

To demonstrate how language and literacy learning experiences might be integrated to provide maximum opportunity for conversation, we take you inside Terri's classroom in late October when her students are explor-

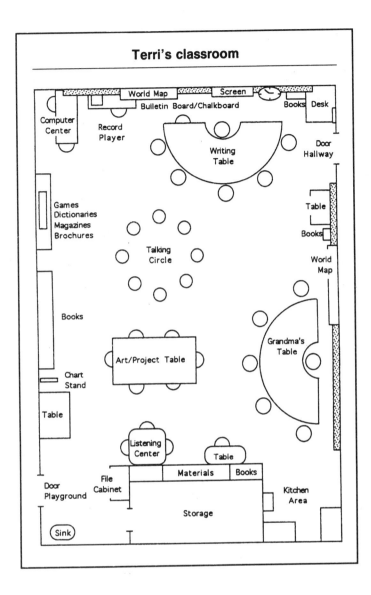

ing the topic "house." The physical setting of the conversational ESL classroom has been designed to encourage talk and interaction between all its participants and to produce a stimulating and experiential language-learning atmosphere. At this point Terri is striving to create a learning community among these children that allows them to integrate their backgrounds, interests, strengths, and prior knowledge of language with useful strategies that promote second language and literacy acquisition.

With the entire class of "beginning" students (those speaking little or no English) grouped in a circle, Terri begins by showing the book cover of *Our House on the Hill* (Dupasquier, 1988) to introduce the new topic and then reads the story aloud. While they talk about the story, Terri writes some of the new words mentioned by students, including names of furniture and household items. Afterwards, while some students draw pictures of houses, others copy the words from the chalkboard.

Next day after reading and talking about *Maggie Doesn't Want to Move* (O'Donnell, 1987), which includes extensive vocabulary about household items, Terri plays a record with the song "Show Me" by Hap Palmer (1975). This activity requires that children sing along and point at different objects around the classroom (e.g., table, chair, door) as they are named. Students sing along and point at objects; when the song is over they ask to hear it again and again (and again). And so Terri plays it five times! By the last round, students know almost all the objects in the song and are able to predict which object is going to be mentioned next.

Children were using their second language as a tool for communicating their own experiences.

As a follow-up activity, students draw pictures of houses in which they live in Florida and in their home countries. Encouraged by Terri, amid the ensuing conversation, some students add labels to their pictures (e.g., door, window, lamp) and others write brief sentences. For example, third grader Ji-Hae asks a volunteer teacher for several words to label the objects depicted in her picture. As Ji-Hae points at the flowers, planters, and curtains, the volunteer teacher enunciates and writes the new words on a piece of scrap paper. After student and teacher read the new words in unison, Ji-Hae adds them to her drawing.

Then Terri gives the children a chance to practice their new vocabulary in context. She invites them to explain something to the whole group about their remembered houses or their present houses in Florida. Some students say one or two sentences. Others, like Ji-Hae, are brief: "house in Korea many many

flowers." Still other students "read" from their drawings as they share one thing about their houses.

What does this brief glimpse into Terri's conversational ESL classroom reveal about an integrated approach to second-language learning? Take Ji-Hae's experience as an example. Literacy activities provided her with the minimal yet functional vocabulary needed to talk about her house in Korea. In the course of reading about houses and writing about her own house Ji-Hae had (a) explored a key word (flower), (b) practiced how to pronounce it, (c) written the new word, (d) used the word within an oral context, and (e) read it aloud. In short, she was beginning to speak, read, and write in a second language. She was becoming literate in English within a supportive context that promotes using literacy and language for authentic, meaning-making, message-sharing purposes—even when students are speaking and writing in a language they have not yet mastered. The oral language shared with students (e.g., through the discussion of the book cover, throughout the story, in the song "Show Me," during small group work) afforded them a considerable amount of information about their second language and how it works. As a result children like Ji-Hae were starting to use their recently acquired language as a tool for communicating their own experiences both orally and in print.

Described as the "speech-print connection" by Enright and McCloskey (1988), an integrated approach such as Terri's highlights the importance of providing second language students with meaningful and interesting learning activities that foster and allow for links between oral and written language. Students like Ji-Hae bring with them a wealth of oral experiences and abilities in both English and their first language. This wealth of experiences can be used to integrate oral and written discourses in their second language. Cook-Gumperz and Gumperz (1981) highlight the importance of this kind of oral-written connection when discussing native English speakers' transitions to literacy:

> Children need experiences in school that favor the learning of written culture through the medium of the oral culture, thus building on the interpretative skills and linguistic understandings that children bring to the school experience, as a basis for fur-

ther reading.... In fact, children need a saturation experience of orally transformed "written prose" in as many culturally "neutral" ways as possible (such as through the teaching of science) in order to transform, for themselves, the rhythms of spoken language into the written modes. (pp. 107-108)

Like their native English-speaking peers, second language learners also need the kinds of oral-written connections that Cook-Gumperz and Gumperz (1981) propose—opportunities to integrate their new experiences (e.g., house in Florida) and past experiences (e.g., house in Korea), using the second language as a medium of expression.

Literacy-based strategies that support conversation in ESL classrooms

Of course our brief look at Terri's ESL classroom during several days in late October offers only a small sampling of literacy-based techniques that support second language learning strategies and foster development. In the following we overview five such techniques with further examples from Terri's classroom. As you will quickly note, these techniques work equally well with native speakers and contribute to the development of learning communities that include all learners.

• *Using a thematic focus*

The use of themes or topics as focal points for organizing instruction is not new (Enright & McCloskey, 1988). In classrooms such as Terri's, well-selected themes are used as overall concepts around which different subject areas are integrated and different materials, resources, and activities are utilized. Thematic units can be very beneficial in classrooms with second language learners for several reasons. First, they allow teachers to draw on their language minority students' backgrounds, interests, and strengths, since topics and activities can be negotiated. Second, theme-based collaborative projects are excellent ways to motivate students, gain their attention, and involve them in a variety of interactive activities. As a result, students work together on projects that naturally promote the use of both oral and written language to question, discuss, inform, negotiate, and communicate with others. Hence, themat-

ic instruction creates excellent opportunities for students to use and develop their oral language as they read, write, and share insights and ideas.

In Terri's classroom, activities are developed around weekly themes. These topics range from those dealing with key terms, such as *house, school,* and *directions,* to more complex topics, such as *country, city,* and *communication.* Every unit or new topic within a unit begins with Terri posing a problem or inviting students to discuss a theme. This is generally followed by the teacher reading a story related to the topic. Often, several books are read throughout the week. In addition, library books relevant to the topic are brought into the classroom for students to read during class or take home.

Take for example the discussion of the theme "friendship." Some of the books that sparked these students to think about the meaning of love, loyalty, and comradeship included *Frog, Duck, and Rabbit* (Gretz, 1992), *Lon Po Po: A Red-Riding Hood Story from China* (Young, 1989), and *Together* (Lyon, 1989). Favorite stories like *The Jolly Postman, or Other People's Letters* (Ahlberg & Ahlberg, 1986), *Frog and Toad Are Friends* (Lobel, 1970), *Charlotte's Web* (White, 1952), and *The Handmade Alphabet* (Rankin, 1991) were obvious choices for discussions about language and communication.

• *Constructing and sharing a classroom culture*

Books can do more than provide opportunities to hear and practice the new language. They can give students both a very special kind of shared experience and the basic English words and phrases needed to talk about it. Since children from different countries and cultures might not come to school with a set of joint encounters, reading a story, talking about it, and relating it to personal happenings can help them experience a sense of shared culture.

When students can relate to the topic of discussion and when they can make use of the new vocabulary acquired through repeated readings and discussion of a book, then their sense of competence and their desire to communicate increases. This confidence, in turn, increases students' willingness to communicate and to take risks with the new language. A case in point is given in the following description of activities constructed around the country/city theme—a topic that is of particular relevance for immigrant students.

In Terri's classroom (as in many classrooms) some students come from rural homes and others from densely populated urban centers. The exploration of the country/city topic allowed students to talk about their previous and present towns and countries and to compare and contrast their experiences in old and new places. In other words, the discussion of this topic helped students bridge their past and present experiences.

As part of the initial activities for this unit, students and teacher read books such as *City Mouse Country Mouse* (Bishop, 1978) and *Tar Beach* (Ringgold, 1991), among others. Then students created a variety of projects related to this topic. One involved making maps of the city on butcher paper and adding paper houses built by the students. Students took their jobs as urban designers very seriously. For example, they spent several hours immersed in discussions about where to locate the mall, church, park, school, and fast food restaurant. They added street signs, billboards, and "neon" signs. Even cars had symbols identifying their make and trucks had signs indicating a business. In sum, city models were packed with print! Later these models were exhibited in the school library; students were very proud of their accomplishments. Other projects related to the country/city theme included drawing or writing about the children's hometowns, comparing and contrasting urban and rural settings, and working on science and art projects.

Throughout these different activities— and while students were learning a great deal about urban and country settings—Terri was learning about the lives and circumstances of her students. Furthermore, both teacher and students were sharing meaningful experiences that scaffolded the development of a unique classroom culture.

• *Reading aloud*

Reading aloud to students has a significant effect on language and literacy acquisition (Cochran-Smith, 1984; Wells, 1986). Second language learners can greatly benefit from listening to stories, since they provide large, cohesive, uninterrupted chunks of language. Books that include attractive and strong illustrations allow students to follow the continuing thread of the plot. In addition, the patterned and repetitive language and the predictable story structure of many children's books are factors that facilitate meaning making. For ESL students, listening to the language as they both follow and talk about the thread of the story is an important way to make connections between oral and written texts, to try out recently acquired vocabulary, and to discover new ways of deploying communicative resources.

Books for the very young can serve well for older students who are in the first stages of learning English. In these early stages, many students can relate to internationally known versions of *Little Red Riding Hood* or *Cinderella* whose Chinese counterparts, for example, are *Lon Po Po* (Young, 1989) and *Yeh-Shen* (Louie, 1982), because they are familiar with the plot. For language minority students, even those with a minimal knowledge of the English language, stories enable them to focus on experiences that can be framed within the structure, conventions, and components of different written genres.

The following account illustrates how ESL students can benefit from listening to and talking about a story like *Brown Bear, Brown Bear, What Do You See?* (Martin, 1967). Earlier in the year Terri read this story to her group of beginning ESL kindergarten students. During the second reading, that same day, the children were able to name most of the colorful characters (e.g., yellow duck, red bird, black sheep). All students were completely involved throughout the reading of this patterned story, listening attentively, predicting and naming characters, and mouthing the words. Later, as they were drawing animals to be displayed on the bulletin board, students were constantly talking about and making fun of their animals by using the new words and language patterns learned from the story.

• *Publishing books*

Current research documents the similarity of writing processes for both first and second language writers (Edelsky, 1986; Hudelson,

1986, 1987). For example, at the early stages, children writing in a second language support their efforts with drawings (Hudelson, 1986) just as their first language peers do (Dyson, 1982). Thus, for beginning learners of English, publishing a book might involve dictating a story to the teacher or organizing a set of drawings.

The benefits of writing and publishing books go beyond the literacy realm. Students not only have a chance to practice and improve their writing, but they also have the opportunity to develop meaningful collaboration with peers as they organize, write, revise, edit, and publish their work. In the "spirit of collaboration" numerous opportunities for using oral language with purpose are generated.

One successful activity in Terri's classroom involved a group of fifth graders publishing legends from their countries. After reading several folktales and legends, these students, in their second year in the ESL program, were asked to discuss with their parents legends from their native countries. Next day, after orally sharing their legends, students generated a first draft. As students wrote several drafts and requested feedback from peers, teachers, and parents, they also worked on their illustrations. After legends were typed and illustrations completed, each was individually bound. The original copies were kept by the students, one copy of each stayed in the class library, and a second copy went to the school library. These copies were indexed and treated like books published commercially. Topics for these legends ranged from Wei-Jue's account of why people in her home country use firecrackers during the Chinese New Year to Gabor's story about a Hungarian magical reindeer.

Through these legends, students were able to learn more about their countries and traditions, to involve parents in their learning, and to share with others their rich cultures. Furthermore, students were able to draw on the funds of knowledge that they bring to school (Heath, 1993; Moll, 1992) that seldom find their way into traditional classroom activities.

• *Literary framework*

Second language learners may also bene-fit from using traditional literary language formats as places to experiment with language in authentic ways. For example, during the second and third weeks of January, a group of first-year students in Terri's classroom learned a variety of nursery rhymes. At the end of the second week and after reading, drawing, reciting, and writing an array of nursery rhymes Hyun-Tae, a fourth-grade student from Korea, responded to an invitation to make a birthday card for Terri, his ESL teacher. This is what he wrote:

> Dear Mrs. S.
> Happy Birthday
> Mrs. S
> I love this classroom.
> I'm a sheep
> You are
> a Little Bo Peep.
> I'm a dog
> You are
> a old mather Houber
> Have a good day
> January 1990, 18 Thursday
>
> Hyun-Tae

Hyun-Tae's card shows clearly that part of the content, vocabulary, and language structure included in his text was drawn from the rhymes he had learned. More important, this example illustrates how writing arises from and relates to current, ongoing interests as children talk, read, and in this case, learn nursery rhymes.

Conclusion

For Terri's students, reading and writing have become pathways to conversational English competence. Rather than designing neat activities, which are seen as isolated

---

Children learn a second language not by practicing drills, but by using it to communicate.

---

lessons unrelated to students' expanding literacy repertoires, teachers like Terri offer students invitations to talk, read, and write around purposeful tasks and within collaborative contexts. Language learning experiences are organized so as to create authentic opportunities for oral and written expression and for connecting what is known with what school has to offer (Ernst, 1993). This is appropriate for the ESL classroom, indeed for any classroom, and should come as no surprise, since children learn their first language not by practicing structured drills, trying to get a sentence right, or communing with a book, but by using language as a means to communicate with real people and in real situations. The same applies for students who are learning a second language. As Ebele notes, "When I was writing I was talking a lot. I like it because I get a chance to talk…. When we talk we learn English." Clearly students learning English as a second language gain substantially in classrooms where oral and written activities are regarded as integral to the process of negotiating knowledge, exchanging personal experiences and thoughts, and using language for authentic, meaning-making purposes.

Ernst heads the bilingual/ESL education program at Washington State University, where Richard is currently a graduate student. Ernst may be contacted at Washington State University, Bilingual/ESL Education, College of Education, Pullman, WA 99164-2122, USA.

References

Cochran-Smith, M. (1984). *The making of a reader.* Norwood, NJ: Ablex.

Cook-Gumperz, J., & Gumperz, J. (1981). From oral to written culture: The transition to literacy. In M.F. Whiteman (Ed.), *Variation in writing: Functional and linguistic-cultural differences* (pp. 89-109). Norwood, NJ: Ablex.

Dyson, A.H. (1982). The emergence of visible language: Interrelationships between drawing and early writing. *Visible Language, 16,* 360-381.

Edelsky, C. (1986). *Writing in a bilingual program: Había una vez.* Norwood, NJ: Ablex.

Enright, D.S., & McCloskey, M.L. (1988). *Integrating English: Developing English language and literacy in the multilingual classroom.* Reading, MA: Addison-Wesley.

Ernst, G. (1993). A multicultural curriculum for the 21st century. In C.G. Hass & F.W. Parkay (Eds.), *Curriculum planning* (6th ed., pp. 84-90). Boston: Allyn and Bacon.

Ernst, G., Castle, M., & Frostad, L. (1992). Teaching in multilingual/multicultural settings: Strategies for supporting second-language learners. *Curriculum in Context, 20*(2), 13-15.

Freeman, Y.S., & Freeman, D.E. (1992). *Whole language for second language learners.* Portsmouth, NH: Heinemann.

Heath, S.B. (1993). Inner city life through drama: Imagining the language classroom. *TESOL Quarterly, 27,* 177-192.

Hudelson, S. (1986). ESL children's writing: What we've learned, what we're learning. In P. Rigg & S. Enright (Eds.), *Children and ESL: Integrating perspectives* (pp. 25-54). Washington, DC: TESOL.

Hudelson, S. (1987). The role of native language literacy in the education of language minority children. *Language Arts, 64,* 827-841.

Moll, L.C. (1992). Bilingual classroom studies and community analysis: Some recent trends. *Educational Researcher, 21*(2), 20-24.

Palmer, H. (1975). *Learning basic skills through music: Vocabulary.* Freeport, NY: Educational Activities.

Wells, G. (1986). *The meaning-makers: Children learning language and using language to learn.* Portsmouth, NH: Heinemann.

Children's books cited

Ahlberg, J., & Ahlberg, A. (1986). *The jolly postman, or other people's letters.* Boston: Little, Brown.

Bishop, D.S. (1978). *La souris de la ville et la souris de la campagne/The city mouse and the country mouse.* Lincolnwood, IL: National Textbook Co.

Dupasquier, P. (1988). *Our house on the hill.* New York: Viking Krestel.

Gretz, S. (1992). *Frog, duck, and rabbit.* New York: Four Winds.

Lobel, A. (1970). *Frog and toad are friends.* New York: Harper.

Louie, A. (1982). *Yeh-Shen.* New York: Philomel.

Lyon, G.E. (1989). *Together.* New York: Orchard.

Martin, B. (1967). *Brown bear, brown bear, what do you see?* New York: Holt, Rinehart and Winston.

O'Donnell, E.L. (1987). *Maggie doesn't want to move.* New York: Four Winds.

Rankin, L. (1991). *The handmade alphabet.* New York: Dial.

Ringgold, F. (1991). *Tar beach.* New York: Crown.

Young, E. (1989). *Lon Po Po: A Red-Riding Hood story from China.* New York: Putnam.

White, E.B. (1952). *Charlotte's web.* New York: Harper.

Buddy Journals for ESL and Native-English-Speaking Students

Karen Bromley

I want to be friends with these kids. I want to help them learn to speak English. I feel sorry about what happened down in Iraq with Saddam Hussein killing them all. Some of their families died. If I were them I would like to know more language and American.

These are the feelings of Keith, an 11-year-old native-English-speaking student, about several Kurdish children who recently enrolled in his school. Nearly 20% of the students in Keith's middle school in Johnson City, New York are new immigrants who either do not speak English or have limited proficiency.

The number of migrant, immigrant, and refugee children in the United States who have little knowledge of English is increasing at a tremendous rate. As many as one in three students in some of our nation's largest school districts have limited English proficiency, and the numbers of these students in smaller school districts are growing daily (Fitzgerald, 1993). Keith's principal estimates that 25% of his school's population next fall will be immigrant children.

These students have much to offer monolingual, mainstream classrooms. They bring rich cultural and ethnic histories, varied family traditions and experiences, assorted languages, different ways of thinking, and unique views of the world. In this kind of classroom environment, all students can learn to celebrate their own uniqueness and expand their perspectives. When students from diverse backgrounds work and learn together in school, they are preparing to work and live together in an increasingly multicultural world.

The success experienced by many students from diverse backgrounds in school and in the work world depends to a large degree on their English literacy. Many of these students either did not attend school in their native country or were not there long enough to become literate in their own language, making them at risk for reading and writing failure here. Fortunately, native-English-speaking students like Keith can help classroom teachers and specialized teachers (ESL teachers, reading teachers, resource room teachers) develop the English literacy of these diverse learners.

In addition, through authentic reading and writing engagements with ESL students, Keith and his peers serve as language models and mentors as they become more self-reliant and

Page from journal of One (ESL student) and Hanh (native-English-speaking student)

From *TESOL Journal,* Spring 1995, pp. 7-11. © 1995 by Teachers of English to Speakers of Other Languages, Inc. Reprinted by permission.

Hi Autumn Howareyo
Doyou like dog
I like.little dogs?
  Autumn Do You like rabbits
I like small white rabbits.
  Autumn Do you like to read books?
I like books about birds.

Vu

Ten-year-old Vu's Drawing and Journal Entry and Autumn's Response

Dear Vu
  yes i do like dogs. I
like a germing shepard.
What is your favorite
food. Mine is pizza fro
Puggies and pizza
hut.

sincerly autumn

Dear Tyrone

Yes I have favorit car.
it is Toyota.

Yes they drive it in

califorha.

I Live on the nine street
I city

Nizar

Nizar's Collaboration with his Teacher
Nizar told his ESL teacher what to write and she drew dots which Nizar followed to write his entry.

begin to develop their own literacy. This article explores one such authentic engagement, the buddy journal.

What Is a Buddy Journal?

The buddy journal is a diary in which two students write back and forth to each other over time (Bromley, 1989). It is an outgrowth of the dialogue journal, a written conversation between a teacher and a student that is self-generated, cumulative, and functional (Atwell, 1987; Gambrell, 1985). Dialogue journal writing is often used with ESL students because it develops their writing fluency and personalizes writing instruction (Peyton, 1987; Young, 1989). Dialogue journals also link reading and writing and provide a real audience and accurate model for ESL students to imitate as their fluency and form improve.

Although the dialogue journal is widely used with ESL students, it has drawbacks. First, it is time consuming for teachers to respond personally and in detail to student entries on a daily, biweekly, or even weekly basis. Second, dialogue journals represent communication between teachers and students who do not have equal status, so writing may be characterized by a lack of shared interest and enthusiasm or even fraught with anxiety and intimidation. Third, there is some evidence that exposure to standard writing conventions in dialogue journals does not necessarily improve linguistically diverse students' use of these conventions (Reyes, 1991).

Buddy journals, however, have the advantage of a peer audience. Students practice literacy use as they write to a peer about what is important to them. In this nonthreatening context, peers not only provide authentic reasons for reading and writing, but also give direct, immediate feedback on the content and form of a buddy's writing. Students generate their own topics, share feelings, describe activities, ask questions, make requests, explore ideas, and solve problems together. Students get to know one another without fear of evaluation or grades.

In addition, journal entries provide insights into how students use writing to communicate meaning and the use of specific writing skills. Because buddy journals do not require the time commitment of dialogue journals, teachers can use this information to offer more explicit writing instruction.

Why Buddy Journals Work

Effective literacy instruction needs to be relevant, serve a real purpose, and be meaningful to the language learner (Goodman, 1986), whether the student is a native English speaker or an ESL student. In particular, we know ESL students need to be involved in tasks that achieve their own intentions, have purposes from their own perspectives, and make use of all language systems (Edelsky, 1986). ESL students also need classrooms where they can acquire language naturally and try out language in low anxiety settings (Allen, 1991). Buddy journals give ESL students a vehicle for communicating during the "silent" period when they are acquiring oral language but are not yet ready to use it (Krashen & Terrell, 1983).

Benefits

Current theory and research point to the importance of peer interaction for literacy learning. ESL students benefit from supportive environments in which they are immersed in reading and writing activities that create relationships between themselves and native-English-speaking students (Fitzgerald, 1993; Short, 1990). As students collaborate they

4|6|93

Dear Diyar,
How is E.S.L.?
Do you like school?
Who is your favort
tacher. See you
tomrow Bye.
from [Kurdish script]
[Kurdish script]
[Kurdish script]
[Kurdish script]

Keith's entry to Diyar in both English and Kurdish

begin to see reading and writing as ways to create and share meaning with each other, not just the teacher.

There are other benefits to written interactions. Buddy journals provide a risk-free context for learning to read and write, which encourages confidence and proficiency. Students who write to geographically distant buddies gain world knowledge, motivation to read and write, self-esteem, and confidence (Newman, 1989). In addition, written letters between students of different backgrounds in separate schools can build positive relationships and remove racial barriers (Foster, 1989).

Buddy journals make a natural connection between reading and writing and provide a real audience for student writing. They furnish opportunities for learning and social interaction through personal written communication as students practice literacy and develop their understandings of each others' cultures.

Implementing Buddy Journals

Keith's teachers, in a Grades 5-7 team setting, and the teachers in a nearby Grades 1-4 elementary school with similarly diverse students, wanted to promote literacy and build bridges between their native-English-speaking students and ESL students. Using buddy journals was only one of the ways the teachers in these two schools fostered cultural sensitivity and understanding. For example, classes read

and shared folktales, information books, and other stories about students' cultural or ethnic backgrounds and participated in an ethnic festival. As part of the festival and with the help of ESL teachers and interpreters, students created books about themselves with written studies of their backgrounds, family folktales, recipes, and copies of important family documents.

Setting Goals

But the teachers still saw rifts between their ESL and native-English-speaking students. They wondered how buddy journals, which had been introduced to all Grades 1-7 teachers in an in-service workshop, might help build relationships and support literacy development. The workshop discussion first focused on the goals of buddy journals, which are to:

• provide a safe context for writing

• develop writing fluency and audience awareness

• build peer relationships and friendships

• establish understanding and respect for other cultures

• develop knowledge of other countries and languages.

The teachers also talked about student involvement, journal mechanics, potential problems, and benefits. They looked at sample buddy journal entries and discussed issues of journal content and privacy.

Creating Guidelines

Several days later, eight teachers decided to try buddy journals for the remaining months of the school year. Four elementary school teachers decided the journals would be a class activity and four middle school teachers asked for student volunteers to engage in buddy journaling. Journals were introduced in each classroom and most students, except first- and second-grade classes who used spiral notebooks, made their own journals by stapling wallpaper covers to sheets of lined paper.

Each teacher and class decided on their own method of management and mechanics, such as length of entries, when and how often writing would occur, how journals would be swapped and where they would be stored. One group of 11-year-old students brainstormed a list of topics to write about **and rules for journal writing (see pp. 74–75).**

In each of the eight classrooms described here, teachers allotted 10-20 minutes for writing at a time that best fit their schedules. This varied, with first and second graders writing first thing every morning, while older students wrote at the end of the day or every other day during language class.

Matching Students

The teachers matched students in a variety of ways. Third- and fourth-grade teachers allowed students to choose their own buddies. A first-grade teacher paired buddies according to strengths and needs in writing. The middle school teachers had the ESL students choose native-English-speaking volunteers as buddies.

Another way to match buddies in classrooms where students sit in groups of several desks, is to have students select a buddy from the group and rotate every 2 or 3 weeks until each student has written to everyone in the group. Or, students can be matched randomly across classes or grades so they converse with someone they may not know. In schools with self-contained classrooms, establishing buddies either within a class or across classes is beneficial for building relationships. Often students in the same class do not have time in the regular day to get to know one another well. Cross-class buddies help build ties within a school and can result in other types of interclass collaborations related to curriculum.

Getting Started

Some teachers modelled entry writing for their students. They shared information, posed questions, gave answers, and included dates and signatures. Purposely, one teacher

Dear nizar
Do you like
T.V.? DO
you Have
a favrot
t.v. show?
from
Tyrone

Tyrone's punctuation

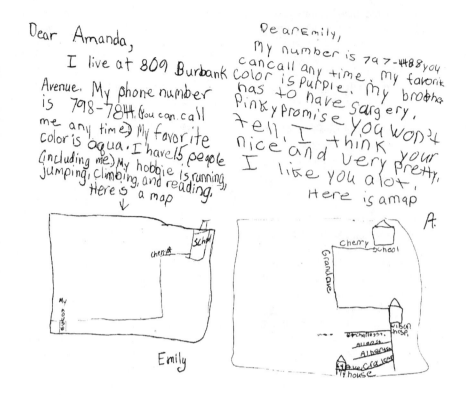

Dear Amanda,
I live at 809 Burbank Avenue. My phone number is 798-7844. (You can call me any time.) My favorite color is aqua. I have 15 people (including me.) My hobbie is running, jumping, climbing, and reading.
Here is a map ↓

Emily

Dear Emily,
My number is 797-4488 you can call any time. My favorite color is purple. My brother has to have sargery. Tell Pinky promise you wont tell. I think your nice and very pretty, I like you a lot.
Here is a map

A.

Emily's model for Amanda

environment. Some ESL students wrote in their native language and ESL teachers or interpreters translated their work into English

Evaluating the Writing

It is important that students know buddy journals are not entirely private. Teachers told students that journals would be monitored regularly, so entries should reflect this semiprivate nature. Some older students felt this was an invasion of privacy, but teachers felt that without monitoring, inappropriate topics might appear.

Teachers read journals weekly or biweekly and praised the content of journal conversations and reminded buddies about the importance of legibility and form when necessary. After daily journal writing in second grade, the teacher gave positive oral feedback to volunteers, still sitting side by side, who read their entries to the class. This was a popular activity and an invaluable motivator for writing as well.

Reading entries orally gives students an opportunity to share their written conversations and to practice using proper inflection and juncture in oral reading. It also allows students who write or label pictures in their native language to read their own language while their English-speaking buddies read the English translation or provide English labels. This practice helps students develop appreciation for each other's language. It also helps teachers better understand the literacy development of their students.

wrote illegible entries for students to read so they could see how handwriting affects the message.

The first- and second-grade teachers had two buddies write in one spiral-bound note-book (see p. 71). These teachers encouraged buddies to sit side by side as they wrote so each could help the other. This worked well for ESL buddies with limited English literacy since they had a ready resource to aid their writing. The reverse also occurred. ESL students were often observed pointing out unclear messages or incorrect spelling for their native-English-speaking peers.

Other teachers had each student keep a journal so there were always two conversations in progress. This succeeds when buddy journals are a class activity because everyone can write at the same time. For buddies who are beginning English learners, it can be a challenge because writing is slow and laborious for them. As students gain English proficiency, however, it is easier for them to do the writing necessary for two simultaneous conversations.

Students were encouraged to write in a variety of ways. Some students, like Vu, drew pictures, and buddies added labels or made their own drawings (see p. 72). An ESL teacher provided Nizar with dots to follow as a guide

in forming letters and words (see p. 72). In the beginning, several students practiced the alphabet and wrote words they were learning to speak, while others copied print from the

Sample Topics For Buddy Journals Generated by 11-year-olds

yourself	problems
where you live	adventures
your family	pets
hobbies and interests	sports
friends	tv shows
favorite books	your past
favorite foods	weather
weekend activities	jokes and riddles
problems	school styles
wishes and dreams	favorite movies
habits	favorite songs
jobs	favorite singing groups
collections	favorite colors
poetry	nature vacations
questions	animals

Sample Rules Created by 11-year-olds

1. Volunteers only, but once you commit you must continue for 3 wks.
2. Choosing buddies:
   - 1st time—Choose name from hat.
   - 2nd time—You pick your buddy.
3. Write during last 15 minutes of reading class.
   - If you don't participate, you read a book.
   - Ice cream social or pizza party during April test week.
4. Entries should include:
   - Date
   - Greeting
   - Closing
   - Signature
5. Occasionally someone will read your journal. Say nothing that shouldn't be said in school!

Allowing for Midcourse Corrections

Writing to the same buddy for a few weeks may be long enough for some students to need a change and want to write to a different buddy. Besides making time for buddy journal writing, this was the biggest problem these teachers encountered. When buddies were within the same classroom, many students wanted to change buddies after a few weeks. After getting started, these teachers planned for regular changes in buddies.

Time for partners to talk together and read journal entries to each other allows students to get to know one another as they practice language use. Socialization can strengthen student relationships as well as personalize writing.

Although the relationship between Keith and Diyar is probably not typical, it seems remarkable enough to mention again here. Although the two boys knew each other before they began the buddy journal, after they started writing they said they often visited each other and played together after school and on weekends. Diyar taught Keith how to write in Kurdish and Keith occasionally wrote his entries in both English and **Kurdish (see p. 73). Keith learned some com**mon Kurdish phrases that he proudly used. The experience of these two boys clearly indicates that the connections they made through buddy journals extend beyond reading, writing, and literacy.

The native-English-speaking students who kept these buddy journals practiced and developed their own literacy as they wrote to their ESL peers. While evidence of writing growth was not always apparent during the 3 months buddy journals were used, the following examples show what did happen for two students. Tyrone, who had not typically used punctuation in his writing, included question marks, periods to mark abbreviations, and commas (see p. 73). He said these helped him when he read his message to Nizar. Amanda, a fourth grade English-speaking student who was not an avid writer, began to write more, perhaps because of the fluent model that Emily, an ESL student, provided her in their buddy journal (see p. 74).

Buddy journals can also be alternated with a variety of other types of journals (Bromley, 1993). In science, social studies, or math journals, students can share new knowledge with each other as they summarize, reflect, and process information or receive answers to questions they ask. Students can also keep home-school journals, dialogue journals, literature response journals, or stop journals altogether for a time if interest wanes.

Conclusion

The interactive writing that occurs in buddy journals helps build a community of learners and encourages collaborative relationships that help students see reading and writing as ways of creating and sharing meaning with each other, not just the teacher. Buddy journals that pair ESL students with native English-speaking students can create enthusiasm for writing, develop written fluency and audience awareness, build peer relationships, and establish cultural understanding and respect.

References

Allen, V. G. (1991). Teaching bilingual and ESL children. In J. Flood, J. M. Jensen, D. Lapp, and J. R. Squire (Eds.), *Handbook of research on teaching the English language arts* (pp. 356-364). New York: Macmillan.

Atwell, N. (1987). *In the middle: Reading, writing and learning with adolescents.* Portsmouth, NH: Heinemann.

Bromley, K. (1993). *Journaling: Engagements in reading, writing, and thinking.* New York: Scholastic.

Bromley, K. (1989). Buddy journals make the reading-writing connection. *The Reading Teacher, 43,* 122-129.

Edelsky, C. (1986). *Writing in a bi-lingual program.* Norwood, NJ: Ablex.

Fitzgerald, J. (1993). Literacy and students who are learning English as a second language. *The Reading Teacher, 46,* 638-647.

Foster, L. A. (1989). Breaking down racial isolation. *Educational Leadership, 47,* 76-77.

Gambrell, L. (1985). Dialogue journals: Reading-writing interaction. *The Reading Teacher, 38,* 512-515.

Goodman, K. (1986). *What's whole in whole language?* Portsmouth, NH: Heinemann.

Krashen, S. D., & Terrell, T. D. (1983). *The natural approach: Language acquisition in the classroom.* Haywood, CA: Alemany Press.

Newman, J. M. (1989). Online: From far away. *Language Arts, 66,* 791-797.

Peyton, J. K. (1987). *Dialogue journal writing with limited-English-proficient (LEP) students.* Washington, DC: Center for Applied Linguistics/ERIC Clearinghouse on Language and Linguistics.

Reyes, M. L. (1991). A process approach to literacy using dialogue journals and literature logs with second language learners. *Research in the Teaching of English, 25,* 291-311.

Short, K. G. (1990). Creating a community of learners. In K. G. Short & K. M. Pierce (Eds.), *Talking about books: Creating literate communities* (pp. 33-52). Portsmouth, NH: Heinemann.

Young, T. A. (1989). The dialogue journal: Empowering ESL students. *Writing notebook: Creative word processing in the classroom, 8,* 16-17.

Author

Karen Bromley is Professor in the School of Education and Human Development at the State University of New York at Binghamton, where she teaches graduate courses and conducts research in literacy and learning.

Entering the Fictive World: Enhancing the Reading Experience

Karen L. Ogulnick
Sharon Shelton-Colangelo
Cheryl N. Williams

Karen Ogulnick, PhD, is an assistant professor and program director of TESOL and Bilingual Education at C. W. Post College, Long Island University.

Sharon Shelton-Colangelo, PhD, is an assistant professor of Education at and director of field experiences at SUNY in Old Westbury in New York.

Cherly N. Williams, MA, is director of HEOP at Medgar Evers College, City University of New York.

Introduction

English as a second language and language arts teachers often search for ways to enrich the literary experience for students. Specifically, we ask ourselves, how can we make reading a more active, interactive, and empowering experience that validates individual interpretations while maintaining a sense of community in the multicultural classroom? There are a variety of enhancement activities that help to facilitate engagement in a text. For instance, students might be involved in performing dramatic scenes of a story, transforming a piece of literature into a collage, musical composition, or a dance, or trying to imagine the work from a different point of view.

In this article we will discuss an approach we have used that enables students to experience multiple voices of a text by entering into a character and creating dialogues with other characters. This approach is called hotseating. Our use of hotseating in English classrooms is based on Deweyian and Vygotskyan notions that learning should be social and experiential, and modeled on the ways people learn and interact in "the real world." These beliefs are in direct contrast to the artificial nature of teacher-dominated classrooms that dictate when students may speak and what they say. It also goes further by encouraging students to explore critically their own problems and issues while learning language and literacy. This method is grounded in Freirian ideas that education should give students the freedom to envision and create alternatives to oppressed conditions in their lives. Drawing on whole language learning and liberatory principles, we believe instruction should:

Proceed with the concrete, lived experiences of the learners;

Engage everyone as teachers and learners;

Develop shared leadership through group process skills;

Construct new knowledge rather than transmitting old;

Draw on emotions and feelings as points of learning;

Combine a variety of approaches and language modes to appeal to different learning styles and senses.

From *Cultural Circles,* Vol. 3, Summer 1998, pp. 125-133. © 1998 by Karen L. Ogulnick, Sharon Shelton-Colangelo, and Cheryl N. Williams. Reprinted by permission.

Hotseating

Hotseating combines reading and drama by asking participants to take on the roles of fictive characters in a text and to respond to questions in the role. After reading a short story or other narrative, readers form small groups, each of which focuses on one character in the piece. These groups explore in more depth the motivations, feelings, attitudes, conflicts, and values of the person they have chosen to portray. After creating a character sketch, each group tries to anticipate questions that might be asked of their assigned character. One person from each group is chosen to sit in the "hotseat," forming a panel. Those remaining become the audience and pose genuine questions that they raised in their groups, as opposed to questions imposed by a teacher or textbook editor. Typically, the teacher facilitates the group discussions, although participants can moderate while s/he joins in the questioning or role playing. Hotseating can be used in a variety of ways in different settings. For example, there are many possibilities for writing exercises, such as rewriting the ending, writing a detailed character sketch, and writing from the perspective of another character. Once students learn the technique, hotseating can also be used more informally. For example, as part of a class discussion, one student may be asked to go into the hotseat, so to speak, as a means of clarifying a character's motivation.

An Example

"The Visit Home" by Rosemary Cho Leyson is one of the stories we've used often. It examines the sometimes destructive impact that life in a hostile environment can have on an immigrant family. We believe this story and other such multicultural texts are valuable for all learners, whether they live in diverse or homogeneous, urban or suburban, settings to help them become more aware of the realities that many immigrants face. Specifically, the story deals with the conflicts engendered by supplanting one's native language with English, the impact of changing loci of power between and among family members, and the desire to both maintain and change one's personal identity.

Briefly, the story chronicles Maree, a young woman of Korean and Filipina descent, who visits "home" and her old neighborhood in San Francisco where her parents still reside. As she rides the bus, she reflects on unhappy memories of discrimination which she experienced as an immigrant child in America, "a country that ridiculed their accents and the color of their skin" (Leyson, p. 133). The occasion for her visit is to celebrate the demise of Ferdinand Marcos; however, as usual, the visit turns into a painful reminder of loss and shame that have resulted from the family's internalization of the negative image the dominant society projected on them. They are so depressed they are no longer able to celebrate because they have taken "the frustrations the world put upon them, swallowed them and turned them on themselves" (Leyson, p. 133).

After giving copies of "The Visit Home" to our students, we ask that as they read, they think of the textual ambiguities they would like to clarify and then jot down questions they would like to ask any of the six characters, given the opportunity. We randomly form groups by counting off, and then assign each group one of the major characters to focus on. Each group is given the task of creating a character sketch and anticipating questions others might ask about the motivations, behaviors, feelings of the character. Questions do not have to be limited to information included in the story. They could include hypothetical situations that might have occurred or could occur in the future. Characters might also be asked to elaborate on issues only hinted at in the story. Often students become so engrossed in their discussions and preparations for the hotseating panel that they ask for more time. The students' lively, animated discussions reflect the excitement that is generated by the prospect of stepping into their character's shoes.

The panel is composed of one representative from each group, who takes on the role of a major character. The remaining people become the audience, whose role it is to address questions to individual panelists in the hotseat. For example, Maree might be asked why she left home. A question often posed to the mother is, "Why did you ban Korean, your mother tongue, from being spoken in your household?" The sister may be asked, "Did you resent that Maree left home?"

As people begin to play their characters, they often become less self-conscious in their responses to questions. A real dialogue emerges, and it appears that the panelists become the characters. There is a collaborative sense among the audience and panelists as questions build upon questions, and audience members take issue with characters, address them by name, commiserate, offer advice and sympathy; in other words, a genuine exchange develops. Sometimes the panelists themselves begin to address one another in role or panelists and questioners try to reach a resolution to the conflicts the characters face.

Student Responses

Finding appropriate readings is a common concern of ESL teachers, particularly at the college level. The problem is compounded in public urban institutions where ESL students are often from backgrounds that are not only linguistically but also educationally diverse. Many are immigrants who have not received the solid academic foundation typically found among foreign students who frequently represent their nations' most academically prepared. In our classrooms, the writers have avoided the bland adapted novels published for ESL classes in favor of unabridged works of fiction. A difficulty of this practice is the danger of selecting works that frustrate the readers. When asked to describe their reactions to their first hotseating experience, one of the most common observations of ESL students is that the activity enables them to better comprehend complex texts. The following comments were made by intermediate level students writing in-class journals describing how hotseating enhanced their reading of "The Visit Home."

Having studied English extensively in this country's most prestigious high school, Fritz (a pseudonym) was demoralized at being placed in an ESL class and sometimes showed annoyance at the unsophisticated literary interpretations made by some of his classmates. Distrustful of the reader response approach used in the class, Fritz sought correct analyses from the teacher. Always frank, Fritz admitted in his journal that initially he had not taken the activity seriously. He wrote:

> After reading the story my imagination did not go so far. I read it, tried to understand it but I never went behind the scene. This hotseating session widely opened my view about the real life Maree and her family were living; certain reactions like the mother's, Melinda's and the more important understandings, the reasons of such reactions.

He concluded by saying:

> For a first time, the try is a success even (though) some of the questions (are) the cause (result) of misunderstanding or are not correctly answered. The main thing is by questions and answers, fellow classmates use mind and sight for more comprehension of a text what (which) can be helpful in the writing of future narrative essays.

Marcia, a less academically prepared but equally conscientious student wrote:

> That was a good idea to act the passage like that. I enjoy it because it helps me to understand better the passage. By the questions from the others, the answers make it clear for me when I go back to the lecture [reading]. I think I will have more comprehension and learn a lot from different opinions to the characters.

Her comment suggests that for Marcia decoding rather than analysis is the primary challenge. By reenacting the story, she is assisted in making sense of the text. It is significant that she plans to return to reread the story.

Coming from countries in turmoil as many immigrant ESL students do, they consistently bring a heightened awareness of the political to the reading. While Leyson only mentions the Marcos regime peripherally, it sometimes becomes a central focus for students coming from similar circumstances. Yves, a Haitian refugee commented:

> According to me, I think it really important to [for] each one to know, whatever the reason, no one has no right to push someone else out of his own country. I feel the pain of Maree in my heart like many others in my country when Duvalier had the power.

At the center of the various strands of reader response theories is the belief that texts are malleable, taking form only as viewed through the lenses of each reader. Carla, a mature woman whose own family life has been unhappy, identified with the dysfunctional family Maree cannot abandon. Carla commented:

> I can really feel the pain the family was going through, especially the poor mother with her drinking husband and her ran away daughter. I believe the characters, it is a true story, because I know so many families going through that same problem. I feel like I am a new person, and I feel more stronger than before to deal with life and its problems.

Assisting students to construct new knowledge and refraining from merely transmitting received information is a principle of liberatory education. We have found that by structuring the hotseating activity so that all class members, including the teacher, participate, we are able to better facilitate this outcome. It should not be assumed that all students accept all interpretations, not even the teacher's. After stating how much she had learned from and enjoyed the process, Iman, a single mother who herself left an unhappy marriage, wrote of the teacher's portrayal of the mother:

> I want to say I don't think Maree's mother was as hard with her husband as you [the teacher] was (Smile). I think she was a more lay back person . . . but I will say with [by] the same token, she was a strong woman. I say a strong woman because I know I would

have not stay in the relationship, don't matter what. Hotseating did not change my opinion about the story, what it did was open my mind more to it.

Of her classmates' performance. Theresa stated:

They did a good job but it doesn't mean that other people would react the same way. I think we should be doing that kind of practice after reading a story because it help people understand better.

One of the most encouraging comments came from Mario, a reflective engineering student:

Beforehand I read the story without any interest. While performing in class a big difference between by lecture and my participation in class has been made . . . I am not really believed in the characters. Very often people are always in their self defense. The truth is often hidden. My opinion is not an easy changeable thing. A deep judgment is always made over a thing on both sides by me before changing my point of view. I enjoy working like that. That helps me get a skill in thinking and talking.

Reader Response Theory

That people begin their observations with personal connections to the story is in keeping with Louise Rosenblatt's notion that all meaning arises out of the transaction between personal experiences and the text. In her book, *Literature as Exploration*, Rosenblatt (1983) talks at length about the integral relationship between the reader and the text. As the following excerpt indicates:

The teacher realistically concerned with helping his [sic] students to develop a vital sense of literature cannot, then, keep his eyes focused only on the literary materials he is seeking to make available. He must also understand the personalities who are to experience this literature. He must be ready to face the fact that the student's reactions will inevitably be in terms of his own temperament and background. Undoubtedly these may often lead him to do injustice to the text. Nevertheless, the student's primary experience of the work will have had meaning for him in these personal terms and no others. (p. 51)

While we believe that the student's primary experience of the work is valuable, the hotseating activity also surfaces different readings reflecting diverse social identities in a public forum. This not only validates individual voices, but enables students to hear a multiplicity of interpretations. Moreover, students can develop an awareness that their readings are culturally based.

Like Rosenblatt, Terry Eagleton (1983) calls into question the traditional privileging of the writer over the reader. As he says:

The reader has always been the most underprivileged . . . strangely, since without him or her there would be no literary tests at all. Literary texts do not exist on bookshelves: they are processes of signification materialized only in the practice of reading. For literature to happen, the reader is quite as vital as the author. (p. 74)

Prior to the development of reader response theory, a prevailing notion was that there was a single *truth* residing in the text, waiting to be discovered by the reader. This truth could be apprehended, for example, through determining authorial intention or formally examining the structure of the text without considering the larger society that produced it. Readings that were valid were those that had exclusive fidelity to the text, or to the authorial intention. In English classrooms, interpretations that strayed from the officially prescribed "meaning" were often dismissed as invalid, but this didn't mean that students' personal interpretations didn't have great significance for them nor that there was no room for resistance within this confining structure.

Unlike Rosenblatt, who focuses primarily on the undifferentiated individual reader, Eagleton examines how power [is] engendered by social stratification's impacts on the act of reading. The complex interplay between power, identity, and language has important implications for teachers in multicultural classrooms, which are in fact all classrooms, if we define "culture" as including gender, race, class, sexuality, and other categories that shape our perspectives of the world and our places in it. Thus, instead of legitimizing only the interpretations of the undifferentiated idealized readers, we, like Eagleton, seek to include and learn from the interpretations of an ever widening circle of readers.

Implications for ESL students

ESL teachers often search for ways to motivate students to speak in class discussions. One way to create this opportunity, particularly for students who are reluctant to speak publicly, is to give them a role to play. All class members may be surprised to hear that the quieter students have profound and powerful insights, which can change stereotypical perceptions that often contribute to a person's shyness, or reluctance to speak in certain settings. Moreover, hotseating provides an entree to students who may not want to compete for conversational space.

Many of our beliefs are borne out in comments expressed in our students' own words. For example, in terms of engaging multiple voices, one student wrote, "It makes a student want to participate in the classwork. Students were able to speak out their mind, and this one can learn from others." In terms of the power of entering a role to overcome shyness, "I do not like speaking in a crowd because it makes me nervous, but with this activity I have more confidence." In terms of developing empathic responses to the characters, "I can really feel the pain the family was going through, especially the poor mother with her drinking husband and her runaway daughter."

Conclusion

We entered into this exploration questioning how we as English teachers can make reading a richer and more active experience. We want literature to make a difference in our students' lives. In this article we proposed one method of enabling students to become more aware of their own and alternative realities. Indeed, hotseating can lead to the "empowerment" and impetus for change that Freire and other liberatory theorists have placed at the heart of the educational process itself. While we don't claim this kind of transformation will be universal or automatic, our students' comments frequently indicate that activity and collaboratively entering the fictive world can be an important first step.

POINT-COUNTERPOINT

Editors and coauthors: James Flood
Diane Lapp
San Diego State University, California, USA

Guest coauthors: Josefina Villamil Tinajero
Sandra Rollins Hurley
The University of Texas at El Paso, Texas, USA

Literacy instruction for students acquiring English: Moving beyond the immersion debate

Point
The best way to teach children English literacy skills is to immerse them completely in English.

Counterpoint
The best way to teach children English literacy skills is through their native language.

Much of the debate surrounding the education of language minority students has focused on whether or not those immersed in English will fare better than those initially taught in their native language. Some argue that immersion quickens second language acquisition by stressing only the new target language (e.g., Chavez, 1991; Imhoff, 1990; Porter, 1990). Others claim that a gradual transition to English via instruction in the native language assures student success (e.g., Collier, 1995, Cummins, 1993; Lapp & Flood, 1992; Thomas & Collier, 1995).

The controversy that swirls around second language education in the United States can be traced to deeply held ideas among many Americans, the educational community not excepted. In this column we examine several of these ideas in light of current research,

dispelling some as myths and challenging others.

Myths about second language education

Myth 1: Immersion works for everyone. Many Americans believe that yesterday's immigrants prospered without special programs and that the public schools successfully weaned students from their native languages by immersing them in English. Educational attainment data on immigrant Americans, however, show neither of these beliefs to be true. Indeed, bilingualism was an accepted fact of life among the early immigrants to the U.S. New arrivals strived to preserve their heritage by preserving their native language. Europeans established schools in the New World that provided instruction in native languages.

Immigrant groups, including Italian, Polish, Czech, French, Dutch and German, introduced their languages into elementary and secondary schools, either as separate subjects or as the language of instruction (Crawford, 1989). According to Crawford, German-speaking Americans operated schools in their own tongue as early as 1694 in Philadelphia, a practice that prevailed

until the early 20th century. For much of the 19th century, the structure of American public education allowed immigrant groups to incorporate linguistic and cultural traditions in the schools, which supported the transition to second language programs.

Nevertheless, immigrant children were more likely to sink than swim in English-only classrooms, where they experienced considerable difficulty. Historically, English-only instruction has been nationally ineffective. According to Crawford (1989),

> in study after study, a non-English background has been correlated with higher rates of falling behind, failing, and dropping out. Language minority youths are one and a half times more likely than their English language counterparts to have discontinued school before completing twelve years, and Hispanic youths are more than twice as likely. (p. 14)

As recently as 1994 the dropout rate for Hispanics (ages 14–34) was 31% compared to 7% for Anglos. Also, language minority children are placed in special classes for the educationally handicapped in disproportionate numbers. In 1980, Hispanic children in Texas, for example, were overrepre-

From *The Reading Teacher*, December 1996/January 1997, pp. 356-358. © 1996 by the International Reading Association. Reprinted by permission.

sented by 315% in the learning disabled category (Crawford, 1989). These data certainly are ample evidence to dispel the myth that immigrants have or can learn English without special programs.

Myth 2: Native language programs are detrimental to literacy growth. Some educators argue that students in bilingual programs do not learn English and that they never do well enough in academic subjects to join the mainstream. Yet research has found that children who participate in properly designed bilingual programs reach satisfactory levels of competence in all academic areas (Krashen & Biber, 1988).

Moreover, the use of the native language to develop the academic skills of students acquiring English appears beneficial for helping students avoid cognitive confusion and achievement lags in their school performance (Hakuta & Diaz, 1984; Krashen & Biber, 1988; Thomas & Collier, 1995). Data from bilingual programs in California, for example, show that children who participate in properly designed bilingual education programs acquire English rapidly and typically achieve at grade level norms and above in English and mathematics after 3–5 years. From these data, it can be concluded that bilingual education may be the best means to develop English as a second language programs.

Myth 3: The sooner students are transferred out of native language instruction the better. Too often, U.S. policy makers mistakenly believe that the first and only thing that language minority students must do is learn English. Studies by Ramirez, Yuen, and Ramey (1991) and Collier (1995) found that "late-exit" bilingual education programs, where students received native language instruction at least through the elementary grades, were most successful for helping students achieve academic success in English. Postponing the teaching of academics until students develop the academic proficiency in English they need to learn subject content does not appear educationally worthwhile. It takes students longer to acquire English when there is less native language support (Thomas & Collier, 1995).

Myth 4: Teaching children to read in their native language hinders learning to read in English. Some educators and policy makers think that diverse bilingual education is an obstacle to literacy achievement and produces students who are illiterate in two languages. The research literature does not support this myth, but in fact substantial research has shown that "the fastest route to second language literacy is through the first language" (Krashen & Biber, 1988, p. 22). Empirical evidence has shown that children who are dominant in a language other than English acquire academic language and literacy skills rapidly and better in both the native language and English when they attain literacy proficiency in the first language. Many researchers (Cummins, 1989; Krashen & Biber, 1988) have found that instruction in the students' native language simultaneously promotes the development of literacy skills in both the native language and a second language.

The linguistic interdependence principle asserts that certain processes are basic to reading and that once learned they can be applied to reading any or almost any language (Krashen & Biber, 1988; Ramirez, Yuen, & Ramey, 1991). Specifically, when children learn about the intricacies of print relationships through materials that highlight their own language and social reality, the linguistic interdependence principle predicts that they will be able to extend their repertoire of literacy expertise to a range of language and social contexts in their second language (Pardo & Tinajero, 1993). Therefore children who learn to read in their native language need not totally relearn to read in English. Learning to read in the native language is beneficial, not detrimental, because students apply many of the skills and strategies they acquired to read in their native language to reading in English.

For more than 25 years, the issue of how best to address the needs of students acquiring English has been vigorously debated. But the debate has never clearly focused on pedagogical issues, having run amok in political sentiment and controversy. However, given recent demographic trends, which suggest that in the near future, language minority and limited English proficient students will compose a greater proportion of the U.S. school-age population than monolingual English speakers, we must move beyond the immersion debate to a more pressing concern about how to provide powerful learning environments for students acquiring English. This topic must have our attention if we are to responsibly and creatively meet the challenge of effective instruction for second language learners. Our failure to realize the potential benefits of native language instruction has kept us from focusing on the most effective ways to teach children.

Fortunately a substantial knowledge base on literacy instruction for non-native speakers has been developed by educators and researchers over the past 2 decades. It has yielded excellent instructional practices that teachers can use with confidence. These best practices include recommendations related to program, methods, materials, and parental involvement.

Program

Rather than attempting to eradicate students' native languages, we must use, affirm, and maintain children's native languages as a foundation for academic success. To build program capacity, three initiatives show promise:

- change the "quick-exit" mentality of bilingual programs to "late-exit," which gives students the opportunity to develop high levels of proficiency in both the native language and English before being mainstreamed.
- implement more two-way programs in which bilingualism is promoted for *all* students.
- replace traditionally taught ESL-only, pullout programs with quality programs that integrate state-of-the-art second language instructional practices with continuous staff development and emphasize respect for students' native language and culture (Collier, 1995).

Methods

In the past 2 decades reading and language arts educators' thinking about children's reading and writing development has changed dramatically (e.g., Flood, Jensen, Lapp, & Squire, 1991). As a result of new understandings, a learner-centered, holistic perspective has emerged. The result, a "new literacy" with new practices, has influenced instruction in English, in native languages, and in ESL. This new view of language and literacy development includes interactive practices such as:

- pairing students heterogeneously for activities such as partner "reading" of big books, story retelling, story mapping, illustrating a new ending to a story, or character mapping;
- using wordless picture books to elicit language and encourage students to produce longer, more detailed, coherent, and cohesive texts;
- incorporating language experience activities to integrate children's ideas, interests, experiences, and natural languages;
- using shared reading activities to expose children to the written and oral forms of language and to provide them with numerous opportunities to develop listening, speaking, reading, and writing skills;
- using songs, poems, stories, games, role plays, story theater, puppetry tapes, dramatizations, and storytelling activities (which encourage physical, visual, and oral participation) to allow students to use natural English while providing a meaningful, motivating, and enjoyable context for learning;
- using authentic literature to nurture children's language development and to provide language models.

Materials

In these days of limited budgets, funds must be invested wisely in instructional materials that support practices found to influence academic achievement. Look for materials and programs that

- organize the literature and grade-level content into thematic units keyed to curriculum goals;
- connect grade-level content with multilevel strategies;
- incorporate a wide array of hands-on learning activities designed to build academic language proficiency;
- give students access to the core curriculum;
- include a simple, effective teaching plan with authentic assessment to

organize, manage, and monitor student progress; and
- incorporate a comprehensive plan for recent immigrants (newcomers) (Tinajero & Schifini, 1996).

Parental involvement

It is important to view parents as assets to the school program and welcome them as important partners in the education of their children. Parents have many talents and experiences. When we tap into these talents, a wealth of information can be shared.

We need to view parents as teaching partners in the classroom. Classrooms can become places where literacy and positive cultural understandings are nurtured and supported with their assistance. In the classroom, parents need to be encouraged to share ideas orally, stimulating conversations about topics that are important to the day's learning goals. Parents can help children who are still developing literacy in their first language by reading and responding to journal entries. Parents can read books in the children's languages and tell stories from their oral traditions. When children see their parents providing valuable experiences for their peers, they not only feel a sense of pride but also share positive feelings about their language and culture.

A final word

The "bilingual education is detrimental vs. bilingual education is beneficial" debate is over. Ample evidence favors bilingualism, bilingual education, and literacy in children's native languages as the means to help children grow academically. What must ensue is a new and vigorous debate that centers on *how* our students who are acquiring English might best learn the literacy strategies and skills they need to participate fully, in school and out.

References

Chavez, L. (1991, December 30). Let's move beyond bilingual education. *USA Today,* pp. 63 – 64.

Collier, V.P. (1995, Fall). *Acquiring a second language for school. Directions in language & education.* National Clearinghouse for Bilingual Education, 1(4), 1 – 12.

Crawford, J. (1989). *Bilingual education: History, politics, theory and practice.* Trenton, NJ: Crane.

Cummins, J. (1989). *Empowering minority students.* Sacramento, CA: California Association for Bilingual Education.

Cummins, J. (1993). Empowerment through biliteracy. In J. Tinajero & A. Ada (Eds.), *The power of two languages: Literacy and biliteracy for Spanish speaking students* (pp. 9 – 25). New York: Macmillan/McGraw-Hill.

Flood, J., Jensen, J., Lapp, D., & Squire, J. (1991). *Handbook of research on teaching the English language arts.* New York: Macmillan/McGraw-Hill.

Hakuta, K., & Diaz, R.M. (1984). The relationship between degree of bilingualism and cognitive ability. A critical discussion and some new longitudinal data. In K.E. Nelson (Ed.), *Children's language* (Vol. 5, pp. 319 – 344). Hillsdale, NJ: Erlbaum.

Imhoff, G. (1990). The position of U.S. English on bilingual education. In C.B. Cazden & C.E. Snow (Eds.), *English plus: Issues in bilingual education* (pp. 48 – 61). The Annals of the American Academy of Political and Social Science. (ERIC Document Reproduction Service No. ED 372 594)

Krashen, S., & Biber, D. (1988). *On course: Bilingual education's success in California.* Sacramento, CA: California Association for Bilingual Education.

Lapp, D., & Flood, J. (1992). *Teaching reading to every child (*3rd ed.). New York: Macmillan.

Pardo, E.B., & Tinajero, J.V. (1993). Literacy instruction through Spanish: Linguistic, cultural, and pedagogical considerations. In J. Tinajero & A. Ada (Eds.), *The power of two languages: Literacy and biliteracy for Spanish speaking students* (pp. 26 – 36). New York: Macmillan/McGraw-Hill.

Porter, R.P. (1990). *Forked tongue: The politics of bilingual education.* New York: Basic Books.

Ramirez, J.D., Yuen, S.D., & Ramey, E. (1991). *Final report: Longitudinal study of structured English immersion strategy, early-exit and later-exit transitional bilingual education programs for language-minority children.* U.S. Department of Education, Contract No. 300-87-0156. San Mateo, CA: Aguirre International.

Thomas, W.P., & Collier, V.P. (1995). *Language minority student achievement and program effectiveness.* Manuscript in preparation.

Tinajero, J., & Schifini, A. (1996). *Into English!* teacher's guide. Carmel, CA: Hampton-Brown.

Multicultural Children's Literature: Canon of the Future

Suzanne S. Monroe

According to Native American scholar Paula Gunn Allen:

Literature is one facet of culture.The significance of a literature can be best understood in terms of the culture from which it springs....A person who was raised in a given culture has no problem seeing the relevance, the level of complexity, or the symbolic significance of the culture's literature.We are all from early childhood familiar with the assumptions that underlie our own culture and its literature and art.(54)

For the past seven years,I have been teaching Children's Literature as part of our university's teacher preparation program. Most of my students are of Anglo and Hispanic heritage with smaller numbers of students of Native American, African American, and Asian American ancestry. First languages for these students have included English,Spanish,Navajo,Tewa,German,and Vietnamese. I try to emphasize the cultures and languages represented in each classroom community as well as the more predominant culture/language communities of the Southwest.

I want to share four personally rewarding approaches which have contributed to my fascination and respect for this growing body of multicultural children's literature: (1) Genre Approach, (2) Author-Illustrator Studies,(3) Theme Approach, and (4) Issues Approach. The power of these approaches lies in the underlying assumption that students learn best through self-selection of tradebooks and regular opportunities for transacting with literature. They are inspired by classroom visits with published authors and illustrators. Additional benefits have included the empowerment of diverse personal voice, authentic alternatives to a traditionally biased canon, and the transformation of family and community stories from oral tradition into print.

Genre Approach

A successful approach to studying multicultural children's literature is through genre. A variety of authors, publications, and cultural themes are included in each featured genre. In this way, writers of diverse backgrounds are viewed as an integral part of genre development and enhancement (Monroe1995).

Examples of such diverse poetry might include *Honey, I Love* and *Nathaniel Talking* by Eloise Greenfield; *Dancing Teepees* by Virginia Driving Hawk Sneve; *Arroz Con Leche* and *Las Navidades* by Lulu Delacre.These poets have evolved a particular style influenced by personal experience, language, and cultural background. In featuring tradebooks reflective of diverse ethnic, racial, and linguistic backgrounds, I provide

From *Language Arts Journal of Michigan,* Vol. 12, No. 1, Spring 1996, pp. 43-48. © 1996 by LAJM. Published by the Michigan Council of Teachers of English (MCTE). Reprinted by permission.

the opportunity to experience poetry from a global perspective, integrating different world views.

The genre of traditional literature also provides a natural framework for the continuing study of diverse world views. It lends itself to the study of global stories while emphasizing the contemporary phenomena of translating oral tradition into print.

The following tradebooks are examples of traditional literature included in this genre study: *In the Beginning: Creation Stories From Around the World* and *The People Could Fly* (African American) by Virginia Hamilton; *Who Speaks for Wolf* (Iroquois) by Paula Underwood Spencer; *The Woman Who Outshone the Sun: The Legend of Lucia Zenteno* adapted from a poem by Alejandro Cruz Martinez (Spanish/English); *Monster Slayer* and *Monster Birds* (Navajo) by Vee Browne; *Spider Woman* (Inuit) by Anne Cameron; *Why Mosquitoes Buzz in People's Ears* (African) by Verna Aardema; *Fables* (Northern European) by Arnold Lobel; *La Llorona* by Joe Hayes (Spanish/English); *Hawaiian Folktales of Earth, Sea and Sky* by Vivian Thompson; *Pecos Bill* and *Paul Bunyan* (Anglo American) by Steven Kellogg; and *Cut From The Same Cloth: American Women of Myth, Legend and Tall Tale* by Robert San Souci. In using such a variety of traditional literature, I am able to integrate the cultural and linguistic contributions of diverse experience while providing examples of tall tales, fables, proverbs, por quoi, and stories of creation, transformation, and warning.

Author-Illustrator Studies

One of the most effective ways to encourage reluctant readers is to provide transactional experiences with ideas and the creators of these ideas. Over the past several years, I have developed the practice of author-illustrator studies. Within this framework, students get to know a particular author or illustrator of diversity very well. Some students write or call the publisher for biographical and publication materials. Others write or call the author or illustrator. A few have chosen to conduct personal interviews and supported these with self-recorded audio or video tapes. Several students have even arranged for their subject of study to visit our classroom!

The process of research begins very early in the semester and culminates in a final paper and presentation. Students provide a rationale for choice, an extensive biographical sketch, a synthesis of the writer or artist's evolving style, and a summary of reader response and personal comments. They frequently bring to the classroom visual supports such as posters, publications, slides of illustrator's work, and a colorful hand-out!

Authors and illustrators of diversity who are providing exciting biographical and publication material worthy of in-depth study include Rudolfo Anaya, Donald Crews, Carmen Lomas Garza, Virginia Hamilton, Patricia McKissack, Pat Mora, Jerry Pinkney, Patricia Polacco, Faith Ringgold, Allen Say, Virginia Driving Hawk Sneve, Gary Soto, Mildred Taylor, and Baje Whitethorne.

These are only a few of many outstanding creators in the field of multicultural children's literature. They have provided many traditional as well as contemporary ideas in a variety of genres. They have also contributed to the popular format of "family stories." Examples of innovative work based on personal and family stories include *The Keeping Quilt* by Patricia Polacco, *Grandfather's Journey* by Allen Say, *Family Pictures/Cuadros de Familia* by Carmen Lomas Garza, *Big Mama's* by Donald Crews, *Tar Beach* by Faith Ringgold, and *Sunpainters: Eclipse of the Navajo Sun* by Baje Whitethorne. These tradebooks suggest that everyone carries the seed of a personal story waiting to be discovered, nurtured, and shared with others. The emergence of these "family stories" supports the concept of authentic authorship and provides diverse role models for young readers and writers.

Theme Approach

I have used a theme approach to encourage students to see the circular connections that exist between ideas and experiences. Currently, I have been emphasizing the theme of quilts as a framework for family and community stories. I have used my own grandmother's quilt as the basis for introducing this unit. The response to this piece of material culture has been overwhelming in this region of the High Plains, an isolated expanse of dry and sparse land in Eastern New Mexico and West Texas.

Because quilts have been valued in local families and passed down through generations, students can easily identify with Patricia Polacco's *The Keeping Quilt*. I have used this story of Jewish tradition as well as several quilt stories from African-American and Hawaiian communities to built a network of inter-cultural "quilt" stories. I have also used Faith Ringgold's *Tar Beach* as an example of picturebook format which emerged from an original story quilt, and *Sam Johnson and the Blue Ribbon Quilt* by Tony Johnston to develop students' sensitivity to stereotypes as well as the importance of gender equity in creative expression.

These tradebooks suggest that everyone carries the seed of a personal story waiting to be discovered, nurtured, and shared with others.

The following tradebooks may be useful in developing a multicultural collection on this theme: *Sam Johnson and the Blue Ribbon Quilt, The Patchwork Quilt, The Quilt Story, The Keeping Quilt, The Josefina Story Quilt, Eight Hands Round: A Patchwork Alphabet, A Quilt for Kiri, Sweet Clara and the Freedom Quilt, Luka's Quilt,* and *Bess's Log Cabin Quilt.*

Historically, the quilt has been recognized as a multi-faceted symbol of women's culture. It is significant as an indigenous American art form which crosses racial, ethnic, language and class lines. It has been created largely, but not exclusively, by women.

For each of us, there is a permanent collection of "scraps" and "pieced patchwork" within our memories. To respond to the call to sort, sift, and resurrect these wonderful stories is the opportunity to make visible the "hidden dimension" of our individual and common inheritance. (Monroe 1994)

Issues Approach

An issues approach has been most successful with graduate students who are willing to look at the deeper issues of racism, sexism, ageism, and invisibility in children's tradebooks. Students often formulate an issue question after reading many multicultural books and noting patterns, trends, or actual gaps in writing and publishing. Students have pursued research on self-selected topics, completed a review of literature, initiated a shelf search of appropriate books at libraries and bookstores, and developed an annotated bibliography of recommended books.

A continuing issue for me has been the invisibility of Native American female protagonists in children's literature. Since the early 1930s, the majority of images have been traditional ones, often stereotyped. This trend has regularly been perpetuated by uninformed and insensitive authors as well as illustrators, publishers, and the media. I encourage my students to look beyond the narrow, often unauthentic and commercialized image of "Pocahontas." I challenge them to search for more authentic and contemporary images of Native American girls and women in settings of home, school, career, and literacy context.

Among the many publications most representative of life in contemporary rural and urban settings are the following: *Jenny Redbird Finds Her Friends* (Ojibway), *The Spider, The Cave and the Pottery Bowl* (Hopi), *Lucy Learns to Weave* (Navajo), *Alive Yazzie's Year* (Navajo), *Red Ribbons for Emma* (Navajo), *Not Just Any Ring* (Pueblo), *Goodbye, My Island* (Inuit), *A Promise Is a Promise* (Inuit), *Children of Clay* (Pueblo), *Kinaalda* (Navajo), and *A First Clay Gathering* (Pueblo). Each of these books presents Native American women of both youth and age in strong and positive roles, and a realistic image of the balance between traditional culture and contemporary social and political issues.

In addition to selections which feature Native American female protagonists, I also feature Native American women writers and their works. Three Native American women are continuing to contribute to the quality and authenticity of Native American children's literature. Virginia Driving Hawk Sneeve (Lakota Sioux) has written

Dancing Teepees:Poems by American Indian Youth and *The Sioux: A First Americans Book*. Paula Underwood Spencer (Iroquois) has published *Who Speaks for Wolf*, a community-learning story based on several thousand years of oral tradition. Vee Brown (Navajo) has collaborated with illustrator Baje Whitethone, Sr. (Navajo) on two tribal creation stories of "Changing Woman" entitled *Monster Slayer* and *Monster Birds*.

Students are encouraged to become familiar with Native American authors and illustrators through author studies, author visits, genre studies, and issues approach. These are all legitimate ways of learning more about the culture, language and world view. In contrast, the theme approach is limiting to the study of Native America simply because it has been over-used, often insensitively. As an alternative to this erroneous imaging of Native America as a culture of the past, I attempt to present more authentic and contemporary images of a living and dynamic people!

Resource Development

The following resources have been most useful in the development of a graduate course in Multicultural Children's Literature as well as workshops for in-service teachers. I have used *Teaching Multicultural Children's Literature K-8* edited by Violet Harris, as a required text. I have supplemented this basic text with two additional resources: *Multiethnic Children's Literature* by Gonzalo and Janet Lee Ramirez, and *Kaleidoscope* by Rudine Sims Bishop. All of these resources address recent multicultural publications. A major resource for updating my classroom collection of tradebooks have been issues of *Language Arts*, particularly the March, 1992 issue. Other resources I have used include *Multicultural Voices in Contemporary Literature* by Francis Ann Day and *Instructor* magazine, which has featured lengthy author-illustrator studies with fold-out photo-biographical sketches. I am currently using the December, 1995 issue of *Instructor* which features the article "How to Choose the Best Multicultural Literature" (Murry) as a resource for updating our classroom and library collections of books.

In conclusion, multicultural children's literature is not an isolated genre as featured in most traditional texts. It should be integrated throughout the curricular year rather than being taught just prior to holidays or monthly celebrations. It is more than food, festivals, and ceremonial dress. Multicultural children's literature is the very "fabric" of contemporary life in a multicultural and global society. With our continued nurturing, it will become the established canon of the future!

Works Cited

Aardema, V. *Why Mosquitoes Buzz in People's Ears*. New York: Dial Books for Young Readers, 1975.

Allen, P. G. *The Sacred Hoop*. Boston: Beacon Press, 1986.

Bishop, R. S. *Kaleidescope: A Multicultural Booklist For Grades K-8*. Urbana, IL: NCTE, 1994.

Browne, V. *Monster Slayer*. Flagstaff, AZ: Northland,1994.

———. *Monster Birds*. Flagstaff, AZ: Northland,1994.

Cameron, A. *Spider Woman*. Madiera Park, B.C.: Harbour Publishing Company, 1988.

Clymer, E. *The Spider, the Cave and the Pottery Bowl*. New York: Atheneum, 1972.

Coerr, E. *The Josefina Story Quilt*. New York: Dial, 1989.

Crews, D. *Big Mama's*. New York: The Trumpet Club,1991.

Cruz-Martinez, A. *The Woman Who Outshown the Sun*. San Francisco: Children's Book Press, 1991.

Day, F. A. *Multicultural Voices in Contemporary Literature*. Portsmouth, NH: Heinemann, 1994.

Delacre, L. *Arroz Con Leche*. New York: Scholastic, 1989.

———. *Las Navidades*. New York: Scholastic, 1990.

Driving Hawk Sneve, V. *Dancing Teepees*. New York: Holiday House, 1989.

———. *The Sioux: A First Americans Book*. New York: Holiday House, 1993.

Ernst, L.C. *Sam Johnson and the Blue Ribbon Quilt*. New York: G. P. Putnam's Sons, 1985.

Flourney, V. *The Patchwork Quilt*. New York: Dial, 1985.

Greenfield, E. *Honey, I Love*. New York: Harper Collins, 1978.

Greenfield, E. *Nathaniel Talking*. New York: Black Butterfly Children's Books, 1988.

Guback, G. *Luka's Quilt*. New York: Greenwillow, 1994.

Haller, D. *Not Just Any Ring*. New York: Alfred Knopf, 1982.

Hamilton, V. *In the Beginning: Creation Stories From Around the World*. New York: Harcourt Brace Jovanovich, 1988.

Hamilton, V. *The People Could Fly*. New York: Alfred Knopf, Inc., 1985.

Harris, V. *Teaching Multicultural Literature in Grades K-8*. Norwood, MA: Christopher Gordon Publishers, Inc., 1992.

Hayes, J. *La Llorona: The Weeping Woman*. El Paso, TX: Cinco Puntos Press, 1987.

Hoffman, V. *Lucy Learns To Weave*. Phoenix, AZ: Navajo Curriculum Press, 1974.

Hopkinson, D. *Sweet Clara and the Freedom Quilt*. New York: Alfred Knopf & Sons, 1993.

Johnston, T. *The Quilt Story*. New York: G. P. Putnum, 1995.

Kellogg, S. *Paul Bunyan*. New York: W. Morrow, 1984.

———. *Pecos Bill*. New York: W. Morrow, 1986.

Language Arts. Theme Issue: Multicultural Children's Literature. March 1993.

Lobel, A. *Fables*. New York: Harper & Row, 1988.

Lomas Garza, C. *Family Pictures/Cuadros de Familia*. San Francisco: Children's Book Press, 1990.

Long, D. *A Quilt For Kiri*. Wellington, New Zealand. Learning Media, Ministry of Education, 1991.

Love, D. A. *Bess's Log Cabin Quilt*. New York: Holiday House, 1995.

Maher, R. *Alice Yazzie's Year*. New York: Coward, McCann and Geoghegan, Inc., 1977.

Melton, D. *How To Capture Live Authors and Bring Them To Your Schools*. Kansas City, MO: Landmark Editions, Inc., 1986.

Monroe, S. "Quilt Scraps: A Framework for Family and Community Stories." *New Mexico Journal of Reading*, 14.3 (1994): 4-7.

Monroe, S. "Spider Woman's Intent: Reweaving the World Through Voice and Vision." *New Mexico Journal of Reading*, 14.2 (1995): 7-11.

Munsch, R. *A Promise Is a Promise*. Toronto: Annick Press, Ltd., 1988.

Murry, W. "How to Choose the Best Multicultural Literature." *Instructor*. December 1995: 46-53.

Naranjo-Morse, N. *A First Clay Gathering*. Cleveland, OH: Modern Curriculum Press, 1994.

New Mexico People & Energy Collective. *Red Ribbons For Emma*. Stanford, CA: New Seed Press, 1981.

Paul, A.W. *Eight Hands Round: A Patchwork Alphabet*. New York: Harper Collins, 1991.

Polacco, P. *The Keeping Quilt*. New York: Simon and Schuster, 1988.

Ramirez, G., and J. L. Ramirez. *Multiethnic Children's Literature*. Albany, N.Y: Delmar Publishers, Inc., 1994.

Ringgold, F. *Tar Beach*. New York: Crown Publishers, 1991.

Roessel, M. Kinaalda: *A Navajo Girl Grows Up.* Minneapolis, MN: Lerner Publications Company, 1993.

Rogers, J. *Goodbye, My Island.* New York: Greenwillow, 1983.

San Souci, R. *Cut From The Same Cloth.* New York: Philomel Books, 1993.

Say, A. *Grandfather's Journey.* New York: Houghton Mifflin Company, 1993.

Spencer, P. U. *Who Speaks For Wolf.* San Anselmo, CA: A Tribe of Two Press, 1991.

Swentzell, R. *Children of Clay.* Minneapolis, MN: Lerner Publications Company, 1992.

Thompson, V. *Hawaiian Myths of Earth, Sea and Sky.* Honolulu: University of Hawaii Press, 1966.

Whitethorne, B. *Sunpainters: Eclipse of the Navajo Sun.* Flagstaff, AZ: Northland Publishing, 1994.

Young, B. et al. *Jennie Redbird Finds Her Friends.* Independence, MO: Independence Press, 1972.

Suzanne S. Monroe is Associate Professor of Reading and Early Childhood at West Texas A&M University, Canyon, Texas. She received her doctorate from the University of Arizona in 1988, and has since continued teaching, research, and publication in Children's Literature. This article is based on her seven years of teaching graduate and undergraduate courses at Eastern New Mexico University, Portales, New Mexico.

Unit Selections

14. **Effective Math and Science Instruction—The Project Approach for LEP Students,** Joseph Vigil
15. **Below the Tip of the Iceberg: Teaching Language-Minority Students,** Vivian Fueyo
16. **Learning Strategy Instruction in the Bilingual/ESL Classroom,** Robin Stergis and Jeanne Perrin
17. **Teaching and Learning Languages through Multiple Intelligences,** Mary Ann Christison
18. **The Social Studies Video Project: A Holistic Approach for Teaching Linguistically and Culturally Diverse Students,** Inez A. Heath

Key Points to Consider

❖ How can a teacher plan instruction to meet all students' needs equitably?

❖ What types of activities empower students to take an active role in the learning process?

❖ What are some ways in which teachers can develop their teaching to include all members of the class, regardless of linguistic or cultural backgrounds? What methods seem most relevant for a multilingual, multicultural classroom?

 **Links**   **www.dushkin.com/online/**

18. **Computer Enhanced Language Instruction Archive (CELIA)**
http://www.latrobe.edu.au/www/education/celia/celia.html
19. **Cutting Edge CALL Demos**
http://www-writing.berkeley.edu/chorus/call/cuttingedge.html
20. **Dave's ESL Café on the Web**
http://www.pacificnet.net/~sperling/
21. **ESL Student Page**
http://www2.wgbh.org/mbcweis/ltc/telecom/esl.html
22. **Interactive Internet Language Learning**
http://babel.uoregon.edu/yamada/interact.html

These sites are annotated on pages 4 and 5.

The increasing cultural and linguistic diversity of children entering schools in the United States has led to new challenges for teaching that require rethinking ways of providing high-quality, equitable education to meet the needs of all students. Teachers of limited-English-proficient (LEP) students must facilitate and encourage language acquisition while simultaneously providing comprehensible course instruction. Furthermore, students from minority language backgrounds may enter the American school system with widely diverse educational backgrounds, including nonexistent or interrupted schooling. These cultural, linguistic, and educational variables are important elements for teachers to consider when preparing instruction.

Teachers and educational researchers have risen to the challenge of providing minority language students with successful learning experiences in a number of innovative and integrative ways. The following articles include descriptions of teaching strategies and methods designed to enhance the learning of minority language students across the areas of the curriculum. The ideas presented in these articles focus on rethinking the roles of such students in the classroom. This newly perceived role considers the value of students' prior experiences, both cultural and linguistic, which are viewed as resources for the teacher and the other students. As learners who are valued for their experiences, these students have more flexibility to explore their own learning styles, thereby assuming a more central role in the educational process. The end result is children who are empowered in setting the stage for their own educational outcomes.

When students are actively learning in the classroom, they are putting their own ideas to work in the educational context. The use of play learning and cooperative learning groups enables teachers to provide a structure in which students may formulate their own hypothesis about learning material. They use their newly found knowledge to practice communicating effectively in heterogenous groups. Interacting naturally, the children have the opportunity to provide one another with the resources for learning and assisting one another in the learning process. Meanwhile, the teacher is always close at hand to facilitate learning through supervising students' interactions, providing necessary linguistic and contextual support, and offering guidance and information when necessary. In this way the students become the main actors in the classroom, and the learning experience is an active and meaningful one for them.

The use of thematic teaching units and integrated language and content instruction also provides students with the necessary tools to begin to comprehend instruction in a holistic and contextualized environment. These articles provide direction for teachers who are interested in implementing an integrated approach to instruction that supports language development while providing students with comprehensible content instruction. By assessing students' content-specific language needs, maintaining opportunities for language use within content areas, and teaching strategies to students that enable them to predict learning outcomes and to categorize new information within specified frameworks, teachers are helping students to succeed both linguistically and academically in a culturally sensitive learning environment.

EFFECTIVE MATH AND SCIENCE INSTRUCTION –
THE PROJECT APPROACH FOR LEP STUDENTS

Joseph Vigil, M.S.

The "project approach" to instruction is becoming popular for providing enriching, cognitively demanding experiences for limited-English-proficient (LEP) students. The project approach involves any type of group learning activity that brings about a sustained period of self-reliant effort by learners to achieve a clearly defined goal.

The approach is most productive to invite students to express themselves in the language they use most comfortably. While extra time may be needed for translation so that all students can understand each other, the benefit is that students are learning to communicate using math and science language that can be transferred as students' English proficiency increases. The translation process can produce greater English fluency. Homework that takes the form of hands-on projects and problem solving promotes students' language and thinking skills and helps parents support the value of learning math and science for real-world applications.

The language needed to communicate ideas in math and science classes can be difficult for LEP students to master. Science vocabulary is key to most science instruction. By one estimate, students in the average high school biology class are exposed to more than 2,400 new terms in one year – more new words than they would be asked to learn in the typical high school French class (Vigil, 1996).

The hands-on project approach can motivate all students to communicate using math and science language in order to produce a final product. For example, teachers in Gallup, New Mexico, are receiving training from the Intercultural Development Research Association (IDRA) on how to implement the project approach to enhance instruction and motivate students to learn math and science concepts.

"We put students first here in Gallup and will adopt strategies that will enhance student learning and achievement," said Melinda Swain, coordinator for language acquisition and staff development for the Gallup-McKinley County Schools (CS). Teachers are not throwing away their textbooks. They are using the solar car project to demonstrate real-world applications of key concepts and to have students communicate these concepts while participating in social interactions with other students, teachers and mentors.

The solar car project approach covers valuable real-world engineering design experiences, math and science concepts, and other experiences including:

Engineering Design Experiences
- Definition of customer and needs
- Performance criteria and contacts
- Research
- Synthesis
- Analysis
- Design
- Prototype construction
- Testing
- Evaluation
- Presentation

Math and Science Concepts
- Metric units
- Force at a point
- Circumference (radius times two times π)
- Torque (force times lever arm; $T=FL$)
- Gear ratio
- Velocity ($V=D/t$)
- Revolutions (rotations per minute or radians per second)
- Friction
- Center of gravity
- Graphing
- Frontal area
- Specific weight of air
- Acceleration of gravity
- Aerodynamic drag
- Solar panel and motor

Other Experiences
- Working as members of a team
- Troubleshooting experiences
- Sportsmanship
- Promoting an event
- Knowing it is okay if something does not work
- Working with Sprint solar car software
- Internet research

Students have such a good time with the project that they often do not see the math and science as school work, but as a tool to create a product. The project drives the math and science content, and communication increases, fostering greater English fluency for LEP students as well as for all students involved. Administrators and parents in Gallup will assist since the solar car project can culminate in a solar car competition that requires many volunteers and assistance from outside the classroom. Community and local businesses will contribute by providing support for the promotion of the event.

Technology is not just something added to this project approach. It is truly

From the *IDRA Newsletter,* March 1998, pp. 1-2. © 1998 by the Intercultural Development Research Association. Reprinted by permission.

integrated into every aspect of the experience. Students will use solar car software that animates key science and math concepts to provide them with background information. The National Renewable Energy Laboratory will provide on-line research for students at <www.nrel.gov/>. Photovoltaic information for teachers and students is featured in an on-line quiz found at <www.nrel.gov./pv/whatispv.html>. An example of student work may be viewed on Chris and Grant's Solar Page at <www.teleport.com/~chrisdb/project/>. This student page was created for a school science project and provides background information on photovoltaic cells, home applications and solar car highlights.

On-line mentors will be utilized to assist students and teachers with the project. Engineers from the Los Alamos National Laboratory will provide expertise on the mechanics of the solar car project and the overall design process. Professional staff from IDRA and the Southwest Comprehensive Center Region IX will provide Gallup-McKinley CS teachers with on-line expertise on topics such as the following:

- Bilingual education and English as a second language (ESL),
- Education technology,
- Instruction and curriculum,
- Multicultural education,
- Family involvement and participation,
- Professional development, and
- Evaluation and assessment.

Two resources that provide educators with ESL strategies are *Teaching Content: ESL Strategies for Classroom Teachers* and *Starting Today...Steps to Success for Beginning Bilingual Educators* developed by Frank Gonzales, Ph.D., a senior education associate at IDRA. These resources point out that the most important tenet of bilingual education is that knowledge is transferable. Content area instruction early in school should be done in the primary language to develop a strong cognitive base in one language, which then transfers to the second language.

The project approach can enhance students' learning of math and science concepts. It provides a rich environment for using math and science language that can be transferred as students' English proficiency increases.

Resources

Gonzales, F. *Starting Today...Steps to Success for Beginning Bilingual Educators* (San Antonio, Texas: Intercultural Development Research Association, 1995).

Gonzales, F. *Teaching Content: ESL Strategies for Classroom Teachers* (San Antonio, Texas: Intercultural Development Research Association, 1995).

Vigil, J. "What is Science Literacy?" *IDRA Newsletter* (San Antonio, Texas: Intercultural Development Research Association, November-December 1996).

Joe Vigil, M.S., is an education associate in the IDRA Division of Professional Development. Comments and questions may be sent to him via e-mail at idra@idra.org.

Below the Tip of the Iceberg

TEACHING

Language-Minority Students

Vivian Fueyo

I believe she doesn't come out because she is afraid to speak English, and maybe this is so since she only knows eight words. She knows to say: He not here for when the landlord comes, No speak English if anybody else comes, and Holy smokes. I don't know where she learned this, but I heard her say it one time and it surprised me.

My father says when he came to this country he ate hamandeggs for three months. Breakfast, lunch, and dinner. Hamandeggs. That is the only word he knew. He doesn't eat hamandeggs anymore. (Cisneros, 1989, p. 77)

Have you met the characters in Cisneros' story? Do they remind you of any of your students? Of their parents?

Language-minority students, children from homes in which English is not the primary language, may come to you from many cultures and languages, with a range of skills and proficiency in written and spoken English (Wong Fillmore, 1991). Academic failure among these students is disproportionately high when compared to students in the general population (Garcia & Ortiz, 1988).

Language-minority students are often misidentified as having learning difficulties or speech and language disabilities. They may be taught with inappropriate strategies by teachers unprepared to teach them, teachers who fail to understand second-language acquisition or cultural differences (Ortiz & Yates, 1983). According to Bos and Reyes (1996), "When language-minority students struggle with academic learning, particularly with language and literacy development, teachers oftentimes use special educators as a resource or refer students for special education services" (p. 344).

From *Teaching Exceptional Children*, September/October 1997, pp. 61-65. © 1997 by The Council for Exceptional Children. Reprinted by permission.

What Is Context-Reduced Versus Context-Imbedded Instruction?

Classroom language used in content instruction varies in the amount and number of cues or context clues that it provides. Here are some examples:

Context-embedded: Telling a student to follow along in the storybook, while holding up the book and pointing to it, gives the student lots of hints as to what's expected.

Context-reduced: Giving the student written instructions describing a four-step research project assignment, with no visual or gestured clues, provides few clues to the student and demands understanding of complex language (Faltis, 1993).

As the number of language-minority children in our classrooms increases, all teachers need to take a more active role in educating these students.

As educators, we need to be able to create a classroom atmosphere accepting of linguistic differences; we need to separate the students' conversational skills from the skills necessary for school success; and we need to develop systematic sequences for language instruction. We don't want our students to have to eat hamandeggs every day.

Commonalities Among Teachers

Several common assumptions already exist between educators of language-minority children and special educators. Both promote diversity and the understanding of individual differences among students who have not been well served by the public school system (Utley, 1995). Both recognize the importance of working in teams with other professionals, parents, and community members to meet the needs of the learner. Both teach students who share similar experiences or discrimination because of cultural characteristics—poverty, language, and/or their disabling condition (Gollnick & Chinn, 1990). Language-minority students and students with mild disabilities suffer from many of the same stereotypical attitudes, expectations, and practices (Amos & Landers, 1984).

Educators of language-minority students and special educators also recognize the importance of keeping well informed. To teach their students well, they need to know about critical issues in their fields and about research findings affecting instructional practices.

Language-minority students are often misidentified as having learning difficulties or speech and language disabilities.

Content Leading and Second Language Acquisition

Cummins (1984) has presented a framework for understanding English-language proficiency and second-language acquisition. His model helps to explain why language-minority children may have difficulty learning content in an all-English classroom. It also helps to explain why language-minority children's skills in English may seem to fluctuate radically throughout the school day—speaking English fluently when out on the playground but unable to utter a single phrase in English during a class discussion.

In studying the first- and second-language skills of second-language learners, Cummins found that the children were often able to speak appropriately to their peers in both languages. At the same time, their literacy skills in both languages were significantly below age-appropriate levels. He explained these differences in language proficiency by distinguishing two types of communication:

- *Surface fluency*—language proficiency in the context of everyday face-to-face communication (context-embedded). These Cummins called "basic interpersonal communication skills."
- *Conceptual-linguistic knowledge*—the language skills required for academic achievement in the absence of context clues (context-reduced). Cummins labeled these skills "cognitive academic language proficiency."

Cummins' (1984) research found that students who have initial reading and writing experiences in a meaningful context, directly related to the child's previous experience, are more likely to be successful. The same principle holds true for second-language instruction. The model in Figure 1 may help illustrate better the following example. Children who have developed the ability to manipulate and interpret challenging language structures in their native language, such as being able to analyze information into its component parts to see their relationships to each other, have already formed these linguistic relationships. To form them in English, therefore, will be simply a matter of learning the new vocabulary to express them.

But if the student is still at the conversational level in his or her primary language and is only able to use his or her native language to recognize and use information, then learning to use English to express more challenging academic concepts will take much longer. Cummins' findings provide a strong rationale for encouraging the language development of all students, particularly students whose first language is not English.

95

Implications for Instructional Programs

Imagine an iceberg with a small portion visible above the water while its greater mass lies below the surface. The visible, surface forms of the language are the most familiar and most evident. Examples of basic interpersonal communication skills include student conversations with teachers and friends, labeling objects, and following a sequence of verbal commands. Students use basic vocabulary, grammar, and pronunciation to recognize and recall information, understand the meaning of information, and use information. They use context cues in the environment or in the classroom.

The less visible and less easily measured aspects of language proficiency for cognitive academic tasks lie much deeper (see Figure 1). Students proficient at this level are able to follow complex written directions, write a story, or listen to a lecture and complete a written activity based on its information. Students demonstrate their language proficiency by dissecting information into its component parts to see their relationship, putting components together to form new ideas, and judging the worth of an idea, notion, theory, thesis proposition, information, or opinion. Students fluent at this level require few context cues. Most instruction focuses on the tip of the iceberg despite the fact that the language needed for critical thinking—for academic success—is below the surface.

Language-minority children quickly master basic interpersonal comunication skills in English from their friends, the media, and their day-to-day experiences (see A and B in Figure 2); but in assessing their language proficiency, we must recognize the distinction between those skills and more complex language skills (see C and D in Figure 2). "If we fail to recognize this difference, we may incorrectly assume that children have acquired sufficient proficiency in English to succeed in a classroom where only English is used, when in fact they have not" (Lessow-Hurley, 1996, p. 54).

Cummins' (1984) theory helps explain the dynamics of school-related language proficiency. It helps explain why Huen so clearly described to you in English the story she read, using surface fluency, but

Figure 1
Levels of Language and Thinking Skills

Basic Interpersonal Communication Skills

Cognitive Process

Knowledge: Recognizing and recalling information

Comprehension: Understanding the meaning of information

Application: Using information

Language Process

Pronunciation: Reproducing sounds

Vocabulary: Using labels and words in context

Grammar: Using rule-governed language structures

Cognitive/Academic Language Proficiency

Analysis: Dissecting information into its component parts to see their relationship

Synthesis: Putting components together to form new ideas

Evaluation: Judging the worth of an idea, notion, theory, thesis, proposition, information, or opinion.

Semantic Meaning: Relying on the context of the language for meaning

Functional Meaning: Understanding language in a meaningful way across setting, topics, and breakdowns in communication

Note: Adapted with permission from Cummins, J. (1984). *Bilingualism and special education: Issues in assessment and pedagogy.* San Diego, CA: College-Hill Press.

was unable to compare the characters in the book she read to the ones in the chapter book you read aloud to the class that morning, requiring cognitive-academic language structures. The language of classroom instruction differs significantly from the style of communication of other daily experiences and communication. Much academic instruction relies heavily on written and verbal explanations in the absence of concrete clues. It is often context-reduced. In addition, classroom tasks require thinking and are cognitively

demanding. Students must focus on tasks that are new and challenging.

In school, many tasks required of language-minority children are new. New tasks tend to require more thinking. They are cognitively demanding. As a task becomes more familiar, it requires less thinking, thus becoming cognitively less demanding. For example, letter writing is generally an automatic skill for most adults. Children learning to write, however, are engaged in a cognitively demanding activity (Lessow-Hurley, 1996). Classroom language used in content in-

Figure 2
Students' Communication and the Need for Support

A. High contextual support (context-embedded), low cognitive demand
- Holds everyday conversations with teachers and friends; participates in conversations about movies, holidays, and so on.
- Interprets nonverbal communication correctly (anger, approval, frustration).
- Watches others to determine appropriate behavior; responds appropriately when spoken to in a group.
- Follows spoken directions with the assistance of props and concrete objects.

B. High contextual support (context-embedded), high cognitive demand
- Talks about school subjects, establishes appropriate content and sequence of events (e.g., talks about or answers questions about Columbus' voyage).
- Follows a sequence of verbal commands with the assistance of visual props and concrete pictures or objects.
- Repeats verbal directions when asked.
- Works with others to complete a cognitively demanding task (e.g., uses manipulatives to solve math work problems).
- Participates with friends in games and sports activities.

C. Reduced contextual support, low cognitive demand
- Follows simple written direction; completes simple paper-and-pencil activities.
- Associates letters/words with sounds or objects (e.g., reads *mat,* is able to pick up the *hat*).
- Listens to recorded stories and follows sequence of events; plays simple individual games.
- Associates time of day with appropriate activities (e.g., knows when it's lunchtime, playtime, reading time).

D. Reduced contextual support, high cognitive demand
- Follows complex written directions (directions that are written with several steps that are written without pictorial clues).
- Writes a story (follows plot structure); writes a formal letter.
- Takes study notes or outlines a chapter in a book; reads a story and prepares a written report.
- Solves word problems independently.

Note: Adapted with permission from Fradd, S., & Tikunoff, W. (Eds.). (1987). *Bilingual education and bilingual special education.* Boston: Little Brown.

struction varies along a continuum from following daily classroom routines (cognitively undemanding) to analyzing character development in a novel (cognitively demanding) (Cummins, 1984; Faltis, 1993).

Figure 2 presents characteristics of student communication using Cummins' framework. Frames A and B are examples of students' surface fluency. Frames C and D are examples of student communication in more complex, academic language.

Strategies You Can Use for All Students

To meet the academic and linguistic needs of the language-minority students in your classroom, make your instructional language easy to understand for learners at all levels, yet relevant and interesting for native English speakers. Encourage students to use their cognitive-academic language skills as much as possible, providing encouragement and support for language use in both their native language and English. Be an active observer of the language of content instruction in the classroom. Create opportunities for all students to express their knowledge in ways that are appropriate to their levels of English.

Strategies for Teaching Language-Minority Students

When Planning Instruction

Ask yourself the following questions:
- What kinds of instructional language will be required of the students? Will it encourage use of both their conversational fluency as well as more challenging structures?
- What is the language of classroom instruction?
- What will be required of the students' comprehension? Is it context-embedded or context-reduced?
- Is the level of language sensitive to the students' level of proficiency?

Prepare a script to help you meet your goals. Plan to record your lessons on video or audiotape to enable you to systematically analyze both your language and the students' language during instruction.

To Increase Comprehension During Instruction

Slow down the rate of speech during instruction. Articulate more clearly. Use longer pauses. Use high-frequency words. Use fewer pronoun forms. Use more gestures and visuals to accompany words. Use shorter, simple sentences. Increase repetition and rephrasing.

Add context to learning activities to increase their ease of understanding. Provide visual supports, pictures, media, real objects, puppets, flannel boards, and manipulatives. Put labels everywhere in the classroom. Emphasize comprehension.

Use signals with explicit cues that you provide throughout the lesson to let students know when to begin, transition, or end: "Let's begin," or "Let's go on," or "Let's put our books away."

To Increase and Sustain Verbal Interaction During Instruction

Ask the learner for further clarification, phrasing the request in the form of information questions (who, what, where, how, when, why, etc.). For example, *the learner says*, "The order rogical . . . "

The native speaker says, "The what? Please repeat."

The learner says, "The order uh rogical."

The native speaker says, "The order is logical? I see." Confirm with the learner in a nonthreatening way that the utterance has been correctly understood or heard.

For example, *the learner says*, "All many outside went."

The native speaker confirms and models the correct grammar, "All went outside?" And the learner responds, "Yes."

Infuse higher-order thinking skills into all aspects of classroom activity. Challenge students to think and use language to describe their thinking. Encourage them to use their language with other students.

After You Teach

Listen to or view the tape of your verbal behavior during instruction. Listen to the students' verbal behavior. Make notations about the amount of context you provided, the level of cognitive demand required, and the students' responses. Review these records frequently to monitor the students' language proficiency, as well as to evaluate and review your language during instruction. (Refer to Figures 1 and 2 for more information.)

Language-minority children are best served when the classroom environment encourages the use of language, when their language use is systematically observed, and when the results of these observations are used as a basis for planning subsequent instruction. The language of instruction supports language-minority students when it is simple, clear, and supported by cues, context-embedded, and cognitively challenging. Effective instructional strategies emphasize comprehension and encourage verbal interaction.

Aren't you already doing some or all of this? The major difference is that you now know what lies below the tip of the iceberg.

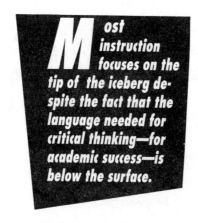

Most instruction focuses on the tip of the iceberg despite the fact that the language needed for critical thinking—for academic success—is below the surface.

Learn More About It

Adger, C., Wolfram, W., & Detwyler, J. (1993). Language differences: A new approach for special educators. *TEACHING Exceptional Children, 26*(1), 44-67.

Baca, L., & Almaza, E. (1991). *Language minority students with disabilities.* Reston, VA: Council for Exceptional Children. (ERIC Document Reproduction Services No. ED 339 171).

Bos, C., & Reyes, E. (1996). Conversations with a Latina teacher about education for language-minority students with special needs. *The Elementary School Journal, 96*(3), 344-351.

Carrasquillo, A., & Baecher, R. (Eds.). (1990). *Teaching the bilingual special education student.* Norwood, NJ: Ablex.

Gersten, R., & Woodward, J. (1994). The language-minority student and special education: Issues, trends, and paradoxes. *Exceptional Children, 60*(6), 310-322.

Klingner, J., & Vaughn, S. (1966). Reciprocal teaching of reading comprehension strategies for students with learning disabilities who use English as a second language. *The Elementary School Journal, 96*(3), 275-293.

National Center for Research on Cultural Diversity and Second Language Learning, Pathways Home Page [on line]. Available: http//www.ncrel.org/skrs/areas/issues/educatrs/leadrshp/le4ncred.htm.

Salend, S. (1997). What about our schools, our languages? *TEACHING Exceptional Children, 29*(4), 38-41.

References

Amos, O., & Landers, M. (1984). Special education and multicultural education: A compatible marriage. *Theory into Practice, 23*(2), 144-150.

Bos, C., & Reyes, E. (1996). Conversations with a Latina teacher about education for language-minority students with special needs. *The Elementary School Journal, 96*(3), 344-351.

Cisneros, S. (1989). *House on Mango Street.* New York: Vintage Books.

Cummins, J. (1984). *Bilingualism and special education: Issues in assessment and pedagogy.* San Diego, CA: College-Hill.

Faltis, C. (1993). Joinfostering: Adapting teaching strategies for the multilingual classroom. New York: Merrill/Macmillan.

Fradd, S., & Tikunoff, W. (Eds.). (1987). *Bilingual education and bilingual special education.* Boston: Little Brown.

Garcia, S., & Ortiz, A. (1988). Preventing inappropriate referrals of language minority students to special education. *New Focus, 5: Occasional Papers in Bilingual Education.* Washington, DC: National Clearinghouse for Bilingual Education.

Gollnick, D., & Chinn, P. (1990). *Multicultural education in a pluralistic society.* New York: Merrill.

Lessow-Hurley, J. (1996). *The foundations of dual language instruction.* White Plains, NY: Longman.

Ortiz, A., & Yates, J. (1983). Incidence among Hispanic exceptionals: Implications for manpower planning. *Journal of the National Association of Bilingual Education, 7*(3), 41-53.

Utley, C. (1995). Culturally and linguistically diverse students with mild disabilities. In C. Grant (Ed.), *Educating for diversity: An anthology of multicultural voices* (pp. 301-322). New York: Allyn & Bacon.

Wong Fillmore, L. (1991). Language and cultural issues in the early education of language minority children. In S. Kagan (Ed.), *The care and education of America's young children: Obstacles and opportunities. Nineteeth Yearbook of the National Society for the Study of Education, Part 1* (pp. 30-49). Chicago: University of Chicago Press.

Vivian Fueyo *(CEC Chapter #311), Professor, Elementary Education, Florida State University, Tallahassee*

Address correspondence to the author at Department of Educational Theory and Practice, Florida State University, 115 Stone Building, Tallahassee, FL 32306-4065. (e-mail: vfuevo@mailer.fsu.edu).

Successful Practices

Column Editor: Dr. Anne Homza, Boston Public Schools, Boston, MA

Learning Strategy Instruction in the Bilingual/ESL Classroom

by Robin Stergis, Ed.D and Jeanne Perrin, M.Ed.

Taking a Look at Learning Strategy Instruction

As you enter the foyer of the middle school, the brightly colored Learning Strategy poster proclaiming "Listen Selectively" is difficult to miss. This is the fifth in a series of learning strategy of the month posters which grace the walls of corridors and classrooms in both English and Haitian Creole. These posters serve as not so subtle reminders of learning strategy instruction based on the *Cognitive Academic Language Learning Approach (CALLA)* going on daily in ESL and bilingual classrooms.

Created by Ana Chamot and J. Michael O'Malley (1987), CALLA is based on research suggesting that effective instruction for English language learners integrates language and content (Genesse, 1987; Mohan, 1986) and includes explicit instruction in learning strategies to accomplish academic tasks (Chamot & O'Malley, 1987, 1994, 1996; Oxford, 1990). Originally designed to help English language learners make a successful transition to monolingual-English classrooms, CALLA has been adapted to different instructional settings including bilingual education classrooms (Chamot & O'Malley, 1994). Let's take a look inside several such classes.

Haitian Students are Taught to Listen Selectively

In a seventh grade beginning ELS class, Haitian bilingual students are being introduced to a unit entitled "Welcome to School" with learning objectives of school vocabulary, reading a school map and listening to school announcements. The learning strategy being introduced is Listen Selectively, a metacognitive learning strategy which helps students to plan their own learning. In the instruction of metacognitive learning strategies, students are first asked in their native language to reflect on the following questions:

*   How do I learn?
*   How can I learn better?

Students and teacher then discuss action steps to plan what the students will do to achieve the learning goals. The teacher guides the students through a discussion of what it means to listen selectively, such as attending to key words and phrases, words or themes that repeat or words that give clues, such as first, finally, for example, and so forth. Then the students listen as the teacher reads, in this case, school announcements, and fill in a chart which they have previewed before the listening activity. The chart provides the students with a framework to begin practicing the listening strategy. (See Figure 1.)

Figure 1. This chart from <u>Building Bridges: Content and Learning Strategies for ESL</u>, is used to help students learn to listen selectively.

Vietnamese Students Learn How to Use What They Know

Sixth grade Vietnamese bilingual students begin an investigative unit on Native Americans in the U.S. The bilingual classroom teacher introduces the unit with pictures and a film strip and then teaches in Vietnamese the learning strategy of Elaborate Prior Knowledge, or "Use what you know." Elaborate Prior Knowledge, a cognitive learning strategy, is reinforced by instructing students to use what they know in order to establish conceptual connections between previously acquired knowledge and new information. In the teaching of cognitive strategies, students are instructed to reflect on the questions:

Figure 2. This K/W/L chart is shown in the finished version. Typically, students complete the K (know) and W (want to know) columns prior to the beginning of instruction and the L (learn) column at the conclusion of the unit.

From *NABE News,* March 15, 1997, pp. 25-28. © 1997 by the National Association for Bilingual Education (NABE). Reprinted by permission.

- How can I understand?
- How can I remember?

The teacher guides the students through writing two columns of a K/W/L chart to elicit students' prior knowledge on the topic. Once the chart is completed, students use both Vietnamese and English to orally share with the group what they already know about Native American history, culture and customs and what they would like to learn. In the example shown, a K/W/L chart is used to reinforce Elaborate Prior Knowledge. (See Figure 2.)

Haitian Students are Taught to Summarize

In another Haitian bilingual class, students summarize the story "The First Thanksgiving" using a story map. The ESL teacher reads the story orally to the class, and then using their text, students summarize the action by completing a story map. The use of a graphic organizer, such as a story map, is another way to help students remember and reflect upon what they have read through the cognitive learning strategy of Summarize. (See Figure 3.)

Vietnamese Students Learn to Cooperate

In the Vietnamese bilingual program, students continue their study of Native Americans. Students are instructed to work in pairs to complete a Venn diagram based on an eight page reading of "American Indians of the Eastern Woodlands" from the National Geographic Society. The students compare Northeast Native Americans with Southeast Native Americans. The Social-Affective learning strategy of Cooperate is employed to assist students in better understanding new written information. As students work together, they share knowledge of vocabulary and check one another to ensure the collected information is complete, accurate and makes sense. (See Figure 4.)

Social-Affective learning strategies are designed to assist students in accomplishing academic tasks through collaboration and peer support. In the instruction of Social-Affective strategies, students are asked to reflect on the following questions:

- How can I help others learn?
- How can others help me learn?

In all learning strategy instructions, students are typically asked to reflect on their learning experiences and their use of learning strategies to accomplish classroom tasks. At the completion of the unit on Native Americans, the students' responses to the question "How does cooperating with a partner help you learn?" are as follows:

- Because we can share ideas and learn to work together
- I help my partner to get smart and work hard and not say the wrong words. And we have to cooperate the work — we do it for homework and classwork
- When I work by myself I feel lonely. But when I work with a partner I feel happy.

Getting Started with Learning Strategy Instruction

As teachers in the Transitional Bilingual Education (TBE) Program of the Boston Public Schools (BPS), we have spent several years implementing learning strategy instruction in bilingual and ESL classrooms. Learning strategy instruction is designed to provide students with problem-solving techniques to

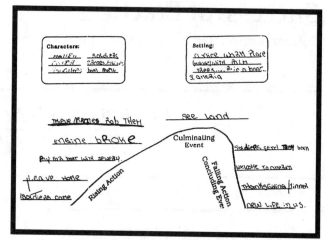

Figure 3. This story map is used to help students learn to summarize a story from their Social Studies lesson.

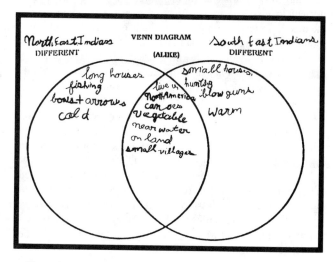

Figure 4. This Venn diagram is used to help students learn to cooperate as they compare two Native American tribes.

accomplish content-area tasks and is ideally suited to bilingual classroom settings. Learning strategies represent higher-order thinking skills that can be promoted in students' native languages. With teacher guidance and support, students can apply learning strategies to a variety of academic tasks in their native language and English.

We decided to implement learning strategy instruction based on the difficulties some of our students were experiencing in accomplishing academic-language tasks such as analyzing and synthesizing information. Previous attempts at assisting these students did not achieve the desired results so we looked for an approach that would provide our students with the tools for academic success in both bilingual and monolingual classroom settings.

Our efforts were directed at students who were enrolled in Vietnamese and Haitian TBE classes in two middle schools and three high schools. Bilingual teachers in these schools had received extensive training and follow-up support in learning strategy instruction. Participating teachers also attended workshops and graduate courses in the areas of ESL and bilingual education methods and materials and multicultural education.

We created a series of classroom activities that were designed to reinforce learning strategies from classroom units in *Building Bridges: Content and Learning Strategies for ESL* (Chamot, O'Malley & Kupper, 1992). This CALLA-based series was used by TBE teachers in our schools. The classroom activities focused on the three types of CALLA learning strategies: metacognitive, cognitive and social-affective.

Involving the Whole School Community in Learning Strategy Instruction

We found that learning strategy instruction provides an effective vehicle for interdisciplinary collaboration among teachers in our schools. CALLA-trained TBE staff have presented the learning strategy approach to colleagues during after school workshops and monthly school-based meetings. These sessions provided a valuable opportunity for teachers from different academic specialties to share knowledge and expertise regarding the learning needs of their students. Content area, special education and foreign language staff discussed applications of learning strategy instruction to their respective classroom settings.

School staff from a variety of disciplines and programs collaborated to organize school-wide learning strategy activities. Grade-level field trips were planned with learning strategy activities. With administrative support, learning strategy of the month posters in students' native languages and English were displayed throughout school buildings. (See Figure 5.) The district-wide after-school cable T.V. show, designed to help students with homework assignments, introduced learning strategy activities across grade levels and languages.

Involving Parents in Learning Strategy Instruction

We provide an opportunity for parents and their children to practice CALLA-based learning strategies that were emphasized in TBE classrooms. We created a series of cooperative tasks centered around the home and community for parents and their children. All of the activities were designed to reinforce CALLA-based metacognitive, cognitive and social-affective learning strategies.

We introduced the activities to parents at the school-based monthly meetings of the bilingual parent advisory council (PAC). Parent coordinators were present to translate information and to discuss the activities with parents. During our meetings with parents, we always began by discussing CALLA and its implementation. We then introduced and modeled a particular activity and its corresponding learning strategy. We also participated with parents in the activities before asking them to try them at home. Parents were asked to implement one of the activities with their children and report on its effectiveness at a future meeting. While our emphasis was on the oral engagement of parents and their children, parents were also invited to keep a written record of their impressions of the activities in a log or journal.

For each activity, we prepared a one-page handout for parents

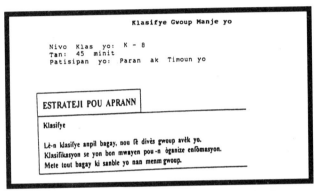

Figure 5. This learning strategy poster in Haitian Creole reinforces the cognitive learning strategy "use what you know" or Elaborate Prior Knowledge.

Figure 6. This handout for Haitian parents provides instructions for an activity that reinforces the cognitive learning strategy "classify."

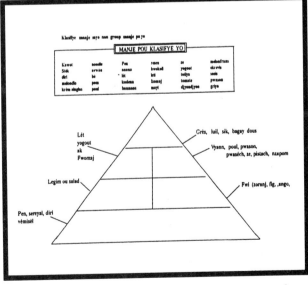

Figure 7. This food pyramid was distributed to Haitian parents to assist them in an activity with their children that reinforces the cognitive learning strategy "classify." Here the families discussed the food they ate and assigned them to categories in the food pyramid.

written in the native language and English. The topic, the time required, the suggested grade level of children and the procedures for doing the activity were indicated. Following CALLA procedures, the particular learning strategies to be reenforced were named and defined. Each handout included space for parents and their children to record their ideas in written form on charts, tables or graphic organizers. (See figures 6 & 7.)

Generally, the learning strategy activities for families helped to establish connections between parents and their children's education. Parents who were introduced to the activities and implemented them with their children found them to be an effective method of assisting with school work. In addition, student enthusiasm and motivation for classwork and were clearly heightened with this approach.

Recommendations for Learning Strategy Instructions

We have the following suggestions for teachers who are interested in implementing learning strategy instruction in their classrooms:

- Teach learning strategies in students' native languages; then introduce similar learning strategy activities in English.
- Provide students with a repertoire of learning strategies for each academic task.
- Choose learning strategies to reflect subject-matter and instructional goals.
- Ensure that students have ongoing guidance and support in order for them to develop proficiency in the use of learning strategies.
- Become knowledgeable about learning strategy instruction through professional training and peer support.

Concluding Remarks

Overall, our experience suggests that learning strategy instruction assists bilingual and ESL students in accomplishing academic tasks. However, the above examples are just a sampling of the learning strategies that we teach in bilingual and ESL classrooms.

There are additional metacognitive, cognitive and social-affective learning strategies that we have found effective in assisting our students to achieve academically. For additional resources and to learn more about other learning strategy activities, we recommend *The CALLA Handbook,* cited below.

References

Chamot, A.U. & O'Malley, J.M. (1987). "The Cognitive Academic Language Learning Approach: A bridge to the mainstream." *TESOL Quarterly,* 21, pp. 227-249.

Chamot, A.U. & O'Malley, J.M. (1994). *The CALLA Handbook, Implementing the Cognitive Academic Language Learning Approach.* Reading, MA: Addison-Wesley Publishing Company.

Chamot, A.U. & O'Malley, J.M. (1996). "The Cognitive Academic Language Learning Approach: A model for linguistically diverse classrooms." *The Elementary School Journal, 96,* (3), pp. 259-273.

Chamot, A.U. & O'Malley, J.M. & Kupper, L. (1992).*Building Bridges, Content and Learning Strategies for ESL.* Boston, MA: Heinle and Heinle.

Genesee, F. (1987). *Learning Through Two Languages: Studies of Immersion and Bilingual Education.* Rowley, M.A.: Newbury House.

Mohan, B.A. (1986). *Language and Content.* Reading, MA: Addison-Wesley.

Oxford, R. (1990). *Language Learning Strategies: What Every Teacher Should Know.* New York: Newbury House.

Robin Stergis, Ed.D., has experience as a bilingual program supervisor, ESL teacher and college instructor. Jeanne Perrin, M.Ed., has served as an administrator, staff developer and consultant in the bilingual/ESL program of the Boston Public Schools. They gratefully acknowledge the contributions of teachers and students from the Boston Public Schools.

Teaching and Learning Languages Through Multiple Intelligences

Mary Ann Christison

When I first began teaching, I remember being surprised to find out that the young man who was doing so poorly in my language class was the best student in math, and the young woman who was my best language student was struggling in physical education. A third student did poorly in both math and English but was an outstanding musician. At that time, I did not consider differences in intelligence profiles or learning styles in planning my lessons. My students struggled to adapt themselves to my teaching style and the activities and materials I chose for them.

The first objective is to learn to use the seven intelligences in problem situations and the second is to discover that using different intelligences creates a deeper, richer, and more varied approach to learning.

Although many ESL/EFL teachers today recognize and appreciate diversity in the students they teach, they are faced with several difficult problems in their workplace situations. The first problem is that embedded in many educational practices are policies and procedures that lead individuals toward uniformity, such as standardized achievement tests, grading on the curve, textbook adoptions, and curriculum guides. Also, the traditional second or foreign language classroom has favored visual and verbal delivery systems—lectures, worksheets, written papers, pictures, graphic organizers, slides, videos, and student art. Using primarily visual and verbal cues, teachers can miss the elusive qualities of learning demonstrated by some of our ESL/EFL students who are not strongly verbal or visual.

There are signs, however, that a paradigm shift is beginning. More and more ESL/EFL teachers are addressing diversity in their classrooms. Our profession is becoming increasingly cognizant of the enormous range of human skills and capacities.

Howard Gardner's (1983) theory of multiple intelligences has great potential for helping revolutionize our concept of human capabilities. Gardner's basic premise is that intelligence is not a single construct: Individuals have at least seven distinct intelligences that can be developed over a lifetime. Gardner's multiple intelligences (MI) theory is very important to EFL/ESL teachers; because we work with such diverse learners, we can nurture intelligences in many different ways. MI theory helps educators create an individualized learning environment. The sidebar ["The Seven Intelligences"] is a thumbnail sketch of the seven intelligences.

Understanding How MI Theory Applies to Your Teaching

MI theory offers ESL/EFL teachers a way to examine their best teaching techniques and strategies in light of human differences. There are two important steps to

---

The Seven Intelligences

Verbal/Linguistic Intelligence: The ability to use words effectively both orally and in writing. Sample skills are remembering information, convincing others to help, and talking about language itself.

Musical Intelligence: Sensitivity to rhythm, pitch, and melody. Sample skills are recognizing simple songs and being able to vary speed, tempo, and rhythm in simple melodies.

Logical/Mathematical Intelligence: The ability to use numbers effectively and reason well. Sample skills are understanding the basic properties of numbers, principles of cause and effect, and the ability to predict.

Spatial/Visual Intelligence: Sensitivity to form, space, color, line, and shape. Sample skills include the ability to graphically represent visual or spatial ideas.

Bodily/Kinesthetic Intelligence: The ability to use the body to express ideas and feelings and to solve problems. Sample skills are coordination, flexibility, speed, and balance.

Interpersonal Intelligence: The ability to understand another person's moods, feelings, motivations, and intentions. Sample skills are responding effectively to other people, problem solving, and resolving conflict.

Intrapersonal Intelligence: The ability to understand yourself, your strengths, weaknesses, moods, desires, and intentions. Sample skills are understanding how one is similar to or different from others, reminding oneself to do something, knowing about oneself as a language learner, and knowing how to handle one's feelings.

---

follow in understanding how MI theory applies to TESL/TEFL. The first step is to identify the activities that we frequently use in our classes and categorize them. Which ones help develop verbal/linguistic intelligence? musical intelligence? logical/mathematical intelligence? When I did this for my own teaching, I came up with such items as the following. (This list is by no means exhaustive.)

Verbal/Linguistic Intelligence
note-taking
listening to lectures
reading books
storytelling
debates

Musical Intelligence
singing
playing recorded music
playing live music (piano, guitar)
Jazz Chants

Logical/Mathematical Intelligence
science demonstrations and experiments
logic puzzles and games
story problems with numbers
logical/sequential presentation of
    subject matter

Spatial/Visual Intelligence
using charts and grids
videos, slides, movies
using art
using graphic organizers

Bodily/Kinesthetic Intelligence
hands-on activities
field trips
role-plays

Interpersonal Intelligence
pair work or peer teaching
board games
group brainstorming
group problem solving
project work

Intrapersonal Intelligence
activities with a self-evaluation
    component
interest centers
options for homework
personal journal keeping

Once we come to an understanding of where our activities fit into the multiple intelligence taxonomy, the next step is to track what we are doing in our lesson planning and teaching. I used the accompanying TESL/TEFL Multiple Intelligences Weekly Checklist to help me do this. I used at least one form for each class for each week and tracked my classes for 2 weeks.

My analysis for the 2-week period indicated that I had not included any activities for logical/mathematical or musical intelligences. The other categories were quite evenly distributed. There were now two options available to me. The most obvious option, of course, was to expand classroom activities to include the neglected intelligences. The other option was simply to use the exercise to come to an awareness of how MI theory could inform language teaching and learning.

Teaching Language Learners About MI Theory

The more aware students become of their own intelligences and how they work, the more they will know how to use that intelligence to access the necessary information/knowledge from a lesson. In order to help students connect their daily activities to MI theory, I employ an inventory (see "Student-Generated Inventory for Secondary-Level and Young Adult Learners"). (I have several inventories: this one is for secondary-level and young adult ESL learners. There are two more, one for young children and one for nonacademic adults.) My students participated in the design of this inventory, which comprises statements they gave me when I asked them how they used the different intelligences in their daily lives. Over time, I collected the statements and eventually created the survey.

I seldom use an inventory in its entirety, as there is too much to digest. In using the inventory, I feature one intelligence during the week. The week's lessons begin with the inventory. The students work independently on the lists and then share with partners. There is always much animated talk during the sharing portion of the activity. They are also eager to share their discoveries with me and the larger group. As a follow up to this activity, I ask the students to help identify the classroom activities for the week that support the intelligence being focused upon. This type of activity is another way in which the students extend their understanding of how MI theory relates to their daily lives in the academic setting.

In addition to making use of this inventory for teaching students about MI theory, I have devised a large number of activities that are designed to help students recognize the seven intelligences in themselves and others. Below, I describe one of the activities I use and how students react to them.

Intelligence Problems

There are two objectives for this activity related to solving problems. The first objective is to learn to use the seven intelligences in problem situations and the second is to discover that using different intelligences creates a deeper, richer, and more varied approach to learning.

In this activity, the first step is to conduct a short discussion about the problems students have in their own lives. I asked the students to help me make a list of problems and to write the list on

TESL/TEFL Multiple Intelligences Weekly Checklist

Course_____   From_____ To_____

	Monday	Tuesday	Wednesday	Thursday	Friday
Verbal/Linguistic					
Musical					
Logical/Mathematical					
Spatial/Visual					
Bodily/Kinesthetic					
Interpersonal					
Intrapersonal					

the board. Then, I ask them to choose one of the problems. Next to this problem, I write this question: What would you do to solve the problem? I number from one to five. The group as a whole must think of at least five different solutions to the problem. Most of my students have found this difficult at first. Often they see only one way to solve the problem. Because not all students will see the solution in quite the same way, alternatives are eventually generated. For example, when given the problem of a stolen bicycle found in the possession of a neighborhood child who claimed the bike was hers, several solutions were possible:

> Go to the police.
> Take the bicycle back.
> Go talk to the child.
> Talk to the child's parents.
> Give the bike to the child.
> Write down clearly why you know the bicycle is yours.

Some of the students told me after class how surprised they were at some of the solutions. At first, they thought that their classmates were simply wrong. Later, they came to see other solutions as possible alternatives. Once students understand the idea of multiple solutions, you can divide them into small groups and give each group a problem handout. Their task is to find seven solutions to the problems and to identify the different intelligences used. Allow time for each team to share and discuss their different solutions. My experience has been that this activity encourages students to offer opinions and ideas, so there is always ample discussion and talk.

Problems for Grades 3–6
List seven ideas. What could you do to help if someone has . . .
> lost money?
> broken a toy?

Problems for Secondary Students
List seven ideas.
What could you do if you . . .
> had a fight with a good friend?
> are accused of doing something you didn't do?
> have run out of allowance money and you need money for an important date?

Problems for Adults
List seven ideas.
What could you do if . . .
> you are being blamed for something you didn't do?
> you had an accident with a friend's car?

you find out your friend has a life-threatening disease?

Applying MI Theory in ESL/EFL Lesson Planning

There are four stages to lessons that teach with multiple intelligences. The developmental sequence (Lazear, 1991) is as follows:

Stage 1: Awaken the Intelligence: A particular intelligence can be activated or triggered through exercises and activities that make use of sensory bases (the five senses), intuition, or metacognition.

Stage 2: Amplify the Intelligence: This part of the lesson focuses on improving and strengthening the intelligence. Like any skill, intelligences improve with use and practice.

Stage 3: Teach for/with the Intelligence: Structure lessons for multiple intelligences, emphasizing and using different intelligences in the teaching/learning process.

Stage 4: Transfer of the Intelligence: This stage is concerned with going beyond the classroom, with the integration of intelligence into daily living, such as solving problems and challenges in the real world.

All of these stages need to be present in an ESL/EFL lesson designed to emphasize the different ways of knowing. The model activities that follow illustrate what you can do at each of the four stages. The activities themselves can promote more than one intelligence.

Stage 1: Awaken the Intelligence

Object Riddles (Intelligences: Verbal/Linguistic, Interpersonal)

This lesson begins with a riddle or brain teaser. Verbal intelligence immediately kicks into gear, searching for clues within the linguistic structure of the riddle or brain teaser, trying to make connections between the riddle and prior knowledge and looking for word associations.

I begin by introducing the idea of a riddle or brain teaser to the entire class. After the students form small groups, I give each group a series of riddles, such as the one that follows (Christison & Bassano, 1995).

> I am both the longest and the shortest, the fastest and the slowest. I am the thing that people waste the most; yet, they need me more than they need anything else. (time)

The students should be given 5 to 10 minutes to work together to guess the answers. The small group usually starts slowly. Students need time to think and to process the information. Don't worry if the students don't say much at first. Ask each group to appoint a secretary to record their ideas. This technique encourages communication among group members. After the small-group working sessions, conduct a large-group brainstorm on possible answers to the riddles. I usually write the answers on the board. Groups will often come up with answers to the riddles that make sense, but aren't the traditional answers. I ask the groups to explain their answers as best they can and accept them. When I use this activity, my students usually volunteer riddles of their own.

Stage 2: Amplify the Intelligence

Describing Objects (Intelligences: Verbal/Linguistic, Interpersonal, Musical, Logical/Mathematical, Bodily/Kinesthetic)

Practice with the awakened intelligence will improve it. The intelligence will become stronger, students will become more familiar with it, and they will begin to understand how it works. In this activity, I give students a formula for describing common objects. I first conduct a short brainstorming session by asking the students to help me describe a common object such as a pencil, eraser, book, pencil sharpener, or clock. I remind the students that in order to describe something, they must learn to recognize its properties—properties of sight, sound, smell, touch, and use. I ask them how many of these properties they included in their description. It's important for students to understand that using properties in describing objects is a logical formula that they can follow.

At first the students seem a little embarrassed, but once they realize that everyone is humming at the same time and that they need only hum softly, they relax.

Next, I ask the students to think of objects they have with them. Then, I ask them to answer the following questions about their objects, but not to show the objects to each other.

1. How does your object look? Color? Size? Shape?
2. Does your object make a sound?
3. How does your object smell?
4. How does it feel?
5. What is it used for?

When they have answered the questions, I ask them to get into small groups. I do this by giving them a piece of paper with the title to a common song written on it. I make certain these are songs the students will know. Usually they are songs that I have either taught in class or know that another teacher has used. I ask the students to hum the tune to the song. Their task is to walk around and find the other people who are humming their same song. At first the students seem a little embarrassed, but once they realize that everyone is humming at the same time and that they need only hum softly, they relax. Once students find their partners, their task is to describe their objects by giving their partners the answers to the questions. When they have given answers to all of the questions, their partners should be able to easily guess the name of the object. Students seem to enjoy this activity immensely. They enjoy describing their objects because the logical formula gives them confidence, and they enjoy listening and guessing because their curiosity is piqued.

Stage 3: Teach for/with the Intelligence

What Am I? (Intelligences: Verbal/Linguistic, Bodily/Kinesthetic, Interpersonal, Logical/Mathematical)

In this activity, each student can use the intellectual skill for describing objects that was taught in Stage 2. I prepare 20 (or more) index cards, with the names of animals or objects written on the cards. The names can range from easy or common—*tree, grass, cat, dog*—to more difficult and uncommon—*juicer, backrest, penguin, cockatoo*. I then tape a card to each student's back. It's a good idea to get student helpers to assist you. Students do not know what is on the cards taped to their backs. Once all of the students have a card, they can mill around, showing their cards to other students and moving from partner to partner until they have spoken with five students. With the partners, students will ask and answer questions.

Each student will ask yes/no questions about the object or animal on

---

Student-Generated Inventory for Secondary-Level and Young Adult Learners

Directions: Rank each statement 0, 1, or 2. Write 0 if you disagree with the statement. Write 2 if you strongly agree. Write 1 if you are somewhere in between.

Verbal/Linguistic Intelligence
____1. I like to read books, magazines, and newspapers.
____2. I consider myself a good writer.
____3. I like to tell jokes and stories.
____4. I can remember people's names easily.
____5. I like to recite tongue twisters.
____6. I have a good vocabulary in my native language.

Musical Intelligence
____1. I can hum the tunes to many songs.
____2. I am a good singer.
____3. I play a musical instrument or sing in a choir.
____4. I can tell when music sounds off-key.
____5. I often tap rhythmically on the table or desk.
____6. I often sing songs.

Logical/Mathematical Intelligence
____1. I often do arithmetic in my head.
____2. I am good at chess and/or checkers.
____3. I like to put things into categories.
____4. I like to play number games.
____5. I love to figure out how my computer works.
____6. I ask many questions about how things work.

Spatial/Visual Intelligence
____1. I can read maps easily.
____2. I enjoy art activities.
____3. I draw well.
____4. Movies and slides really help me learn new information.
____5. I love books with pictures.
____6. I enjoy putting puzzles together.

Bodily/Kinesthetic Intelligence
____1. It is hard for me to sit quietly for a long time.
____2. It is easy for me to follow exactly what other people do.
____3. I am good at sewing, woodworking, building, or mechanics.
____4. I am good at sports.
____5. I enjoy working with clay.
____6. I enjoy running and jumping.

Interpersonal Intelligence
____1. I am often the leader in activities.
____2. I enjoy talking to my friends.
____3. I often help my friends.
____4. My friends often talk to me about their problems.
____5. I have many friends.
____6. I am a member of several clubs.

Intrapersonal Intelligence
____1. I go to the movies alone.
____2. I go to the library alone to study.
____3. I can tell you some things I am good at doing.
____4. I like to spend time alone.
____5. My friends find some of my actions strange sometimes.
____6. I learn from my mistakes.

---

the cards, such as: *Is it as small as a dime store novel? Is it soft? hard?* The task is to ask questions about the object in such a way that other students will give you the information you need in order to know what is on your card. I ask the students to sit down once they find out what is on their cards. After about 10 minutes, I ask the students who are still milling around to return to their seats.

In the large-group discussion that follows, students always mention how important it is to sequence the questions so that they make a logical progression. Students who had difficulty in

discovering what was on their card come to realize that their trouble stemmed from lack of a formula or system of discovery (adapted from Christison & Bassano, 1995).

Stage 4: Transfer the Intelligence

Reflecting (Intelligences: Verbal/Linguistic, Intrapersonal, Interpersonal)

There are two goals for the transfer part of a lesson. The first goal is to help the students reflect on their learning in the previous stages. The second goal is to help the students make the lesson content relevant to their lives outside the classroom. Below are suggestions for achieving these goals.

I give the students the following questions and ask them to work alone and give me thoughtful answers. When they have finished, I ask them to find a partner and take turns sharing. In order to facilitate the sharing, I put the questions on the board: *What parts of the lesson were easy for you? What was difficult? What was fun? What did you learn? What did you learn about yourself? About your classmates? How will you use these ideas in your life outside of this classroom?*

After the partner sharing, I usually conduct either a large-group discussion or spend a few minutes with each pair, finding out what they learned. When I tried this activity recently with secondary school students, they were very thoughtful and insightful about their own learning experiences and about their use of the intelligences. Most of them knew what they didn't know. They felt the process of sharing this information with their partners and teacher was helpful. Some of them were unsure of how to learn what they didn't know, but they received good suggestions from others. They also learned that they weren't the only ones who were having trouble. They commented on how the logical step-by-step process could be applied to other classes. I worked with the students to create the following list.

We can use the logical step-by-step process for . . .

1. recording observations for the theater class.
2. looking at and analyzing an object in science class.
3. looking at ourselves and our responses in the communication class.
4. writing descriptive paragraphs for our writing class.
5. writing about a cooperative experience in our college survival class.

In summary, I was surprised at the insightful comments and the sophistication of the ideas. The students told me how much they had enjoyed this lesson, how much about themselves they felt they had learned from it, and how beneficial it had been for their language learning.

I realize that no two ESL/EFL teachers are alike and no two ESL/EFL teachers will apply MI theory in their classrooms in quite the same way. Some of you may have read this article because you are looking for an exact plan, some of you may wish to tinker with the ideas I present here, some of you may be looking for a catalyst. If you began this article knowing nothing about the subject, I hope the article has whetted your appetite to learn more about MI. If you were already familiar with the topic, I hope it has given you a few new ideas to work with. Jean Houston's (1987) comment, "Never has the vision of what human beings can be been more remarkable" takes on an even more profound meaning as we consider Gardner's theory. I hope you will join me in embracing a language classroom that continues to develop a vision for expanding intelligent behavior.

References

Christison, M. A. (1995, October). *Multiple intelligences in the second language classroom.* TeleTESOL Conference, Alexandria, VA.

Christison, M. A., & Bassano, S. (1995). *Look who's talking!* Burlingame, CA: Alta.

Gardner, H. (1983). *Frames of mind: The theory of multiple intelligences.* New York: Basic Books.

Houston, J. (1987). *The search for the beloved: Journeys in sacred psychology.* Los Angeles, CA: J. P. Tarcher.

Lazear, D. (1991). *Seven ways of teaching.* Palatine, IL: IRI/Skylight Training and Publishing.

Author

Mary Ann Christison is Professor in the Department of ESL, and Director of the International Center, at Snow College, in Ephraim, Utah, in the U.S. She has published widely and is President-Elect of TESOL.

The Social Studies Video Project

A Holistic Approach for Teaching Linguistically and Culturally Diverse Students.

INEZ A. HEATH

The increase in limited-English proficient (LEP) students in today's classrooms is presenting unique academic and social challenges in education. Teachers who lack experience and training in working with linguistically and culturally diverse students must make a commitment to address these students' needs by learning strategies that can fulfill the dual function of presenting academic content while also providing opportunities for the limited-English proficient students to develop their language skills naturally. To this end, diversity in our classrooms represents opportunities for expanding ideas, for learning about language, and for cultural exchange among students. The cultural and racially diverse classroom is a natural resource, yet few teachers realize the educational benefits that can be attained through understanding how diversity enhances the learning experience, especially when teachers are striving to develop a global perspective.

The demand on teachers working

INEZ A. HEATH is an associate professor of social studies and multicultural education in the Department of Early Childhood and Reading Education at Valdosta State University in Valdosta, Georgia.

with linguistically diverse students in the middle grades (grades 4–8) is further compounded by having to address issues related to social awareness, prejudice, and peer acceptance among the students, in the process of implementing the curriculum. Allen and Stevens (1984) noted that changes among students in middle grades become evident as their interpersonal relationships take on new dimensions, shifting the base of affiliation from teacher and family to the peer group. This shift in affiliation is also affected by cultural values, as students' perceptions of themselves and others become entangled in issues of cultural and racial identity.

The social studies video project discussed in this article provides evidence to support the use of technology that is student centered and focused on developing interpersonal and academic linguistic proficiency. Furthermore, this technology is effective in enhancing the learning experiences of all students, regardless of their linguistic and cultural backgrounds. Such opportunities provide a learning environment that is conducive to the promotion of tolerance and understanding among various ethnic and racial groups.

Many technologies exist to reinforce and enhance learning. The video is one

option that offers many exciting possibilities for middle-grade teachers working with linguistically diverse student groups. The opportunity for students to study academic content by researching issues and topics that are relevant and meaningful to them encourages them to use their natural sense of inquiry in the learning process. This leads to linguistic, academic, and social growth. Video technology can be an especially effective tool for teaching linguistically diverse groups because it can be used to develop informal and formal language skills within the academic content. It is also a comfortable and familiar medium for all students.

The teaching of social studies content poses many problems for teachers of LEP students. The difficulties lie in the students' inability to compete academically because of problems in comprehending text, synthesizing information, and expressing ideas orally in discussion. It is little wonder that LEP students often lose interest in these subjects as the demand for cognitive academic language skills increases. Langston (1995) suggested that with determination and informed effort, teachers can meet the challenge of making social studies at grade level comprehensible and accessible to their limited-

From *The Social Studies*, Vol. 87, No. 3, May/June 1996, pp. 106-112. © 1996 by the Helen Dwight Read Education Foundation.

English proficient students. Langston noted that history textbooks often present LEP students with more information than they can process. She refers to this as information overload. Because this experience is especially discouraging to students who have linguistic difficulties, she recommends that social studies be approached at three levels of intensity. The first, Level A, represents the "big picture" or the main idea. Level B delves further into the who, why, where, and what; and finally Level C considers the elaboration of the ideas through anecdotes, primary source information, and multimedia experiences.

To implement an approach such as Langston's, teachers must understand the process that LEP students undergo in their transition from their native language (L1) to their second language (L2). The teachers should also be aware of how the LEP students' life experiences differ from those of students born in the United States. Inquiring about these experiences can help the teacher include the student in the learning process and give him or her a sense of being involved in the topics the class is studying. Teachers also need to allow time for the LEP students to "make sense" of the information being presented. By encouraging the participation of LEP students in the process of studying a social studies topic, the teacher creates an opportunity for enriching the learning experience of all students in the class.

The Second-Language Acquisition Process

The acquisition of a second language is a difficult and complex process. Of critical importance are two distinctions that are involved in this process, the distinctions that relate to the function and purpose of language. The first involves functional language—that which is used in daily interpersonal communication; the second, more challenging to the learner and the teacher, is cognitive academic language—the language that is essential for success in the academic setting.

I emphasize these two distinctions in second-language acquisition because many of the frustrations a teacher experiences when teaching the content of a subject can be directly attributed to linguistic factors. The teacher's lack of knowledge about these critical factors can be detrimental to a student's success in learning the content. Therefore, every effort should be made to educate teachers about these differences.

Collier (1995) explains that second-language acquisition is a complex phenomenon and a lifelong developmental process. The second-language learning process is similar to the first-language acquisition process. Collier stresses that the acquisition of a language, whether first or second, is a dynamic, creative, innate process that is developed through contextual, meaningful activities that focus on language. Because no two students are at the same stage of second-language development, regardless of the similarity of their learning experiences, the teacher must often deal with individual problems that only become evident when the LEP students are challenged by content that is rich in high cognitive demand. The teacher who understands the nature of language acquisition can incorporate strategies into the content that will help individual students develop both cognitively and linguistically.

The terms *basic-interpersonal communication skills* (BICS) and *cognitive academic linguistic proficiency* (CALP) were introduced by the applied linguists Cummins and Swain (1986) and Cummins (1991) to distinguish linguistic proficiency levels of non-native English-speaking students, who were assessed for their ability to function in their second language within the school and the nonschool (work or social) settings.

Basic interpersonal communication skills, which also include basic communication within the social or peer group, apply to getting things done. Many individuals, both non-native and native English speakers can function and succeed comfortably at this level. However, in order to meet more rigorous cognitive demands within the academic setting, a person must develop his

or her language skills to higher and more complex levels. In developing research skills, for example, the individual must be able to find information that is imbedded in text, make inferences, synthesize information, evaluate various opinions, make decisions, and finally, present the research in the second language.

Consequently, the need to focus on cognitive academic linguistic proficiency within the content becomes an essential part of the teaching process. Teachers should not, however, disregard the importance of social language. Collier (1995) writes that "a good teacher includes social and academic language in every lesson." New knowledge, she says, is developed and applied through active tasks that stimulate cognitive and academic development. Because we are unclear about how communication strategies are developed, Dornyei (1995) suggests that teachers consider a broad spectrum of techniques in developing communication strategies, focusing on social and real-life experiences as part of the second-language acquisition process. The importance of balancing social and cognitive academic language encourages formal and informal language learning to evolve, which provides the skills necessary for success in life.

Ramirez (1992) found that early exit from bilingual/ESL instruction leads to difficulties in content learning. Collier (1992) emphasized the importance of teachers encouraging their LEP students to maintain their native language through interaction with family in the home. She noted that teachers should continue to reinforce linguistic concepts in the process of learning the second language within the content. In his observation of English-only classroom teachers working with recently mainstreamed LEP students, Ramirez found that teachers were not as active in involving their LEP students in higher-order language development skills. Instead they consistently used listening and basic recall in their interaction with those students. Ramirez and Collier's research supports the need for ESL strategies that develop higher-level thinking to be implemented with bilingual students for at least six years before the students are fully mainstreamed into an English-only classroom.

The literature is replete with examples of successful approaches for teaching content. Salient to the success of a program is its consideration of the "whole" individual as a learner. Such programs involve learning that requires social interaction and focuses on making learning relevant. Open-ended questions are also encouraged. These types of strategies are helpful in satisfying individual academic needs and abilities, thus allowing for flexibility and student-directed learning.

Developing Linguistic and Social Skills through Videos

The importance of technology is emphasized by Collier (1995), Gaer and Ferenz (1993), O'Neil (1993), and Penfield (1987). They state that working on the computer or passively watching a film or video is not an effective use of technology. Technology must be used to integrate learning while it stimulates students' interest and helps them to find meaning and relevance in what they are studying.

The success of videos as a medium for teaching and learning is dependent on one's ability to entertain and communicate effectively to the intended audience (Worth 1991 and Winston and Keydell 1984). Through the video medium, ideas are naturally developed and communicated. Hess and Penfield-Jasper (1995) noted that the visual medium attracts and engages. It is especially appropriate for LEP students because it gives them the "push" they need to become committed to learning.

Worth (1984) suggests that involvement in video productions can provide us with several options and some unique advantages for communication that are not possible or as likely with other media. For example, a video

• provides a way to teach and reinforce specific concepts. As a natural language teaching situation, it presents opportunities for clarifying questions that are relevant to grammar and syntax usage.

• provides a sense of "being there" and sharing in the activity. Even though we are sitting in our classroom, we still are somehow transferred to the experience, especially when the students are viewing themselves or their peers.

• provides a sense of timeliness. Videos that are developed by students are current and are live sources of information.

• provides action, accompanied by color and sounds, that can enhance and involve the viewer in what is happening and what is being said.

Today video cameras and VCRs are part of the common media equipment that is available in most schools. The problem is that most teachers are unaware of the value of this equipment as an effective instructional resource. The teacher's awareness and understanding of the possibilities of how academic content can be presented through use of this resource are the magic aspects of this medium.

In the following section, I will describe a social studies video project that involved my fourth- and fifth-grade intensive-English students in a cooperative effort with the fifth-grade students from the mainstream classes. The four-week project had many positive results. Among them was its value in affecting changes in attitudes among the different racial and ethnic groups in our school. It also elicited a genuine sense of understanding about culture and respect for others' values.

Description of the Project

Participants in the project, entitled "This Is My Flag," included eleven limited-English-proficient fifth-grade students, whose linguistic levels varied from low to moderate proficiency. These students had been in my content-based sheltered English class for periods ranging from six months to one year. The eleven students had come from seven countries. These students worked with twelve African American students, one Native American, and five Anglo-European white students who had been selected by their teachers from the mainstream fifth-grade classes.

From the planning stage to final product, the project took four weeks to complete. When it was completed, we presented lessons to other classes, using the video to teach world cultures from a primary perspective. The video was also catalogued in our media center and became a resource for teachers and students.

LEP students working together to gather material for their video presentation.

In planning the video production, members of the initial design team (seven students from each country) met with me to plan the project. Each team member was part of one of the cooperative groups. As experts and primary sources of information about the country being researched, the design team had the responsibility of organizing and listing areas they felt would be interesting and important to discuss in the video.

The other students who were in the cooperative groups gathered resources and information on their group's respective country. The groups were formed according to the members' interest in the country and their native-English proficiency. One of the primary objectives of the project was to develop, through research, the oral and written communication skills of all the students. Their success was based on their ability to produce a video segment on their country that was accurate, well written, and interesting to the students.

Each team consisted of four students. At least one student—the content expert—was a native of the country being studied. At least one student was selected on the basis of his or her language-arts skills and had been recommended by the mainstream classroom teacher. The two other students in the group were selected because of their interest in the topic and their ability to use language effectively. In some cases, two content experts from the country being researched worked on one team.

By using an approach similar to Langston's three-tiers strategy, working with basic knowledge, and working through the where, why, when, and so forth that lead to higher levels of understanding, all students on the teams were able to engage in the learning process with confidence. I believe that Langston's (1995) approach serves as a good model for cooperative research projects because it allows students at varying linguistic levels to communicate ideas and encourages thinking that moves from a lower to higher order. In using this approach to develop the videos, I found that students were more likely to ask open-ended questions and to apply ideas that had relevance and meaning to their own experiences.

The technological aspect of the production was also very important. This provided the students with a natural opportunity to use language in a social, as well as an academic, context in which they discussed the issues and the content they had researched. All students were involved in the making of the video.

Observations

As the process developed, students became interested in other related areas of social studies, such as economics, government policies, social mores and traditions, art, and music. Students in the groups asked questions and tried to learn more about the topics from the experts who were natives of the countries being studied. Parents of the LEP students and parents of the native English-speaking students from the mainstream classroom became involved with the project. Some of the younger siblings of the LEP students, who were in the intensive English program, were also included in the video production. The students who were involved in the process shared their enthusiasm with their peers and teachers in other classes.

To confirm what they were learning from their research, the native English speakers asked many questions of the "experts" representing the various countries. The students used a variety of communication strategies in the process of developing their video presentations. These strategies were as basic as drawing diagrams and pointing to pictures and maps; talking slowly, and using body language. Some students depended on bilingual dictionaries in an attempt to introduce and define new vocabulary. Other communication strategies included reinforcing through repetition and questioning and negotiating for meaning in conversation. The students who had been in the intensive English program for a longer period of time and were more bilingual acted as translators for their less-proficient peers, yet another way for ideas to develop. All students in the intensive English program had enough functional English to communicate basic ideas. The use of these strategies allowed for the natural development of language and expanded the non-native speakers' vocabulary, grammar, and syntax.

Because the emphasis was on the communication and clarification of ideas, everyone was benefiting linguistically from this experience. Because the native English speakers had the responsibility of being the "language experts," they also became more conscious of the correct usage and pronunciation of English. They became actively involved in teaching the non-native speakers. Through this experience, many realized the value of language as a critical tool for communication. The students understood, and were more sensitive to, the difficulties that non-English-speaking students were experiencing.

Alley (1992), a middle-school media specialist, found that learning about media production involved her students as active learners in a holistic process. Our video project also reflected this, because students were totally immersed in the process. They were empowered by their ability to influence and control their own learning. Through the video experience, they became the creators who shaped their product.

The program followed a show-and-tell format, with the students sharing information, comparing and contrasting life and customs in their respective countries with those of the United States, and sharing language differences that might be interesting to the audience. To introduce themselves to the others in the school, the students used flags as a colorful way to invite interest and encourage curiosity about their countries. Figure 1 provides a brief outline of the program.

The opportunity to observe students as they worked together, researched information, and presented their findings on camera provided new insights into how the students developed their thinking skills and the process of expanding language to articulate ideas related to the content. Throughout the project, the students showed genuine interest in learning the content and an eagerness to share their knowledge with others through the video. They strived to be clear in communicating and were open to suggestions from teachers and peers.

Summarizing the Process

Although the assessment of this process was informal, it provided a great deal of diagnostic information, as well as opportunities for clarification and remediation. In spite of this, the teachers with whom I discussed our project expressed concern about how to grade students. When asked if they would use our video as a resource in their classes, many said that they would. They thought, however, that students would more likely prefer professionally developed commercial products to ours.

Students involved in making the video were surveyed, along with all fourth and fifth graders who viewed the video. Overwhelmingly the responses from those students were favorable and supportive of the video as a resource. Contrary to the teachers' beliefs, the students showed preference for the class-made materials.

Many students remarked that they enjoyed learning about these countries from students in their school, and they liked being able to ask them questions about the things they said on the videos. Students were also fascinated by the many personal things that had relevance to them, such as information about play, school, clothing, language, traditions, and family. They felt a sense of connection with these "far-away" places.

Figure 2 shows the results of our survey of the students. The percentages on questions 1 through 4 are based on the total number of the students who viewed the video and those involved in the video project, a total of 63 students. Question 5 was answered only by those involved in the production of the video, 28 students. Several of the native–English-speaking students expressed interest in learning other languages, something they had never considered prior to this experience. The project provided

the students with an opportunity for sharing and learning from one another.

Building Understanding and Tolerance

An incident that occurred in the beginning of the year was the motivating factor in my developing this activity and involved the native–English-speaking students making fun of the languages and appearance of the students in the intensive English program. This experience was evidence of the students' lack of exposure to other cultures. The animosity between students from the two groups was especially evident in mainstream classes, such as music, art, physical education, and in the lunchroom.

The experience of having to work together to develop the video instilled pride and encouraged the native–English-speaking students to take leadership roles in accepting and welcoming the students from the intensive English program into their social group. Those who watched the video in their social studies classes were intent on the information that the students were present-

FIGURE 1—Program Outline for "This Is My Flag"

Country	Topics/Concepts	Language I	Culture	Visual Aids
Iceland—Symbolism and colors of the flag	• Midnight Sun • living in a cold climate • transportation • fishing industry	• greetings • comparing English to Icelandic	• foods • school • recreation	• clothes • salted fish dish • pictures taken during different seasons
Japan–Symbolism of the flag	• maps • cars • working and corporations	• greetings • bowing • family • teachers • familiar foods	• tea ceremony • origami	• tea set • kimono and shoes
Peru–Symbolism of the flag	• Incas • maps • climate • Andes mountains	comparing Ketchua and Spanish objects found in ruins	comparing people of the cities with the people living in the mountains	• photographs of Cuzco and Machu Pichu • dish made with potatoes
Commonwealth of Puerto Rico—Symbolism of the flag	• part of the U.S. • island • bilingualism • government • education • maps	• island • Spanish • "Spanglish" • family • Spanish words for American holidays	life on a tropical paradise	• rice for dinner and rice for dessert • pictures and art from Loiza Aldea
Poland—Symbolism of the flag	• democracy in Poland • Lech Walesa	• poem: How Polish sounds different from English • words similar to English	• religion • the Pope • families in Poland • Christmas	• pictures from school and family gatherings
Saudi Arabia—Symbolism of the flag	• maps • the Middle East • Oil • gender roles	• Arabic sounds and script • writing • math problems	• religion • how to act when visiting Saudi Arabia • Ramadan	• pictures of Mecca • clothing • school • school books • math problems • money • toothbrush
Thailand Symbolism of the flag	• maps • temples • monarchy	• Thai words • Thai names	• religions • good luck • harvest rice festival	• pictures of costumes and rice noodles

FIGURE 2—Survey

1. When watching video instructional programs, I prefer watching

a. myself	49%
b. people I don't know	8%
c. adults and teachers	3%
d. other kids like myself	40%

2. I feel I learned more from

a. the educational program on culture from around the world	47%
b. the students' presentations on countries of the students in the intensive English class	53%

3. Whose presentation do you think you understood better?

a. the presentation made by fifth-grade students and students in the intensive English class in "This is My Flag"	68%
b. the video "Faces of Culture"	32%

4. I feel that being videotaped is

a. a lot of fun	81%
b. something I do not like it	9%
c. OK, sometimes	10%

5. I prefer learning in school

a. by watching videos and reading books and doing worksheets	32%
b. by making our own videotapes and teaching others	58%
c. it doesn't make any difference to me.	10%

ing. They actively participated in repeating words in the students' native languages. Because their friends were involved in the process, they too wanted to be involved in the next video production.

The project was catalogued as a library resource and was used the following year. It also served as a model for developing other resources for teaching about culture. New students entering the intensive English program, and their parents, also viewed the video as part of their orientation. The overwhelming response from parents and school board members, who viewed the video program at a Parent Teacher Association meeting, was also positive.

Learning to work with others requires the ability to communicate across linguistic, social, and cultural barriers. A teamwork approach encourages the crossing of such barriers. Like any method, however, it is only effective when everyone is involved in the process as well as the product. Teachers must be able to facilitate the integration of strategies and content so that all students can benefit through their participation. Adams, Carlson, and Hann (1992) realized the value of a video for integrating technology, scholarship, and interpersonal development and viewed it as the "winning combination that can boost our educational and societal future" (165).

Given the cultural, linguistic, and racial diversity of the students in our classrooms today, it is important for teachers to consider the value in developing academic language skills within the content while also emphasizing language that focuses on communicating and developing social skills that have practical application for future success in society and the workplace. By exploring the various technological resources that allow students to practice their language skills and apply their content knowledge in a natural, open-ended manner, teachers are also providing a nurturing environment for promoting empathy, respect, and tolerance of racial and ethnic diversity.

REFERENCES

Adams, D., H. Carlson, and M. Hamm. 1990. *Cooperative learning and educational media.* Englewood Cliffs, N. J.: Educational Technology Publications.

Alley, L. 1992: Become the catalyst so that school and camera work converge. *Florida Media Quarterly* 17(1): 18-19.

Allen, M., and R. Stevens. 1994. *Middle grades social studies: Teaching and learning for active and responsible citizenship.* Boston: Allyn and Bacon.

Collier, V. P. 1992. A synthesis of studies examining long-term language minority student data on academic achievement. *Bilingual Research Journal.* 16 (1 and 2): 187-212.

———. 1995. *Promoting academic success for ESL students: Understanding second language acquisition for school.* Elizabeth, N.J.: NJTESOL-BE.

Cummins, J. 1992. Bilingual education and English immersion: The Ramirez report in theoretical perspective. *Bilingual Research Journal* 16(1 and 2): 91-104.

Cummins, J., and M. Swain. 1987. *Bilingualism and education: Aspects of theory, research and practice.* London: Longman.

Dornyei, Z. 1995. On the teachability of communication strategies. *TESOL Quarterly* 29(1): 55-85.

Gaer, S., and K. Ferenz. 1993. Telecommunications and interactive writing projects. *CAELL Journal* 4(2): 2-5.

Hess, N., and S. Penfield-Jasper. 1995. A blending of media for extensive reading. *TESOL Journal* 4(1): 7-11.

Langston, L. 1995. Helping students make sense of social studies. Ideas for excellence: The Newsletter for ESL/Bilingual Education 3(3): 1-3.

O'Niel, J. 1993. Using technology to support authentic learning. ASCD Update 35(8)1: 4-5.

Penfield, J. 1987. The media: Catalysts for communicative language learning. Reading, Mass.: Addison Wesley.

Ramirez, J. D. 1992. Executive summary. Bilingual Research Journal 16(1 and 2): 1-62.

Winston, B., and R. Keydel. 1986. Working with video: A comprehensive guide to the world of video production. New York: Knowledge Industry Publications.

Worth, R. 1981. Creating cooperative audio-visual presentations: How to commission and manage successful projects. New York: Quorum Books.

Unit 5

Unit Selections

19. **Alternative Assessment: Responses to Commonly Asked Questions,**
Ana Huerta-Macías
20. **Moving toward Authentic Assessment,** J. Michael O'Malley and Lorraine Valdez Pierce
21. **Portfolio Assessment in Second Language Teacher Education,** Karen E. Johnson
22. **Assessing Integrated Language and Content Instruction,** Deborah J. Short

Key Points to Consider

❖ What challenges do we face when assessing English-language learners?

❖ How does English-language proficiency affect assessment of content knowledge?

❖ How can we best assess the language proficiency and content knowledge of English-language learners?

❖ What factors should be considered when developing an evaluation program for English-language learners?

 **Links** — **www.dushkin.com/online/**

23. **Dr. Helen Barrett's Bookmarks**
http://transition.alaska.edu/www/Portfolios/bookmarks.html
24. **Performance and Portfolio Assessment for Language Minority Students**
http://www.ncbe.gwu.edu/ncbepubs/pigs/pig9.htm
25. **Portfolio Assessment**
http://www.eduplace.com/rdg/res/literacy/assess6.html

These sites are annotated on pages 4 and 5.

Assessment and evaluation of student achievement is an integral component of the teaching learning process. Assessment is how we measure what a student has learned or the effectiveness of our teaching. Formal assessment usually takes the form of standardized tests in which short answers or multiple-choice formats are used. Textbook tests most often employ this approach. Alternative or authentic assessment, however, which is a holistic and open-ended approach, emphasizes the application of learning within the natural environment.

Since authentic or alternative assessment is differently structured, it is very important that the teacher be clear about the objectives and the expected outcomes. For example, a kindergarten child who can tie a shoe on demand is providing information about the child's fine-motor development as well as the ability to learn a basic procedure that requires several steps. Children who can write sentences on a certain subject are also providing information about their language skills within a content area. This requires knowledge about the subject as well as the ability to communicate thoughts clearly in writing. Both examples provide the teacher with alternative ways to assess learning that is meaningful and relevant. By examining the language that is used to express thoughts, the teacher gains a deeper understanding of the children's linguistic development as well as their ability to communicate what they know about a subject. The process is natural and real, or "authentic."

There are many alternative types of assessment that can provide teachers who are working in multilingual, multicultural settings with valuable information about their own effectiveness as teachers, as well as about their students' ongoing progress. Portfolio assessment is a holistic approach that has gained acceptance as an effective alternative assessment instrument.

Portfolios have the advantage of giving students many opportunities in a variety of contexts to demonstrate their ability to perform certain tasks or activities. Portfolios are especially effective with language learners at all levels, because they are thorough and adaptable. They allow the students time to grow and mature. For the ESL learner, time is essential in the transition process from the first language to the second.

Traditional language tests that use discrete items to assess elements such as grammar or vocabulary tend to ignore the intricate relationship of language to thought and culture. Linguists agree that these elements are inseparable.

Graphic organizers enable the teacher to see the thought processes of the student expressed in "information chunks." This teaching tool is useful with students in the emergent or transitional stages of second-language acquisition. Either with the help of the teacher in a cooperative group, with peers or independently, students write short phrases that express their thoughts, views, and perceptions about a subject or topic. Graphic organizers emphasize knowledge, the ability to organize information, and students' perceptions or opinions over language structure and form. They are especially useful in assessing content learning and in enhancing language development.

Historically, students with culturally and linguistically diverse backgrounds have scored poorly on traditional standardized tests. Discouraged teachers, who lack appreciation of the importance of language in assessing learning, lack knowledge of the complexity of second-language acquisition. They are unaware of cultural factors that interfere or inhibit student performance, and they have developed negative attitudes about these students as learners. Many of these students have dropped out of school, with little hope for a bright employment future.

However, recent interest in rethinking assessment practices has led to using authentic assessment to assist students in learning about their own needs and to help them find new opportunities to continue their education. Sound evaluation practices can help improve the way we deliver instruction to students, as well as helping students to take responsibility for their learning.

The recent trend in alternative assessment is by no means a panacea. Many tough questions remain. While traditional tests do offer an easier, quicker, more objective way of comparing student performance, most standardized tests are not designed to include the minority language population. Thus the information gathered from these tests is of little value when applied to students who are not able to compete academically due to limited linguistic proficiency. Although alternative assessment often gives a more accurate and whole picture of students' competency, educators are still concerned about the issues of reliability and validity of these measures. Even more difficult are the questions of how to accurately observe, classify, and objectively report all the data that are obtained through this process.

The design of the evaluation and assessment component of the teaching/learning process should meet the needs of English-language learners as well as all others. Assessment practices that are effective result in positive teaching and learning experiences. The articles selected for this section focus on alternative assessment that provides choices for teachers who are working with minority language students.

Alternative Assessment: Responses to Commonly Asked Questions

Ana Huerta-Macías

I was picking up my fourth-grade daughter after school one afternoon when, as she jumped into the car, she exclaimed, "Mom, I've never in my life had none of the above!" I thought for a moment and then realized just what she was talking about—a multiple choice test. Surely enough, as she continued to talk she expressed her frustration at a science test she had taken that afternoon. The teacher had decided to add the choice of "none of the above" to several of the questions, a choice my daughter had not understood. Never having before seen it on a test, she decided it meant that she was not to circle any of the choices listed for the questions that offered "none of the above" as a response. Consequently, she failed the test.

The previous anecdote illustrates but one problem that is found in contrived tests—including standardized tests as well as teacher-made tests such as the one my daughter took. In this case the student knew the concept being tested, but was unfamiliar with the language and format of the test. Thus, her test taking skills were what was lacking, not her scientific knowledge. Other problems that have been discussed in the literature with relation to traditional, standardized tests include norming on a population unlike the one being tested and cultural and language biases (García & Pearson, 1992, 1994; Wrigley & Guth, 1992). In addition, the testing situation itself often produces anxiety

within the student such that she is unable to think clearly. The student may also be facing extenuating circumstances (e.g., personal problems or illness) at the time she is being tested, thus also hampering the student's performance on the test. The problems associated with traditional testing often mask what the student really knows; or in the case of ESL, what the student can do in her second language. What, then, are the alternatives? How can we assess a student's acquisition of a second language in a valid and reliable way? Are there alternatives that can be adapted to all levels? In this article I will offer responses to these questions by (a) describing alternative assessment procedures; (b) addressing issues related to validity, reliability, and objectivity that are often raised as objections to alternative assessment; and (c) discussing the power of alternative assessment to provide knowledge about a student.

Alternative Assessment Procedures

Alternative assessment has been described as an alternative to standardized testing and all of the problems found with such testing. There is no single definition of alternative assessment. Rather, a variety of labels has been used to distinguish it from traditional, standardized testing. García and Pearson (1994) include the following in their review of these labels: performance assessment,

authentic assessment, portfolio assessment, informal assessment, situated (or contextualized) assessment, and assessment by exhibition. They also state that alternative assessment consists of all of those "efforts that do not adhere to the traditional criteria of standardization, efficiency, cost-effectiveness, objectivity and machine scorability" (p. 355).

Alternative assessment is different from traditional testing in that it actually asks students to show what they can do. Students are evaluated on what they integrate and produce rather than on what they are able to recall and reproduce. The main goal of alternative assessment is to "gather evidence about how students are approaching, processing, and completing 'real-life' tasks in a particular domain" (García & Pearson, 1994, p. 357). Alternative assessment, most importantly, provides alternatives to traditional testing in that it (a) does not intrude on regular classroom activities; (b) reflects the curriculum that is actually being implemented in the classroom; (c) provides information on the strengths and weaknesses of each individual student; (d) provides multiple indices that can be used to gauge student progress; and (e) is more multiculturally sensitive and free of norm, linguistic, and cultural biases found in traditional testing.

Alternative assessment procedures are nonintrusive to the classroom because they do not require a separate block of time to implement them, as do traditional tests. Moreover, the same day-to-day activities that a student is engaged in (e.g., writing, role playing, group discussion) are the basis for alternative assessment. Thus, there is little or no change required in classroom routines and activities in order to implement alternative assessment. Because alternative assessment is based on the daily classroom activities, it also reflects the curriculum, unlike traditional, standardized tests that often test skills incongruent with classroom practices. Because the data collected are based on real-life tasks, furthermore, alternative assessment provides information on the strengths as well as the weaknesses of a student. A work sample, for instance, may tell an instructor that a student's strong points are with the mechanics of English but that she needs additional work on vocabulary and organization of a written piece. Alternative assessment provides a menu of possibilities, rather than any one single method for assessment. Thus, student growth can be more reliably assessed because information from various sources is included in the process. Finally, alternative assessment procedures are multiculturally sensitive. They are particularly suited for the diverse ESL populations because they are free of those biases found in traditional testing. They are not normed instruments, and they are based on student performance in real-life tasks.

Alternative assessment includes a variety of instruments that can be adapted to varying situations. Because the literature (Anthony, Johnson, Mikelson, & Preece, 1991; Goodman, 1991; Holt, 1994; Navarrete, Wilde, Nelson, Martínez, & Hargett, 1990; Wilde, Del Vecchio, & Gustke, in press) provides ample discussion and illustrations of these procedures, I will only briefly mention them here. Although it is unlikely that any one instrument will fit the needs of a given group of students, the idea is to adopt and/or adapt existing instruments in such a way that they reflect the goals of the class and the activities being implemented in that classroom to meet those goals. Alternative assessment procedures include, for example, the use of checklists of student behaviors or products, journals, reading logs, videos of role plays, audiotapes of discussions, self-evaluation questionnaires, work samples, and teacher observations or anecdotal records. The instructor and students can collaboratively decide which procedures are to be used for assessment in a given class. Individual students are also often given the responsibility of selecting specific products of their work (published pieces, for instance) on which they will be assessed.

Validity, Reliability and Objectivity

Objections to alternative assessment are often voiced in terms of *validity, reliability, and objectivity*—terms that have been most often associated with standardized tests. Questions that focus around these issues are (respectively):

- Does the test measure what it is supposed to measure?
- Is the test consistent in its measurement?
- Is the test unbiased? (García & Pearson, 1991)

Proponents of alternative assessment do not suggest that we overlook these criteria, for any high quality assessment must adhere to them. Rather, the suggestion is that we apply new words that have been borrowed from the literature on qualitative research. Concerns with validity and reliability of assessment instruments have been addressed in qualitative research through the use of the term *trustworthiness*. An instrument is deemed to be *trustworthy* if it has *credibility* (i.e., truth value) and *auditability* (i.e., consistency). In other words, does it measure what it is supposed to measure and would the instrument give the same results if replicated? (Guba & Lincoln, 1981).

Kirk and Miller (1986) write that "In the best of worlds, a measuring instrument is so closely linked to the phenomena under observation that it is 'obviously' providing valid data" (p. 22). Alternative assessment represents the best of all worlds in that it looks at actual performance on real-life tasks, such as writing, self-editing, reading, participation in collaborative work, and doing a demonstration in front of a group. The procedures in and of themselves are, therefore, valid. Written work samples and published pieces in an ESL class, for instance, will inform a teacher as to how well the student can write in English. The pieces themselves will serve as evidence of the student's ability to express his ideas in writing in an organized fashion, to use appropriate mechanics, transitions, and vocabulary.

What about reliability, or consistency? It follows that if a procedure is valid, then it is reliable in that it will consistently produce the same results if audited or replicated. The probability is very high, for example, that a student's written retelling of a story will share the same or at least highly similar characteristics in his writing from one week to the next. Two instructors or even the same instructor who is trained in the use of a holistic evaluation scale will more than likely find that two pieces, written a week apart by a student, will exhibit like characteristics.

Thus, the rater will assign the same or a similar score on the scale because the descriptors that best fit the two pieces will most probably be the same ones.

Wilde, Del Vecchio, and Gustke (in press) further suggest the following to ensure reliability in alternative assessments:

- design multiple tasks that lead to the same outcome
- use trained judges, working with clear criteria, from specific anchor papers or performance behaviors
- monitor periodically to ensure that raters use criteria and standards in a consistent manner

Reliability, or consistency, in qualitative research is often ensured through yet another means, *triangulation*. In qualitative research, triangulation refers to the combination of methodologies to strengthen a study design (Patton, 1987). When applied to alternative assessment, triangulation refers to the collection of data/information from three different sources/perspectives. In the case of an ESL public school class, for instance, a teacher would want to assess students' literacy development in English. In order to do this, she could collect data that would paint a picture of each student's growth by describing, for example, his (a) background, (b) use of English (reading, writing, speaking, listening) in academic tasks within the classroom as well as in situations outside the classroom, and (c) ability to use literacy behaviors such as inferencing, obtaining meaning from context, and skimming through a text before reading it. In this case, the sources of data might be the parents, the students, and the teacher herself (see above). Data from the parents might include information gathered through conversations, surveys, or informal interviews on the student's linguistic and cultural background, length of residence in the U.S., language(s) spoken at home, language(s) spoken with friends, amount of reading in English and the native language done at home, among other items. From the student, the instructor might put together a portfolio that includes data such as written work samples, audiotapes of the student engaged in conversation, a video of a role play, a reading log, and self-evaluation sheets. The instructor would then include his own perspectives by adding, for instance, observations or anecdotes of events in the class that demonstrate English proficiency, teacher journals, and checklists on performance.

Triangulation can be applied in varying contexts. Consider, for example, an adult workplace literacy class focusing on work-related English that will assist employees to

Triangulation of Data: Alternative Assessment for ESL Public School Class

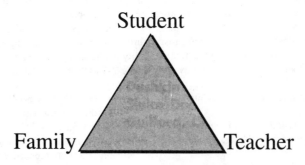

Student

Family

Teacher

more effectively carry out their duties. Triangulation in this case might be achieved by gathering data from the instructor, the student, and her employer or fellow co-workers (see below). Data from the instructor and the student would include the same types of information described above. The employer/co-worker might provide additional information on a student's growth in ESL. This can be done by using surveys, informal phone or personal interviews where the instructor asks about the student's use of English in varying contexts at the workplace—such as at meetings or informal discussions. In addition, work-related samples, such as forms that were filled out by the student at the workplace, may also be included as data from the workplace.

Another concern that is often raised with respect to alternative assessment is the lack of objectivity. Yet, even though standardized tests are described as objective, the notion of objectivity has been challenged. As humans, we all have biases, whether we're aware of them or not. A standardized test merely represents agreement among a number of people on scoring procedures, format and/or content for that specific test. In other words, these individuals are not really objective; they just collectively share the same biases. Therefore, in this sense, a standardized test is no more objective than an alternative assessment instrument. One might argue, moreover, that quantitative data—as from standardized tests—can be more subjective because the numbers or statistics can be manipulated to reflect certain biases on the part of the researcher. There is no reason, then, to consider alternative assessment any less objective than traditional testing.

Conclusion

I've discussed alternative assessment as consisting of valid and reliable procedures that avoid many of the problems inherent in traditional testing including norming, linguistic, and cultural biases. There is yet another advantage to the use of alternative assessment: It has the power to tell a story. The data compiled on individual students provides a clear picture of each student's development through the various work samples and products collected. As an educator looks at this picture, she can determine growth, areas of weakness, and areas of strength. She can also inform herself about the student's background, interests, and goals through his journals, compositions, conversations, and observations. In short, the educator becomes acquainted with this person. Thus, contrary to traditional testing, which typically provides only a set of numbers, alternative assessment documents a story for every student—and what is the ultimate goal of evaluation but to give us the knowledge to be able to reflect upon, discuss, and assist a student's journey through the learning process?

Alternative assessment gives us the power to do all three.

References

Anthony, R., Johnson, T., Mickelson, N., & Preece, A. (1991). *Evaluating literacy: A perspective for change.* Portsmouth, NH: Heinemann.

García, G.E., & Pearson, P.D. (1991). The role of assessment in a diverse society. In E.F. Hiebert (Ed.), *Literacy for a diverse society* (pp. 253–278). New York: Teachers College Press.

García, G.E., & Pearson, P.D. (1994). Assessment and diversity. In L. Darling-Hammond (Ed.), *Review of research in education* (pp. 337–391). Washington, DC: American Education Research Association.

Goodman, Y.M. (1991). Informal methods of evaluation. In J. Flood, J.M. Jensen, D. Lapp, & J. Squire (Eds.), *Handbook of research on teaching the English language arts* (pp. 502-509). New York: Macmillan.

Guba, E.G., & Lincoln, Y.S. (1981). *Effective evaluation: Improving the usefulness of evaluation results through responsive and naturalistic approaches.* San Francisco: Jossey–Bass.

Holt, D. (1994). *Assessing success in family literacy projects: Alternative approaches to assessment and evaluation.* Washington, DC: Center for Applied Linguistics.

Kirk J., & Miller, M.L. (1986). *Reliability and validity in qualitative research.* Newbury Park, CA: Sage.

Mitchell, R. (1979). Less than words can say. Boston: Little, Brown.

Navarrete, C., Wilde, J., Nelson, C., Martínez, R., & Hargett, G. (1990). *Informal assessment in educational evaluation: Implications for bilingual programs.* Washington, DC: National Clearinghouse for Bilingual Education.

Patton, M.Q. (1987). *Creative evaluation.* Newbury Park, CA: Sage.

Wrigley, H. S., & Guth, G.A. (1992). Bringing literacy to life: Issues and options in adult ESL literacy. San Mateo, CA: Aguirre International.

Wilde, J., Del Vecchio, A., Gustke, C. (in press). Alternative assessments for Latino students. In M. González, A. Huerta-Macías, & J. Tinajero (Eds.), *The schooling of Latino students: A guide to quality practice.* Lancaster, PA: Technomic Publishing.

Triangulation of Data: Alternative Assessment for Adults in a Workplace ESL Class

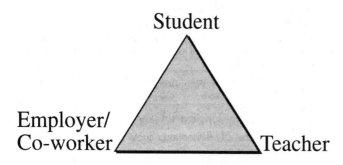

Student

Employer/ Co-worker

Teacher

Author

Ana Huerta-Macías currently coordinates the TESOL program in the Department of Curriculum and Instruction at New Mexico State University. She completed her PhD in 1978 at the University of Texas, where she specialized in Applied Linguistics. During the past 18 years she has conducted research and published in the areas of bilingual education, family literacy, bilingualism, and TESOL.

MOVING TOWARD AUTHENTIC ASSESSMENT

J. MICHAEL O'MALLEY AND LORRAINE VALDEZ PIERCE

Over the past decade we have seen a rapid expansion of interest in alternatives to traditional forms of assessment in education (Aschbacher 1991; Herman, Aschbacher, and Winters 1992). The form of assessment used for both standardized testing and classroom assessment for as long as most educators can remember is the multiple-choice test. While this type of test has been a mainstay of educational programs, educators from all backgrounds have raised concerns about its usefulness as a primary measure of student achievement and are seeking alternatives through multiple forms of assessment. These educators are also seeking assessments that more closely resemble instructional activities in classrooms.

Alternative assessment consists of any method of finding out what a student knows or can do that is intended to show growth and inform instruction, and is an alternative to traditional forms of testing, namely, multiple-choice tests (Stiggins 1991). Alternative assessment is by definition criterion-referenced and is typically authentic because it is based on activities that represent classroom and real-life settings. We use the term *authentic assessment* throughout this book* to describe the multiple forms of assessment that are consistent with classroom goals, curricula, and instruction.

The increased interest in authentic assessment is based on two major issues: current assessment procedures do not assess the full range of essential student outcomes, and teachers have difficulty using the information gained for instructional planning. Educators have questioned "fill in the bubble" or multiple-choice tests because these forms of assessment are not adequate to assess the full range of higher-order thinking skills considered important in today's curriculum. Further, these types of tests do not represent recent improvements in our understanding of what and how students learn (Resnick and Klopfer 1989). Multiple-choice tests, while objective and highly reliable for most students, have emphasized the assessment of discrete skills and do not contain authentic representations of classroom activities. The tests therefore lack the content validity considered important to en-

sure student interest and motivation during assessment. In their classrooms, students read interesting literature, write papers, integrate resource information with personal viewpoints, work on projects cooperatively, share information while summarizing their conclusions, and use information from one content area (like mathematics) to solve problems and display information in other content areas. Little of the knowledge and strategic processes needed to accomplish these tasks is captured in multiple-choice or single-answer tests.

Teachers question the overdependence on a single type of assessment because test scores sometimes disagree with conclusions they have reached from observing how students actually perform in classrooms. Teachers need information to gauge whether students are making progress, if they respond to instructional approaches and materials, and if they accomplish the kinds of complex learning expected in today's curriculum. The information teachers need for instructional planning concerns the very type of complex and varied student learning that is difficult to assess with multiple-choice tests. Teachers need information about integrative language and content knowledge rather than isolated pieces of knowledge and skills. What teachers gain from daily contact with students is an understanding of the processes by which students learn as well as the products of their learning. They also rely on multiple ways of collecting information that provide them with the type of feedback they need to monitor student progress and to plan for instruction.

In addition to the issues raised by teachers, administrators and education policy analysts have been concerned that the knowledge and skills students will need to function effectively in a future technological and complex society are inadequately represented in multiple-choice tests. Because teachers tend to focus instruction on the skills emphasized in testing, multiple-choice tests have had the long-term effect of limiting the curriculum to isolated and lower-level skills (Resnick and Klopfer 1989). The ability to accurately select one of a number of options to brief questions does not reflect what students will be called on to do in solving complex problems, communicating significant ideas, persuading others on important positions, organizing information and managing human resources, and working cooperatively with others in the workplace (Wiggins 1989, 1993). Policy analysts and administrators are looking for evidence of accountability that schools are successful in producing a new generation of students with skills that will be required in the decades to come. Because teachers and administrators both sense the need for new forms of assessment, the development of new measures has become all the more important and is likely to thrive as an important component of instructional programs.

While there has been a high degree of interest in authentic assessment in general education, as evidenced by the number of articles and books appearing on the topic, there are relatively few articles and monographs on alternative assessment with language minority students (students who speak a language other than English as their first language and/or come from an environment where a language other than English is spoken). The more general articles and books on alternative assessment, while often useful, do not focus on the specific needs of language minority students and often fail to provide specific examples that teachers can use in classrooms. Thus, schools must search deeply to find the information they need to assess these students and to monitor their educational progress. In addition to these instructional needs in assessment, school districts continually have difficulty in making effective decisions about the level of English language proficiency necessary for the participation of English language learning[1] (ELL) students in district or statewide testing programs (O'Malley and Valdez Pierce 1994).

Assessment of English Language Learning Students

For at least three decades, teachers and program administrators have struggled to identify appropriate procedures to assess the knowledge and abilities of ELL students. The path has been difficult in part because of the need to identify varying levels of knowledge and proficiency in English and in part because the purposes of assessment with language minority students are so varied and complex. Assessment information is needed by administrators, teachers, staff developers, students, and parents to assist in determining appropriate program placements and instructional activities as well as in monitoring student progress.

Accurate and effective assessment of language minority students is essential to ensure that ELL students gain access to instructional programs that meet their needs. The failure of assessment and instruction to interact effectively is most evident when inappropriate assessment approaches lead to inaccurate identification, improper program placements, inadequate monitoring of student progress, and the long-term failure of instruction (Cummins 1984). Conversely, appropriate assessment has the potential to ensure that these students are on course to becoming literate and able participants in English language classroom settings.

With ELL students, assessment is far more complex and challenging than with native speakers of English. Assessment is used for at least six purposes with ELL students:

1. *Screening and identification:* to identify students eligible for special language and/or content area support programs
2. *Placement:* to determine the language proficiency and content area competencies of students in order to recommend an appropriate educational program
3. *Reclassification or exit:* to determine if a student has gained the language skills and content area competencies needed to benefit from instruction in grade-level classrooms[2], (i.e., from all-English programs not specifically designed to address the needs of ELL students)
4. *Monitoring student progress:* to review student language and content area learning in classrooms
5. *Program evaluation:* to determine the effects of federal, state, or local instructional programs
6. *Accountability:* to guarantee that students attain expected educational goals or standards, including testing for high school graduation

---

1. The term *limited English proficient* or *LEP* is typically used to describe non-native speakers of English who experience difficulty in profiting from instruction in English. We prefer the term *English language learners (ELLs)* or *English language learning (ELL)* students because of the more positive emphasis on what the students are learning rather than on their supposed limitations. ELL students are part of a larger population of language minority students who speak a language other than English as their first language and/or who come from a background where a language other than English is used. We use the term *language minority* because of its broader implications in the United States population even though language minority groups may be dominant in some local school districts.

---

2. The term *grade-level classrooms* is borrowed from Enright and McCloskey (1989) and refers to classrooms with grade-appropriate content materials. In grade-level classrooms, reclassified ELL students learn along with native English-speaking students. We prefer the term *grade-level* over *mainstream,* which has connotations from special education and may be inappropriate where the local student population is largely from language minority backgrounds.

Many schools assess skills in the student's native language as well as in English, thereby expanding the range of assessment with ELL students. Because of these varying purposes and audiences, consensus on the appropriate procedures for assessment of language minority students has been difficult to attain.

In spite of this general lack of agreement, most educators do agree that standardized, norm-referenced tests are inappropriate for ELL students. Traditional forms of assessment such as standardized tests are inappropriate for ELL students for a variety of reasons. Standardized tests use multiple-choice items, a format that may be unfamiliar to students with limited experience in U.S. public schools. Moreover, multiple-choice items assume a level of English language proficiency that ELL students may not have acquired. The subtle distinctions made on various items for vocabulary, word analysis, reading, and listening subtests may produce information on what the student *does not* know but little information about what the student *does* know. This gives the teacher an incomplete picture of student needs and strengths. The language components of standardized tests mainly assess reading and vocabulary knowledge and ignore progress in written and oral language, important components of language-based instructional programs. Standardized tests in content areas, such as math and science, may not assess what ELL students know because of the complexity of the language in which the questions are asked. These tests have not been effective in assessing the higher-order thinking skills students use in solving problems, analyzing texts, or evaluating ideas (Resnick and Klopfer 1989). Virtually all schools administer standardized tests once a year, leaving teachers without regular information throughout the school year on what students have learned. Even formal language testing for oral proficiency is typically conducted only once annually. Without additional assessments tailored to the needs of ELL students, teachers are unable to plan instruction effectively or make accurate decisions about student needs and progress.

The previous discussion does not suggest that there is no role for standardized testing in school district or state assessment programs or in the assessment of former ELL students. Standardized tests have an important role in at least four components of an overall testing program: (1) to compare individual or group performance with an external normative group, (2) to identify relative strengths and weaknesses in skill areas, (3) to monitor annual growth in skills, and (4) for program evaluation (Hoover 1995). With former ELL students, standardized tests can be used for accountability to ensure that these students are progressing effectively in grade-level classrooms once they no longer need special language and/or content area supports (O'Malley and Valdez Pierce 1994). As we have noted, however, these uses of standardized tests do not cover the full range of assessment needs for ELL students.

Past critics of standardized testing with language minority students have had limited success in proposing acceptable alternatives, except to suggest administering tests in the student's native language. Unfortunately, the same type of tests have been recommended in the native language as are typically administered in English, thereby not extending the argument into new areas of assessment and not allowing for multiple ways of assessing knowledge and skills. Recently, educators have offered more varied suggestions for improving the assessment of ELL students (e.g., Fradd, McGee, and Wilen 1994; Garcia and Ortiz 1988; Navarette et al. 1990; O'Malley and Valdez Pierce 1991; Valdez Pierce and O'Malley 1992; Short 1993).

Definition of Authentic Assessment

We use the term *authentic assessment* to describe the multiple forms of assessment that reflect student learning, achievement, motivation, and attitudes on instructionally-relevant classroom activities. Examples of authentic assessment include performance assessment, portfolios, and student self-assessment.

Performance assessment consists of any form of assessment in which the student constructs a response orally or in writing (Feuer and Fulton 1993; Herman, Aschbacher, and Winters 1992). The student response may be elicited by the teacher in formal or informal assessment contexts or may be observed during classroom instructional or non-instructional settings. Performance assessment requires students to "accomplish complex and significant tasks, while bringing to bear prior knowledge, recent learning, and relevant skills to solve realistic or authentic problems" (Herman, Aschbacher, and Winters, p. 2). Students may be called on to use materials or perform hands-on activities in reaching solutions to problems. Examples are oral reports, writing samples, individual and group projects, exhibitions, and demonstrations.

Some of the characteristics of performance assessment are the following (adapted from Aschbacher 1991; Herman, Aschbacher, and Winters 1992):

1. *Constructed Response:* students construct a response, provide an expanded response, engage in a performance, or create a product
2. *Higher-order Thinking:* the student typically uses higher levels of thinking in constructing responses to open-ended questions
3. *Authenticity:* tasks are meaningful, challenging, and engaging activities that mirror good instruc-

tion or other real-world contexts where the student is expected to perform

4. *Integrative:* the tasks call for integration of language skills and, in some cases, for integration of knowledge and skills across content areas
5. *Process and Product:* procedures and strategies for deriving the correct response or for exploring multiple solutions to complex tasks are often assessed as well as (or sometimes instead of) the product or the "correct" answer
6. *Depth Versus Breadth:* performance assessments provide information in depth about a student's skills or mastery as contrasted with the breadth of coverage more typical of multiple-choice tests

Performance assessment often requires teacher judgment of student responses. To aid in making the judgments accurate and reliable, a scoring scale referred to as a *rubric* is used, in which numerical values are associated with performance levels, such as 1 = Basic, 2 = Proficient, and 3 = Advanced. The criteria for each performance level must be precisely defined in terms of what the student actually does to demonstrate skill or proficiency at that level. One of the characteristics of performance assessment is that the criteria are made public and known in advance (Aschbacher 1991). Accordingly, students can participate in setting and using the criteria in self-assessment of their own performance.

Portfolio assessment is a systematic collection of student work that is analyzed to show progress over time with regard to instructional objectives (Valencia 1991). Examples of portfolio entries include writing samples, reading logs, drawings, audio or videotapes, and/or teacher and student comments on progress made by the student. One of the defining features of portfolio assessment is the involvement of students in selecting samples of their own work to show growth or learning over time.

Student *self-assessment* is a key element in authentic assessment and in self-regulated learning, "the motivated and strategic efforts of students to accomplish specific purposes" (Paris and Ayers 1994, p. 26). Self-assessment promotes direct involvement in learning and the integration of cognitive abilities with motivation and attitude toward learning. In becoming self-regulated learners, students make choices, select learning activities, and plan how to use their time and resources. They have the freedom to choose challenging activities, take risks, advance their own learning, and accomplish desired goals. Because students have control over their learning, they can decide how to use the resources available to them within or outside the classroom. Students who are self-regulated learners collaborate with other students in exchanging ideas, eliciting assistance when needed, and providing support to their peers. As they go about learning,

these types of students construct meaning, revise their understandings, and share meaning with others. These students take pride in their efforts and in the new meanings they construct because they see the connection between their efforts and learning success. Finally, self-regulated learners monitor their own performance and evaluate their progress and accomplishments (Paris and Ayers 1994). Self-assessment and self-management are at the core of this type of learning and should be a regular part of instruction.

Because we believe assessment is inextricably tied to instruction, our suggestions for using authentic assessment imply changes in instruction. For example, you cannot use portfolios without changing your philosophy of teaching and learning from one which is transmission-oriented to one which is learner-centered. Student input and ownership are defining elements in portfolios and in authentic assessment in general. In learner-centered classrooms, students have input not only into what they learn, but also into how they will be assessed. Student self-assessment and reflection are critical to the view of assessment and learning we propose.

Authentic assessment is important for ELL students as well as for students in grade-level classrooms. Teachers of language minority students have benefited from the interest of the general education community in authentic assessment and are adding to this repertoire of new assessment procedures. With ELL students, teachers using authentic assessment can assess students at all levels of proficiency for language and content knowledge in both English and in their native language.

The use of authentic assessment places greater demands on teachers than the use of single-answer tests. Time and management skills are needed to design and use these assessments, and judgment is required in reaching conclusions about student learning and student progress. Because authentic assessment is relatively new, few teachers have had sustained professional development opportunities on the design, creation, and use of these assessment procedures. The changing models of student learning and instruction also require teachers to understand the reasons for the new directions in assessment and how to link assessment with instruction.

Purposes of This Book* and Target Audience

This book* is designed for teachers, teacher trainers, administrators, and assessment specialists who work with ELL students. We present an overview and rationale for authentic assessment and a framework for the assessment of ELL students at all grade levels. The book* focuses on portfolios and practical examples of assessment procedures used to collect information on ELL students in English as a second language (ESL) and bilingual programs, and in grade-level classrooms. We describe assessment procedures for second language learners in language arts and in the content areas. The examples we use are largely K–12, although the assessment procedures are often applicable to early childhood and adult settings. We have tried to introduce a variety of assessment procedures and a number of ways of looking at student performance that will provide teachers with a balanced view of learning. We also describe assessment procedures that can be used for identification and placement of English language learners, monitoring of student progress, and reclassification of students who are ready to exit special language programs and enter grade-level classrooms.

The assessment procedures described in this book* will benefit all teachers working with students who need to strengthen their language skills. In addition to ELL students, these include students in any second language context and Title I students. Teachers may use these assessment procedures whether they work in their own classroom, on interdisciplinary teams, or with content area teachers in collaborative settings.

While teachers spend as much as 20–30 percent of their professional time involved in assessment-related activities (Stiggins 1988), pre- and in-service programs to date have not familiarized teachers with issues in authentic assessment, nor have they prepared them to design and use this type of assessment for instructional planning. Teachers in some states are not required to take an assessment course, and most college and university courses in assessment tend to be very traditional. Such courses cover the different types of tests used in education, various standardized tests, different types of test items, the meaning of test scores, test construction in classrooms, some rudimentary statistics necessary for classroom testing, and grading practices. These courses do not cover the design, construction, and use of performance assessments, student portfolios, anecdotal records, reading logs, running records, and other types of assessment discussed in the performance assessment literature and covered in this book.* Furthermore, these courses for the most part do not address the assessment of language minority and ELL students in any significant manner.

Authentic assessment places heavy demands on teachers' professional skills. In comparison to multiple-choice testing, where judgments are made based on a curve or on the percent of correct items, these new assessment procedures call for more independent judgment and interpretation of student performance (Herman, Aschbacher, and Winters 1992). Furthermore, authentic assessments take time and careful planning to be used effectively. Teachers need staff development and support to design and use performance assessments that effectively address multidisciplinary understanding and critical thinking skills (Khattri, Kane, and Reeve 1995). Without opportunities to collaborate with other teachers, to try out new assessments, and to discuss the assessments they are using, teachers will almost certainly have problems in advancing beyond rudimentary uses of these new approaches.

Overview of the Book*

We have introduced this book* by presenting some background information about general assessment issues, about authentic forms of assessment, and about specific issues in the assessment of language minority students. We view assessment and instruction as interlocking parts of educational programs and believe that assessment must be an integral part of instruction.

We continue in Chapter 2 by presenting an overview of authentic assessment, including performance and portfolio assessments. We describe specific types of authentic assessment and issues in designing these assessments, and bring essential assessment concepts of reliability and validity together with authentic assessment procedures. We also discuss how to design authentic assessments and lay out a series of steps that teachers can apply in working with other teachers to design and use performance assessments and portfolios. This chapter is particularly important for teachers working in grade-level or school teams on authentic assessments and contains suggestions for staff development.

In Chapter 3 we present a more detailed overview of portfolio assessment and explain how to integrate the information collected from classroom assessment in a portfolio. We describe different types of portfolios, the purposes of portfolio assessment, issues that are relevant to the use of portfolios, specific steps in portfolio design, and suggestions for using portfolios in instruction. Throughout this chapter we describe the changing role of teachers and students in using portfolios. We also discuss procedures for communicating information about portfolios to parents so that portfolios are useful in helping parents understand their children's progress.

Chapters 4–7 discuss assessment approaches that have special relevance to teachers of ELL students and show how these procedures can be used in conjunction with portfolio assessment in classrooms. These chapters focus on assessment of oral language (Chapter 4), reading (Chapter 5), writing (Chapter 6), and assessment in the content areas (Chapter 7). Teachers looking for assessment at the different grade levels will find examples addressing their needs throughout these chapters. The use of separate chapters on the language skills is a convenience only, and does *not* imply that we believe these skills should either be taught or assessed in isolation.

We begin Chapters 4–7 with an overview of the instructional context in each area and highlight advances in thinking about instruction that urge the use of authentic assessment. We review the purposes of assessment in each subject for administrative or instructional applications. We then define specific assessment approaches, give examples that teachers can use, and provide sample scoring rubrics for various assessment procedures. In each of these chapters we point out the importance of self-assessment and indicate methods teachers can use to support student self-assessment. We include numerous tables and figures containing scoring rubrics and assessment techniques throughout the book.* At the conclusion of each chapter we discuss how teachers can use the assessments in instruction. While teachers use performance assessment during instruction in a variety of ways—to share performance expectations with students and to introduce project-based tasks (Khattri, Kane, and Reeve 1995)—we also emphasize uses to monitor student progress and to assist in planning for future instruction.

The final chapter provides examples from the classroom in which teachers have used authentic assessment. In these examples, teachers have embedded assessment in instruction so that the result appears to the students (or to an observer) as nothing more than an interesting instructional activity. From these activities, however, teachers and students derive feedback on student performance from self-assessment, from peer evaluation, and/or from the teacher's assessment of the student. These examples illustrate that setting time aside to conduct authentic assessment in classrooms requires the creative integration of assessment with an instructional activity the teacher had already planned. The teachers in these examples relied on their professional leadership qualities to introduce and use innovative approaches to assessment when their background may not have prepared them for using authentic assessment, when other teachers in their school held to more traditional assessment approaches, and when careful preparation and sustained commitment were required to communicate student performance on the new assessments to parents.

*[Book referenced in text is *Authentic Assessment for English Language Learners: Practical Approaches for Teachers*, O'Malley and Pierce (Reading, PA: Addison-Wesley Publishing Co., 1996).—**Ed.**]

Portfolio Assessment in Second Language Teacher Education

Karen E. Johnson

One of the most common criticisms of teacher education programs is that we continue to assess teachers based on observable teaching behaviors, or through paper and pencil tests that assess knowledge about teaching instead of assessing how novice teachers use their knowledge while actually teaching. If teacher educators wish to assess how teachers use their knowledge about teaching, we need an approach to assessment that

- examines how teachers make sense of what they are learning
- values what teachers think, not simply what they do
- allows for multiple opportunities for teachers to demonstrate their competencies
- recognizes the true complexities of learning to teach.

One such approach is portfolio assessment.

The concept of portfolio assessment comes from the field of fine arts in which portfolios are used to demonstrate the depth and breadth of an artist's talents and capabilities. However, portfolios are not just a collection of materials stuffed into a folder. Each piece of the portfolio must be created, collected, and organized in such a way as to demonstrate certain competencies. Barton and Collins (1993) propose three critical components to portfolio design and development. These include purposes, evidence, and assessment criteria.

Component 1: Purposes

Before implementing portfolio assessment, teacher educators must decide on the purposes of their teacher education program and how the requirements of their program enable students to meet those purposes. Thus, purposes must be established in order to determine what the portfolio will be used to measure. For example, novice teachers clearly need a methods course, but what is it specifically about methodology that they need to know, or more importantly, what is it that they need to be able to do with this knowledge? And how do the requirements of the methodology course enable them to demonstrate what they can do with this knowledge?

What is it that we really want our students to know and be able to do as a result of a teacher education program?

Establishing clearly articulated purposes may be the single most difficult aspect of implementing portfolio assessment. To do so, teacher educators must begin by asking themselves: What is it that we really want our students to know and be able to do as a result of this teacher education program? For example, as a teacher educator, I may believe that novice teachers need to reflect on, critically analyze, and evaluate their own teaching. I may believe that novice teachers need to be aware of the unique needs and learning styles of their students and be sensitive to the social factors that may affect their students' learning. I may believe that novice teachers need to see the subject matter they are teaching from the perspective of their students and to be able to anticipate areas of difficulty that their students may have. The particular purposes that you identify will depend on who you are

and what you believe about teachers and teaching. In addition, the purposes you select will depend on who your students are, where they have come from, and where they will end up teaching.

Component 2: Evidence

Once the purposes of the portfolio have been established, you then need to determine how students can demonstrate that they have accomplished these purposes. Collins (1991) classifies four types of evidence that are appropriate to assess the knowledge, skills, and dispositions of teachers. These include artifacts, reproductions, attestations, and productions.

Artifacts

Artifacts are documents produced during the normal course work of the teacher education program. An artifact could be a paper written for a course, field notes from a series of classroom observations, a case study based on the field experience, or a self-analysis of a videotaped lesson.

Reproductions

Reproductions are documents about typical events in the work of preservice teachers that are not captured in artifacts. For example, a reproduction might be an audiotape of a discussion with an experienced teacher about classroom management, or a collection of journal entries about a particular student in the preservice teacher's class, or an interview with a student about his or her perceptions of the preservice teacher's instructional activities.

From *TESOL Journal*, Winter 1996, pp. 11-14. © 1996 by Teachers of English to Speakers of Other Languages, Inc. Reprinted by permission.

Attestations

Attestations are documents about the work of the novice teacher prepared by someone else: for example, a cooperating teacher's final written report, a peer's written observation of the novice teacher, or the university supervisor's evaluation of a classroom observation.

Productions

Productions are documents prepared especially for the portfolio and include three kinds of materials: goal statements, reflections statements, and captions. A goal statement is a personal description of the focus of the portfolio. A reflection statement provides a summary of the documents in the portfolio and requires that students trace how they have captured and portrayed their competencies. Captions are statements attached to each document that describes what it is, why it is evidence, and what it is evidence of.

An Example: Sam's Case

To illustrate what sort of evidence might meet a specific set of purposes, consider the following case developed by Sam (a pseudonym), a student in one of my graduate seminars. In this seminar, I identified four purposes for my students' portfolios. The first is that novice teachers need to be able to reflect on, critically analyze, and evaluate their own teaching. The second is that they need to be aware of the unique needs and learning styles of their students and be sensitive to the social factors that may affect their students' learning. The third is to use their knowledge of theory to inform their instructional practices. And, the fourth is to participate in professional collaborations with other teachers.

It is no accident that these solutions are based on the theoretical principles that I cover in my seminar.

As part of this seminar, students have the option of constructing a case study about any aspect of their field experience. Case studies are like stories that contain some sort of dramatic tension

that must be resolved. Case studies are not general but instead specific to a particular context, so they are situated and include events within a particular time and place. Most importantly, case studies reveal something about the workings of the teacher's mind, in that they illustrate the complex variables that are considered as teachers sort out, make sense of, and justify the use of particular actions (Shulman, 1987). Sam's case contains three parts: the context, the problem, and the solution.

The Context

Sam teaches ESL in an Adult Community Education Program in a midsize university town. The program caters to two types of ESL students: newly settled immigrants who work for local manufacturing companies located on the outskirts of the town, and spouses of graduate students enrolled in degree programs at the university. The course is a beginning-level conversational English class and meets twice a week in the evenings at a local community center. There are 11 students enrolled in this course. Five of the students, three males and two females, are Puerto Rican and are enrolled in the course as part of a work-based literacy program supported by their employer. Four of the students are Japanese women. Three are homemakers, and one holds a clerical job in one of the undergraduate libraries on campus. The remaining two students are Russian and are husband and wife. They recently moved to the area through a church-based resettlement program. The husband works as a mechanic in a local gas station, and the wife is a homemaker.

The Problem

During the first 2 weeks of class Sam notices that the students with similar first languages tend to sit together and socialize with each other. During large-group activities, the Spanish speakers tend to ask and answer most of the questions and dominate most of the student talk. Moreover, because the Spanish speakers work together they tend to talk about things that happen at work. The Japanese speakers tend to be very quiet. Sam feels strongly that everyone in his class should have equal opportunities to participate. It is through participation, Sam believes, that his students will acquire English, and he realizes that for most of his students, this class is one of the few opportunities they have to actually speak English. Last week Sam tried an activity in which he paired up

different first language speakers, but he found that the Spanish speakers dominated, while the Japanese speakers sat quietly, and when it was their turn to speak, they appeared to be very uncomfortable. As soon as the activity was over, the students reorganized themselves according to first language groups again. Sam is pleased with the Spanish speakers' eagerness to participate and does not want to squelch their opportunities to speak, but he is very concerned about providing opportunities for the Japanese speakers to participate in class. Sam is also concerned about the Russian speakers because they tend to sit together and speak Russian to one another. Sam is at a loss for how to arrange his instructional activities to foster equal student participation.

As part of developing this case, Sam asked his classmates, who are also novice teachers, to consider the case and discuss possible solutions. The students began by talking about cultural differences in classroom participation. They suggested ways of making instructional activities predictable because this helps minimize the risk that students may experience as they attempt to participate. They reminded Sam of the importance of students' feelings of competence because the extent to which students are willing to participate depends on how they think their contributions will be received. They encouraged Sam to help his students make sense of new information by filtering it through what they already know, in other words, building on his students' prior knowledge. They encouraged Sam to explicitly tell his students exactly what is expected of them, perhaps even in the form of a concrete model or demonstration. They reminded Sam of the importance of providing ample opportunity for students to prepare for an activity and to encourage students to use exploratory talk to formulate their ideas before having to make their ideas public in front of the class.

It is no accident that these solutions are based on the theoretical principles that I cover in my seminar. The students were trying to make sense of these principles in terms of their own teaching, and therefore, they became the basis for their discussions and for Sam's decisions about how to foster classroom participation.

The Solution

In writing up the solution for this case, Sam described three things he did with his students. First, in their dialogue journals, Sam explained his expectations for classroom participation and asked each student to describe his perceptions, feelings, or concerns about participating in class. Thus, Sam initiated and sustained a private dialogue with each student about classroom participation.

Second, Sam devoted some class time to an open discussion about classroom participation. He explained why he feels it is important for students to participate in class, and he allowed the students to describe their perceptions of classroom participation. As a result of this discussion, the class generated a set of participation rules that everyone agreed to follow for the remainder of the semester. These had to do with rules for turn-taking in both small- and large-group discussions.

Third, Sam attempted to make his instructional activities predictable so as to foster more student participation. Below is a portion of Sam's solution, written in the context of one particular lesson, that illustrates how he organized his instruction to foster more classroom participation.

An Excerpt from Sam's Write Up

While planning a lesson on polite ways of making and accepting invitations, Sam recalled that his students are much more willing to participate when they are given an opportunity to relate what they are learning to their own experiences. Therefore, he planned to begin the lesson with a large-group discussion in which he would ask his students to share their own personal experiences of having to make and accept invitations. However because his previous attempts at large-group discussions were not very successful (i.e., the Puerto Rican students tend to dominate while the others sit quietly), Sam decided to ask the students to complete a journal assignment (prior to class) in which they were to write about their own personal experiences either making or accepting invitations. He hoped the Japanese and Russian students would be more willing to participate in the large-group discussion if they had an opportunity to rehearse what they would be expected to say in writing. Sam also wanted his students to know exactly what was expected of them, so before assigning the journal assignment, he shared his own personal example of when he reluctantly accepted an invitation for a blind date. His model contained some background information about the social situation and the status of the speakers, and illustrated how he accepted the invitation.

On the day of the lesson, Sam placed his students in pairs and asked them to share their journal assignments with one another. He hoped this activity would give them an opportunity to rehearse telling their personal experiences before being asked to speak in front of the entire class. He also encouraged the students to ask questions or request further information from their partners if some aspect of the story was unclear. He then explained that when they were finished they would be expected to retell their partner's story to the class. Sam decided to use a retelling activity because he felt it would reinforce listening comprehension skills and generate more authentic language.

After the retelling activity, Sam played three audiotaped dialogues that illustrate making and accepting invitations in different social contexts. Knowing that his students' listening comprehension skills are weak, Sam broke the listening task into smaller parts, assigning individual students the task of listening for one specific piece of information. For example, two students were asked to listen for how the speaker introduced the invitation, two other students were asked to listen for how the actual invitation was made, and two others were to listen for how the listener accepted the invitation. After each dialogue, Sam allowed the two students to compare what they had heard and then to share that information with the class.

As a final activity, Sam placed the students in pairs and asked them to create a scenario in which they had to make and accept an invitation. Because, once again, Sam felt it was important for his students to see a model of what they were expected to do, Sam and a student volunteer modeled a scenario for the class. In preparation for the performance activity, Sam placed two pairs together in a group of four, and ask[ed] each pair to perform their scenario for the other. He then asked the pairs to switch and, once again, perform their scenario for a new pair. Once the pairs had rehearsed their scenarios several times, he asked for volunteers to perform their scenario in front of the entire class. During the performance activity, Sam asked the class to listen for how the speaker introduced the invitation, how the actual invitation was made, and how the listener accepted the invitation. This information became the basis for the follow-up discussion after each pair performed their scenario.

Returning to the initial purposes, we see the extent to which Sam's evidence has met the purposes. Clearly, Sam was able to reflect on, critically analyze, and evaluate his own teaching. This is evident in the recognition of the problem and obvious in the development of the solution. It appears that Sam is aware of the unique needs and learning styles of his students and is sensitive to the social factors that affect their learning. In fact, this is what prompted Sam to address the problem of classroom participation in the first place. But the way Sam organized his activities also reflected his awareness of and concern for his students' unique needs. Moreover, it appears that Sam is able to use his knowledge of theory to inform his instructional practices because he based much of the solution on the theoretical principles of making classroom instruction predictable. Finally, to arrive at the solution, Sam participated in professional collaborations with other teachers.

Because Sam chose to include this case in his portfolio, he became responsible for identifying how he met the purposes for this piece of evidence. Thus, Sam's productions about the case tell us not only what Sam learned from this experience but how he used the information that he learned throughout the process of developing this case to inform his own teaching.

Obviously, a single case, no matter how detailed, does not constitute an entire portfolio. Therefore, Sam included other evidence that demonstrated his competencies. For example, he included a videotape of his own teaching, in which he identified when and how he organized his instruction to increase classroom participation (an artifact). He included a written observation from his cooperating teacher who specifically focused on how he managed and encouraged classroom participation (an attestation). He included a written summary of his discussions with his classmates about the case (a reproduction). And, he conducted an interview with one of his Japanese students in which he asked her how she felt about classroom participation and if Sam's instructional activities had helped her feel more comfortable participating in class (a reproduction). For each piece of evidence, Sam was responsible for identifying how it met the purposes established for the portfolio.

Assessment Criteria

If the initial purposes for a portfolio have been clearly articulated, the assessment criteria should simply reflect those purposes. There are two ways to determine this. The first is technical; for example, does the portfolio have a goal statement and a reflection statement?

Does each piece of evidence have a caption? The second is substantive; for example, am I convinced that the student has met or made progress toward the established purposes? If the answer is no, the question then becomes: What would I need to see added to this portfolio in order to be convinced that the purposes have been met?

Ultimately, this means assessing the process more than the product and valuing pedagogical reasoning more than teaching behaviors.

There tend to be two ways that students fail to provide enough evidence of growth. Either they include too little information in the portfolio, or they fail to demonstrate an explicit link between the evidence provided and the established purposes. To maintain some sense of interrater reliability, the same faculty who establish the purposes for the portfolios should be involved in assessing whether or not the portfolios meet the established purposes. In my own seminar, I find that when I am explicit with students about what I want, I tend to get it. And, when I am clear with myself about what I am looking for, I find that my professional judgments are more than adequate for assessing my students' portfolios.

Conclusion

Portfolio development and assessment can create opportunities for novice teachers to use their knowledge about teaching in ways that are similar to how they will use that knowledge once they enter their own classrooms. In addition, it can help teacher educators assess how novice teachers make sense of what they are learning in terms of themselves, their classroom practices, and the social contexts within which they teach. Ultimately, this means assessing the process more than the product and valuing pedagogical reasoning more than teaching behaviors. It means moving away from assuming there are right answers about teaching to accepting multiple perspectives. It means providing multiple opportunities for teachers to demonstrate their competencies. And finally, it means carrying out assessment that is less like external judgment and more like internal sense-making and self-analysis.

References

Barton, J., & Collins, A. (1993). Portfolios in teacher education. *Journal of Teacher Education, 44.* 200–210.

Collins, A. (1991). Portfolios for biology teacher assessment. *Journal of Personnel Evaluation in Education, 5,* 147–167.

Shulman, J. H. (1987). *Case methods in teacher education.* New York: Teachers College Press.

Author

Karen E. Johnson is associate professor of speech communication at The Pennsylvania State University, where she teaches in the MATESOL program. Her research focuses on teacher cognition in second language teacher education, and she is the author of Understanding Communication in Second Language Classrooms *(Cambridge University Press).*

Assessing Integrated Language and Content Instruction

Deborah J. Short

Center for Applied Linguistics

Integrated language and content instruction has become a popular alternative to traditional ESL instruction. Researchers have recommended this instructional approach to develop students' academic language ability and facilitate their transition to mainstream classes. Practitioners have also favored this approach for several reasons: to prepare students for mainstream classes, increase student motivation and interest with content themes, and make ESL students feel part of the mainstream school curricula. Over the past 10 years, much progress has been made in developing, implementing, and refining strategies and techniques that effectively integrate language and content instruction. However, the issue of assessment is still being resolved. Neither traditional language tests nor content achievement tests are adequate. The difficulty with assessment centers on isolating the language features from the content objectives so one does not adversely influence the other. This article addresses the issue of assessment in integrated classes and provides a framework for organizing assessment objectives. It recommends using alternative assessment measures, such as checklists, portfolios, interviews, and performance-based tasks. Examples of the framework being implemented in elementary and secondary school integrated language and content classes are also included.

The integration of language and content instruction has come of age. No longer the new trend in methodologies, content ESL—or sheltered English, or language-sensitive content instruction as it is variously known—has assumed a valued and dynamic place in many school curricula. Language teachers have forged common ground with subject-area educators in implementing content-based syllabi. These educators recognize that although the need to prepare language minority students for a rigorous academic program is great, in many school settings, the time for such preparation is brief.

The demographic picture in the U.S. is revealing. The fastest growing sector of the school population comprises language minority students. Within the language minority student body, the underschooled group is the fastest growing. Educators can no longer rely on transfer of knowledge and skills as students learn English and then enter a mainstream track because so many students come to U.S. schools underprepared for the required grade-level work. In response, language and subject-area educators have been joining forces to get language minority students involved in the regular curricula before they have fully mastered the English language. There simply is no time to delay academic instruction until these students have developed high levels of English language proficiency if they are to stay in school, succeed in their classes, and graduate with a high school diploma. In a recent report, the Council of Chief State School Officers (CCSSO, 1992) notes: "For limited English proficient (LEP) students success in school hinges upon gaining access to effective second language learning opportunities, and to a full educational program" (p. 4). The report goes on to say that whereas language assistance programs help in developing English proficiency, they should, at the same time, "ensure that these students continue to learn and expand their knowledge of new content and therefore do not fall behind peers whose native language is English" (p. 6).

In many U.S. schools, bilingual education programs have been perceived as the answer to keeping students on grade level for content objectives while developing enough language proficiency for students to be mainstreamed eventually. Unfortunately, this ideal is rarely fulfilled in bilingual programs for several reasons. First, most of the programs are "early exit." Students exit the program after 2 years, often on the basis of oral proficiency tests, before they have the academic language skills needed to master the demands of the regular classroom. (See Cummins, 1980a, and Collier, 1989, for a fuller discussion.) Second, bilingual programs are found primarily in the elementary schools, leaving secondary-aged students without that form of native language support. Third, a bilingual approach is not feasible in schools where the LEP students speak many different native languages. In these last two situations, students are often placed in ESL programs. However, traditional ESL programs, where the focus is on language development with little attention to subject-area curricula, are not serving the current influx of language minority students well.

As a consequence, the integration of language and content objectives in lesson plans has been implemented and accepted by a wide range of teachers and administrators as one solution to the dilemma of how to teach English to linguistically and culturally diverse students while preparing them for grade-level curricula. A number of teacher resource manuals and student textbooks have been written to guide instruction in this approach.[1] Preservice and in-service training have increasingly focused on the integration of language and content around the country. Journal articles and conference presentations abound. The U.S. Department of Education is sponsoring a national study, which, in its first phase, collected data from more than 1,500 programs in the U.S. that have an integrated language and content program in one school or more (Center for Applied Linguistics, 1993). The overall goal of the study will be to describe the range of practices for content ESL and identify key program features that produce effective educational results.

In content-based language instruction, language teachers use content topics, rather than grammar rules or vocabulary lists, as the scaffolding for instruction. Frequently, language teachers collaborate with content-area colleagues to plan instruction that complements and/or reinforces instruction occurring in the regular content course. In language-sensitive content instruction, such as in sheltered science, content teachers have been trained in ESL techniques, enabling them to adjust their instruction to meet the needs of language minority students. These techniques include increased use of visuals and demonstrations, emphasis on graphic organizers and thinking/study skill development, and promotion of student participation and communication through all four language skills—listening, speaking, reading, and writing. Moreover, most language and content teachers are using cooperative grouping, thereby enabling language minority students to access additional support from their peers. By providing students opportunities to use language in meaningful contexts—studying the academic subject matter while they develop language proficiency—teachers create an ideal learning environment for facilitating the transition of these students into mainstream courses.

How to teach academic content has been the first barrier to cross in order to improve educational practice for language minority students, but a second remains—how to assess student comprehension of subject matter and student language skill development. Students and teachers realize that most assessment instruments actually test both content concepts and language ability, particularly reading comprehension and writing. Because language and content are intricately intertwined, it is difficult to isolate one feature from the other in the assessment process. Thus, teachers may not be sure whether a student is simply unable to demonstrate knowledge because of a language barrier or whether, indeed, the student does not know the content material being assessed. Yet, a distinction needs to be drawn, especially if a student is not succeeding in a course. This article will address the second barrier by providing a framework for teachers to use as they measure students' content mastery and language skill and seek to determine whether content objectives have not been mastered or whether language is interfering with a student's acquisition and application of information.

ASSESSMENT REFORM

At present, assessment dominates the educational reform dialogue. Inadequacies in current practices have led many educators and observers of educational progress in the U.S. to call for changes in assessment procedures. (See, e.g., Linn & Baker, 1992; NCEST, 1992; NCRMSE, 1991.) The emphasis on assessment reform comes from many fronts: teachers, administrators, government officials and politicians, researchers, education consultants, and business leaders. At the local level, it is tied to accountability, program evaluation, programmatic support, community support, student achievement, student promotion, and credibility. Beyond the school district boundaries, it is linked to college entrance requirements, the national standards movement, and workplace skills. It affects teacher and administrator careers, public funding of programs, school choice, and more.

There are several reasons to assess student learning in the classroom: to place students in classes, to measure student progress and achievement, to guide and improve instruction, and to diagnose student knowledge of a topic before it is taught. Such assessment must be carried out carefully. Educators now acknowledge that standardized tests with short answer or multiple-choice items do not provide an accurate picture of student knowledge as a whole (Ascher, 1990; CCSSO, 1992; MSEB, 1991); therefore, it is inappropriate to base placement, achievement levels, and instructional plans solely on standardized test results. In addition, a task force commissioned by the National Center for Research on Evaluation, Standards and Student Testing (NCRESST, 1992) has recognized that student diversity and educational equity play a role in test performance. In the monograph it is preparing, the task force plans to recommend nonstandardized, alternative assessment approaches for measuring student ability. Although school systems will continue to use standardized tests to measure and compare student progress, alternative assessment must also become part of the student evaluation package.

The demand for assessment alternatives to paper-and-pen multiple-choice tests has grown among language and content educators who want more accurate measures of their students' knowledge. For some educators, alternative measures may simply entail incorporating open-ended questions and essays into existing tests. For others, alternative assessment would be organized to permit students to demonstrate their knowledge and abilities over a long period of time, as through portfolios. Still others look at *authentic* assessment as the solution—requiring students to conduct tasks that mirror the use of the concept or operation or manipulative (e.g., microscopes, geoboards, or fraction bars) in the real world.

The charge to revise curriculum and evaluation practices in the U.S. began with the publication of *Curriculum and Evaluation*

---

[1]Teacher resources include, among others. Brinton, Snow, & Wesche, 1989; Cantoni-Harvey. 1987; Crandall, 1987; Mohan, 1986; and Short, 1991. Student textbooks include, among others, Chamot, O'Malley, & Kupper, 1992; Crandall, Dale, Rhodes, & Spanos, 1989; Fathman & Quinn, 1989; Johnston & Johnston, 1990; and Short, Seufert-Bosco, & Grognet, 1991.

Standards for School Mathematics by the National Council of Teachers of Mathematics (NCTM, 1989). In these standards, NCTM recommended that students be taught to communicate mathematically and called for a new way of thinking about assessing mathematics, including making assessment integral to instruction and using multiple measures to evaluate student learning. Lajoie (1991) offered several ideas and principles for designing authentic assessment tasks that conform to the new standards. In 1992, NCTM devoted an issue of *Arithmetic Teacher* (NCTM, 1992b) and of *Mathematics Teacher* (NCTM, 1992a) to alternative assessment with articles describing assessment trends, classroom strategies, and grading procedures. In addition, NCTM has recently begun developing assessment standards to be published in a separate volume to accompany the organization's standards publications.

Other subject-area professional organizations have taken up the charge and are in the process of revising their assessment practices, many calling for more performance-based measures. A case in point is the National Science Teachers Association's (NSTA) Scope, Sequence and Coordination of Secondary School Science project. As the informational brochure explains:

> The assessment will require students to demonstrate why they believe something, how they know something is correct, and what terms mean, using real objects and phenomena. (NSTA, no date)

The National Research Council is also looking at science assessment and has established the National Committee on Science Education Standards and Assessment to work on national standards for science that "guide judgements about and the development of science curriculum, teaching and assessment" (NSTA, 1992, p. 3).

The National Council for the Social Studies (NCSS), like NCTM, devoted a special section of its journal, *Social Education* (NCSS, 1992), to assessment. Articles addressed issues of testing and teacher involvement with alternative measures such as performance tasks and portfolios. In his book, Parker (1991) advocated authentic assessment in social studies education that corresponds to instructional activities, requires higher order thinking, and sets out performance-based criteria that define the levels of student knowledge.

Assessment reform has not been unheralded among language educators either. With the introduction of a whole language perspective into elementary classrooms, assessment of student progress has been reconsidered. No longer could traditional spelling tests, for example, serve their familiar function in a classroom where *intended* spelling was the norm.[2] In fact, the use of portfolio assessment in K–12 language arts classes has its origins in the whole language movement (Harp,

1991; Tierney, 1991). With portfolios (as this article discusses below), students exhibit their writing progress and proficiency through meaningful and contextual activities that they have selected and compiled.

ESL and bilingual educators have had to attend to a wider range of assessment practices than most other classroom teachers. Besides measuring student achievement within the course, assessment has always played a gatekeeping role in deciding which students would be placed in which class and, later, when a student would exit from that class. In the not too distant past, students frequently entered and exited ESL/bilingual (BE) education programs on the basis of their oral language proficiency test scores. Over time, however, we have learned that these tests are imprecise measures of students' ability to do grade-level subject-matter work in a nonnative language (see Cummins, 1980b). Many former ESL/BE students who passed these tests were not ready for the academic language tasks (e.g., expository reading and writing assignments) required in mainstream classes, and they did not succeed. One common solution was to place these students in the lowest track courses. Some students' solution was to drop out. Neither solution solved the problem of students being underprepared for the academic rigors of the mainstream curriculum. This realization gave impetus to ESL and bilingual teachers to use content-based language instruction and subsequently to recognize the need for additional assessment instruments more commensurate with the academic demands of the mainstream curricula.

Further support for assessment reform has come from U.S. business and industry reports of deficiencies in the skills of the workforce (see Johnston & Packer, 1987). Once students move into the workplace, they discover the need for communication skills in the context of writing, reading, and social tasks and for document and quantitative literacy skills such as interpreting graphs and schedules, or performing accounting procedures and balancing budgets, respectively. The instructional and assessment practices many of these students experienced in school have not corresponded well to the application of their knowledge in the work setting. Seeking to employ a better prepared workforce, the business sector has called for educational improvements including the incorporation of alternative or authentic assessment into an overall policy (Berryman & Bailey, 1992; Secretary's Commission on Achieving Necessary Skills, 1991). In one response, the American College Testing program is working on a "skills assessment tool to link school instruction with workplace needs" (AAAS, 1991, p. 1). This assessment tool considers the academic skills of reading, writing, and computation along with workplace skills such as problem solving, reasoning, teamwork, and oral communication.

ASSESSING THE INTEGRATION OF LANGUAGE AND CONTENT

Government, school, and business sectors in the U.S. have joined in their support for assessment reform. Alternative assessment, in its diverse formats, has become the trend. Most

---

[2] In a whole language classroom, children who are learning to read and write are encouraged to write before they have mastered spelling. They often write words based on the sounds they hear and, through pictures and reading aloud, they share their intent with the audience. Some educators refer to this process as *invented* spelling. I prefer the expression *intended* spelling to acknowledge that students are not just combining letters in any order but rather are making progress toward the actual spelling.

educators are experimenting with it in some form in their class-rooms. Some states, such as Vermont and California, are mandating it for all students. (See Blank & Dalkilic, 1992, for a review of state policies.) Parents are becoming informed about alternative assessment; students are responding positively to it. As assessment increasingly reflects instruction that is occurring in the classroom, teaching to the test has been deemphasized. Good assessment is recognized as that which reflects actual classroom practices, not a one-time standardized exam.

The many varieties of alternative assessment include performance-based tests, portfolios, journals, projects, and observation checklists. Although these measures allow better demonstration of student knowledge, they can nonetheless confound teachers of language minority students. Complications arise first because teachers must determine whether the language or the content is being assessed in these alternative measures. Then teachers must distinguish between the language and content knowledge of the students and decide if one is interfering with the demonstration of the other.

For instance, students who can solve math computation problems correctly and thereby demonstrate mastery of mathematical operations may be unable to solve a math word problem requiring the same computations if their English proficiency is not at a level capable of understanding the words and assumptions in the problem. Conversely, students who can write a well-constructed essay about their country's agricultural practices and thereby demonstrate mastery of paragraph development with topic sentences and supporting details may be unable to write an essay on the decline of the U.S. automobile industry if the topic, its relevant vocabulary, and notable people and events are unfamiliar.

Clearly, educators of language minority students grapple with this dilemma every day. As a result, one strong recommendation has emerged: Objectives should be defined before designing or choosing any instructional procedure, ranging from a lesson plan to an exam. Although it is not uncommon to find teachers assigning two grades to a writing sample such as an essay—one for form (e.g., grammar, vocabulary, spelling, topic sentences) and one for content (e.g., topical, accurate, interesting)—this practice does not work for all subject areas or testing situations. Instead, it is more advisable to focus on a single objective, be it content or language specific. Some assessment tools can be used exclusively for checking content comprehension, whereas others can be designated as language development measures. A word of caution is in order: Even within a language assessment instrument, teachers must make a choice whether to measure fluency or accuracy.

A second recommendation from field experience concerns flexibility. School systems should include both formal and informal measures in their overall assessment plan and must support teachers who develop and implement a diverse repertoire of assessment tools. Although all students can benefit from a wide range of assessment procedures, variety is particularly important for language minority students because they (a) are often unfamiliar with the type of standardized tests usually required in U.S. schools, (b) may have different learning and testing styles, and (c) may be unable to demonstrate the extent

of their knowledge at a single sitting on one designated testing day. Further, particularly in the case of standardized tests, language minority students should be given more time for completion because they must process both language and content information embedded in the test.

The remainder of this paper proposes an assessment framework with the underlying philosophy that alternative measures should be incorporated into lesson planning frequently and informally as a significant part of instruction. Successful implementation of the framework requires that (a) students be given frequent opportunities to demonstrate the growth of their knowledge base; (b) assessment tools be varied to meet individual learning styles, needs, and current skill levels; and (c) students be made aware of the assessment objectives in advance. (There may be times when an educator wishes to prepare a test in a more formal manner to compare the achievement of students receiving content-based instruction with those receiving traditional ESL instruction; e.g., see the systematic discussion of content-based language test design by Turner, 1992.)

AN ASSESSMENT MATRIX

Overall, assessment should be viewed holistically but in an integrated language and content course, where students are asked to demonstrate knowledge and ability in several areas, it is important to separate language issues from subject-area concepts. The following matrix (Figure 1) is offered to language and content educators as a guide for selecting their assessment-tool and for determining in advance their assessment objective: language or content. (Some of the categories have been derived from work conducted by the author and colleagues at the Center for Applied Linguistics, from Griffiths & Clyne, and from work by Kessler & Quinn, 1992.) This matrix examines what might be assessed and how the assessment might be done. It is a first step in distinguishing between these two categories of learning for a language minority student.

The objectives of an integrated language and content course can be divided into the following categories: problem solving, content-area skills, concept comprehension, language use, communication skills, individual behavior, group behavior, and attitude. These areas can then be assessed through some of the following alternative measures: skill checklists and reading/writing inventories, anecdotal records and teacher observations, student self-evaluations, portfolios, performance-based tasks, essay writing, oral reports, and interviews.

Some overlap will occur between the language and content distinctions when some of the objectives, such as certain problem-solving activities, require that language (oral or written) be demonstrated. If students solve a mixture problem in algebra but are asked to explain and justify the steps taken, language is required to do so. They must recall the vocabulary terms, articulate coherent sentences, and make use of transition markers such as *then* and *next*. The overlap can be clarified, however, by varying the assessment alternatives and categorizing the objective areas for assessment, as the divisions in Figure 1 show. The key is to select the type or types of assessment

FIGURE 1
Integrated Language and Content Assessment: What and How

| | | H O W | | | | | | |
	Checklist, inventory	Anecdotal record, teacher observation	Student self-evaluation	Portfolios	Performance, manipulatives	Written essays, reports	Oral reports	Student interviews
Problem solving								
Content-area skills								
Concept comprehension								
Language use								
Communication skills								
Individual behavior								
Group behavior								
Attitudes								

carefully and to focus consistently on the objective. For instance, by looking at the process a student undertakes when solving a problem through anecdotal records kept during class, a teacher can note that the student made estimations before seeking a solution and checked the work before turning it in. When checking on language use, the teacher may have the student report orally on a solved problem and listen for appropriate use of technical terms.

The matrix also distinguishes between individual and group work. As indicated earlier, content and language teachers often engage students in cooperative activities, and this practice benefits language minority students. However, all students must also be able to complete tasks individually. When language minority students are placed in mainstream classes, they will be expected to work on group and individual assignments; thus, assessing their preparation in these areas is important.

The final category of the matrix considers student attitude toward content subjects. Determining a student's attitude toward a subject can be enlightening for a teacher in terms of selecting curricula and promoting student participation. There is ample anecdotal evidence that if students like a subject and/or recognize its importance, they will be motivated to work hard and perhaps be more successful in that course.

SKILLS ASSESSED

The skill categories shown in the matrix in Figure 1 are as follows.

Problem Solving

Within this category, students show the ability to solve problems. Examples include drawing diagrams, sorting and classifying, using manipulatives as models, explaining to other students, finding/accepting alternate solutions, designing one's own problems, checking one's work.

Content-Area Skills

Here, students demonstrate content skills. Examples include adding mixed numerals, graphing points on x- and y-axes, simplifying algebraic expressions, creating a timeline, following directions on a map, balancing a chemical reaction equation, identifying elements of a cell.

Concept Comprehension

Students show understanding of content concepts and when and where to apply this knowledge. Examples include determining whether to use multiplication or addition, distinguishing between area and perimeter, representing information graphically, recognizing patterns, comparing the monetary systems of two ancient civilizations, arranging organisms into a food chain.

Language Use

Students are assessed on their ability to use academic language appropriately. Examples include using correct technical vocabulary; recognizing similar terms such as *decrease, diminish,* and *minus;* writing a paragraph with a topic sentence and supporting details.

Communication Skills

Students must convey information or opinions about the work done or the subject area studied. Examples include the ability to explain steps taken in an experiment, sharing ideas, discussing math concepts, debating health issues, giving and justifying opinions.

Individual Behavior

Students conduct and complete work individually. Examples include planning and carrying through an assignment, researching a topic and preparing a report on it, exhibiting self-motivation, discipline, and independence.

Group Behavior

Students demonstrate successful communicative and social skills and complete group tasks. Examples include working collaboratively with other students in a group, contributing to the discussion, explaining to others, using social skills.

Attitude

Teachers can assess student attitude toward the subject. Examples include being comfortable doing content work, exhibiting confidence, showing a willingness to take risks, recognizing the relevance of a content area in one's life. If the attitude is negative, teachers may want to modify their instructional approach.

ASSESSMENT MEASURES

Many of the alternative assessment measures of this matrix have been described in detail elsewhere. (See ASCD, 1992; Hamayan & Pfleger 1987: Pierce & O'Malley, 1992, and Short, 1991.) In this article, they will be briefly explained, noting some advantages and disadvantages. It is important to recognize that this list is not exhaustive but representative of teacher options that take into account student skill levels, learning styles, and presentation modes.

Skill and Concept Checklist, Reading and Writing Inventories

A teacher can use a checklist or an inventory during the lesson as students are working and mark off skills students demonstrate. The checklist could also be used after the lesson, upon reflection, or based on student work that has been turned in.

Advantages

This quick measure can be completed while walking around during individual or cooperative learning activities. It helps meet some curricular objectives, such as covering grammar items, within the context of a communicative, content-based lesson where items appear in context, not as discrete variables.

Disadvantages

Because this is often a yes-or-no measure, the student demonstrates the skill or doesn't; it is hard to show student progress for a specific skill. This limitation could be overcome by defining three increments such as *unable, making progress,* and *mastery* of a skill or concept.

Anecdotal Record, Teacher Observations

A teacher may reflect on a student's work or behavior during the day or over a short period of time and record impressions and anecdotes that pertain to the student's learning progress.

Advantages

Such records and observations help capture the learning process vividly; they can be an insightful commentary on student progress.

Disadvantages

This measure may not satisfy the requirements of accountability. Anecdotal records are not always considered valid evidence of student progress and achievement. Moreover, such observational records take time but need to done regularly.

Student Self-Evaluation

Students may evaluate a specific piece of their own work or judge their learning progress using a checklist, scale, or written description.

Advantages

Self-evaluations offer students opportunities for reflection. Moreover, they encourage students to take responsibility for assessment.

Disadvantages

Once again, the question of accountability is raised. Self-report data are not always considered valid measures. Also, students may need to be trained to judge their own work and that of classmates.

Portfolios

Students, sometimes with teacher, peer, or parental assistance, are given the responsibility to select a variety of work products and arrange them in a portfolio that demonstrates their knowledge growth. Students are often asked to justify their selections.

Advantages

Portfolios allow students to demonstrate progress over time. As such, they encourage student participation and accountability. An additional advantage is that they can be assembled according to specifications such as "include a first draft and final copy of a report" and "include something you think was not done well and explain how you could improve it."

Disadvantages

Developing and evaluating portfolios is time-consuming; they do not provide a quick picture of student knowledge. Another drawback for some is that scoring is subjective and teachers need training in how to score consistently.

Performance-Based Tasks, Manipulatives

It should be noted that some educators use the term *performance assessment* to include all activities that assess skills contextually. Some also use *performance* interchangeably with *authentic* and *alternative* assessment. For the purposes of this article, performance has this more limited, task-based definition. In this measure, students must perform an assigned task, such as setting up equipment for a science experiment, miming the events in a story, following oral or written directions. This type of assessment often involves physical movement and manipulatives.

Advantages

These tasks help students with low literacy skills. As well, they meet the needs of tactile and kinesthetic learners; assessment is process oriented.

Disadvantages

This kind of assessment is time-consuming; students must be assessed individually or in small groups, and scoring may be subjective.

Written Essays, Reports, and Projects

Students present their knowledge pictorially or in writing through essays, research reports, or long-term projects.

Advantages

These measures give students time to prepare. They may also allow for different modes of presentation (written or pictorial). Essays, reports, and projects are suitable for group work.

Disadvantages

Research may require high literacy skills in reading and writing. It is also time-consuming.

Oral Reports and Presentations

Students report and present orally knowledge they have acquired.

Advantages

Oral presentations give students time to prepare in advance. They allow low-literacy-level students to participate in assessment and are suitable for group work.

Disadvantages

Some students are uncomfortable with public speaking. Again, oral assessment is time-consuming.

Interviews

A teacher may conduct an individual or group interview to ascertain student knowledge or attitude.

Advantages

Interviews give teachers opportunities to probe student knowledge or rephrase questions; they provide students with a chance to ask and clarify questions. Interviews do not require high literacy skills.

Disadvantages

It is time-consuming to interview each student individually. As well, interviews require oral comprehension and production skills.

ASSESSMENT ACTIVITIES

At this point, it may be useful to demonstrate the use of this matrix by describing some activities that might occur in several cells. For illustrative purposes, various subject areas and classes found in the U.S. school system are represented. Figure 2 indicates which cells will be discussed.

1. Problem Solving: Anecdotal Record
Objective: To determine if students make use of problem-solving techniques

In an integrated language and mathematics class, the teacher has asked students to solve some word problems. As the teacher walks around the room, s/he notes that some of the students are drawing diagrams as they work out their solutions. The teacher records in a notebook students who try several diagrams, those who compare diagrams with others, and those who do not draw diagrams.

2. Problem Solving: Essays, Reports
Objective: To evaluate student ability to analyze and describe problem-solving processes

Students are shown an algebraic word problem and two correct but different solutions written by other students. They are asked to write an essay describing the steps each student took to generate their solution to the problem. Then they are shown a third student's solution which resulted in an incorrect solution and are asked to explain where and how that student erred.

3. Problem Solving: Interview
Objective: To have students reflect metacognitively on steps taken to solve a health problem

In an integrated language and health class, the teacher has set up the following scenario.

> A village in India uses a common well as its source of drinking water. The water has become polluted and villagers are getting sick. You students are the scientists given the task of determining the source of the pollution.

The teacher allows students to discuss the problem in groups and then interviews several students individually. During the interview, the teacher asks the students what hypotheses they have generated, what steps they will take to solve the problem, and why they chose those steps.

4. Content Skills: Skill Checklist
Objective: To determine if students are able to use science equipment properly

In the first quarter of the year, the physical science teacher introduces the class to various scientific instruments that will be used in experiments throughout the year. During this time, the teacher maintains a skills checklist for each student. (See Figure 3 for some sample items.) As the students use the equipment in class, the teacher records the date and his/her evaluation of the student's ability.

FIGURE 2
Integrated Language and Content Assessment: What and How

				H O W				
		Checklist, inventory	Anecdotal record, teacher observation	Student self-evaluation	Portfolios	Performance, manipulatives	Written essays, reports	Oral reports	Student interviews
W H A T	Problem solving		1				2		3
	Content-area skills	4		5					
	Concept comprehension				6	7			
	Language use	8						9	
	Communication skills				10		11		
	Individual behavior		12			13			
	Group behavior			14				15	
	Attitudes	16							17

5. Content Skills: Student Self-Evaluation

Objective: To measure the ability to perform mathematical computations

At the beginning of the school year, the teacher in an ESL math class decides to give students a checklist to report their computation skills. (See Figure 4 for some sample items.) The teacher plans to use this checklist as a diagnostic assessment tool along with other measures, such as a placement test, to guide whole class, small-group, and individual instruction for the first quarter. To help some students, the teacher reads the checklist aloud as the students fill it out.

6. Concept Comprehension: Portfolios

Objective: To assess student knowledge of ways protest has influenced social change

One objective of a U.S. history class is to recognize the role of protest in engendering change in society, such as legislation or revolution. In the third quarter of the year, the teacher asks students to prepare a portfolio that demonstrates their awareness of different types of protest and their subsequent results. Students are required to collect newspaper clippings of current events and comment on the protests described. They are encouraged to analyze the motives behind the protests and make predictions about resulting future change, drawing on historical comparisons. To accommodate different language abilities, the teacher allows the students to write their comments or record them on audiotape to include in the portfolio. At the end of the quarter, the teacher will review the portfolios, looking for student historical knowledge and conceptual comprehension.

FIGURE 3
Science Equipment Skills Checklist (Sample)

	Mastery of skill	Needs assistance	Unable to do
1. Read a graduated cylinder			9/16
2. Use a pipette			
3. Read a metric ruler	9/10		
4. Read a thermometer	9/13	9/10	
5. Use a balance			

FIGURE 4
Student Self-Evaluation Checklist (Sample)

	YES	NO	SOMETIMES
I can add a column of four numbers. I can multiply two-digit numbers. I can divide by a three-digit number. I can add fractions. I can divide fractions. I can change a percent to a decimal.			

7. Concept Comprehension: Performance

Objective: To measure student ability to distinguish between regular and irregular polygons

In a geometry class, the teacher distributes paper, scissors, yarn, and several geoboards. Because the teacher wants to minimize the language barrier that might interfere with the students' performance, the teacher provides written and oral instructions for each task. Beginning with the paper and scissors, students are instructed to cut out geometric shapes, such as an isosceles triangle, an irregular pentagon, and a circle. Next, they are told to create a square, a rectangle, and an irregular six-sided figure with their geoboards and yarn. Scanning the room, the teacher can quickly assess the students' comprehension of these polygons.

8. Language Use: Checklist

Objective: To determine student familiarity with synonymous terms for mathematical operations

The pre-algebra teacher has drawn up a checklist of terms that s/he would like the class to know for the operations of addition, subtraction, multiplication, and division. To determine if they can link the terms to the symbols, the teacher designs a paired activity based on a technique in the *Pre-Algebra Lexicon* (Hayden & Cuevas, 1990). One partner receives a sheet with the operational symbols, the other the terms

in verbal mathematical expressions (see Figure 5). The partner with the expressions reads them aloud. The other partner circles the correct symbol for the operation. In reviewing the worksheets, the teacher indicates on her checklist the terms students know and do not know.

9. Language Use: Oral Presentation

Objective: To measure student knowledge of key vocabulary terms, question formation, and sentence structure

In an elementary-level family life course, students have been studying hygiene. Their assignment has been to interview family members and neighbors about their dental hygiene habits and prepare an oral presentation of their findings. The teacher has encouraged them to prepare some charts or graphs to share. During the presentation, the students are expected to relate their interview questions, the subjects' responses, and their conclusions about dental hygiene habits. While they present, the teacher listens for key terms and grammatical questions and answers.

10. Communication: Portfolios

Objective: To evaluate student knowledge of genetics through several modes of communication

The high school biology class began a unit on genetics recently. On the first day, the teacher distributes a K-W-L chart

FIGURE 5
Vocabulary in Mathematics Operations

Partner A: Read the Expressions below to your partner.	Partner B: Circle the symbol of the operation you hear.			
Expression	*Operation*			
1. Thirty minus eleven	+	−	×	/
2. Sixty-five times two	+	−	×	/
3. The quotient of sixty-four and eight	+	−	×	/
4. One less than ninety-six	+	−	×	/
5. Four increased by eighteen	+	−	×	/
6. One third of twenty seven	+	−	×	/

FIGURE 6
Genetics Portfolio Assignment

A. For your Genetics Portfolio, please include the following six items.

1. Design a tree diagram tracing the genetic history of eye color in your family for three generations.
2. Write a prediction and explanation for your child's eye color if your spouse has gray eyes.
3. Explain the difference between fraternal and identical twins. Draw pictures to illustrate the difference.
4. Select one lab report from the genetics experiments we conduct in class. Explain how the experiment increased your knowledge of genetics.
5. Write a dialogue between two or three people discussing a genetic disease.
6. Complete the What I Learned section on your K-W-L chart for the genetics unit and include it in your portfolio.

B. Choose two additional items to show me what you know about genetics.

and had the students fill in the What I Know about genetics and the What I Want to Learn sections. (The final section, What I Learned, will be part of a portfolio.) Based on what students put in their charts, the teacher generates a list of objectives for the portfolio. Three days later the teacher explains the portfolio procedure that would be used over the next 4 weeks and the list of items to include. (See Figure 6.) The teacher explains that students should begin working on the items and emphasizes that the objective is to see if students can create a portfolio that communicates the knowledge they have acquired about genetics.

11. Communication: Written Essays

Objective: To determine student ability to write a persuasive letter about a community issue

In a civics class, students read a hypothetical newspaper article about the county government's decision to allow a local developer to raze some old apartment buildings and build expensive, single family homes and a small shopping center. The article explains that the low-income building housed poor families but was in disrepair. Students are then instructed to take a position for or against the development plan and write a letter to the county government or to the newspaper outlining their position and making recommendations.

12. Individual Behavior: Anecdotal Record

Objective: To measure student ability to conduct research

The middle school language arts teacher has been focusing on research study skills in class. The teacher has introduced students to the library and reviewed the process for conducting research, including generating a research question. Each student has reflected on a piece of literature previously read in class and comes up with a question he or she would like to answer, perhaps about the historical background of the story. While the students conduct their research, the teacher records vignettes of student actions. The teacher notes if students use the card catalogue, if they consult with the librarian for addi-

tional sources, if they make note cards, and so forth. At the end of the research activity, the teacher will have some insight into which individuals are able to conduct research and which need more practice in the process.

13. Individual Behavior: Performance

Objective: To determine student knowledge of the scientific observation

At the conclusion of a unit on the senses, during which groups of students conducted several experiments, students work individually on a lab practical to demonstrate their observation skills. Each student is given water, clear plastic or glass cups, and colored, nontoxic fizzy tablets. They are told to place the tablets in water, observe what happens, and then write down their observations. The teacher will give credit for observations that were accurate and used sensory methods such as sight, taste, smell, and hearing.[3]

14. Group Behavior: Student Evaluation

Objective: To use social skills during group tasks

After a week-long social studies project that resulted in a group presentation on several inventions designed during the Industrial Revolution and their impact on the students' lives today, the teacher distributes a group evaluation sheet to the students. (See sample items in Figure 7.) They are asked to complete it individually at first and then meet with the group to resolve any differences among group members.

15. Group Behavior: Reports

Objective: To evaluate students' abilities to work in a group to prepare an oral presentation

---

[3]This example is derived from an item on the international performance assessment conducted by the Center for Assessment of Educational Progress. See Semple, 1992.

FIGURE 7
Group Evaluation Form (Sample)

Please respond to the following statements. Circle A for *All*, M for *Most*, S for *Some*, and N for *None*

	All	Most	Some	None
How many members brainstormed ideas for the report?	A	M	S	N
How many members followed his/her assigned role?	A	M	S	N
How many members prepared the final report?	A	M	S	N
How many members praised the ideas of the others?	A	M	S	N
How many members stayed on task during class most of the time?	A	M	S	N

[3]This example is derived from an item on the international performance assessment conducted by the Center for Assessment of Educational Progress. See Semple, 1992.

In the second semester of the year, small groups of elementary school students are assigned the task of studying one class of animal (e.g., reptile, fish, bird) and preparing an oral report. These students had participated in cooperative learning activities previously. To facilitate the first phase of the process, the teacher asks each student to research a different representative animal and share that knowledge with group mates. In the second phase, the teacher suggests the students choose roles such as illustrator, recorder, reporter, and so forth. The students are expected to prepare and present the report collaboratively. During the class time devoted to the project, the teacher evaluates the group process and notes whether (a) all the students participated, (b) they stayed on task, (c) they pooled their information, (d) they selected roles and followed them, and (e) their final report was a balanced representation of their work.

16. Attitude: Reading Inventory

Objective: To determine student attitude toward an instructional technique that promotes reading

In a language arts class with LEP students, the teacher uses sustained silent reading (SSR) twice a week. To determine student attitude towards this reading activity, the teacher may use a reading inventory such as the REACH scale in Figure 8. (See Hamayan & Pfleger, 1987, for a full discussion.)

The dimensions most revealing about student attitudes are E (*Enthusiastic* about SSR), A (*Attentive* and on task during the activity), and C (easily *Choosing* books to read).

17. Attitude: Interview

Objective: To assess student recognition of the role of geography in society

World geography has been an elective course in one high school but became required for graduation this year. Anticipating discontent among the seniors forced to take the course,

the teacher decides to conduct group interviews. Within the first 2 weeks of school, the teacher asks small groups of students their feelings about the geography course, their knowledge of other countries' natural resources and land features, and geography's importance in their lives now and in the future. At the end of the course, the teacher asks the students similar questions to determine if their attitudes have changed and whether the teaching has been successful in helping students gain an appreciation of geography.

DISCUSSION

It is unlikely (and unnecessary) for all cells of the matrix to be filled during any one curricular unit or course. The matrix should be used to display the distribution of alternative assessment practices and the objectives teachers have measured. By keeping track of the filled-in cells, teachers can gauge their efforts at meeting the learning and testing styles of students and make adjustments if the choice of assessment measures has been unbalanced—all content skill measures or all written reports, for example.

The suggested assessment tools allow for oral, written, pictorial, and physical demonstrations of knowledge on the part of the students. They also balance control and responsibility for assessment outcomes between teachers and students. The checklists and observations are information and teacher controlled; students need not know they are being assessed. The interview process incorporates opportunities for clarification and probing by both the teacher and the students. The other tools are student controlled. Students make their own decisions about the amount of effort they expend to complete the tasks.

Teachers may want to use measures for assessing students beyond those described in the matrix. Journals, profiles, reading logs, and simulations, for instance, may be substituted in the columns or added to the matrix. The increasing use of

FIGURE 8
Evaluating SSR Performance (The REACH[a,b]Scale)

Student Name	Week of:					Week of:					Week of:					Week of:				
	R	E	A	C	H	R	E	A	C	H	R	E	A	C	H	R	E	A	C	H
1																				
2																				
3																				
4																				
5																				
6																				
7																				
8																				
9																				
10																				

[a]*Dimensions*
R = Reading orally
E = Enthusiastic
A = Attentive
C = Choosing books easily
H = How many books read

[b]Rate the REACH dimensions along the following scale:
1 = Not able to/not at all
2 = Adequate
3 = Very well/very much so
NA = Not applicable

multimedia technology in the language classroom offers additional avenues for assessment. Video- and audiocassette tapes, which may be made at regular intervals and preserved, can capture student oral language development as well as growth of content knowledge. Computers, with tracking and branching capabilities, can individualize student assessment and monitor student progress. Computer simulations with interactive screen and audio components can engender assessment designs that measure all four language skills, problem solving, mastery of content objectives, and more.

The framework recommended in this article involves a time-consuming process. In setting up and implementing the matrix, teachers have to plan ahead and delineate their assessment objectives as they teach because assessment should be linked closely to instruction. Flexibility is important and insight into student learning styles is crucial. In some instances, teachers will need guidance in evaluating some of the measures. Scoring a portfolio or performance-based task, for example, often requires listing criteria and developing a rating scale in advance. Furthermore, because some administrators and funding authorities prefer quantitative data when making program decisions, teachers should be aware that these individuals may need some training in interpreting the information some of these qualitative assessment tools reveal.

CONCLUSIONS

We must always remember that in integrated language and content courses we are doubly burdening our students. We are demanding that they learn enough English—academic En-glish—to be mainstreamed and that they receive, process, and retain content information, much of which will be unfamiliar in terms of their prior schooling and life experiences. But, we have little choice. Time and interest take their toll on our students' educational careers: time because many students do not have 5–7 years to master English before approaching a content course in the U.S. educational system; interest because a grammar-based curriculum is not particularly appealing to a student who wants to fit into the school environment.

Our profession, therefore, has accepted the integration of language and content as an approach to assisting students with limited English proficiency. No approach is without drawbacks, and even if assessment is the weak link in the integrated language and content approach, the framework offered in this paper aims to strengthen that aspect of instructional practice. Clearly, some standardized tests and paper-and-pencil chapter tests will continue to be used, but they are no longer satisfactory as the sole measures of student achievement.

After all, at the heart of instruction is the desire to help our language minority students learn, and at the heart of assessment is the need to determine whether our students have learned. We must assist them in that process by trying new alternatives that are not so language bound, time restrictive, or autonomous. Further, we must advocate assessment practices that mirror instructional practices. Let us focus on our students' strengths and give them opportunities to demonstrate ability, skill, and knowledge through the medium that suits them best, whether oral or written or even, in the case of beginner students, pictorial. Let us familiarize them in advance with the assessment measures and give them adequate time to complete the tasks. Let us help them take some responsibility for their own evaluation, especially through tools such as student checklists, reports, and portfolios. Let us become alternative assessment advocates for our language minority students.

ACKNOWLEDGMENTS

I would like to thank my copresenters in *Assessment of Content-Based Language Instruction: Issues and Ideas,* a colloquium conducted at the 26th Annual TESOL Convention (Vancouver, Canada, 1992), where I presented some of the ideas in this paper: Bernard Mohan, Mary Ellen Quinn, Carolyn Kessler, David Freeman, and Lorraine Valdez Pierce. Richard Mott and Vickie Lewelling also provided helpful comments on earlier drafts.

THE AUTHOR

Deborah J. Short is Associate Division Director for ESL at the Center for Applied Linguistics. She is interested in the integration of language and content and has conducted research and teacher preparation in that area. She also develops integrated curricula and materials.

REFERENCES

AAAS (American Association for the Advancement of Science). (1991). *Science Education News, 9*(1, 2).

ASCD (Association for Supervision and Curriculum Development). (1992). Using performance assessment [Theme issue]. *Educational Leadership, 49*(8).

Ascher, C. (1990). Can performance-based assessments improve urban schooling? *ERIC Digest.* New York: ERIC Clearinghouse on Urban Education.

Blank, R. K., & Dalkilic, M. (1992). *State policies on science and mathematics education 1992.* Washington, DC: Council of Chief State School Officers, State Education Assessment Center.

Berryman, S. E., & Bailey, T. R. (1992). *The double helix of education and the economy.* New York: Columbia University, Teachers College, Institute on Education and the Economy.

Brinton, D., Snow, M. A., & Wesche, M. (1989). *Content-based second language instruction.* New York: Newbury House.

Cantoni-Harvey, G. (1987). *Content-area language instruction: Approaches and strategies.* Reading, MA: Addison-Wesley.

Center for Applied Linguistics. (1993). *A descriptive study of content-ESL practices* (Final data analysis report, Contract No. T291004001). Washington, DC: U.S. Department of Education, Office of Bilingual Education and Minority Languages Affairs.

Chamot, A. U., O'Malley, J. M., & Kupper, L. (1992). *Building bridges: Content and learning strategies for ESL* (Books 1–3). Boston, MA: Heinle & Heinle.

Collier, V. (1989). How long? A synthesis of research on academic achievement in a second language. *TESOL Quarterly, 23*(3), 509–532.

CCSSO (Council of Chief State School Officers). (1992). *Recommendations for improving the assessment and monitoring of students with limited English proficiency.* Washington, DC: CCSSO.

Crandall, J. A. (Ed.) (1987). *ESL in content-area instruction.* Englewood Cliffs, NJ: Prentice Hall Regents.

Crandall, J. A., Dale, T. C., Rhodes, N., & Spanos, G. (1989). *English skills for algebra.* Washington, DC/Englewood Cliffs, NJ: Center for Applied Linguistics/ Prentice Hall Regents.

Cummins, J. (1980a). The cross-lingual dimensions of language proficiency: Implications for bilingual education and the optimal age issue. *TESOL Quarterly 14*(2), 175–187.

Cummins, J. (1980b). The entry and exit fallacy in bilingual education. *NABE Journal, 4*(3), 25–29.

Fathman, A., & Quinn, M. E. (1989). *Science for language learners.* Englewood Cliffs, NJ: Prentice Hall Regents.

Griffiths, R., & Clyne, M. (1991). *Books you can count on: Linking mathematics and literature.* Portsmouth, NH: Heinemann.

Hamayan, E., & Pfleger, M. (1987). *Developing literacy in ESL: Guidelines for teachers of young children from non-literate backgrounds* (Teacher resource guide). Washington. DC: National Clearinghouse on Bilingual Education.

Harp, B. (Ed.) (1991). *Assessment and evaluation in the whole language classroom.* Norwood, MA: Christopher-Gordon.

Hayden, D., & Cuevas, G. (1990). *Pre-algebra lexicon.* Washington, DC: Center for Applied Linguistics.

Johnston, J., & Johnston. M. (1990). *Content points* (Books A–C). Reading. MA: Addison-Wesley.

Johnston. W. B., & Packer, A. H. (1987). *Workforce 2000: Work and workers for the 21st century.* Indianapolis IN: Hudson Institute.

Lajoie, S. (1991). A framework for authentic assessment in mathematics. *NCRMSE Research Review, 1*(1), 6–12.

Linn, R. L.. & Baker, E. L. (1992, Winter). Testing as a reform tool? *The CRESST Line.* Los Angeles: National Center for Research on Evaluation, Standards. and Student Testing.

Kessler, C.. & Quinn. M. E. (1992). Assessment techniques for science. In D. J. Short (Chair), *Assessment of content-based language instruction: Issues and ideas.* Colloquium conducted at the 26th Annual TESOL Convention, Vancouver, Canada.

MSEB (Mathematical Sciences Education Board). (1991). *For good measure: Principles and goals for mathematics assessment.* Washington. DC: National Academy Press.

Mohan, B. A. (1986). *Language and content.* Reading, MA: Addison-Wesley.

NCRMSE (National Center for Research in Mathematical Sciences Education). (1991). Perspectives on assessment. *NCRMSE Research Review, 1*(1), 3.

NCRESST (National Center for Research on Evaluation. Standards, and Student Testing). (1992, Spring). Authentic assessments—The challenge of diversity and equity. *The CRESST Line.* Los Angeles: Author.

NCSS (National Council for the Social Studies). (1992). Student assessment in education [Special section]. In P. Nickell (Ed.), *Social Education, 56*(2), 89–108.

NCTM (National Council of Teachers of Mathematics). (1989). *Curriculum and evaluation standards for school mathematics.* Reston, VA: Author.

NCTM. (1992a, November). Alternative assessment [Focus issue]. *The Mathematics Teacher, 85*(8).

NCTM. (1992b, February). Assessment [Focus issue]. *The Arithmetic Teacher, 39*(6).

NCEST (National Council of Education Standards and Testing). (1992). *Raising standards for American education.* Washington. DC: Author.

NSTA (National Science Teachers Association). (1992, October/November). *NSTA Reports!* Washington. DC: Author.

NSTA. (no date). *Scope, sequence and coordination of secondary school science* [Brochure]. Washington. DC: Author.

Parker, W. C. (1991). *Renewing the social studies curriculum.* Alexandria, VA: Association for Supervision and Curriculum Development.

Pierce, L. V., & O'Malley. J. M. (1992). *Performance and portfolio assessment for language minority students.* Washington. DC: National Clearinghouse for Bilingual Education.

Secretary's Commission on Achieving Necessary Skills. (1991). *What work requires of schools: A SCANS report for America 2000.* Washington, DC: U.S. Department of Labor, Author.

Semple, B. M. (1992). *Performance assessment: An international experiment* (Report No. 22-CAEP-06). Princeton, NJ: Educational Testing Service, Center for the Assessment of Educational Progress.

Short, D. J. (1991). *How to integrate language and content instruction: A training manual* (2nd ed.). Washington, DC: Center for Applied Linguistics.

Short, D. J., Seufert-Bosco, M., & Grognet. A. G. (1991). *Of the people: U.S. history.* Washington, DC/Englewood Cliffs, NJ: Center for Applied Linguistics/Prentice Hall Regents.

Tierney, R. J., Carter, M. A., & Desai, L. E. (1991). *Portfolio assessment in the reading-writing classroom.* Norwood, MA: Christopher-Gordon.

Turner, J. L. (1992), Creating content-based language tests: Guidelines for teachers. *CATESOL Journal, 5*(1), 43–58.

Unit Selections

23. **Low Income Does Not Cause Low School Achievement: Creating a Sense of Family and Respect in the School Environment,** Anita Tijerina Revilla and Yvette De La Gorza Sweeney
24. **Parents as First Teachers: Creating an Enriched Home Learning Environment,** Abelardo Villarreal
25. **The Education of Hispanics in Early Childhood: Of Roots and Wings,** Eugene E. Garcia
26. **Attending to New Voices,** Chris Liska Carger

Key Points to Consider

❖ Identify some of the problems teachers have with linguistically diverse students and their families.

❖ What are some of the attitudes or behaviors that are rooted in deep cultural values that can affect the home/school relationship?

❖ What are some activities that can help parents to become involved in their children's learning experience in the new school?

❖ How can teachers help parents who lack literacy skills to work with their children?

❖ How important are the influences of the native language and culture on the development of the child?

❖ Compare the adult who has a dual linguistic and cultural frame of reference with an adult who has grown up in the United States in a monolingual home.

 **Links** | **www.dushkin.com/online/**

26. **Internet Resources**
    http://ericps.ed.uiuc.edu/clas/links.html
27. **Prospects: The Congressionally Mandated Study of Educational Growth and Opportunity**
    http://www.ed.gov/pubs/Prospects/index.html
28. **The Rice School/La Escuela Rice**
    http://riceinfo.rice.edu/armadillo/Rice/dev.html

These sites are annotated on pages 4 and 5.

Multicultural dynamics influencing demographic changes across our country have forced educators to reexamine the institution of the family and its important role in education. Many of the new questions being raised reflect concerns about the effectiveness of parents in shaping school policies and influencing educational reforms. These questions are especially complex when we consider the minority language family whose cultural values shape their perceptions of home, school, and community relationships.

Recognized as the salient factor affecting a child's success in school, this important relationship between the family and school is woven into the curriculum. A child's interest in learning encompasses a variety of experiences. Attitudes and perceptions about learning and getting along with others in the world are heavily dependent on the child's parents and teachers, who are major life influences. By working together, they can provide positive support for the child's physical, cognitive, social, emotional, and moral development.

Teachers who work with second-language learners and their parents are especially challenged to communicate in unusual ways and to make a special effort to include parents with limited English proficiency in their classrooms in nonthreatening ways. Through the assigning of work activities that are done in the home, parents of older students also have opportunities to share in their child's learning.

The benefits of positive home/school partnerships can make the difference between success and failure in school, especially for those children whose families experience difficulty adjusting to a new way of life. Already feeling anxious about learning a new language, as well as experiencing academic and social pressures, minority language students must also face the stress of moving between two contrasting worlds—home and school. Daily, they are challenged linguistically as well as culturally.

Albeit difficult, the impact of having to move between two cultures and languages on a daily basis places students at a distinct advantage over their parents. The continual contrast of experiences between home and school encourages flexibility in dealing with difficulties of cultural assimilation. For the parents, however, acculturation to a new and different system of values and beliefs can be difficult and complicated, especially if they are unemployed and spend most of their time in the home. To expect parents to be enthusiastic about school issues when they are involved in daily survival is unrealistic. Teachers who are unaware of these problems often assume that parents are not interested in their children's education, which is seldom the case. Many teachers become discouraged by parents who do not respond to their efforts to bridge the home and school.

There are many things that teachers can do to encourage parents to become involved in their children's school experience. While the literature seems to focus more on parent/school relationships in the primary grades, it is also important that teachers in the middle grades make special efforts to consider the importance of involving parents in school-related activities whenever possible. Home/work activities such as helping a parent to cook a favorite family recipe and writing the ingredients, or asking parents to send pictures or items from their country for social studies class can extend the home to the school in a natural way.

The many hats worn by teachers also require a commitment to their community. They should be knowledgeable about programs that can help parents make the transition to the new culture and language as smoothly as possible. Information on community programs and social agencies that can help parents to learn the language or receive special job training should also be available at the school.

Keeping the lines of communication open between student and parents and parents and teacher are critical, especially in the early stages of second-language development. When the family is undergoing so many challenges, relationships among family members can become strained, yet they are most crucial. The teacher should make every effort to show respect for the child and the family. The teacher should also encourage the child to show special appreciation and respect for the parents, who may be feeling inadequate or insecure about their limited educational experience or lack of competency in the second language.

In this unit we consider these issues through articles that provide examples of ways in which teachers, administrators, and school professionals can develop and improve their communication with families of minority language students.

Parental Involvement in Bilingual Education

Column Editor: **Aurelio Montemayor, IDRA, San Antonio, TX**

Low Income Does Not Cause Low School Achievement: Creating a Sense of Family and Respect in the School Environment

by Anita Tijerina Revilla, M.A., and Yvette De La Garza Sweeney

Current research on the performance of low-income schools has not only served to dispel the myth that low income equals low academic achievement, it has also proven that, when the certain schoolwide strategies are implemented, all schools and all children can be high performing. In this article, the results of three major studies are summarized and combined into a table which highlights the five major factors that created success at these campuses. The results of the studies can provide ideas for school administrators and staff, particularly in schools that are in the process of developing school improvement plans and low-income schools with low academic achievement.

Students in low-income schools often deal with obstacles in the school environment that stem from cultural and power dynamics. Antonia Darder, author of *Culture and Power*, states:

> [Bicultural students] must contend with (1) two cultural systems whose values are very often in direct conflict and (2) a set of socio-political and historical forces dissimilar to those of mainstream students and the educational institutions that bicultural students must attend (Darder, 1991).

For example, most methods of academic assessment of students in U.S. classrooms are rooted in a middle-class model based on middle-class values. Thus, students who have learning styles, communication skills or home environments that are dissimilar to this middle-class model are believed to be disadvantaged or at-risk primarily because they are different. Darder advocates cultural democracy in the classroom, a concept she defines as follows:

The right of individuals to be educated in their own language and learning style and the right to maintain a bicultural identity— that is, to retain an identification with their culture of origin while integrating, in a constructive manner, the institutional values of the dominant culture (Darder, 1991).

The same should be true for the parents of these students. If schools and teachers expect parents to be involved in the schooling process, they must respect and encourage the parents to maintain their own cultural values and practices and to utilize them as they come into contact with the school environment. Otherwise, students often begin to reject the authority and knowledge of their parents, resulting in lessened parental involvement and the devaluation of the home as a learning environment.

For example, in 1982 Richard Rodriguez wrote of his embarrassment as a "scholarship boy." He wrote:

> 'Your parents must be so proud of you.' People began to say that to me by about the time I was in sixth grade. Shyly, I'd smile, never betraying my sense of the irony: I was not proud of my mother and father. I was embarrassed by their lack of education. It was not that I ever thought that they were stupid, though stupidly I took for granted their enormous native intelligence. Simply what mattered to me was that they were not like my teachers (Rodriguez, 1982).

Rodriguez and others have experienced great shame because of the fact that schools often do not value each child's home language and culture. It is up to the educator, the parent and society to assure children

that their bicultural knowledge and existence is regarded positively, not shamefully. Therefore, parental involvement and schoolwide inclusivity depends on mutual respect on the part of the student, the parents and the school personnel.

A study by the Charles A. Dana Center at the University of Texas at Austin, *Successful Texas Schoolwide Programs*, identifies several factors that account for successful schoolwide programs for low-income students (Charles A. Dana Center, 1997). One of the key indicators of success found was the "sense of family" created in the school environment. The researchers reported:

> Beyond the inclusivity evidenced by the schools, [they] observed a powerful sense of family. Not only were students, parents and all school personnel included as a part of the team, they were also included as part of the school family (Charles A. Dana Center, 1997).

According to the Dana Center study, it was exactly that type of mutual respect that aided the success of several low-income schools in Texas. The most common traits of the high performing, low-income schools are related to creating a sense of family.

The schools examined in the Dana Center study achieved state recognition for high performance while having a high percentage of low-income students. These schools, by example, showed that low income does not equate with low performance. On the contrary, students at these schools, who were highly valued and respected in the classroom regardless of their economic background or academic preparation, proved to be high achievers.

Project Pathways was a statewide collaborative formulated in 1993 between the

Creating High Performance Schools

Factor

❶ Create and nurture a familial environment
❷ Educate the "whole" child
❸ Celebrate cultural and linguistic diversity
❹ Assume responsibility for teaching
❺ Communicate and involve parents

Examples Cited by Research and Experience

❶ Create and nurture a familial environment

Students were given respect.

Counselors, nurses, social workers and family liaisons worked together to ensure that students' basic needs were met.

The sense of family was all inclusive among students, parents and school staff. Each staff member was highly valued as an individual.

Everyone who came in contact with students participated in ensuring their success.

Everyone on the campus was involved in the students' learning process.

The school was considered to be a family, more than just a system for learning.

School staff ensured that students knew they were held in high esteem.

❷ Educate the "whole" child

Each teacher's priority was the student's total development, not only performance on standardized tests.

Emphasis was placed on ensuring positive academic achievement for *every* child.

Failure was not tolerated, expectations were not lowered.

Teachers avoided stigmatizing students and categorizing or labeling them.

All accomplishments were praised and recognized.

Students were allowed to become actively involved in decisions relating to their school experiences.

Strategies such as cooperative learning and peer-to-peer tutoring allowed students to take possession of their learning.

❸ Celebrate cultural and linguistic diversity

Cultural and linguistic diversity was integrated into school activities and curriculum.

Teachers and staff provided a school environment similar to that of the local community.

The home culture of minority families was respected and valued.

Students were encouraged to use their native language in order to communicate effectively.

Teachers utilized students' native language to help them develop proficiency in the new language.

❹ Assume responsibility for teaching

Teachers created their own assessment tools to determine which methods would contribute positively to higher academic achievement.

Academic success for *every* child was the highest priority when teachers developed lessons.

Curriculum was aligned with standardized test objectives.

Teachers experimented with creative activities in an effort to improve student success while maintaining high expectations.

Teachers practiced team teaching.

One particular goals were achieved, higher goals were defined.

A stable environment was provided through continuum of classes.

Limited-English-proficient (LEP) students were not segregated from native English-speaking students.

Students practiced literacy development activities.

Schools created a program that assists LEP students with language acquisition.

Schools had a strong, integrated curriculum.

Administrative leadership was strong.

Campuses practiced shared decision making.

Schools advocated high morale and schoolwide support for students' academic achievement.

Schools provided master teacher tutoring and reading, writing and math labs.

❺ Communicate and involve parents

Parents were highly valued members of the school environment, and they knew they were an important part of the school family.

It was important to school staff that parents were able to communicate their views and concerns. Educational jargon was avoided and parents were not spoken to in condescending ways.

Teachers avoided forcing parents into traditional parenting roles.

Outreach to parents was extensive, ensuring high parent participation.

Schools maintained open door policies and created a welcoming environment, especially for parents.

The cultural and linguistic diversity of office staff enabled LEP parents to feel more comfortable and a part of the team.

- Developed by IDRA from research conducted by IDRA, the Charles A. Dana Center, at the University of Texas at Austin and Beverly McLeod.

Intercultural Development Research Association (IDRA); the Center for Success and Learning (CSL); the Texas Association for Supervision, Curriculum and Development (TASCD); and Educational Services Centers I, IV, X and XX, funded by the Texas Education Agency (TEA), designed to address the needs of the students at the secondary level who do not pass the Texas Assessment of Academic Skills (TAAS) test (Adame-Reyna, 1993). IDRA created seven Project Pathways training sessions emphasizing strategies that better prepare minority students to be successful on the TAAS test.

To inform the development of the Project Pathways program, IDRA set out to identify the characteristics and needs of students and schools with poor TAAS performance by studying diverse school districts (rural and urban, small and large, high and low minority student enrollment, high and low performance on the TAAS) from four regional education areas.

IDRA published the study, entitled *Project Pathways: Programs That Work*, that found that state-recognized high performing campuses share several characteristics that have resulted in improved TAAS test achievement (IDRA, 1993). The critical elements outlined in the study include the following:

- solid and supportive administrative leadership
- positive expectations of students
- strong, integrated curriculum
- shared decision making
- campus-wide responsibility for teaching and success (see box)

Many of the schools that had high TAAS performance also had high percentages of minority and low-income students. Contrary to the widespread belief that these students could not achieve high test scores, the statistics showed that the high TAAS performance at these campuses included all students. This study once again documented that the value of a student must be held high if high achievement is desired because any child who is devalued in the classroom becomes a child "at-risk."

A study by Beverly McLeod, funded by the U.S. Department of Education, provides a basis for understanding various types of reforms that provide limited-English-proficient (LEP) students with "equal access to an academic program of high quality" (McLeod, 1996). The study focused on various areas of educational reform such as curriculum, parental and community involvement, and student diversity. Eight primary and secondary schools with high percentages of LEP students participated in the study. Each of the schools involved developed and implemented several methods for achieving positive academic outcomes in which every student received an equal opportunity for academic success.

The five major factors practiced by the high performing schools that contributed to the high achievement of low-income and/or linguistic and cultural minority students include the following:

- Created and nurtured a familial environment.
  A non-threatening school environment was created. The entire school staff was involved in assuring individual success while also maintaining a sense of family.

Critical Elements of High Performing Campuses

Certain elements are critical to assuring that high poverty schools become high performing schools. Activities alone will not notably improve student performance. Activities intended as minimal or remedial responses start from weak premises, they assume that students "don't care," "can't learn," or "won't make the effort," and they quickly lose strength. In direct contrast, activities gain strength from the critical elements (listed below). This is because the elements themselves derive from sound educational precepts: the valuing of students, their education and teachers. The critical elements assume that *properly supported students can learn and teachers can teach.*

Effective administrative leadership — The principal sets the pace of change and promotes standards, exemplifies and encourages a positive atmosphere and enthusiasm for learning, expects creative problem solving from teachers, shares decision making with faculty, encourages academic leadership, supports professional development, evaluates programs, gives innovative programs time to work, and seeks faculty and student opinions.

Positive expectations — The principal is finely tuned to negative attitudes among students and faculty and reverses them.

Strong, integrated curriculum — The principal works with the faculty to develop a long-term campus plan with specific expected outcomes.

Shared decision making — The principal maintains close contact with the site-based management teams to coordinate goals and objectives. Decision-making teams include department chairs or core teachers, counselors and at-risk coordinators.

Campus-wide responsibility for teaching and success — Within the context established by other critical elements, successful schools initiate emphasis on reading, writing and mathematics across the curriculum.

- Educated the whole child.
  Each individual child's academic success was important. No child could be left behind. Respect, support, encouragement and the child's total development were all priorities.
- Celebrated cultural and linguistic diversity.
  Sensitivity to diversity was demonstrated within the school population and community. Accommodations

were made to ensure two-way communication among students, parents and school personnel.

- Assumed responsibility for teaching.

  Teachers, administrators and school districts exhibited active participation in students' success. Adopted techniques were continually assessed by a reflective practitioner. Students were given the opportunity to become actively involved in the learning process.
- Communicated and involved parents.

  Parents were valued and involved in the educational process. They were respected and appreciated, and they were actively encouraged to be a part of the school family.

In summary, there is a myth that has inappropriately been attached to low-income students; that is, low-income students cannot reach high academic standards. The three studies summarized in this article serve as concrete examples that dispel the myth. Low-income and minority students have demonstrated high performance in schools, yet there are several responsibilities that school administrators and staff must accept in order to ensure that success. The factors listed in this article are techniques that work. School families, highly valued students and parents, and strong, supportive administrations do create success.

Resources

Adame-Reyna, Ninta. "Project Pathways: Innovative Teaching Strategies for Improving LEP Students' TAAS Scores," *IDRA Newsletter*. San Antonio, Texas: Intercultural Development Research Association, October 1993, pg. 3.

Cantu, Linda. "TAAS Math Performance," *IDRA Newsletter*. San Antonio, Texas: Intercultural Development Research Association, June-July 1996

Charles A. Dana Center. *Successful Texas Schoolwide Programs*. Austin, Texas: Charles A. Dana Center, University of Texas at Austin, February 1997.

Darder, Antonia. *Culture and Power in the Classroom: A Critical Foundation for Bicultural Education.* Westport, Conn.: Bergin and Garvey, 1991.

Intercultural Development Research Association, *Project Pathways: Programs That Work.* San Antonio, Texas: IDRA, 1993.

McLeod, Beverly. *Educating Students from Diverse Linguistic and Cultural Backgrounds.* Santa Cruz, Calif.: The Bilingual Research Center, Internet posting, 1996.

Rodriguez, Richard. *Hunger of Memory: The Autobiography of Richard Rodriguez.* New York, N.Y.: Bantam Books, 1982.

Anita Tijerina Revilla is an education assistant in the IDRA Division of Professional Development. Yvette De La Garza Sweeney is a student in the division of bilingual/bicultural studies at the University of Texas at San Antonio. Comments and questions may be sent to them via E-mail at idra@idra.org.

Parental Involvement

Column Editor: Dr. Aurelio Montemayor, Intercultural Development Research Associates, TX

Parents as First Teachers: Creating an Enriched Home Learning Environment

by Abelardo Villarreal, Ph.D.

By the end of the first semester of second grade, Emilio was so fed up with his performance in school that he decided to play sick every morning. His teacher blamed Emilio and his parents for his poor performance, and his parents angrily accused school personnel for the inadequate education that he was receiving. At the losing end of this dichotomy was Emilio and his future.

Unfortunately this is not uncommon. Ill-defined roles and responsibilities for school personnel and parents and an inadequate instructional program for Emilio kept his educational well-being in abeyance. Numerous articles have been written to help school personnel reform their practices to assume a more responsible role in the education of all children and, in particular, the children who speak a language other than English or who share a different culture (TEA, 1994; Díaz-Soto, 1991; Villarreal, 1993). Although schools are still struggling to become more responsive to all students, this lack of success is not always due to lack of information (Cárdenas, 1995).

Parents, on the other hand, decry the lack of access to information for them to play their part as children's first teachers (Schoonmaker, 1992). The purpose of this article is to provide school personnel with insights for use in parenting workshops on enriching learning opportunities during their children's formative years (ages three to five).

Parenting involves taking responsibility seriously, taking advantage of every opportunity to enhance children's learning, and providing children with challenges. Children absorb life experiences indiscriminately. To a large extent, these life experiences form children's character, feelings and values, and they provide the window through which they will view the world (Scott, 1992; Villarreal, 1993). In other words, through interaction with their children and the experiences that they provide them, parents can influence and guide children's growth and development.

By age five children will be exposed to school life. Parents can either provide learning experiences haphazardly or unknowingly (with good intentions, but with little knowledge and no plan) or they can conscientiously plan for quality experiences to occur and exercise their obligation in a more responsible manner. There are three major tasks that parents can do to improve the learning environment at home. These tasks are discussed below.

Task 1: Learn More About How Children Learn

Parents who have been successful in their role as the first teachers of children share a similar philosophy about children's learning. This philosophy is defined by eight key assertions about parenthood and learning (Bredekamp, 1987). The following outlines these major thoughts that are instrumental for parents to be successful as children's first teachers.

A. Children are always ready to learn.

Children have an inborn capacity to learn (Forman and Kuschrer, 1983). They start learning from the time that they are in the mother's womb. The fact that children ask many questions or are eager to touch all that they see is an expression of their readiness to receive input from the environment. This innate willingness to learn could be nourished or weakened by childhood experiences from the environment. Parents must be vigilant and expose their children to the "right experiences."

What Parents Should Do

- Turn as many everyday life experiences as possible into learning opportunities.
- Model learning from everyday experiences.
- Talk about the importance of learning as a self-initiated activity.

What Parents Should Avoid

- Interact with children only when they ask a question ("I don't have time to talk").

B. Children have a curiosity for learning.

Children test the world. When the child jumps from a chair the first time and finds out that it hurts, he or she has learned the consequences of such an act. The responsibility of the parent is to teach the child that risks need to be calculated. Killing curiosity for learning will have serious consequences later in life.

What Parents Should Do

- Take advantage of children's questions to extend learning.
- Capitalize on children's interest in selecting learning experiences.
- Plan the home physical environment with children's needs and desires in mind.
- Purchase toys that are specifically designed to stimulate children's thinking and creativity.

What Parents Should Avoid

- Leave children's learning to chance.
- Tell children you are too busy to answer their questions.

C. Children learn from their environment.

Children learn from all aspects of the environment (Greenman, 1988; Penny-Velázquez, 1993; Adame-Reyna, 1995). The environment is represented by people and objects that surround them. Every experience, whether it is a positive or negative experience, will teach children something. Some experiences that can be used to teach new concepts and develop appropriate behaviors are the following: (1) child sees a mountain and asks about it; (2) child is involved in a fight with another

From *NABE News*, February 1, 1996, pp. 13-17. Originally from *IDRA Newsletter,* April 1995. © 1995 by the Intercultural Development Research Association. Reprinted by permission.

child; (3) sister is reading a book and child sits next to her; (4) child receives a ball of clay; (5) child accompanies parent to the doctor's office; and (6) child watches a cartoon on television.

What Parents Should Do
- Expose children to experiences that teach social, academic and motor skills.
- Capitalize on children's interest in selecting learning experiences.
- Allow children to actively interact with the environment; allow them to explore and ask questions.

What Parents Should Avoid
- Expose children to experiences that focus only on one set of skills.
- Only expose children to experiences interesting to parents.

D. Children thrive in an environment of love and respect.

Children need to feel secure in order to take risks and take advantage of a learning experience (Scott, 1992; González-Mena, 1991; Allen and Mason, 1989). Children are unique individuals whose feelings evolve from their experiences with other people and with the environment that surrounds them. These feelings form the basis for children's self-esteem, love, and an appreciation and an acknowledgment of one's uniqueness.

Feelings can facilitate or hinder learning. Feelings that facilitate learning are based on love and respect. Children who feel a sense of belonging and feel like worthwhile individuals who have unique qualities and characteristics experience love and respect. Parents have the responsibility to sustain an environment full of love and respect and to nourish children's self-esteem when confronted with a hostile or unfriendly environment (Bredekamp, 1987; Scott, 1992; Adame-Reyna, 1995).

What Parents Should Do
- Show love for all their children equally.
- Celebrate the uniqueness of each child.
- Respect children's views of the world.
- Ask and value children's opinions.
- Provide opportunities to excel and experience positive feelings about themselves.
- Model respect for other's beliefs and values.
- Expect children to respect other's beliefs and values.

What Parents Should Avoid
- Be partial to some of your children.
- Criticize children for their actions and behaviors.
- Impose your will without an explanation for your action.
- Demean children because of their actions or beliefs.

E. Children have a potential for acquiring language.

Children learn from their parents or the persons with whom they live. Children have an innate capacity to process and use language (Sosa, 1993; Strickland, 1990; González-Mena, 1991). The process for learning a language is complex, requiring at least 12 years to formalize itself. In homes where the language is Spanish, children will become proficient in Spanish. If children live in an environment where a wide variety of languages are used, they will become very proficient in those languages. Parents, siblings and other adults who spend considerable time with the children become language models.

Parents should make sure that children are exposed to effective language users. Talking and reading with children develops their control of the language. Once children have mastered one language, they can learn a second one quickly. For example, children who have mastered the Spanish language well, have been exposed sufficiently to the English language at the appropriate time, and are not forced to learn the new language, can become proficient users of both Spanish and English. Parents should ensure that children are not prematurely forced to learn a new language.

What Parents Should Do
- Talk to children as often as possible.
- Engage children in conversations.
- Ask for their views about certain topics of interest.
- Increase children's vocabulary on different topics.

What Parents Should Avoid
- Use language to request children's compliance only.
- Criticize children for the way they express themselves.
- Turn down an opportunity to explain or respond to a question.
- Expect children to listen passively.
- Dominate a conversation with children.

F. Children can communicate ideas in many different ways.

Children are versatile individuals who have learned to communicate ideas through language, behaviors and actions (Gandini, 1993; Greenman, 1988). Many have learned that they can communicate ideas on paper. That is, children have learned that people's scribbles communicate an idea. Children who are ready to discover the excitement those scribbles represent begin to scribble themselves. Soon, their scribbling begins to communicate a feeling or an action. When asked, children will talk about the scribbling. Parents can help children master this form of communication by reading and providing them opportunities to scribble and talk about their masterpieces. Displaying their work guarantees acknowledgment of children's unique qualities and characteristics.

What Parents Should Do
- Provide opportunities to communicate ideas through speech or writing.
- Show children ways they can communicate ideas.
- Encourage children to use acceptable behavior.
- Redirect unacceptable behavior.
- Provide opportunities to appreciate art and music.

What Parents Should Avoid
- Criticize or demean cultures or languages that are different from theirs.
- Pressure children to react or respond in one specific way.

G. Children can acquire a love and desire for reading.

Reading is the most efficient way of acquiring information. Reading is a skill that children can develop from a very early age (Strickland, 1990; Greenman, 1988). Children who are exposed to print at a very early age tend to become better readers and learners when they go to school. They develop a thirst for information and knowledge. Parents can help their children by talking about the beauty of reading, by getting books for them to own, and by reading signs, labels and a range of items that have print on them.

What Parents Should Do
- Stress the importance of comprehending what is read.

- Provide opportunities to select topics or books to read.
- Read to children starting at an early age.
- Have print materials (newspapers, books, letters, forms and in whatever language) at home at all times.
- Read all labels and signs to and with children.
- Expose children to different literature styles at an early age.

What Parents Should Avoid
- Ask children to conform with your selection of reading materials only.
- Force children to begin decoding works when they are not ready.
- Criticize children for not liking to read.
- Compare children to other children's accomplishments.

H. Children learn in different ways.

Adults and children use the senses to learn (Forman and Kuschrer, 1983). Some learn by seeing. Others learn by hearing, reading or touching. Some of us are better at learning by using one particular sense or another. For example, some of us can learn better if the reading is accompanied by pictures. Reading about how to put a model together may be sufficient for some. While other children may learn better if presented with a "hands on" activity. Parents should keep this information in mind and determine which is the preferred way of their children to learn. Provide more opportunities for children to learn in their preferred way.

What Parents Should Do
- Provide learning opportunities using all the senses.
- Teach that some questions do not have a right or wrong answer.
- Provide opportunities for problem solving using the different senses.
- Provide with opportunities to role play.

What Parents Should Avoid
- Teaching children to learn only by reading and memorizing materials.
- Teach that one way of learning is better than another.

Task 2: Establish a Vision and Goals

A vision is a mental picture of an event that has not yet occurred. A mental picture allows us to define what children would be able to do within a period of time. Getting there does not happen automatically; parents have to make sure that support is available to help them to get to that point. After hearing about a successful learner who entered school at age five, a parent decided to write down his vision for his three-year-old. The vision went like this:

My son will know about many things. He will be able to talk about them and express his desire to know more about certain things. He will not be afraid to ask if he is unsure of things. He will not be afraid of making mistakes. He will show respect and love for

---

> **Contract with My Children**
>
> During the next six months, I (we) will try out the following five activities:
>   1.
>   2.
>   3.
>   4.
>   5.
>
> I (we) will find out if I (we) have been successful if my children do the following:
>   1.
>   2.
>   3.
>   4.
>   5.
>
> Signed:_____ Date: _____

---

others and will always be happy. He will be highly dominant in Spanish, the language that we speak at home. He will be in the process of learning English in a meaningful manner and not feel frustrated or hurried to learn English immediately.

I challenge parents to do the same. Write or share with someone else a vision that will guide you and your children through the journey of childhood life.

The parent proceeded to write his goals in meeting this responsibility. Goals are like guideposts that define responsibility in making a vision a reality. His goals were:

- Strive to learn more about how children learn by reading articles, books or watching informational television programs.
- Take advantage of every opportunity to engage my children in learning.
- Create a home environment conducive to learning.
- Instill in my children a desire for learning.

These goals served him and his children well. The parent planned activities to ensure that goals were met and the vision was realized.

Task 3: Reflect and Plan an Enriched Learning Home Environment

The third major task is to take stock, reflect and plan the improvement of the home learning environment. The chart on the facing page provides a checklist with activities that promote a positive home learning environment. Parents can use this checklist to reflect on what has been occurring at home. All ratings of "never" or "sometimes" merit some attention by parents. After

Parents as First Teachers Checklist

Rate each item according to the degree that it is practiced in your household, by writing the appropriate number in the blank to the right of the statement. Use the following codes: Always = 1 Sometimes = 2 Never = 3

1. I take advantage of as many learning opportunities for my children as possible. _____

2. I model by taking advantage of as many learning opportunities as possible. _____

3. I talk about the importance of learning from every experience with my children. _____

4. I take advantage of my children's questions by extending learning. _____

5. I capitalize on my children's interests in selecting learning experiences. _____

6. I plan my home physical environment with my children's needs and desires in mind. _____

7. I purchase toys that stimulate children's thinking skills. _____

8. I expose my children to experiences that develop social, academic and/or motor skills. _____

9. I respect my children's views of the world. _____

10. I ask children for their opinions. _____

11. I acknowledge my children's efforts. _____

12. I praise my children's accomplishments. _____

13. I model respect for other's beliefs and values. _____

14. I expect my children to respect others' beliefs and values. _____

15. I talk to my children as often as possible. _____

16. I engage in conversations and discussions with my children. _____

17. I ask for my children's views about certain topics. _____

18. I strive to increase my children's vocabularies in many different topics. _____

19. I provide opportunities for my children to express their ideas in different ways. _____

20. I model how ideas can be expressed in different ways. _____

21. I acknowledge my children's use of acceptable behavior. _____

22. I redirect my children's use of unacceptable behavior. _____

23. I provide opportunities for my children to appreciate art and music. _____

24. I probe to ensure that my children understand the importance of comprehending what is read. _____

25. I provide opportunities for children to select topics or books to be read. _____

26. I read to my children constantly. _____

27. I have print material available at home. _____

28. I read all labels and signs with my children. _____

29. I expose my children to classic literature. _____

30. I provide my children opportunities to use the different senses to learn. _____

31. I teach my children that some questions do not have a right answer. _____

32. I provide my children opportunities for problem solving using the different senses. _____

33. I provide my children opportunities to role play. _____

using the checklist, parents may identify those activities that they propose to improve upon during the next six months. On this form, parents can write down their commitments to improve the learning environment. They can share this contract with their children and other adults and ask them to "check on them" periodically. They should post this contract on the refrigerator or a place where they will see it often. Repeat this process every six months.

Parents as effective teachers play several roles. First, they are good listeners. They listen to everything that children say, and they observe the environment that surrounds them. They respect what children have to say. There are no absurdities; whatever is said is said with a reason. Parents look for the message and question children when the message needs clarity. A good listener promotes the use of language by children. Children appreciate and are prompted to use language when they know that others listen and do not criticize them. One of the major responsibilities of a parent is to initiate conversations and take every opportunity for their children to use language.

Secondly, parents who are resourceful promote learning in many different ways. They have print available for children to see. They model the use of print to communicate ideas. A resourceful parent creates opportunities for learning.

Resources

Adame-Reyna, Ninta. "What Parents Can Do for Their Children's Mathematics Learning," *IDRA Newsletter* (San Antonio, Texas: Intercultural Development Research Association, February 1995).

Allen, JoBeth and Jana M. Mason. *Risk Makers, Risk Takers, Risk Breakers: Reducing the Risks for Young Literacy Learners* (Heinemann Educational Book, Inc., 1989).

Bredekamp, Sue (editor). *Developmentally Appropriate Practice in Early Childhood Programs Serving Children From Birth Through Age 8* (Washington, D.C.: National Association for the Education of Young Children, 1987).

Cárdenas, José A. *Multicultural Education: A Generation of Advocacy* (Needham Heights, Mass.: Simon & Schuster Custom Publishing, 1995).

Díaz-Soto, Lourdes. "Understanding Bilingual/Bicultural Young Children," *Young Children* (January 1991).

Forman, George E. and David S. Kuschrer. *The Child's Construction of Knowledge: Piaget for Teaching Children* (Washington, D.C.: National Association for the Education of Young Children, 1983).

Gandini, Lella. "Fundamentals of the Reggio Emilia Approach to Early Childhood Education" *Young Children* (November 1993).

González-Mena, Janet. *Tips and Tidbits: A Book for Family Daycare Providers* (Washington, D.C.: National Association for the Education of Young Children, 1991).

Greenman, Jim. *Caring Spaces, Learning Places: Children's Environments That Work* (Redmond, Wash.: Exchange Press, Inc., 1988).

Penny-Velázquez, Michaela. "Yo Escribo: Promoting Interactions in the Early Childhood Classroom," *IDRA Newsletter* (San Antonio, Texas: Intercultural Development Research Association, August 1993).

Schoonmaker, Mary Ellen. "When Parents Accept the Unacceptable," *Early Childhood Education* (Guilford, Conn.: the Dushkin Publishing Company, 1992).

Scott, Bradley. "Providing for Strong Roots: The Teacher and Human Relations in the Preschool" *IDRA Newsletter* (San Antonio, Texas: Intercultural Development Research Association, April 1992).

Sosa, Alicia S. *Questions and Answers About Bilingual Education* (San Antonio, Texas: Intercultural Development Research Association, 1993).

Strickland, Dorothy S. "Emergent Literacy: How Young Children Learn to Read and Write," *Educational Leadership* (March 1990).

Texas Education Agency. *First Impressions: Primeras Impresiones* (Austin, Texas: Texas Education Agency, January 1994).

Villarreal, Abelardo. "The Challenge for Site-Based Decision Making Council: Making Quality Preschool Accessible to Language Minority Students," *IDRA Newsletter* (San Antonio, Texas: Intercultural Development Research Association, June 1993).

Abelardo Villarreal is the director of the IDRA Division of Professional Development.

Reprinted with permission from IDRA Newsletter, April 1995.

Editor's Note: *NABE is pleased to announce the appointment of Dr. Aurelio Montemayor as editor of the new regular* **Parental Involvement** *column.*

Research in Review

The Education of Hispanics in Early Childhood: Of Roots and Wings

Eugene E. Garcia

As director of the Office of Bilingual Education and Minority Languages Affairs in the U.S. Department of Education, I sought to engage my *professional* experience and expertise as an educational researcher and my *personal* cultural and linguistic experience to address national education policy. The professional in me has been nurtured at some of the best educational institutions in the United States, while the nonprofessional has been nurtured in a large, rural, Mexican American family. Born in the United States and speaking Spanish as our first language for generations, our family included 10 children— four high school graduates and one college graduate.

Bringing these *personas* (Spanish for "persons") together was not as difficult as I had expected and the mixture was quite helpful to the wide variety of people I interacted with in my national role. Bringing together these personas, I communicated with individuals in ways not possible had I spoken only with one voice or separate voices.

This article presents my intersecting but distinct voices to help further our understanding of life in a diverse society—particularly of Hispanics growing up in the United States during their early childhood years. The historical pattern of the education of Hispanics in the United States is a continuous story of underachievement. It need not continue to be that way.

The three voices here address issues of the past, present, and future. They recognize the multiple selves that not only make up my own persona but those that are a reality for all of us. It is useful to recognize that we walk in varied and diverse cultures. There is great diversity within each individual, just as there is diversity among individuals and the many cultures they belong to or represent. We all live with diversity, some of us more than others. No one escapes this challenge or its advantages and disadvantages.

***Eugene E. Garcia**, Ph.D., is professor and dean of the Graduate School of Education at the University of California in Berkeley. He continues to do research in areas related to language, culture, and schooling. He served as director of the Office of Bilingual Education and Minority Language Affairs in the U.S. Department of Education, 1993–95.*

*This is one of a regular series of Research in Review columns. The column in this issue was invited by **Carol Seefeldt**, Ph.D., professor at the University of Maryland, College Park.*

While English First, an organization committed to English as the official U.S. language, is passionately concerned that multilingualism will produce divisiveness and significant conflict, indigenous people whose roots in the Americas outdistance the "White man's" presence mourn just as passionately the loss of their languages and cultures. As this country and the world shrinks communicatively, economically, socially, and intellectually, diversity is becoming harder to hide, but it has always been there. In the following pages, I address issues related to the education of Hispanics in early childhood with the varied voices within me.

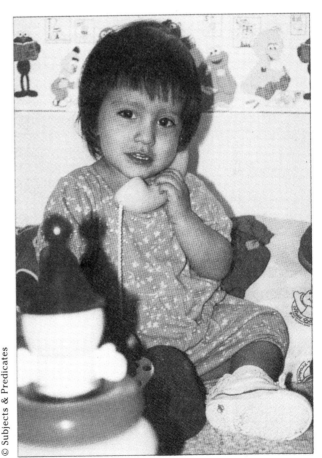

© Subjects & Predicates

The Voices

Eugene. This voice often represents my intellectual upbringing and is recognized primarily by my academic credentials—degrees received and where and when, how successful I was in those environments, academic positions I have held and their status in the academic world, the empirical research I have done, my teaching, and, of course, the articles and books I have written. This set of experiences and accomplishments, at its core, attempts to expand in critical and strategic ways our broader understanding of language acquisition, teaching, learning, and schooling, and the specific relevance of these to language-minority populations—learners who come to the educational enterprise not knowing the language of that formal enterprise and particularly for students like me who are classified as Hispanic in the present jargon of educators and demographers. I did not begin my academic pursuits with this specific population in mind but have naturally gravitated toward using my professional skills to address issues of relevance to it, but not *only* to it.

Gene. Other parts of me are more rooted in the nonacademic world, my social and cultural realities. I am a son, brother, husband, father, and so on. In such social and cultural roles, I have experienced a wonderful family environment, learning much from my father and mother—neither of whom ever had the opportunity to attend school. They taught me to respect them, my elders, my brothers and sisters, and others who were not members of my family—such as my teachers—or not like me, and, most of all, to respect myself. They never gave me a formal lesson about these things; they just lived them, in the harsh realities of poverty and the hard work any migrant or sharecropping family understands. This teaching and learning included experiences of outright racism and subtle institutional racism in which our language, color, and heritage were not always met with either individual or group respect. From these experiences and teachers emerged the voice of Gene (a name used most often by my family and friends).

This persona agreed to work as an undergraduate in the migrant camps, tutoring adults in English and related subjects so that they could earn the GED (general equivalency diploma). This persona realized early that he was different. I spoke primarily Spanish, my peers only English. I and my family worked in the fields; my peers and their families hired us to work in their fields. My peers enjoyed a much higher standard of living—I recall being embarrassed that my family did not take summer vacations or have running water and inside toilets. Quite honestly, most of the time, these differences did not weigh heavy on my mind or affect my behavior—I had lots of friends, some like me and others quite different from me.

It was likely more Gene than Eugene who accepted the invitation to join the Clinton administration and Secretary of Education Richard Riley in the Department of Education. In political/policy roles like this one, I realized that policymakers and practitioners of education do not always act based on the best theory, proven educational practices, or even promising educational innovations. They act mostly out of political interests. I realized the importance of the politics of education. Gene's voice is often dominated by these lessons, although Eugene is not totally unaffected by them.

Gino.

Another voice within me is identified best by the endearing name that my mother used for me—Gino. In my large, quite Catholic family, to baptize a child is a distinct honor and, in recognition of that honor, *los padrinos,* the godparents, are given the authority to name the child. At my birth my parents selected my eldest sister and her husband to serve as my padrinos, and my sister was enchanted with the name Eugene. That is how I came to have a Greek name in a cohort of brothers and sisters named Antonio, Emelio, Cecelia, Ciprianita, Abel, Federico, Tiburcio, and Christina, and born of parents named Lorenzo and Juanita. My mother could not pronounce *Eugene,* so to her and my immediate family I became Gino.

Gino carries a distinct sense of cultural "Hispanic-ness," "Chicanismo," "Latino-ness," or "Raza-ness." These concepts reflect a deep regard for the linguistic and cultural roots that foster identity—best exemplified by a lesson from my father:

> For farmworkers and sharecroppers, winter was a time to prepare for work—there was not much work during this period. One winter in the high plains of Colorado where I was born and raised, my father pointed to an *árbol*—a cottonwood tree. He asked, *"Por qué puede vivir ese árbol en el frio del invierno y en el calor del verano?"* (How can that tree survive the bitter cold of winter and the harsh heat of summer?) My father was a man of few words—relatives often characterized him as quiet and shy—but when he spoke we all listened very carefully. I rambled on about how big and strong the tree was and how its limbs and trunk were like the strong arms and bodies of my elder brothers. Then he kindly provided a different perspective by referring to a common Spanish *dicho/consejo* (proverb): *El árbol fuerte tienen raíces maduros* (A strong tree has mature/strong roots).

In articulating this significant piece of the analysis that was absent from my youthful thoughts, my father made clear that without strong roots, strong trees are impossible—and we don't even see the roots! The roots of many Hispanics in this country have either been ignored or stripped away in the name of growing strong. Many have been directed to stop speaking Spanish, to perceive their culture as a "less-than" one, and to assimilate as quickly as possible so they can succeed in American society (Chavez 1991). Unfortunately, many have suffered the fate of the rootless tree—they have fallen socially, economically, academically, and culturally.

However, to Gino, my mother made it very clear: roots and their concomitant integrity and self-respect were not enough. She wanted the very best for all her children, certainly not the long and painful fieldwork that she had endured for a lifetime. She wanted us *bien educados*—to have a set of formal and marketable skills. She made very clear that children needed wings, like the wings she insisted we children grew every night upon falling asleep, so as to fly to heaven to be with God. "All children," she said, "are angels." In recent stories by Chicano author Victor Villaseñor, his mother elaborates further on this notion (Villaseñor 1991). She says that the children fly to God each night and station themselves as stars in His heaven. Both our mothers expressed a special regard for the sanctity of childhood and required children to have wings to perform their related roles. My mother emphasized that she could not provide the kind of wings that God and a good education could provide. She knew that the teachers and schools would have to take me further than she could personally. Education would need to provide the strong and elaborate wings for me to succeed where she often felt she had failed: "Go to school—strong wings like those of an eagle are also what you need in this world to raise your family and provide for them all that we have been unable to provide for you."

For Hispanics in this country, the emphasis on building wings in school has strategically focused on teaching English language skills: "Teach them English well and then they will succeed." Yet all educators realize that in today's information age, education must provide broad and strong intellectual wings related to fundamental linguistic, mathematical, scientific, and technological literacies. English literacy is important, but it is not enough. Gino feels that Hispanics, such as those he and his family represent, have been educationally shortchanged.

The "Hispanic" debate

Eugene, Gene, and Gino realize that their voices are not alone nor are their views held by all Hispanics in the United States. Most critical of such views of the interactive relationship of "roots and wings" for Hispanics are two well-regarded and influential Hispanic authors, each in her or his own way refuting the importance of roots and the relationship of those roots to the educational development of Hispanics.

Linda Chavez, an adviser in the Reagan White House, journalist commentator, and author of *Out of the Barrio: Toward a New Politics of Hispanic Assimilation,* suggests that

> Every previous group—Germans, Irish, Italians, Greeks, Jews, Poles—struggled to be accepted fully into the social, political and economic mainstream, sometimes against the opposition of a hostile majority. They learned the language, acquired education and skills, and adapted their own customs and traditions to fit an American context. (1991, 2)

The key for Hispanic success in America, Chavez argues, is minimizing the public/governmental recognition of Hispanic roots and the individual and governmental promotion of assimilation. She chides the federal government, particularly federal bilingual education programs, and Hispanic leaders for promoting permanent victim status and vying with Black Americans for the distinction of being the poorest, most segregated, and least educated minority, thereby entitling them to government handouts. These actions in turn, her conclusion advances, encourage Hispanics to maintain their language and culture and their specific identity in return for rewards handed out through affirmative action and federal, state, and local educational policies that thwart assimilation. This does not sound like my father's concern for the importance of roots or my mother's emphasis on wings.

Yet another Hispanic author, Richard Rodriguez, is very eloquent in his description of his upbringing in a Mexican home and a Catholic school where the English-speaking nuns literally beat the Spanish language and the "Hispanic-ness" out of him. His book *Hunger of Memory* (1982) describes this forced assimilation, painful as it was, that propelled him to new heights of educational achievement. Although he himself never articulates the conclusion, he leaves open the suggestion that such treatment of Hispanics is exactly what they need to get over their "problems." Eugene, Gene, and Gino reach a very different conclusion in this discussion. But you should know that the debate exists.

The following discussion indirectly addresses this debate but includes an expanded research-related discussion of vulnerability factors both within and outside the education arena along with data related to the "effective" treatment of this growing population of young children and families. The discussion addresses the following:

1. An overall demographic assessment of factors related to the schooling of culturally diverse populations, including issues of poverty, family stability, and immigrant status;

2. A particular analysis of the challenges associated with the growing number of language-minority students who are Hispanic—children who come to school with limited or no proficiency in English; and

3. A presentation of conceptual and empirical perspectives that sets the stage for a more informed approach to the education of Hispanics in early childhood.

The research

The demographic picture

The Census Bureau in its attempts to provide clarifying demographic information never fails in confusing us. In documenting the racial and ethnic heterogeneity of our country's population, it has arrived at a set of highly confusing terms that place individuals in separate exclusionary categories: White, White non-Hispanic, Black, Hispanic (with some five subcategories of Hispanics). Unfortunately, outside of the census meaning of these terms, they are for the most part highly ambiguous and nonrepresentative of the true heterogeneity which the Census Bureau diligently seeks to document. Therefore, it is important to note at the outset of this discussion that these categories are useful only as the most superficial reflection of our nation's true diversity. I do not know many census-identified "Whites," "Blacks," or "Hispanics" who believe they are "White," "Black," and so on, but given the forced-choice responses allowed them in census questionnaires, they are constrained by these choices.

Having consented to this significant restriction regarding efforts to document population diversity in this country, I still must conclude that an examination of the available data provides a fuzzy but useful portrait of our society and the specific circumstances of various groups within our nation's boundaries. That sketch is one of consummate vulnerability for non-White and Hispanic (usually referred to as "minority") families, children, and students. On almost every indicator, non-White and Hispanic families, children, and "at-risk" students are likely to fall

While English First, an organization committed to English as the official U.S. language, is passionately concerned that multilingualism will produce divisiveness and significant conflict, indigenous people whose roots in the Americas outdistance the "White man's" presence mourn just as passionately the loss of their languages and cultures.

Hispanic Demographics

General demographic character

• Of the approximately 22.7 million Hispanics in the continental United States, the following information characterizes the population's ethnic diversity.

Country/area of origin	Number (in millions)	%
Mexico	14.6	64.3
Puerto Rico	2.4	10.6
Central/South America	3.0	13.4
Cuba	1.1	4.7
Other Hispanic countries	1.6	7.0

• 89.5% of the total Hispanic population in the United States is concentrated in three states: California (26%), Texas (25.5%), and New Mexico (38%). Other states with significant Hispanic populations are Arizona (19%), Colorado (13%), Florida (12%), and New York (12%).

• Average age of the Hispanic population in 1993 was 26.7 years.

• 200,000 Hispanics immigrate legally to the United States annually; Hispanics are 40% of all legal immigrants. (An estimated 200,000 Hispanics immigrate illegally.)

• The Hispanic population grew by 53% from 1980 to 1990, compared to the 9.8% growth in the general U.S. population.

• 17 million Hispanics report speaking Spanish in the home.

• 90% of Hispanics live in metropolitan areas; 52% in central cities.

Indices of "vulnerability"

• Median family income has fluctuated for Hispanics (1982—$23,814; 1991—$24,614; 1992—$23,912), remaining below that of non-Hispanics (1982—$35,075; 1991—$38,127; 1992—$38,015).

• In 1992, 26.2% of Hispanic families lived below the poverty line, compared to 27.2% in 1982. (In 1992, 10.4% of non-Hispanic White families lived below the poverty line.)

• In 1993, 1,239,094 Hispanic families (23.3%) were maintained by a female head-of-household (an increase of .5% from 1983 when it was 22.8% or 827,184); 48.8% of these households lived below the poverty line.

• 72.9% of Hispanics hold unskilled and semiskilled jobs, compared to 50.8% of non-Hispanics.

Education

• Approximately 50% of Hispanics leave school prior to graduation (70% by 10th grade).

• 38% of Hispanics are held back at least one grade.

• 50% of Hispanics are overage at grade 12.

• 90% of Hispanic students are in urban districts.

• 82% of Hispanic students attend segregated schools.

• Hispanics are significantly below national norms on academic achievement tests of reading, math, science, social science, and writing at grades 3, 7, and 11, generally averaging one to two grade levels below the norm. At grade 11, Hispanics average a grade 8 achievement level on these tests.

• Hispanics are placed in special education services six times more often than the general student population.

Sources: U.S. Bureau of the Census, *The Hispanic Population in the United States: March 1993* (Washington DC: U.S. Government Printing Office, 1993); U.S. Bureau of the Census, *Social and Economic Characteristics in the U.S.: 1990 Census of the Population* (Washington DC: GPO, 1990); M.A. Reddy, *Statistical Record of Hispanic Americans* (Michigan: Gale Research, Inc., 1993); and U.S. Immigration and Naturalization Service, *Statistical Yearbook of the Immigration and Naturalization, 1993* (Washington DC: GPO, 1994).

into the lowest quartile on indicators of "well-being": family stability, family violence, family income, child health and development, and educational achievement. Yet this population has grown significantly in the last two decades and will grow substantially in the decades to come. The table on the previous page summarizes these factors for census-derived information on Hispanics.

The demographic transformation that has become more evident in the last decade was easily foreseen at least that long ago. Our schools' future student profile is as predictable: in a mere 40 years, White students will be a minority in every category of public education as we know it today. Unfortunately, the emerging student majority of ethnic and racial background continues to be at risk in today's social institutions. The National Center for Children in Poverty (1995) provided a clear and alarming demographic window on these at-risk populations. Of the 21.9 million children under six years of age in 1990 who will move slowly through society's institutions—family, schools, the workplace—five million (25%) were living in poverty. Although less than 30% of all children under six years of age were non-White, more than 50% of the children in poverty were non-White. In addition, these children continued to live in racial/ethnic isolation. Some 56% lived in racially isolated neighborhoods in 1966; 72% resided in such neighborhoods in 1994; 61% of children in poverty live in concentrations of poverty where 20% of the population is poor.

High school or equivalent completion rates are alarming for these emerging majority student populations. In 1994 the high school completion rate for the U.S. population was 81.1% for 19-year-olds, 86.5% for 24-year-olds, and a very respectable 86% for 29-year-olds. For Blacks and Hispanics the rate of completion in all age groups was close to 60% (U.S. Department of Commerce 1990). With regard to academic achievement, in 1994, 30% of 13-year-old students were one grade level below the norm on standardized achievement measures. However, this differed significantly for emerging majority and White students: 27% for White students, 40% for Hispanic students, and 46% for Black students.

The qualitative description of education presented above is further affirmed for Hispanics by other quantitative descriptions. A recent study reported by de Leon Siantz (1996) uses descriptive data from the Hispanic Health and Nutrition Examination Survey, a national effort sampling stratified populations of Mexican American, Puerto Rican, and Cuban American families in three U.S. regions (southwest, northeast, and southeast). This study reports very small differences in family well-being and child well-being indicators across these groups and regions. The Hispanic population was described as growing, youthful, poor, lacking parental care, and at high risk for AIDS.

Moreover, recent national Head Start data (Phillips & Cabrera 1996) indicate that only one-third of the pro-

Part of the current push for excellence and equity for all students has been increased attention to Hispanic children.

grams had an enrollment characterized by a single language, with a range of 1 to 32 languages represented in programs, while 72% of programs had enrollments of between 2 and 3 languages. The predominant languages represented in these programs were Spanish and English.

Combined with the contemporary educational zeitgeist that embraces excellence and equity for all students, attention to the Hispanic children, families, and students has been significant. Following this theme are recent analyses and recommendations: the California State Department of Education efforts to better train infant and toddler caregivers in state-supported programs (California State Department of Education 1992), the U.S. Department of Education reforms for federally funded education programs (Garcia & Gonzales 1995), the National Academy of Education discussion of standards-based reform (McLaughlin & Shepard 1995), the National Research Council's Roundtable on Head Start Research efforts to provide an issue analysis of research needed to produce a thriving future for Head Start for a highly diverse population of children and families (Phillips & Cabrera 1996), the National Council of Teachers of English and the International Reading Association's treatment of language arts standards (NCTE/IRA 1996), and NAEYC's position statement on linguistic and cultural diversity (NAEYC 1996). All of these publications have attended to the vulnerabilities of Hispanics and have addressed issues of language and culture in light of this country's past treatment of this population and the present conceptual and empirical understanding of the need for institutions to be more responsive. Much of this thinking about policy and practice is based on the issues and research findings that follow.

Our past approach: Americanization

Historically, Americanization has been a prime institutional education objective for Hispanic young children and their families (Elam 1972; Gonzales 1990; Garcia 1994). Schooling practices were adapted whenever the Hispanic student population rose to significant numbers in a community. This adaptation resulted in special programs applied to both children and adults in urban and rural schools and communities. The desired effect of Americanizing was to socialize and acculturate the targeted diverse community. In essence, if public efforts could teach these children and families English and American values, then social, economic, and educational failure could be averted. Ironically, social economists have argued that this effort was coupled with systematic efforts to maintain disparate conditions between Anglos and minority populations. Indeed, more than anything else, past attempts at addressing the Black, Hispanic, Indian, Asian, etc., "educational problem" have actually preserved the political and economic subordination of these communities (Spencer 1988). Coming from a sociological theory of assimilation, Americanization has traditionally been recognized as a solution to the problem of immigrants and ethnicity in the modern industrialized United States. Linda Chavez (1991) continues to champion this solution for Hispanics.

The Americanization solution has not worked. Moreover, it depends on the flawed notion of group culture. The Americanization solution presumes that culturally different children are, as a group, culturally flawed. To fix them individually, we must act on the individual as a member of a cultural group. By changing the values, language, and so forth of the group, we will have the solution to the educational underachievement of students representing these groups. The challenge facing educators regarding Hispanic students is not to Americanize them but to understand them and act responsively to the specific diversity they bring and the educational goal of academic success for all students.

Early childhood practices that meet the challenge

The debate regarding early childhood education of Hispanic students in the United States has centered on the role of cultural and developmental appropriateness of curriculum and pedagogy, along with Spanish language use and the development of English in these early childhood settings. Discussion of this issue has included cross-disciplinary dialogues involving psychology, linguistics, sociology, politics, and education. (For a more thorough discussion of these issues, see Cummins 1979, Troike 1981, Baker and deKanter 1983, Garcia 1983, Willig 1985, Rossell and Ross 1986, Hakuta and Gould 1987, August and Garcia 1988, Crawford 1989, Baker 1990, Kagan and Garcia 1991, Garcia 1994, Cole 1995, Garcia and Gonzalez 1995, and Rossell and Baker 1996.) The central theme of these discussions relates to the specific role of the native language.

Supporters of culturally sensitive and native language instruction are at one end in this debate. Proponents of this specially designed instructional strategy recommend the utilization of the child's native language and mastery of that language prior to the introduction of an English, more mainstream curriculum. This approach (Cardenas 1986; Fishman 1989) suggests that the competencies in the native culture and language, particularly about academic learning, provide important cognitive and social foundations for second-language learning and academic learning in general—you really only learn to read once. At the other end in this debate, introduction to the English curriculum is recommended at the onset of the student's schooling experience, with minimal use of the native language. This specially designed approach calls for English language "leveling" by instructional staff (to facilitate the understanding on behalf of the student with limited English proficiency) combined with an English-as-a-second-language component. In essence, the earlier the student confronts English and the more times he or she is confronted, the greater the English linguistic advantage (Rossell 1992; Rossell & Baker 1996).

The native language debate has ignored the contributions of Friere (1970), Bernstein (1971), Cummins (1979, 1986), Heath (1986), Ogbu (1986), Trueba (1987), Levin (1988), Tharp (1989), Rose (1989), Moll (1991), Garcia (1995), and Krashen (1996), who have suggested that the schooling vulnerability of such students must be understood within the broader contexts of this society's treatment of these students and their families in and out of educational institutions. That is, no quick fix is likely under social and early education conditions that mark the Hispanic-language minority student for special treatment of his or her language difference without consideration for the psychological and social-cultural circumstances in which that student resides. This is not to suggest that the linguistic character of this student is insignificant. Instead, it warns us against the isolation of this single attribute as the only variable of importance. This more comprehensive view of the education, particularly early childhood education, includes an understanding of the relationship between home and school, the sociocultural incongruities between the two, and the resulting effects on learning and achievement (Kagan & Garcia 1991; Garcia 1994).

Recent research findings have redefined the nature of the educational vulnerability of Hispanic children, destroyed common stereotypes and myths, and laid a foundation on which to reconceptualize present educational practices and launch new initiatives. This foundation recognizes the homogeneity and heterogeneity within and between diverse student populations. No one set of descriptions or prescriptions will suffice; however, a set of commonalties deserves particular attention.

Research focusing on early childhood classrooms, teachers, administrators, and parents revealed an interesting set of perspectives on the treatment of children (Hakuta & Gould 1987; Rose 1989; Garcia 1991; Moll 1991; Ramirez et al. 1991; Wong Fillmore 1991; Garcia 1994; Cole 1995). Classroom teachers were highly committed to the educational success of their students; perceived themselves as instructional innovators utilizing "new" learning theories and instructional philosophies to guide their practice; continued to be involved in professional development activities, including participation in small-group support networks; had a strong, demonstrated commitment to student-home communication (several teachers were utilizing a weekly parent interaction format); and felt they had the autonomy to create or change the instruction and curriculum in their classrooms even if it did not meet the district guidelines exactly. Significantly, these teachers "adopted" their students. They had high academic expectations for all their students ("Everyone will learn to read in my classroom") and also served as advocates for their students. They rejected any conclusion that their students were intellectually or academically disadvantaged.

Parents expressed a high level of satisfaction and appreciation regarding their children's educational experience in these classrooms. All indicated or implied that academic success was tied to their children's future economic success. Anglo and Hispanic parents were both quite involved in the formal parent-supported activities of the schools. However, Anglo parents' attitudes were much more in line with a child advocacy view—somewhat distrustful of the school's specific interest in doing what was right for their child. Conversely, Hispanic parents expressed a high level of trust for the teaching and administrative staff.

This recent research addresses some significant practice questions regarding effective academic environments for Hispanic children:

1. *What role did native language instruction play?*

Teachers considered native language use in daily instruction as key. They implemented an articulated native language and literacy effort that recognized language as a tool for learning and not as a learning objective.

2. *Who were the key players in this effective schooling drama?*

Administrators and parents played important roles. However, teachers were the key players. They achieved the educational confidence of their peers and supervisors. They worked to organize instruction, create new instructional environments, assess effectiveness, and advocate for their students. They were proud of their students, reassuring but consistently demanding. They rejected any notion of linguis-

proficiency-as-a-problem approach to an asset inventory and native-language-as-a-resource approach.

Conclusion

Effective early education curriculum, instructional strategies, and teaching staffs recognize that development and learning have their roots in sharing expertise and experiences through multiple avenues of communication. Further, effective early childhood education for linguistically and culturally diverse children encourages them to take risks, construct meaning, and seek reinterpretation of knowledge within the compatible social contexts. Within this nurturing environment, skills are tools for acquiring knowledge, not ends in themselves, and the language of the child is an incredible resource. The curriculum recognizes that any attempt to address the needs of these students in a deficit or subtractive mode is counterproductive. Instead, this knowledge base recognizes, conceptually, that educators must be additive in an approach to these students.

Recent statements about these challenges reinforce this charge. The National Council of Teachers of English and the International Reading Association (NCTE/IRA) in their enunciation of standards for English language arts recognize that

---

> **Be an advocate for our linguistically and culturally diverse children and families by nurturing, celebrating, and challenging them. They do not need our pity for what they do not have; they, like any individual and family, require our respect and the use of what they bring as a resource.**

---

tic, cultural, or intellectual inferiority regarding their students. They were child advocates.

Imbedded in the activities of these educational enterprises for Hispanic students was the understanding that language, culture, and their accompanying values are acquired in the home and community environment; that children come to school with some knowledge about what language is, how it works, and what it is used for; that children learn higher-level metacognitive and metalinguistic skills as they engage in socially meaningful activities; and that children's development and learning are best understood in the interaction of linguistic, sociocultural, and cognitive knowledge and experiences. In particular for students who did not speak English, their native language was perceived as a resource instead of a problem. **In general terms, this research *suggests* moving away from a needs assessment and non-English-**

Students develop an understanding of and respect for diversity in language use, patterns, and dialects across cultures, ethnic groups, geographic regions, and social roles.

Students whose first language is not English make use of their first language to develop competency in the English language arts and to develop understanding of content across the curriculum.

Celebrating our shared beliefs and traditions are not enough; we also need to honor that which is distinctive in the many groups that make up our nation. (1996, 3)

NAEYC echoes these same concerns in its position statement related to educational practices regarding linguistic and cultural diversity in early childhood:

Early childhood educators can best help linguistically and culturally diverse children and their families by acknowledging and responding to the importance of the child's home language and culture. Administrative support for bilingualism as a goal is necessary within the educational setting. Educational practices should focus on educating children toward the "school culture" while preserving and respecting the diversity of the home language and culture that each child brings to the early learning setting. (1996, 12)

In the present era, this challenge must be met within the context of philosophical, ideological, and political debates surrounding our professional efforts to do things right and to do the right things for all children and families. Eugene, Gene, and Gino encourage you in these efforts, particularly for Hispanics, recognizing the significance of your role and regard for their roots and wings. Here are five practical applications that teachers can use to meet this challenge:

1. Know the linguistic and cultural diversity of your students. Like an ethnographer, be very observant and seek information regarding the languages and cultures represented by the children, families, and communities you serve. Learn to pronounce your student's name as the family pronounces it. For each student write down linguistic and cultural information so it becomes as important as the other things you write down.

2. Take on the new challenge of serving linguistic and culturally diverse children with resolve, commitment, and *ganas* (high motivation). Children and families will appreciate your willingness to learn their language—even small phrases of their language. They will also recognize paternalistic attitudes—attitudes that convey the notion that their children should negate their native language and culture.

3. Be up to date on the new knowledge base. We know so much more now about how better to deal with diversity. Most of us grew up or received our formal training in eras when diversity was not an issue. Incorporate personal and formal stories, games, songs, and poems from various cultures and languages into the curriculum.

4. Share the knowledge with the educational and noneducational community. There is so much strong feeling among educators and the general public that diversity is a problem and must be eliminated. Be clear about how you deal with diversity in ways that respect the need for common culture, shared culture, and individual integrity.

5. Above all else, care about and be an advocate for our linguistically and culturally diverse children and families by nurturing, celebrating, and challenging them. They do not need our pity or remorse for what they do not have; they, like any individual and family, require our respect and the use of what they bring as a resource.

References

August, D., & E. Garcia. 1988. *Language minority education in the United States: Research, policy and practice.* Chicago: Charles C. Thomas.

Baker, K.A. 1990. Bilingual education's 20-year failure to provide rights protection for language-minority students. In *Children at risk: Poverty, minority status and other issues in educational equity,* eds. A. Barona & E. Garcia, 29–52. Washington, DC: National Association of School Psychologists.

Baker, K.A., & A.A. deKanter. 1983. An answer from research on bilingual education. *American Education* 56: 157–69.

Bernstein, B. 1971. A sociolinguistic approach to socialization with some reference to educability. In *Class, codes and control: Theoretical studies towards a sociology of language,* ed. B. Bernstein, 146–71. London: Routledge & Kegan Paul.

California State Department of Education. 1992. *The program for infant/toddler caregivers: A guide to language development and communication.* Sacramento: Author.

Cardenas, J. 1986. The role of native-language instruction in bilingual education. *Phi Delta Kappan* 67: 359–63.

Chavez, L. 1991. *Out of the barrio: Toward a new politics of Hispanic assimilation.* New York: Basic.

Cole, R.W. 1995. *Educating everybody's children: What research and practice say about improving achievement.* Alexandria, VA: Association for Supervision and Curriculum Development.

Crawford, J. 1989. *Bilingual education: History, politics, theory, and practice.* Trenton, NJ: Crane.

Cummins, J. 1979. Linguistic independence and the educational development of bilugual children. *Review of Educational Research* 19: 222–51,

Cummins, J. 1986. Empowering minority students: A framework for intervention. *Harvard Educational Review* 56 (I): 18–35.

de Leon Siantz, M. 1996. Profile of the Hispanic child. In *Hispanic voices: Hispanic health educators speak out,* ed. S. Torres, 134–49. New York: NLN Press.

Elam, S. 1972. Acculturation and learning problems of Puerto Rican children. In *The Puerto Rican community and its children on the mainland,* eds. F. Corradasco & E. Bucchini, 116–38. Metuchen, NJ: Scarecrow.

Fishman, J. 1989. Bias and anti-intellectualism: The frenzied fiction of "English only." In *Language and ethnicity in minority sociolinguistic perspective,* ed. Multilingual Matters, 214–37. London: Multilingual Matters.

Friere, P. 1970. *Pedagogy of the oppressed.* New York: Seabury.

Garcia, E. 1983. *Bilingualism in early childhood.* Albuquerque: University of New Mexico Press.

Garcia, E. 1991. *Education of linguistically and culturally diverse students: Effective instructional practices. Education Report #1.* Washington, DC: Center of Applied Linguistics and the National Center for Research on Cultural Diversity and Second Language Learning.

Garcia, E. 1993. Language, culture and education. In *Review of research in education,* ed. L. Darling-Hammond, 51–97. Washington, DC: American Educational Research Association.

Garcia, E. 1994. *Understanding and meeting the challenge of student diversity.* Boston: Houghton Mifflin.

Garcia, E. 1995. Educating Mexican American students: Past treatments and recent developments in theory, research, policy, and practice. In *Handbook of research on multicultural education,* eds. J. Banks & C.A. McGee Banks, 372–426. New York: Macmillan.

Garcia, E., & R. Gonzalez. 1995. Issues in systemic reform for culturally and linguistically diverse students. *College Record* 96 (3): 418–31.

Gonzalez, R. 1990. *Chicano education in the segregation era: 1915–1945.* Philadelphia: Balch Institute.

Hakuta, K., & L.J. Gould. 1987. Synthesis of research on bilingual education. *Educational Leadership* 44 (6): 39–45.

Heath, S.B. 1986. Sociocultural contexts of language development. In *Beyond language: Social and cultural factors in schooling language minority students,* ed. California Department of Education, 143–86. Los Angeles: Evaluation, Dissemination, and Assessment Center, California State University.

Kagan, S.L., & E. Garcia. 1991. Educating culturally and linguistically diverse preschoolers: moving the agenda. *Early Childhood Research Quarterly* 6: 427–43.

Krashen, S. 1996. *Under attack: The case against bilingual education.* Culver City, CA: Language Education Associates.

Levin, I. 1988. *Accelerated schools for at-risk students.* CPRE Research Report Series RR-010. New Brunswick, NJ: Rutgers University Center for Policy Research in Education.

McLaughlin, M.W., & L.A. Shepard. 1995. *Improving education through standard-based reform: A report by the national academy of education panel of standards-based education reform.* Stanford, CA: National Academy of Education.

Moll, L. 1991. *Funds of knowledge for change: Developing mediating connections between homes and classrooms.* Paper presented at the conference on "Literacy, Identity and Mind," University of Michigan, Ann Arbor.

NAEYC. 1996. NAEYC position statement: Responding to linguistic and cultural diversity—recommendations for effective early childhood education. *Young Children* 51 (2): 4–12.

National Center for Children in Poverty. 1995. *Welfare reform seen from a children's perspective.* New York: Columbia University School of Public Health.

NCTE/IRA (National Council of Teachers of English and International Reading Association). 1996. *Standards for the English language arts.* Urbana, IL: NCTE.

Ogbu, J. 1986. The consequences of the American caste system. In *The school achievement of minority children: New perspectives,* ed. U. Neisser, 73–114. Hillsdale, NJ: Erlbaum.

Phillips, D.A., & N.J. Cabrera. 1996. *Beyond the blueprint: Directions for research on Head Start's families.* Washington, DC: National Academy Press.

Ramirez, J.D., S.D. Yuen, D.R. Ramey, & D.J. Pasta. 1991. *Final Report: Longitudinal study of structured English immersion strategy, early-exit and late-exit transitional bilingual education programs for language-minority children.* San Mateo, CA: Aguirre International.

Rodriguez, R. 1982. *Hunger of memory.* New York: Bantam.

Rose, M. 1989 *Lives on the boundary.* New York: Free Press.

Rossell, C. 1992. Nothing matters? A critique of the Ramirez, et al. longitudinal study of instructional programs for language minority children. *Journal of the National Association for Bilingual Education* 16 (1–2): 159–86.

Rossell, C., & K. Baker. 1996. The education effectiveness of bilingual education. *Research in the Teaching of English* 30: 7–74.

Rossell, C., & J.M. Ross. 1986 *The social science evidence on bilingual education.* Boston: Boston University.

Spencer, D. 1988. Transitional bilingual education and the socialization of immigrants. *Harvard Educational Review* 58 (2): 133–53.

Tharp, R.G. 1989. *Challenging cultural minds.* London: Cambridge University Press.

Troike, R.C. 1981. Synthesis of research in bilingual education. *Educational Leadership* 38: 498–504.

Trueba, H.T. 1987. *Success or failure? Learning and the language minority student.* Scranton, PA: Harper & Row.

U.S. Department of Commerce. 1990. *The Hispanic population in the United States: March 1989.* Washington, DC: GPO.

Villaseñor, V. 1991. *Rain of gold.* New York: Delta.

Willig, A.C. 1985. A meta-analysis of selected studies on effectiveness of bilingual education. *Review of Educational Research* 55 (33): 269–317.

Wong Fillmore, L. 1991. When learning a second language means loosing a first. *Early Childhood Research Quarterly* 6 (3): 323–46.

Chris Liska Carger

Attending to New Voices

Listen, observe, visit, read, reflect, and write. All these activities can broaden your understanding of your culturally diverse students.

By the year 2050, the present percentage of Latinos in the U.S. population will almost triple; the Asian population will more than triple; African Americans will increase about 3 percent; the non-Hispanic white population will drop from 76 percent to 53 percent.

The ESL language-minority student population in Illinois will experience a projected 91 percent growth in the greater Chicago area and 141 percent growth outside that area (U.S. Census Bureau).

*T*his is some of the information I give to my classes, composed of prospective and veteran teachers, as we explore the concept of multicultural education. My premise is that, as teachers, we are experiencing these demographics—and we need to learn to appreciate and attend to new voices, new languages, and diverse educational needs among our students. We must go beyond the lip service we often give to multicultural education. Educating multiculturally is more of an approach than a recipe for dealing with diverse students; it requires an individualized, life-long process of learning, discovering, accepting, and trying—a little like developing gourmet cuisine versus ordering fast food.

We need to read multicultural children's literature, invite diverse parents to our classrooms, and reflect on differences and embrace them, not lament them. One way to gather information is to observe our children's families and

Educating multiculturally is an individualized, lifelong process of learning, discovering, accepting, and trying.

communities. We can learn much through such *ethnographic* observations of people living in various cultural groups (Husserl 1970). Dutch researcher and philosopher Max Van Manen emphasizes: "It is a crucial feature of teaching that the educator understands a child's learning and development in the context of the larger biography of the child" (1991, p. 53).

Photos courtesy of Chris Liska Carger

Murals in Chicago's Mexican-American community reflect the rich culture of the families living there.

Children in the Neighborhood

In a study I conducted in Chicago, I set out to become better acquainted with the culture of Mexican-American families of my preschool students. I wondered what these parents desired for their children, what they did to prepare them for their first school experience, and what kinds of toys and books they encouraged. I wanted to know why so many Latino preschoolers lacked what teachers call "readiness skills"—despite my previous observations that these parents were totally attentive and devoted to their children.

Readiness skills, for the purpose of my inquiry, included a familiarity with basic concepts of color, shape, size, and numbers; the ability to attend to oral directions, storytelling, or oral reading for a short period of time; and the ability to express oneself verbally to

From *Educational Leadership*, April 1997, pp. 39-43. © Chris Liska Carger. Reprinted by permission of the author.

communicate basic needs, ideas, and emotions appropriate for a preschool age. Prospects for the Latino pre- schoolers I studied saddened me. Latino students are reported to fall twice as far below grade level as their non-Latino peers. They suffer the highest dropout rate in the United States. In Chicago, the Latino dropout rate has been reported as high as 70 percent (Perez-Miller 1991).

I set about visiting preschool class- rooms, homes, library story times, play- grounds, and neighborhood businesses in the community called Pilsen, which has the highest percentage of Latino people in Chicago. In Pilsen, sights, sounds, and aromas strongly attest to the Mexican-American presence in the community. Tortilla factories send wafts of freshly baked specialties throughout the neighborhood amidst the beat of *salsa* music pouring out of small record shops. Mothers carrying their babies in handmade shawls and blankets, grand- mothers crocheting as they sit outside on kitchen chairs, handpainted murals exploding with color on the sides of old brick buildings—all are common sights in Pilsen. Children are every- where—hanging on to their mothers or fathers' hands, sitting on their grand- mothers' laps, being attended to by aunts, cousins, waitresses, and friendly passersby.

As I pursued my study, I was partic- ularly interested in a 4-year-old girl, Maribel Chavez, who was not flour- ishing in preschool. I arranged for an interview, and my visit to Maribel's home was illuminating.

Maribel at Home

Señora Chavez's oldest son, Fernando, who is 18, peeked through the curtain on the front door window before politely welcoming me into his home. From the outside, I could see a small Christmas tree in the picture window of the one-family, red brick house.

When I walked into the house, Andy, the 7-year-old son, was seated on the

Preschoolers (above) participate in language-learning activities; life-sized portraits of children abound in colorful neighborhood murals (right).

floor about two feet from a color television set. The home was spotless and in perfect order. The first floor consisted of a living room, a large kitchen, two bedrooms (for the older boys), and a bathroom. It amazed me that a house with four children could look so clean and organized.

My impression was that this was not a show put on for a visitor. Señora Chavez had just returned from work 10 minutes before I arrived. Her four children, ranging in age from 4 to 18 years, arrived home before her—yet not even a jacket or book was visible or out of place. Mrs. Chavez turned off the TV and sent her three boys to the basement while we talked.

The basement was completely finished as one large bedroom for herself, her husband, and the two youngest children. She explained that Andy still cries at night (and I noticed that 4-year-old Maribel still sleeps in a crib) and that she didn't want to make separate bedrooms. "They're still very little," she said.

Mrs. Chavez works in a restaurant in downtown Chicago; her husband is a construction worker. They live quite comfortably compared to the humbler homes I have visited in their neighbor- hood.

I introduced myself and gave Mrs. Chavez my usual reassurances of anonymity. Maribel was a small-built 4-year-old. She cuddled into her mother's lap while we talked and remained there without a word until I left. I asked Mrs. Chavez what she looked for in a preschool program for her children, what she hoped they would learn. She answered without hesitation, "My first concern was that it be a full-day program because I work all day and so does my husband." With less certainty, she added, "And, well, I wanted to teach them something useful, you know, better than just being with a baby-sitter."

"Do you read to your children?" I asked. I saw no books, magazines, or newspapers in the house.

"Yes," she answered. "They send me books from school to read—sometimes in English, sometimes Spanish." Mrs. Chavez was bilingual, but as soon as she knew I spoke Spanish she was visibly relieved. "I'm so glad you speak Spanish. My English is not so good," she said.

"What kind of toys do you buy for Maribel?" I continued.

"Dolls, all dolls," she told me, and Maribel grinned. "She's crazy about Barbies. That's all she asks me to buy."

"How do you feel about their school?" I asked. "Are you happy with the program?"

Mrs. Chavez said that she was very happy with the school. She said that they called her a lot to bring or do things. "I just love it when they ask me to do something. Then I know they are paying attention to my children." Mrs. Chavez mentioned no further goals concerning her children's education. Like the other moms I spoke to, she seemed trusting of the educators in her children's school.

After further discussion, Mrs. Chavez told me that I was always welcome in her home. "What a shame you can't stay and eat," she said. I felt that what was a threatening situation for a woman whose children do not do well in school (her sons attended a special reading tutorial), turned out to be a positive experience for Señora Chavez.

I wanted her to realize that she was doing me a favor, that she had valuable information that would help me, and that I thought she was a good mother. I remembered what another Latino parent had said about how important it was to old-fashioned Mexican-American moms that little ones "don't touch." As I was leaving, Maribel stood gazing at their Christmas tree but never laid a finger on it. I told Mrs. Chavez how lovely the tree looked and that I noticed how careful Maribel was with it. Mrs. Chavez beamed and hugged

> In Spanish, "bien educado" connotes a wider sense of being well-bred, mannerly, clean, respectful, responsible, loved, and loving.

her daughter. "She is always good like that," she laughed.

During this whole time, her sons watched TV in the basement bedroom. Mrs. Chavez puts few restrictions on types of shows watched or time spent watching TV. She is on her feet all day, working in a restaurant. Then she rushes home by train to cook dinner.

It must take a lot of time to keep a house as clean and organized as hers is, and this clearly is her priority. If the school asked her to do something or sent home a book, she took care of it; but I did not get the sense that she initiated contact. As Mrs. Chavez talked of her desire to keep her two younger children near her, I found it easy to forget that they are 4 and 7. They are very small for their ages, and Maribel constantly clings to her as Mrs. Chavez runs her fingers through the child's silky black hair. "I waited so long for a girl," she said.

Home/School Expectations

So in school, Maribel's English-speaking teacher struggles to get her to speak more, to be more independent, and to participate in class. At home, Maribel still sleeps in a crib in her parents' room—her mother's youngest child who plays exclusively with dolls and hears no English.

The Latino parenting that I observed in this home and others had a nurturing style. Children were not expected to be independent. The parent's role was clearly emerging as one of caretaker, provider, protector. Preparing children to express themselves verbally, develop fine motor skills, listen and attend to storybooks, partake in structured play activities, amplify vocabulary, or recognize colors was simply not considered a parental responsibility.

In fact, in most interviews I have conducted in this community, the parents expressed a definite hesitancy and uneasiness with schooling. Their early memories of school in Mexico were not positive. They worried that their children would "tire of school" because their experiences with it revolved around rote memorization with few stimulating materials. They wanted their older children to do homework, but did not usually structure a time or space in which to do it.

My research surprised me. I had expected to find that parents had prepared their children with some readiness skills that teachers had overlooked. Instead, I had discovered an important social and emotional support system separate from school goals or objectives. For most Latino children, entrance into the school world brings a more abrupt and total change than it does for other kids. Not only are there new surroundings and expectations, but many preschool activities are unfamiliar. Even typical classroom toys, often emphasizing fine motor development, frequently are not in their background of experiences. Most of their schoolwork is accompanied by a language they do not hear in their homes, and they are taught by teachers who know little about their culture.

In a similar study of an adolescent Mexican-American student (Carger 1996), I experienced another revelation about the strengths possessed by a Mexican-American family.

Alejandro's "Open Wound"

Alejandro Juarez was a student who had tremendous difficulty with literacy. I had met him when he was a 4th grader and returned to conduct a study about his 8th grade experience. His difficulties had mounted over the intervening years despite remedial efforts. Yet in elementary school, he doggedly hung on to his educational program, albeit by a thread, even in the face of embarrassment and punishments for poor-quality schoolwork in a traditional school system.

From Alejandro's mother, Alma, I learned the importance of listening to family stories as she narrated her own struggle to enter the United States to make a better life for herself and her children. She and her husband had made many terrifying trips, in all sorts of transports, to cross the U.S.-Mexican border, which Anzaldúa calls "*una herida abierta* (an open wound), where the Third World grates against the first and bleeds" (1987, p. 3). They made their way through polluted river water, pushing through gaps in fences that sent electrical shocks through their bodies. They paid exorbitant fares to *coyotes,* or smugglers.

Their determination to provide for their family gave me great insights into Alejandro's resilience and persistence in the face of failure at school. I reflected in *Of Borders and Dreams* that "perhaps his parents have taught him a lesson far greater than the textual

> Parental involvement in preschool may increase Latino parents' confidence in actively participating in their children's school experiences.

literacy which they cannot provide. Maybe he has learned from them that if you're strong enough to dive into that river enough times, sooner or later you might just beat the current and succeed in *la lucha* (the struggle)" (Carger 1996, p. 21).

Alejandro persisted in grammar school despite dyslexia; he resisted the gangs that surrounded him; and he remained faithful to his family. As my study drew to an end, high school presented further dangers and temptations that proved insurmountable to him. But his mother never lost hope that he would make something of himself and contribute to the family, even though she feared for his life and eventually had to acknowledge that he would drop out of school. Alma held tenaciously to her maternal goal that her son be *bien educado.*

"Bien Educado"

From my studies of Maribel and Alejandro's families, I learned much more than I expected. What I saw in these Latino families was a comprehensive, inclusive conception of educating children. Latino parents use the term *bien educado.* Translated literally, it means "well educated"; but in Spanish, it connotes a wider sense of being *well-bred, mannerly, clean, respectful, responsible, loved,* and *loving.* Children are an integral, celebrated part of family and neighborhood. They are expected to obediently fulfill the teacher's directives and to respectfully, lovingly fulfill family responsibilities. Rarely did the families refer to specific career or long-range educational plans, but they always hoped that their children would be *bien educado.*

Van Manen (1990) speaks of the necessity of connecting research to the everyday world of the children we seek to educate. Out of my research, I began to see connections that could benefit both teachers and parents. First, it appeared to me that Latino children have often been planted in fertile ground for a cooperative style of learning. They emerge from a culture that has blanketed them with supportive care and that does not emphasize competition and independence. A familiarity with Latino child-rearing practices may positively increase a teacher's understanding of how her students' family expectations and learning styles might blend with educational efforts in the classroom.

Second, I believe that parental involvement in preschool may increase Latino parents' confidence in actively participating in their children's school experiences. This is not meant to emphasize the "deficits" of such families and dwell on weaknesses, but rather to realize differences and help develop areas that will make school success more attainable. Van Manen (1990) laments the loss of "common sense, the sense we have in common, the basic assumptions and values . . . the inexhaustible layers of meaning of everyday living with children in cultures where family traditions have been lost" (p. 142). Here lies a strength still apparent in many Latino families I met: The "layering" from one generation's child-rearing practices merges with the next generation, so that families retain values even in the midst of great cultural adjustments.

I would like to see schools encourage parental involvement that realizes and celebrates the nurturance of the extended Latino family while helping the parents to explore new educational and academic ground. Latino parents can thus integrate new worlds into their child-rearing practices and incorporate new ideas about education into their family networks, which are already strong in integrative and collaborative skills. A goal of *bien educado* has much merit, and I believe it can cross into the academic world as teachers and parents move closer to one another's experiences and expectations.

From Negatives to Positives

For children like Maribel and Alejandro who are from Latino families, many teachers have had negative perceptions of what was (or wasn't) happening in their homes. Teachers have often assumed that these children's parents are not interested in school. But my studies have given me images of caring parents whose styles differed from the mainstream conception, yet were equally valid. My observations gave me a grasp on the concept of *bien educado*.

Integral to gaining understanding from close observations is the activity of writing about them. I would like to encourage teachers to write portraits of their students—and to write responsively and reflectively. We must share this writing—whether at a school level, the district level, or through professional publications. Teachers—and students—need to read immigrant stories, particularly those describing educational experiences. For example, read Sandra Cisneros's (1989) childhood vignettes and glimpses of classroom life, Carmen Tafolla's (1983) poetry on classroom memories, and Luis Rodriguez's (1993) recounting of misplaced Latino students in special

Latino children have often been planted in fertile ground for a cooperative style of learning.

education classrooms and the eventual drift toward gangs. Such works can provide powerful links between the life worlds and school worlds of diverse students.

In the case of young Maribel, the classroom teacher learned to gradually introduce new kinds of toys to her and to lend such toys, along with books, for home use. The teacher also learned not to view Señora Chavez's rare communication with school in a negative light but to realize that Maribel's mother would warmly welcome school initiatives.

In Alejandro's case, some of his teachers and tutors (including myself) learned a great deal about acknowledging diverse parents' strengths even when they are outside the academic realm. Alejandro's parents were eager to share their stories and their strengths. Sadly, Alejandro's schools did not pursue this information. For Alejandro, the huge urban public high school he attended the year after my study proved

to be overwhelmed with issues of security from gang violence and operated on a deficit view of minority students. Unfortunately, it seemed too late to undo the years of misconceptions about urban students and families like Alejandro's.

My goal is to help teachers avoid losing more Maribels and Alejandros to the dropout rate and to encourage appreciation and integration of their families in educational settings. Through listening, observing, and reflecting, I believe we can cross borders and attend to the new voices of our diverse students and their parents.

References

Anzaldúa, G. (1987). *Borders/La Frontera: The New Mestiza.* San Francisco: Spinsters/Aunt Lute.

Carger, C. (1996). *Of Borders and Dreams: A Mexican-American Experience of Urban Education.* New York: Teachers College Press.

Cisneros, S. (1989). *The House on Mango Street.* New York: Vintage Books.

Husserl, E. (1970). *The Idea of Phenomenology.* The Hague: Martinus Nijhoff.

Perez-Miller, A. (1991). *An Analysis of the Persistence/Dropout Behavior of Hispanic Students in a Chicago Public School.* Unpublished doctoral diss., University of Illinois, Chicago.

Rodriguez, L. (1993). *Always Running: La Vida Loca, Gang Days in LA.* Willimatic, Conn.: Curbstone Press.

Tafolla, C. (1983). *Curandera.* Santa Monica, Calif.: Santa Monica Press.

Van Manen, M. (1990). *Researching Lived Experience: Human Science for an Action Sensitive Pedagogy.* New York: State University of New York Press.

Van Manen, M. (1991). *The Tact of Teaching: The Meaning of Pedagogical Thoughtfulness.* New York: State University of New York Press.

Chris Liska Carger is Professor of Elementary Education, Department of Curriculum and Instruction, Northern Illinois University, DeKalb, IL 60115 (e-mail: ccarger@niu.edu).

Unit Selections

27. **Language-Minority Student Achievement and Program Effectiveness,** Wayne P. Thomas and Virginia P. Collier
28. **Two Languages Are Better than One,** Wayne P. Thomas and Virginia P. Collier
29. **School Reform and Student Diversity,** Catherine Minicucci et al.
30. **A Gradual Exit, Variable Threshold Model for Limited English Proficient Children,** Stephen Krashen

Key Points to Consider

❖ What are the commonly used program models for second-language learners?

❖ Why is two-way bilingual education the preferred model?

❖ How is content treated in a two-way bilingual program?

❖ What does the research on language model effectiveness show?

❖ How can two-way bilingual programs be developed to serve both the minority- and majority-language groups in a school district?

 **Links**   **www.dushkin.com/online/**

29. **For All Students: Limited English Proficient Students and Goals 2000**
    http://www.ncbe.gwu.edu/ncbepubs/focus/focus10.htm
30. **Multicultural Education**
    http://www.ceousa.org/multic.html
31. **Mundo Latino—Rincon Literario**
    http://www.mundolatino.org/cultura/litera/
32. **School Reform and Student Diversity**
    http://www.ncbe.gwu.edu/ncbepubs/resource/schref.htm
33. **Schools on the Web: Sites of Interest to Bilingual/Multcultural Educators**
    http://www.ncbe.gwu.edu/classroom/bilschool.htm

These sites are annotated on pages 4 and 5.

The success of any new school program depends on a clear vision that is based on obtainable goals, long-term commitment, and long-term evaluation, which advance and enhance the realization of the vision. Questions regarding program success in ESL and the effectiveness of bilingual education in meeting the needs of linguistically diverse students have been an issue for some time. In this section we present these and other issues that are helping to shape opinions on program reforms in this field.

Since the 1960s, when large numbers of Cuban refugees began entering Florida schools, American educators have grappled with the question of how to teach English quickly and effectively. The Bilingual Education Act of 1968 was enacted to ensure equal opportunity in education for the refugee students. The political problems in Cuba were seen as a temporary crisis, and the bilingual maintenance model adopted at the Coral Way Elementary School in Miami, Florida, was seen as a solution to that temporary problem. The program emphasized teaching English while also maintaining Spanish, with the intention of providing uninterrupted education for the students, thus facilitating their return to their native country once the political crisis in Cuba was resolved. As we now know, the expected resolution did not occur.

Efforts then to provide services to other diverse language groups, including Puerto Ricans in the northeast, Mexican Americans in the southwest and California, as well as Asian refugees entering western states from the war-torn countries of Vietnam, Cambodia, Laos, Korea, and others, led to modifications of bilingual and ESL programs to accommodate the particular needs of each group.

By the mid-1970s, most large urban centers across the nation were being pressured to address cultural and linguistic issues within their schools. The growing consensus among educators that bilingual education was becoming a national reform issue could no longer be ignored. New initiatives in bilingual/bicultural education also motivated the Bureau of Indian Affairs to become active in the educational movement and to seek funding and technical assistance for the badly neglected Indian schools. These new directives in education helped to influence changes in perceptions of America as a multilingual, multicultural nation.

Nearly 30 years have passed since the early publicly funded bilingual programs were established, but many of the same questions remain. Among them are these: Which program model is most effective in helping non-English-speaking children to learn English? How long does it take for a child to learn English as a second language well enough to function successfully and consistently at grade level?

Results of a 12-year longitudinal study by Drs. Virginia Collier and Wayne Thomas have provided important information about bilingual education. Succinctly stated, their research confirms the widely held belief that the acquisition of a second language, like that of the first, is a long-term developmental process lasting 5–7 years. There are no shortcuts to learning anything complex, especially the process by which we communicate our thoughts to others on an interpersonal as well as academic level.

Moreover, effectively acquiring a second language also depends on several other critical factors: balanced instruction in the native as well as the second language, access to English-speaking peers in socioculturally supportive classroom environments, a comfort level that allows students to interact naturally, the utilization of strategies that are collaborative, and an emphasis on cognitively complex learning.

Research has helped to clear up many of the myths about bilingual education and ESL programs, and it is of particular significance as we consider the ongoing pressures of providing effective instruction to all students, including language minority students, under tight budgetary constraints.

Views about program reforms for minority language students have changed over the past two decades. From early perceptions of bilingual education as a temporary solution for refugee students who would be returning to their native countries, we have progressed toward a newfound appreciation of the language minority student as a bilingual-bicultural resource in a monolingual nation.

Until recently, Americans have been short-sighted and ethnocentric in their support of foreign language education and world cultural understanding. The need for program reforms that encourage minority language students to become bilingual is an important educational direction. By maintaining their native language through instruction and by developing comparative cultural perspectives through home experiences as well as through academic study of their culture, these students can also learn to function successfully in English, the second language. This can be accomplished most effectively in two-way bilingual programs. Such an approach should also involve the child born in the United States, who can learn a great deal from minority-language peers. Bilingual education should be a choice for all students.

Along with educators, many politicians and corporate executives appreciate and support educational reforms that encourage a multilingual and multicultural perspective, because they realize its potential to maintain and expand our national as well as global interests. Even more importantly, these reforms can help us recognize and appreciate the value of multicultural differences and similarities and can expand our ability to reach out to others around the world in their respective languages.

Language-Minority Student Achievement and Program Effectiveness

by Dr. Wayne P. Thomas and Dr. Virginia Collier

This series of studies, conducted as collaborative research with the bilingual/ESL school staff in each of five urban and suburban school district sites in various regions of the U.S., focuses on the length of time needed to be academically successful in a second language and the student, program, and instructional variables that influence language minority students' academic achievement. The school systems chosen have language minority programs that are well established and strongly supported, with experienced staff. The research extends the analyses by Collier and Thomas (Collier, 1987, 1988, 1989, 1992; Collier and Thomas, 1988, 1989, 1991, 1992, Thomas, 1992, 1993, 1994) in the field of language minority education. The sample consists of approximately 42,000 language minority student records per school year, with from 8 to 12 years of data from each of the five school systems. The data include language minority student background variables and student academic achievement as measured by standardized tests, performance assessment measures, grade point average, and high school courses in which enrolled. Data sources are all central administrative student records, central testing databases, and bilingual/ESL program databases, as well as any additional data that the school staff decide to collect to answer questions they want answered. Interviews with school staff provide additional information regarding the sociocultural context of schooling and programmatic variations. In addition, we have acquired and re-analyzed portions of the Ramírez (1991) dataset, to compare this data to our findings.

Data analysis of the study includes the use of relational database computer programs to match all historical records of student background variables and educational program treatment variables with outcome measures, in a series of longitudinal cohorts of 3-6 years, for a long-term look that is cross-sectional but that incorporates longitudinal data. Each school district's data has been analyzed separately, using descriptive statistical analyses and hierarchical multiple linear regression, to assess relationships between and among various student variables, program variables, and student outcomes. The interpretations of the data analyses have taken into consideration the sociocultural contexts in which the language minority students function, through interviews and collaborative analyses of the data conducted with school staff. General patterns have emerged in program differences and students achievement across the five school district sites and are reported below.

Key Findings

Three key predictors of academic success appear to be more important than any other variables. These features are more powerful than specific program type or student background variables. Schools that incorporate all three of these factors are likely to graduate language minority students who are very successful academically in high school and higher education:

- Cognitively complex academic instruction through student's first language for as long as possible and through second language for part of the school day;
- Use of current approaches to teaching the academic curriculum through both L1 and L2, through active, discovery, cognitively complex learning; and
- Changes in the sociocultural context of schooling, e.g. integration with English speakers, in a supporting, affirming context for all; an additive bilingual context, in which bilingual education is perceived as the gifted and talented program for all students; and the transformation of majority and minority relations in school to a positive school climate for all students, in a safe school environment.

Examples of programs that have the potential to incorporate these three key factors are the following:

1. For students who are schooled in the U.S. from kindergarten on, the elementary school program with the most success in language minority students' long-term academic achievement, as measured by standardized tests across all the subject

Figure 1

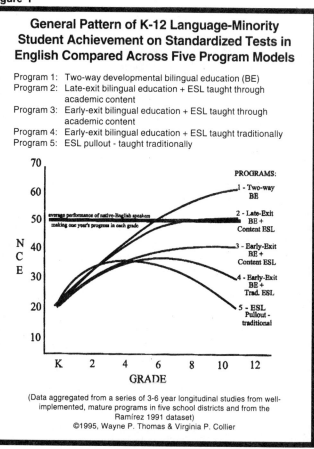

General Pattern of K-12 Language-Minority Student Achievement on Standardized Tests in English Compared Across Five Program Models

Program 1: Two-way developmental bilingual education (BE)
Program 2: Late-exit bilingual education + ESL taught through academic content
Program 3: Early-exit bilingual education + ESL taught through academic content
Program 4: Early-exit bilingual education + ESL taught traditionally
Program 5: ESL pullout - taught traditionally

PROGRAMS:
1 - Two-way BE
2 - Late-Exit BE + Content ESL
3 - Early-Exit BE + Content ESL
4 - Early-Exit BE + Trad. ESL
5 - ESL Pullout - traditional

average performance of native-English speakers making one year's progress in each grade

N C E

GRADE

(Data aggregated from a series of 3-6 year longitudinal studies from well-implemented, mature programs in five school districts and from the Ramírez 1991 dataset)
©1995, Wayne P. Thomas & Virginia P. Collier

From *NABE News*, Vol. 19, No. 6, May 1, 1996, pp. 33-35. © 1996 by the National Association for Bilingual Education (NABE). Reprinted by permission.

areas, is two-way developmental bilingual education. As a group, students in this program maintain grade-level skills in their first language at least through sixth grade and reach the 50th percentile of NCE in their second language generally after 4-5 years of schooling in both languages. They also generally sustain the gains they made when they reach secondary level. Program characteristics are:

- Integrated schooling, with English speakers and language minority students learning each others' languages;
- Perception among staff, students, and parents that it is a "gifted and talented" program, leading to high expectations for student performance;
- Equal status of the two languages achieved, to a large extent, creating self-confidence among language minority students;
- Healthy parent involvement among both language minority and English-speaking parents, for closer home-school collaboration;
- Instructional approaches emphasizing: whole language, natural language acquisition through all content areas, cooperative learning, interactive and discovery learning, cognitive complexity of all lessons.

2. Students in well-taught bilingual classes that continue through at least sixth grade (late-exit or maintenance bilingual programs), with substantial cognitive and academic development through both first and second languages, are also able to reach the 50th percentile of NCE within 4-7 years and maintain their academic performance at secondary level in academic classes taught all in English.

Current Approaches

The second predictive factor, use of current approaches to language and content teaching, provides a clear example of

feasible and effective program change. Students do less well in programs that focus on discrete units of language taught in a structured, sequenced curriculum with the learner treated as a passive recipient of knowledge.

Students achieve significantly better in programs that teach language through cognitively complex academic content in math, science, social studies, and literature, taught through problem-solving, discovery learning in highly interactive class-

room activities. ESL pullout in the early grades, taught traditionally, is the least successful program model for students' long-term academic success. During grades K-3, there is little difference between programs, but significant differences appear as students continue in the mainstream at secondary level, where the instruction and testing become more cognitively demanding.

Secondary Education

For students entering U.S. schools at secondary level, when first language instructional support cannot be provided, the following program characteristics can make a significant difference in academic achievement for English language learners:

- Second language taught through academic content;
- Conscious focus on teaching learning strategies needed to develop thinking skills and problem-solving abilities;
- Instructional approaches that emphasize activation of students' prior knowledge, respect for students' home language and culture, cooperative learning, interactive and discovery learning,

intense and meaningful cognitive/academic development, and ongoing assessment using multiple measures.

How long does it take groups of students to reach the 50th NCE or percentile on standardized tests (including performance assessment) in their second language (L2)? (See Table 1 above)

Both language minority and language majority students, in the very highest quality programs, take this long to reach the level of a native speaker on school tests given in the students' second language. First language literacy and schooling in first language (in home country or in the U.S.) are very important student background variables that are predictors of academic success in second language.

Table 1
Length of Time for Students to Reach 50th Percentile on L2 Standardized Tests

When schooled L2 in the U.S. and tested in L2:

Students with at least 2-3 years of L1 schooling in home country:	5-7 years
Students with no schooling in L1:	7-10 years

When schooled bilingually in L1 and L2 in the U.S.:

Students when tested in L1:	on or above grade level
Students when tested in L2:	4-7 years

Theoretical Model

The research results to date validate our theoretical model illustrated in the form of a prism with four interdependent dimensions: social and cultural processes, as well as language, cognitive, and academic development in L1 and L2. If schools emphasize one dimension to the neglect of another, this may be detrimental to a student's overall growth and academic success.

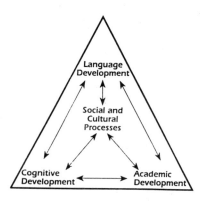

© Virginia P. Collier, 1994

Future Research

We will continue this research with data collection and analyses in the current research sites, and will add five new school districts over the next five years.

Notes

Figure 1 shows the results of some of the data analyses of this study, illustrating general patterns of student achievement on standardized tests in English, compared across several program models. The box (Program Models in Language-Minority Education in the United States) provides an overview of the major variations in program types that have been implemented in the United States for educating language-minority students, focusing on the overall distinguishing characteristic of the amount of instructional support in each language.

Drs. Virginia P. Collier and Wayne P. Thomas are members of the faculty at George Mason University in Fairfax, VA.

Program Models in Language-Minority Education in the United States

(Ranging from the most to the least support through the minority language)

Immersion Bilingual Programs:
Academic instruction through both L1 and L2 for Grades K-12. Originally developed for language majority students in Canada. Used as one model for two-way bilingual education in the U.S.
  Early total immersion (in the U.S., often referred to as the 90-10 model, or the Eastman model in California)
    Grades K-1: All of 90% of academic instruction through minority language
    Grade 2: One hour of academic instruction through majority language added
    Grade 3: Two hours of academic instruction through majority language added
    Grades 4-5 or 6: Academic instruction half a day through each language
    Grades 6 or 7-12: 60% of academic instruction through majority language and 40% through minority language.
  Partial-immersion (in the U.S., the 50-50 model)
    Grades K-5 or 6: Academic instruction half a day through each language
    Grades 6 or 7-12: 60% of academic instruction through majority language and 40% through minority language.

Two-way Developmental Bilingual Programs:
Language majority and language minority students are schooled together in the same bilingual class, with many variations possible, including immersion bilingual education and late-exit bilingual education.

Late-Exit or Maintenance Bilingual Programs:
Academic instruction half a day through each language for Grades K-6. Ideally, this type of program was planned for Grades K-12, but has rarely been implemented beyond elementary school level in U.S.

Early-Exit or Transitional Bilingual Programs:
Academic instruction half a day through each language, with gradual transition to all-majority language instruction in approximately 2-3 years.

English as a Second Language (ESL) or English to Speakers of Other Languages (ESOL) Instruction, with no instruction through the minority language.
  Elementary education
    Structured immersion
      Taught by a bilingual teacher, in a self-contained classroom, but all instruction is conducted through English (all day)
    ESL or ESOL self-contained taught through academic content (all day)
    ESL or ESOL pullout
      Varying from 30 minutes to half a day
  Secondary education
    ESL or ESOL taught through academic content or sheltered English
    ESL or ESOL taught as a subject

Submersion:
No instructional support is provided by a trained specialist.
This is NOT a program model: it is illegal in the U.S. as a result of the Supreme Court decision in Lau v. Nichols.

Wayne P. Thomas and Virginia P. Collier

Two Languages Are Better Than One

Dual language programs help native and nonnative speakers of English speak two languages proficiently— and they do so in cost-effective ways that lead to high academic achievement for all students.

Among the underachieving youth in U.S. schools, students with no proficiency in English must overcome enormous equity gaps, school achievement tests in English show. Over the past three decades, schools have developed a wide range of programs to serve these English learners. After much

Students at Key School/La Escuela Key in Arlington, Va., where learners are united through two languages, stand behind a school banner in Spanish and English.

Photos courtesy of Marjorie W. Myers

experimentation, U.S. schools now have clear achievement data that point to the most powerful models of effective schooling for English learners. What is astounding is that these same programs are also dynamic models for school reform for all students.

Imagine how the 21st century will look. Our world

will surely be in constant change, for we are facing this pattern now. The predictions of the near future also depict an interconnected world, with global travel and instant international communications. Right now, many U.S. businesses seek employees proficient in both English and another language. Students who graduate with monocultural perspectives will not be prepared to contribute to their societies, for cross-cultural contact is at an all-time high in human history as population mobility continues throughout the world (Cummins in Ovando and Collier, in press). Thus, majority and minority language students together must prepare for a constantly changing world.

Tapping the Power of Linguistic Diversity

For more than three decades, as we have struggled to develop effective models for schooling English learners, we have mostly considered the choices available to us from a deficit perspective. That is, we have often viewed English learners as a "problem" for our schools (oh, no—they don't know English), and so we "reme-diate" by sending them to a specialist to be "fixed." In the remedial program, English learners receive less access to the standard grade-level curriculum. The achieve-ment and equity gap increases as native English speakers forge ahead while English learners make less progress. Thus, underachieving groups continue to underachieve in the next genera-tion. Unfortunately, the two most common types of U.S. school services provided for English learners— English as a Second Language (ESL) pullout and transi-tional bilingual education—are remedial in nature. Participating students and teachers suffer often from the social consequences of this perception.

But when the focus of any special school program is on academic enrichment for all students, the school community perceives that program positively, and students become academically successful and deeply engaged in the learning process. Thus, enrichment

From *Educational Leadership,* Vol. 55, No. 4, December 1997/January 1998, pp. 23-26. Reprinted with permission of the Asso-ciation for Supervision and Curriculum Development.

At Key School/La Escuela Key, native English and Spanish speakers are peer language models. At left, students present a science project. Below, students pose enroute to an exchange program in El Salvador

Photos courtesy of Marjorie W. Myers

programs for English learners are extremely effective when they are intellectually challenging and use students' linguistic and cultural experiences as a resource for interdisciplinary, discovery learning (Chiang 1994, Ovando and Collier in press, Thomas and Collier 1997). Further, educators who use the enrichment models that were initially developed for English learners are beginning to see the power of these models for *all* students.

A History of Bilingual Enrichment

These innovative enrichment models are called by varying names—*dual language*, *bilingual immersion*, *two-way bilingual*, and *developmental bilingual education*. We recommend these models as forms of mainstream education through two languages that will benefit all students. Let's examine the history of their development and some basic characteristics of these models.

Initially, the first two 20th-century experiments with bilingual education in the United States and Canada in the early 1960s came about as a result of parental pressure. Both of these experiments were enrichment models. In Canada, English-speaking parents who wanted their children to develop deep proficiency in both French and English initiated what became known as immer-

sion education. Immersion is a commitment to bilingual schooling throughout grades K–12 in which students are instructed 90 percent of the school day during kindergarten and grade 1 in the *minority* language chosen for the program, and 10 percent of the day in the majority language (English). The hands-on nature of academic work in the early grades is a natural vehicle for proficiency development of the minority language.

Immersion programs emphasize the less dominant language more than English in the first years, because the minority language is less supported by the broader society, and academic uses of the language are less easily acquired outside school. Gradually, with each subsequent grade, the program provides more instruction in the majority language until children learn the curriculum equally through both languages by grade 4 or 5. By grade 6, students have generally developed deep academic proficiency in both languages, and they can work on math, science, social studies, and language arts at or above grade level in *either* language. From the 1960s to the 1990s, immersion bilingual schooling has grown immensely popular in Canada and has achieved high rates of success with majority and minority students, students

of middle- and low-income families, as well as students with learning disabilities (Cummins and Swain 1986, Genesee 1987).

About the same time that the first immersion program started in Canada, Cubans arriving in Miami, Florida, initiated the first U.S. experiment with two-way bilingual education in 1963. The term *two-way* refers to two language groups acquiring the curriculum through each other's languages; *one-way* bilingual education refers to one language group receiving schooling through two languages (Stern 1963). Intent on overthrowing Fidel Castro and returning to their country, the Cuban arrivals established private bilingual schools to develop their children's English and maintain their Spanish. The public schools, losing significant enrollment, chose to develop bilingual classes to attract students back. As English-speaking parents enrolled their children in the classes, two-way, integrated bilingual schooling emerged as a new program model in the United States.

These classes provided a half day of the grade-level curriculum in Spanish and a half day in English, now known as the *50-50* model of two-way.

Over time, these two experiments have expanded to many states in the United States as school communities recognize the benefits for all students. The immersion model, originally developed in Canada for majority language speakers, has become known as the *90-10* two-way model in the United States because during the first two years both language groups receive 90 percent of the instruction through the *minority* language.

Students as Peer Language Models

Key to the success of all two-way programs is the fact that both language groups stay together throughout the school day, serving as peer tutors for each other. Peer models stimulate natural language acquisition for both groups because they keep the level of interaction cognitively complex (Panfil 1995). Research has consistently demonstrated that academic achievement is very high for all groups of participants compared to control groups who receive schooling only through English. This holds true for students of low socioeconomic status, as well as African-American students and language-minority students, with those in the 90-10 model achieving even higher than those in the 50-50 model (Lindholm 1990, Lindholm and Aclan 1991, Thomas and Collier 1997).

The Role of Careful Planning

What are other essential characteristics of this school reform? An important principle is clear curricular separation of the two languages of instruction. To maintain a continuous cognitive challenge, teachers do not repeat or translate lessons in the second language, but reinforce concepts taught in one language across the two languages in a

spiraling curriculum. Teachers alternate the language of instruction by theme or subject area, by time of day, by day of the week, or by the week. If two teachers are teaming, each teacher represents one language. When two teachers share and exchange two classes, this is a cost-effective, mainstream model that adds no additional teachers to a school system's budget. In contrast, ESL pullout is the most costly of all program models for English learners because extra ESL resource teachers must be added to the main-

Dual language programs promote collaboration among students of different linguistic backgrounds. Students work together on school events, such as book fairs.

stream staff (Crawford 1997).

Successful two-way bilingual education includes

■ a minimum of six years of bilingual instruction;

■ focus on the core academic curriculum rather than on a watered-down version;

■ quality language arts instruction in both languages;

■ separation of the two languages for instruction;

■ use of the non-English language for at least 50 percent of the instructional time and as much as 90 percent in the early grades;

■ an additive bilingual environment that has full support of school administrators;

■ a balanced ratio of students who speak each language (for example, 50:50 or 60:40, preferably not to go below 70:30);

■ promotion of positive interdependence among peers and between teachers and students;

■ high-quality instructional personnel; and

■ active parent-school partnerships (Lindholm 1990).

Demographics influence the feasibility of two-way programs, because the students in each language group serve as peer teachers for each other. A natural choice for many U.S. schools is a Spanish-English two-way program, because Spanish speakers are most often the largest language group. In the 204 two-way bilingual schools identified in the United States in a 1997 survey, other languages of instruction in addition to Spanish include, in order of frequency, Korean, French, Cantonese, Navajo, Japanese, Arabic, Portuguese, Russian, and Mandarin Chinese (Montone et al. 1997).

Closing the Equity Gap Through Bilingual Enrichment

What makes these programs work? To answer this question, let's look at the students who are initially the lowest achievers on tests in English. Most school policymakers commonly assume that students need only a couple of years to learn a second language. But while these students make dramatic progress in English development in the first two years, English language learners are competing with a moving target, the native English speaker, when tested in English.

The average native English speaker typically gains 10 months of academic growth in one 10-month school year in English development because first language acquisition is a natural work in progress throughout the school years, not completed until young adulthood.

Although some score higher and some lower, on average they also make a year's progress in a year's time in mathematics, science, and social studies. Thus students not yet proficient in English initially score three or more years below grade level on the tests in English because they cannot yet demonstrate in their second language all that they actually know. These students must outgain the native speaker by making one and one-half years progress on the academic tests in their second language for each of six successive school years (a total of nine years progress in six years) to reach the typical performance level of the constantly advancing native English speaker.

When students do academic work in their primary language for more than two to three years (the typical support time in a transitional bilingual program), they are able to demonstrate with each succeeding year that they are making more gains than the native English speaker—and closing the gap in achievement as measured by tests in English across the curriculum. After five to six years of enrichment bilingual schooling, former English learners (now proficient in English) are able to demonstrate their deep knowledge on the academic tests in English across the curriculum, as well as in their native language, achieving on or above grade level (Thomas and Collier 1997).

Bridging the Gap to a Better Tomorrow

Why is such progress for English learners important for our schools? Language-minority students are predicted to account for about 40 percent of the school-age population by the 2030s (Berliner and Biddle 1995). It is in our pragmatic self-interest to ensure their success as young adults, for they will be key to a robust economy to pay retirement and medical benefits for today's working adults. We must close the equity gap by providing enrichment schooling for all. For native English speakers as well as language-minority students, the enrichment bilingual classes appear to provide a constant stimulus and intellectual challenge

similar to that of a gifted and talented class. The research evidence is overwhelmingly clear that *proficient* bilinguals outperform monolinguals on school tests (Collier 1995). Crossing cultural, social class, and language boundaries, students in a bilingual class develop multiple ways of solving human

---

U.S. schools now have clear achievement data that point to the most powerful models of effective schooling for English learners. What is astounding is that these same programs are also dynamic models for school reform for all students.

---

problems and approach ecological and social science issues from a cross-national perspective. These learners acquire deep academic proficiency in two languages, which becomes a valuable resource in adult professional life. And they learn to value each other's knowledge and life experiences—leading to meaningful respect and collaboration that lasts a lifetime.

References
Berliner, D.C., and B.J. Biddle. (1995). *The Manufactured Crisis: Myths, Fraud, and the Attack on America's Public Schools*. Reading, Mass.: Addison-Wesley.
Chiang, R.A. (1994). "Recognizing Strengths and Needs of All Bilingual Learners: A Bilingual/Multicultural Perspective." *NABE News* 17, 4: 11, 22–23.
Collier, V.P. (1995). *Promoting Academic Success for ESL Students: Understanding Second Language Acquisition for School*. Elizabeth: New Jersey Teachers of English to Speakers of Other Languages-Bilingual Educators.
Crawford, J. (1997). *Best Evidence: Research Foundations of the Bilingual Education Act*. Washington, D.C.: National Clearinghouse for Bilingual Education.
Cummins, J., and M. Swain. (1986). *Bilingualism in Education*. New York: Longman.
Genesee, F. (1987). *Learning Through Two Languages: Studies of Immersion and Bilingual Education*. Cambridge, Mass.: Newbury House.
Lindholm, K.J. (1990). "Bilingual Immersion Education: Criteria for Program Development." In *Bilingual Education: Issues and Strategies*, edited by A.M. Padilla, H.H. Fairchild, and C.M. Valadez. Newbury Park, Calif.: Sage.
Lindholm, K.J., and Z. Aclan. (1991). "Bilingual Proficiency as a Bridge to Academic Achievement: Results from Bilingual/Immersion Programs." *Journal of Education* 173: 99–113.
Montone, C., Christian, D., and A. Whitcher. (1997). *Directory of Two-way Bilingual Programs in the United States*. Rev. ed. Washington, D.C.: Center for Applied Linguistics.
Ovando, C.J., and V.P. Collier. (in press). *Bilingual and ESL Classrooms: Teaching in Multicultural Contexts*. 2nd ed. New York: McGraw-Hill (available in Nov. 1997).
Panfil, K. (1995). "Learning from One Another: A Collaborative Study of a Two-way Bilingual Program by Insiders with Multiple Perspectives." *Dissertation Abstracts International* 56-10A, 3859. (University Microfilms No. AAI96-06004).
Stern, H.H., ed. (1963). *Foreign Languages in Primary Education: The Teaching of Foreign or Second Languages to Younger Children*. Hamburg, Germany: International Studies in Education, UNESCO Institute for Education.
Thomas, W.P., and V.P. Collier. (1997). *School Effectiveness for Language Minority Students*. Washington, D.C.: National Clearinghouse for Bilingual Education.

Wayne P. Thomas is Professor of Research and Evaluation Methods, and **Virginia P. Collier** is Professor of Bilingual/Multicultural/ESL Education, Graduate School of Education, George Mason University, MS#4B3, Fairfax, VA 22030-4444 (e-mail: wthomas@gmu.edu; vcollier@gmu.edu). The authors are researchers with the Center for Research on Education, Diversity, and Excellence (CREDE), funded by the Office of Educational Research and Improvement, U.S. Department of Education.

School Reform and Student Diversity

BY CATHERINE MINICUCCI, PAUL
BERMAN, BARRY McLAUGHLIN,
BEVERLY McLEOD, BERYL
NELSON, AND KATE
WOODWORTH

*The authors studied eight
exemplary schools for
language-minority students
in grades 4 through 8.
These cases demonstrate
that, while language-
minority students are
becoming literate in
English, they can learn
the same curriculum in
language arts, science,
and math as native
English speakers.*

ABOUT ONE IN seven of the nation's 5- to 17-year-olds speaks a home language other than English, and the number of such young people is growing.[1] Dur-

CATHERINE MINICUCCI is head of Minicucci Associates, Sacramento, and a research
affiliate with the National Center for Research
on Cultural Diversity and Second Language
Learning, University of California, Santa Cruz.
PAUL BERMAN is president of BW Associates,
Berkeley, Calif. BARRY McLAUGHLIN is director of the National Center for Research on
Cultural Diversity and Second Language Learning, where BEVERLY McLEOD is a research
affiliate. BERYL NELSON is senior researcher
at BW Associates, where KATE WOODWORTH
is a researcher.

ing the 1980s the number of students considered to be limited English proficient (LEP) grew 2½ times faster than the general school enrollment.[2] LEP students are concentrated in large urban areas in a few states — California, New York, Texas, Florida, Illinois, and New Jersey — and in the rural areas of the Southwest.[3]

Nearly all language-minority students are also poor, and many are members of racial or ethnic minority groups as well. Most LEP children live in communities beset by poverty and violence and offering limited economic opportunity. LEP children attending public schools frequently do not have access to adequate nutrition, housing, or health and dental care. The disconnections between the school and the community, coupled with the lack of economic opportunity, create an atmosphere of alienation between the home and the school. For their part, schools cannot predict the numbers, literacy levels, or previous school experience of incoming immigrant students.

It should not be surprising, then, that children who come from cultural- and linguistic-minority backgrounds often founder in American schools. By the time they enter high school, many still lack a solid grounding in reading, writing, mathematics, and science. Moreover, most secondary schools do not offer an academic program in science, math, or social studies that is geared toward LEP students.[4] While dropout rates are not tallied for LEP students per se, it is clear that LEP students in some ethnic groups are dropping out of school

at a high rate. The dropout rate for Hispanic immigrants is estimated to be 43%.[5] As young adults, many LEP students are inadequately prepared for higher education or high wage/high skill employment.

Recent reports have called for making the needs of LEP students more central to the national school reform effort. At a time when America seeks to reform its schools so that all students meet high standards, the challenge of educating language-minority students assumes even greater importance. But many schools undergoing restructuring fail to include LEP students in their attempts to revitalize their curriculum and instruction.[6]

There are schools that have made significant breakthroughs in educating LEP students, however.[7] In our study of student diversity, we examined eight such exemplary school reform efforts for language-minority students in grades 4 through 8 in language arts, science, or mathematics.[8] We identified theory-based and practice-proven strategies that effectively teach language arts, mathematics, and science to students from linguistically and culturally diverse backgrounds.[9]

Solutions Found
In Exemplary Schools

The case studies of eight exemplary schools demonstrate that, while they are becoming literate in English, LEP students can learn the same curriculum in language arts, science, and math as native English speakers. The success of these schools challenges the assumption that students must learn English first, before they learn grade-level science or math. The elements that come together in these schools are 1) a schoolwide vision of excellence that incorporates LEP students and embraces the students' language and culture, 2) the creation of a community of learners engaged in active discovery, and 3) well-designed and carefully executed programs to develop LEP students' skills in English and in their native languages.

While the vision of each exemplary school we studied was unique, they all held high expectations for the learning and personal development of LEP students. The exemplary sites developed a meaningful curriculum that made connections across disciplines, built real-life applications into the curriculum, related the curriculum to student experiences, and emphasized depth of understanding rather than breadth of knowledge. Schools relied on thematic learning that connected science, math, social science, and language arts and validated students' cultural and linguistic backgrounds. Working in teams, teachers developed, assessed, and refined thematic units over a period of years.

The exemplary schools used innovative approaches to help LEP students become independent learners who could take responsibility for their own learning. Teachers understood that they were not the sole sources of information and wisdom, and they acted as facilitators for student learning. The students were the center of classroom activity; they collaborated with their peers and teachers in the processes of inquiry and active discovery. Students understood what was expected of them and viewed each other as resources for learning.

Cooperative learning was used extensively in all eight of the exemplary schools. Cooperative learning strategies are particularly effective with LEP students because they provide opportunities for students to produce language in a setting that is less threatening than speaking before the entire class. Cooperative learning groups promote the development of language related to a subject area, which serves the dual purpose of developing language skills and enhancing understanding of core content.

All the schools were "parent friendly" and welcomed parents in innovative ways. The schools were also "family friendly," and some took unusual steps to bring health care, dental care, counseling, and social services onto their campuses to serve the families

The exemplary schools made special academic support available to LEP students when they were mainstreamed into all-English classes.

of students. The schools embraced the cultural and linguistic backgrounds of students by employing bilingual staff members, by communicating with parents in their native language when necessary, by honoring the multicultural quality of the student population, and by ensuring a safe school environment. The value placed on students' culture pervaded the classroom curriculum, whether taught in the student's native language or in sheltered English.

In order to build consensus through broad-based decision making, the exemplary schools developed new governance structures involving teachers, parents, and community members. The teachers in the exemplary schools were treated as professionals, encouraged to learn from one another, and given the time to develop programs. The schools used the findings of educational research to hone their approaches, and they sought assistance from external partners in curriculum development and professional development. In schools with exemplary science programs, external partners played a very important role in adapting innovative science curriculum materials for LEP students.

The exemplary schools created smaller school organizations, such as "families" or "houses," that strengthened the connections among students and teachers alike. Smaller school units set the stage for cross-disciplinary instruction and enhanced teachers' sense of commitment by allowing them to focus on a smaller group of students. One exemplary school kept students to-

gether with the same teacher for five years. This continuity offers distinct advantages to students who are learning English. Gaps in student learning between grades taught by different teachers were avoided. Parent involvement was enhanced. LEP students in such long-term "continuum" classes became skilled at cooperative learning, were highly responsible for their own learning tasks, and built a remarkable level of academic self-confidence.

The exemplary schools used time in inventive ways. For the most part, teachers controlled their own daily schedules, and they zealously protected students' time to learn. Several exemplary schools extended the school day and year. This added student learning time and freed time for teacher collaboration and professional development. LEP students making the transition to English instruction need additional time to learn, and the schools meet that need through Saturday programs, summer programs, and after-school tutorials.

Exemplary schools paid special attention to the main goal, which is helping students achieve English literacy. The schools used qualified faculty members fluent in the native language of students and trained in second-language learning. Teachers had the flexibility to tailor transitional paths to meet each child's needs. The schools had more than one program path for students to move to English literacy. In these schools native language literacy was universally regarded as a critical foundation for successful attainment of English literacy. The exemplary schools made special academic support (through homework clubs or after-school tutorials) available to LEP students when they were mainstreamed into all-English classes.[10]

The stories of two of these schools will illustrate the dynamic quality of the interplay of school reform, high-quality language development programs, and challenging curriculum for LEP students.

Inter-American School

Inter-American School is a public school enrolling 650 Chicago students from pre-kindergarten to eighth grade. It was founded in 1975 by a small group of parents and teachers as a bilingual preschool under the auspices of the Chicago Public Schools. The parents and teachers envisioned a multicultural school in which children would be respected as individuals and their languages and cultures would be respected as well.

Today, the school is a citywide magnet school whose students are 70% Hispanic, 13% African American, and 17% white. The developmental bilingual program at the school has the goal of bilingualism and biliteracy for all students including native speakers of English. At all grade levels, English-dominant and Spanish-dominant students are assigned to classrooms in roughly equal proportions. In prekindergarten, all core subjects are taught in Spanish to all students. Spanish-dominant students take English as a second language, and English-dominant students take Spanish as a second language. An 80/20 ratio of Spanish to English instruction remains through third grade; then English instruction is gradually increased to 50/50 by eighth grade. Students enrolled in fifth and sixth grades at Inter-American School are fully bilingual and biliterate in Spanish and English.

Much of the school's curriculum is integrated across the disciplines and built around themes that reflect the history, culture, and traditions of students. The school emphasizes the study of the Americas and Africa, especially how African history and culture have influenced the Americas. Teachers at each grade level work together to develop their curriculum around themes. For example, fourth-grade teachers use a thematic unit on Mayan civilization to integrate content across the curriculum. In social studies, students study the geographic spread of Mayan civilization, Mayan religion, and Mayan cultural traditions. In science, students study Mayan architecture and agriculture. In language arts, they read and write stories about the Mayans. A volunteer parent taught an art lesson in which students painted Mayan gods. The unit began with a visit to the Field Museum to see an exhibit on Mayan culture, architecture, and religion.

Throughout the year teachers work together intensively in groups that span two grade levels. The teachers at prekindergarten and kindergarten, grades 1 and 2, and so on, plan together, exchange students across grade levels and classrooms, and work together on thematic units.

Like other Chicago schools, Inter-American School has a local school council that sets school policies, hires and evaluates the principal, interviews prospective teachers, and controls the school budget. The professional personnel advisory committee, made up entirely of faculty members, sets priorities and takes responsibility for the instructional program.

Hanshaw Middle School

Hanshaw Middle School serves 860 sixth- through eighth-graders from a predominantly low-income Latino community in Modesto, California. It opened in the fall of 1991. The Hanshaw student body is roughly 56% Hispanic, 26% white, 11% Asian, and 5% African American. After interviewing 500 families in their homes, the principal and faculty agreed on four principles for the foundation of Hanshaw's program: high expectations for all students, support for the Latino and Chicano experience, a meaning-centered curriculum, and a conscious effort to impart life skills as part of the curriculum. The principal recruited teachers from industry — for example, a former museum director teaches science, and a former wildlife biologist teaches science. Life skills such as patience, flexibility, integrity, initiative, and effort are taught at the start of each school year. Students are rewarded throughout the year for demonstrating life skills.

Hanshaw is organized into five houses, each named for a campus of the California State University system. Each house is made up of from six to nine teachers, led by a team leader. Teams of two teachers (one for the math/science core and one for the language arts/social studies core) teach groups of 30 to 35 students. All students take two 90-minute core classes, one for math/science and one for language arts/social studies. Each year students visit the college campus their house is named after, meet college students from various ethnic backgrounds, hear lectures, and receive a T-shirt and a "diploma." Students identify strongly with the college campus, which provides them with an alternative to gang affiliation. Teachers within each house make decisions about the school's budget.

The curriculum design decisions that Hanshaw teachers make are based on a simple principle: every lesson or skill must be relevant to the students' lives. Teachers strive to help students know the "why" of an answer or of multiple answers or to help them understand multiple ways of getting to an answer. Teachers build on students' own experiences in thematic instruction. Themes unify instruction across science, math, language arts, and social studies, incorporating topics from the California curriculum frameworks.

Hanshaw offers several programs for LEP students: instruction in Spanish in core curricular areas, sheltered instruction for advanced Spanish-speaking LEP students and students who speak other primary languages, and mainstream English instruction for clusters of LEP students who speak the same first language. When LEP students are considered ready to move to full English instruction, they are clustered together in mainstream classes. Many of the teachers of mainstream classes have special training and credentials in second-language acquisition.

Hanshaw teachers use a constructivist approach to teaching math. A mainstream eighth-grade algebra class we observed included 15 LEP students. The math teacher is a former carpenter who had training in second-language acquisition. The spatial math lesson she was conducting challenged students to modify the profile of a building and to graph that profile. Students working in cooperative groups used Lego blocks to re-create the profile in three dimensions. The teacher's role was to set up the challenge and to facilitate the work of cooperative student groups in solving the problem. When students finished the assignment, she asked them to solve it another way. LEP students speaking the same language worked together in both English and their native language in their cooperative groups.

Hanshaw's program is supported by a vigorous relationship with an external partner, Susan Kovalik and Associates from the state of Washington; that partner works with Hanshaw faculty members in intensive summer and weekend retreats. A Kovalik coach assists the school on a monthly basis, designing curriculum, providing instructional coaching, and helping the faculty identify problems and solutions. The school uses both state and federal funds to purchase assistance from Kovalik. Hanshaw also has a comprehensive health and social services center on campus that is staffed by social workers and counselors who are bilingual in Spanish and English.

These two schools provide concrete examples of the broader solutions listed above. Both schools have a schoolwide vision that incorporates high standards for LEP students. Both schools take a number of concrete steps to validate and honor the languages and cultures of their students. Both schools teach challenging academic content to LEP students in their native languages. Both schools use the thematic approach to deliver a meaning-centered curriculum that relates to students' life experiences. And teachers at both schools take responsibility for making decisions about the uses of resources and time.

Exemplary schools, such as Inter-American and Hanshaw, illustrate the way such concepts of school reform as smaller school organizations, protected time for learning, thematic instruction, and teacher collaboration can be harnessed to meet the needs of LEP students. They demonstrate that high-quality LEP programs, which include the development of native language literacy, are certainly compatible with learning science and math through active discovery. The dynamic interplay of greater school autonomy, protected time to learn for smaller groups of students with a small group of teachers, intensive professional development, and development of LEP students' literacy in English and in their native languages holds the promise for success in educating growing numbers of LEP students.

1. General Accounting Office, "Limited English Proficiency: A Growing and Costly Educational Challenge Facing Many School Districts," Report to the Chairman, Committee on Labor and Human Resources, U.S. Senate, Washington, D.C., January 1994; and Diane August and Kenji Hakuta, *Federal Education Programs for Limited-English-Proficient Students: A Blueprint for the Second Generation* (Stanford, Calif.: Stanford Working Group, 1993).

2. Cynthia A. Chavez, "'State of the Play' in Educational Research on Latino/Hispanic Youth," unpublished manuscript, Rockefeller Foundation, New York, N.Y., May 1991. The phrase "limited English proficient" is used to refer to students whose home language is other than English and who have been determined, using tests of oral English fluency, to require special instruction in order to acquire sufficient English skills to participate in all English instruction.

3. *Numbers and Needs: Ethnic and Linguistic Minorities in the United States*, newsletter published by Dorothy Waggoner, Washington, D.C., May 1992; and Lorraine M. McDonnell and Paul T. Hill, *Newcomers in American Schools: Meeting the Education Needs of Immigrant Youth* (Santa Monica, Calif.: RAND Corporation, 1993).

4. Catherine Minicucci and Laurie Olsen, *Programs for Secondary Limited English Proficient Students: A California Study, Focus #5* (Washington, D.C.: National Clearinghouse for Bilingual Education, 1992).

5. *School Success for Limited English Proficient Students: The Challenge and State Response* (Washington, D.C.: Resource Center on Educational Equity, Council of Chief State School Officers, 1990).

6. Laurie Olsen et al., *The Unfinished Journey: Restructuring Schools in a Diverse Society* (San Francisco: California Tomorrow, 1994).

7. See Paul Berman et al., *Meeting the Challenge of Language Diversity*, 5 vols. (Berkeley, Calif.: BW Associates, February 1992).

8. The eight exemplary schools selected after an extensive nationwide search are: Del Norte Heights Elementary School, Ysleta Independent School District (El Paso); Hollibrook Elementary School, Spring Branch Independent School District (Houston); Linda Vista Elementary School, San Diego Unified School District; Inter-American School, Chicago Public Schools; Graham and Parks Alternative School, Cambridge (Mass.) School District; Evelyn Hanshaw Middle School, Modesto (Calif.) City Schools; Horace Mann Middle School, San Francisco Unified School District; and Charles Wiggs Middle School, El Paso Independent School District.

9. *School Reform and Student Diversity,* 3 vols. (Santa Cruz: National Center for Research on Cultural Diversity and Second Language Learning, University of California, in collaboration with BW Associates, September 1995).

10. We conducted focus groups with LEP students who had made the transition to all-English instruction. The students told us that they relied on their bilingual teachers, their older siblings, and their English-speaking peers in learning English and that they benefited from the after-school tutorial opportunities, summer programs, and extracurricular opportunities.

A Gradual Exit, Variable Threshold Model for Limited English Proficient Children

Dr. Stephen Krashen

Dr. Stephen Krashen is a professor in the School of Education at the University of Southern California.

The components of a properly organized program for limited English proficient students are consistent with the concept of comprehensible input, the hypothesis that we acquire language when we understand it. The "reading hypothesis" is a version of the input hypothesis that states that meaningful reading is the source of much of our competence in literacy.

The first language can be used in ways that help English language development, ways that are consistent with the concept of comprehensible input. First, the primary language can be used to supply background knowledge, which can help enormously in making English input more comprehensible. A limited English proficient (LEP) child who has learned math well through the primary language will have a better chance of understanding a math class taught in English than a LEP child who doesn't know math well,

and the former will make better progress in both math and English, because the input she hears in class will be more comprehensible.

A second means of using the first language to aid English development is by developing literacy through the first language. It is extremely efficient to develop literacy first in the child's first language; the transfer to English is rapid, even when the alphabets used are very different. To see this, consider this three step argument:

(1) We learn to read by reading. There is good evidence that we learn to read by understanding the message on the page (Goodman, 1982; Smith, 1995). As noted earlier, this view is similar to the idea of comprehensible input.

(2) If we learn to read by reading, by making sense of what is on the page, it is easier to learn to read a language we already understand.

(3) Once we can read, we can read. The ability to read transfers across languages, even if the writing systems are different. Learning to read any language helps one learn to read any other. There is another

sense in which literacy transfers across languages: The ability to use language to solve problems. This includes discovering new ideas as the writer moves from draft to draft, the ability to read selectively for information relevant to a problem one is trying to solve, the ability to use a library, etc. Clearly, once someone has developed this kind of competence in one language, it transfers to any other language: Once we are educated, we are educated.

Characteristics of Successful Programs

If the principles presented above are correct, they suggest that successful programs for limited English proficient students will have the following characteristics:

1. Comprehensible input in English, provided directly in the form of ESL and sheltered subject matter classes.[1]

2. Subject matter teaching done in the first language, without translation. This indirect help provides

Table 1. The Gradual Exit Plan

	MAINSTREAM	ESL/SHELTERED	FIRST LANGUAGE STAGE
BEGINNING	art, music, PE	ESL	all core subjects
INTERMEDIATE	art, music, PE	ESL, math, science	language arts, social studies
ADVANCED	art, music, PE math, science	ESL, social studies language arts	continuing L1 development
MAINSTREAM	all subjects		continuing L1 development

background information that helps make the English that children read and hear more comprehensible. Methods that use the first language for concurrent translation (the teacher speaking in one language, and then translating what was said into the second language) are not effective in helping children acquire English (Legaretta, 1979, Wong-Fillmore, 1985); when a translation is available, the children do not attend to the input in the second language and teachers do not have to try to make this input comprehensible.

3. Literacy development in the first language, which transfers to the second language.

Children who participate in programs that have these three characteristics do very well, at least as well as children in all-day English programs, and usually better (Krashen and Biber, 1988). A fourth very desirable component is the continuation of the development of the primary language. There are good practical reasons (e.g. international business), and cognitive reasons (bilinguals do better on certain linguistic tasks as well as measures of "divergent thinking") to do this. In addition, a high level of competence in the first language contributes to a healthy sense of biculturalism, an avoidance of the state of "bicultural ambivalence," shame of the first culture and rejection of the second culture (Cummins, 1981).

The Ideal Case

Here is one way to set up a program that meets these characteristics. Sometimes called the "Eastman plan," it is in wide use in California (Table 1). We will first deal with an ideal case, where there is a fairly large concentration of children who speak the same first language, and there are faculty trained to work with them.

The plan has three components and four stages. The stages, however, are very flexible. In the beginning stage, all children—limited English proficient and native speakers of English—are mixed for art, music and physical education. This makes sense for two reasons: It avoids segregation, and much of the English the minority-language children will hear will be comprehensible, thanks to the pictures in art and movement in PE. Also at this stage, children are in high quality comprehensible input-based ESL classes, and are taught all other subjects in the primary language.

The intermediate stage child is defined as the child who understands enough English to begin to learn some content through English. We begin with sheltered subject matter instruction in those subjects that, at this level, do not demand a great deal of abstract use of language,

such as math and science. Subjects such as social studies and language arts remain in the first language, as it is more difficult to make these subjects comprehensible to second language acquirers at this level.[2]

At the advanced level, limited English proficient students join the mainstream, but not all at once: they begin with one or two subjects at a time, usually math and science. When this occurs, social studies and language arts can be taught as sheltered subject matter classes.

In the mainstream stage, students do all subjects in the mainstream, and continue first language development in classes teaching language arts and social studies in the first language. These continuing first language classes are not all-day programs. Rather, they can take the place of (or supplement) foreign language study.

Examine the possible progress of a limited English proficient student: She first studies math in the primary language, then moves to sheltered math, and then finally to the mainstream. At every stage, instruction is comprehensible, and the sheltered class acts as a bridge between the first language class and the mainstream. When she enters the mainstream, this child will know a great deal of math and will be familiar with the special kind of English used in math class.

Gradual Exit

Bilingual educators have been sensitized to the problem of early exit, exiting children from primary language instruction before they are ready (Cummins, 1980). On the other hand, we also have a late exit problem, because we do not always have the resources to provide as much instruction in the first language as we would like to. Our task, therefore, is to make sure we provide primary language instruction where it is most needed.

Of course, some people think there is a different late exit problem:

They think that we keep children in primary language instruction too long, after they speak English well enough to be in the mainstream. As Cummins (1980) has pointed out, this is rarely the case. More typically, children have conversational fluency in English but lack academic language ability (literacy and background knowledge), which is efficiently developed in the primary language.

The plan presented here is a gradual exit program: Children are exited into the mainstream gradually, subject by subject, as they are ready to understand the input. The more easily contextualized subjects are the first to be done as sheltered subject matter and are the first to be done in the mainstream.

Note that children never need to exit the bilingual program: They have the option of continuing first language development.

Variable Threshold

Cummins (1981) has hypothesized the existence of two thresholds in first language development. The lower threshold is the minimum amount of first language academic proficiency necessary to make a positive impact on second language academic proficiency. The higher threshold is the amount of first language competence necessary to reap the cognitive benefits of bilingualism.

The task of the bilingual educator is to ensure attainment of the lower threshold, and, whenever possible, help students attain the higher threshold. This plan accomplishes both of these goals.

The plan employs a "variable threshold" approach for the attainment of the lower threshold: As children reach the threshold for a particular subject matter, they then proceed to follow instruction in English in that subject matter, beginning with sheltered instruction. By providing continuing first language development, the plan also provides

for the attainment of the higher threshold and its advantages.

Modifications

As noted earlier, the plan presented above is for the ideal situation. In the less than ideal situation, we attempt to ensure that the principles underlying the plan are satisfied, even if the full version cannot be done.

A modified gradual exit plan can be used in situations in which the limited English proficient children speak different first languages and/or primary language instruction is not possible for other reasons (e.g. staffing, materials).

In these cases, two thirds of the plan can be carried out: the "mainstream" and "ESL/sheltered" components. This kind of program has the advantage of being comprehensible all day long, but it lacks the advantages of developing literacy in the first language and using the first language to supply subject matter knowledge. It will be better, however, than ESL "pull-out," which means exposure to incomprehensible input most of the day.

Quite often, however, even the modified plan is not possible. This occurs when there are only a few limited English proficient children in the school, and/or when coordination among teachers is not possible. In cases like this, the classroom teacher is faced with great diversity within one classroom.

Before discussing some solutions, some ways of reducing the burden, it needs to be pointed out that many teachers today are facing a degree of diversity, of heterogeneity, that has never been seen before in the history of education. It is not usual to see a single class with native and fluent English speakers, students who speak no English at all (and who have a poor background in the primary language), and students who speak a wide variety of first languages. Traditional solutions will not work: Even if paraprofessionals

are available, teachers must supervise them, and wind up making two, three or even four lesson plans every period. Bilingual teachers sometimes must translate simply to get through the period, an exhausting procedure that does not result in second language acquisition. And we wonder why teachers burn out so quickly! The real solution is to set up a plan similar to the gradual exit plan, with team-teaching. But let us consider the situation in which this is not possible. We will return to the principles underlying successful programs and see to what extent we can work toward them in this situation.

Submersion and Pull-Out ESL

Even in submersion situations, we can mimic the gradual exit plan to some extent. Of course, the art, music and PE parts of the day will be the same regardless of whether the full plan can be used or not: the children will be together for this part of the day. Comprehensible-input based ESL can be of great help, even if it is done on a pull-out basis. The time to pull out the limited English proficient students is the time of day when more proficient English-speakers are doing the subject matter that requires the most abstract use of language and that will be the least comprehensible for the new second language acquirer: language arts and social studies.

When beginners in English are submersed in classes with more proficient English-speakers, we can make life easier on them and us, and help their language acquisition by being consistent with the concept of comprehensible input, e.g. by allowing a silent period, gently encouraging but not forcing production in early stages of second language acquisition, and when the children do begin to speak, by not insisting on complete sentences and not correcting errors. If the teacher understands some of the child's first language, there is no reason not to utilize the natural approach procedure of allowing the child to respond in the first language. This will greatly facilitate communication.

Primary Language Development without Bilingual Education: Home Use of the First Language

When primary language instruction is not possible, there is still a great deal that can be done to get some of the positive effects of bilingual education. First, we can encourage the use of the first language at home. Parents often ask if they should use more English at home, thinking that this will speed up English language development in their children. Unless the parent speaks English extremely well, switching to English has the danger of disturbing parent-child communication, which cripples both cognitive and emotional development (Wong-Fillmore, 1991). This view is confirmed by the research. Several studies show that when parents switch to exclusive use of the language of the country, school performance suffers (Cummins, 1981; Dolson, 1985). We would much rather teach a child in Kindergarten who does not speak English but who is well-adjusted and ready for school than a child who has picked up some English (from an imperfect model) but who has not been communicating very well with his/her parents.

Helpers

Another way we can make use of the first language without a full bilingual program is the judicious use of paraprofessionals and other helpers. All too often, these helpers are used to drill English spelling and vocabulary. If we have a helper who speaks the child's first language, we should use that helper to provide background knowledge and literacy in the child's first language. This help will usually be most effective in those subjects requiring the most use of abstract language: social studies and language arts.

Even when only a little help is available, it can be very valuable. Consider the case of a class with three Korean-speaking children, who know little English. They are progressing fairly well in mathematics, because of their good background in their first language, and because math does not require a high level of language ability in early grades. Social studies, however, is more difficult for them. Assume that a paraprofessional who speaks Korean is available only one morning per week for one hour. My suggestion is that we inform the helper what will take place the following week in social studies. If it is the Civil War, the helper uses the one hour on Monday to provide the children with background information, in Korean, about the Civil War: Who the combattants were, what the issues were, etc. This will make the history lessons that follow during the week much more comprehensible.

Classmates who speak the limited English proficient child's first language can help and sometimes do spontaneously. We should allow this to occur: It is not a good policy to forbid the use of the first language in school: "English only" rules are not good for English. Peer help should be done the same way we do it in bilingual education programs: As a source of background information and academic knowledge in the first language, not as on-line translation.

First Language Use in Class

There is also nothing wrong with an occasional translation in class. Teachers need not waste time in frustrating pantomime and paraphrase when a concept is important, explanation of its meaning resists normal efforts and the teacher or another student can explain the concept quickly in the child's first language. The problem is when the translation is no longer occasional but becomes concurrent translation, and there is no need to listen to the second language input.

Books in the Primary Language

When some books are provided in the primary language, in the classroom and school libraries, they help validate the primary language and culture, can contribute to continued first language development, and can help literate students get subject matter knowledge. Feuerverger (1994) noted that children who made greater use of books in the first language provided by the school had "a greater feeling of security in their cultural background" (p. 143).

Staffing

There are short-term and long-term solutions to the bilingual teacher shortage, and the gradual exit plan can help with both.

First, the plan provides some immediate relief. Because it is gradual exit and does not require full development of all aspects of academic language in the primary language before transition begins, it requires fewer teachers who can teach in the primary language.

Second, the gradual exit plan is well-suited to team-teaching, with those who speak the child's first language teaching in the primary language, and with those who do no teaching in the mainstream and sheltered/ESL sections. I have occasionally witnessed a bilingual teacher teaching a class in English, and, at the same time, down the hall, a non-bilingual who has had a year of Spanish class and a few months in Mexico struggling through a lesson in Spanish. Clearly, there is an easier way. In my view, if a teacher speaks the child's first language well, he or she needs to teach in that language as much as possible, even if that teacher speaks English perfectly. Many bilingual teachers have told me that they are willing to do this; in fact, it makes it easier.

This kind of team-teaching will make life easier for English-language teachers as well. Their limited English proficient students, thanks to their good background knowledge and literacy competence, developed in the first language, will be much easier to teach.

A long-term strategy for reducing the teacher shortage is to encourage the continuing development of the primary language, as is done in the gradual exit plan. As noted earlier, there are very good reasons for doing this, including practical and cognitive reasons. An additional reason is that at least some of the students currently enrolled in bilingual programs will be interested in becoming bilingual teachers. This plan can help them develop the linguistic competence to do so. We can, in other words, grow our own.

Notes

1. In sheltered subject matter classes, intermediate second language acquirers are given comprehensible subject matter instruction in the second language. The focus of the class is on subject matter learning, not language acquisition. Students in these classes typically acquire as much language as students in traditional intermediate classes, and often acquire more, and learn subject matter at the same time (Krashen, 1991).

2. When the limited English proficient children reach the intermediate stage, we might consider additional mixing of children: English-speakers could make occasional visits to ESL classes to join in selected activities. In addition, if a school offers Spanish as a second language, Spanish-speakers could visit the SSL classes to provide some peer input.

Here is an example. Assume that the ESL class is doing an activity such as "The Desert Island" (Christison and Bassano, 1981), in which students, in small groups, discuss what supplies they would take with them if they were stranded on a desert island. Native speakers of English make their strongest contribution in such an activity simply by participating in the groups with the ESL students. The activity constrains the discourse, which helps make input more comprehensible.

Mixing has several advantages. First, it helps the children get to know each other. Second, it is very likely that the Spanish-speakers will make faster progress in English than the English-speakers will make in Spanish. This will certainly have a positive effect on the self-esteem of the Spanish-speakers and inspire some respect for them in the eyes of the English-speaking children.

References

Christison, M. and Bassano, S. 1981. *Look Who's Talking.* San Francisco: Alta.

Cummins, J. 1980. "The exit and entry fallacy in bilingual education." *NABE Journal 4:* 25–60.

Cummins, J. 1981. "The role of primary language development in promoting educational success for language minority students." In *Schooling and Language Minority Students.* Sacramento, CA: California Department of Education, pp. 3–49.

Dolson, D. 1985. "The effects of Spanish home language use on the scholastic performance of Hispanic pupils." *Journal of Multilingual and Multicultural Development 6:* 133–155.

Feuerverger, G. 1994. "A multicultural literacy intervention for minority language students." *Language and Education 8:* 123–146.

Goodman, K. 1982. *Language and Literacy.* London: Routledge and Kegan Paul.

Krashen, S. 1991. "Sheltered subject matter teaching." *Cross Currents 18:* 183–189.

Krashen, S. and Biber, D. 1988. *On Course: Bilingual Education's Success in California.* Ontario, CA: California Association for Bilingual Education.

Legaretta, D. 1979. "The effects of program models on language acquisition by Spanish-speaking children." *TESOL Quarterly 8:* 521–576.

Smith, F. 1994. *Understanding Reading. Fifth Edition.* Hillsdale, NJ: Erlbaum.

Wong-Fillmore, L. 1985. "When does teacher talk work as input?" In S. Gass and C. Madden (eds.), *Input in Second Language Acquisition.* New York: Newbury House, pp. 17–50.

Wong-Fillmore, L. 1991. "When learning a second language means losing the first." *Early Childhood Research Quarterly 6:* 323–346.

This article also appears as a chapter in Dr. Krashen's book, *Under Attack: The Case Against Bilingual Education* (Language Education Associates, Culver City, CA, 1996).

Unit Selections

31. **Cruising the Web with English Language Learners,** Laura Chris Green
32. **Confronting an Embarrassment of Riches: Internet Search Tools,** Dennis Sayers
33. **The Case for Bilingual Education,** Stephen D. Krashen
34. **What's New in Ebonics?** Jacqueline Brice-Finch, A. Duku Anokye, and Bob Reising
35. **Beyond Adversarial Discourse: Searching for Common Ground in the Education of Bilingual Students,** Jim Cummins

Key Points to Consider

❖ How can the Internet be used as a resource in teaching ESL?

❖ What are the problems in assessing minority language students for placement in gifted and talented programs?

❖ How do nonnative students who are learning English perceive regional American dialects?

❖ How are educators addressing issues related to nonstandard or vernacular English in their classrooms?

 **Links** **www.dushkin.com/online/**

34. **Hispanic Online: Latino Links**
    http://www.hisp.com/links.html

35. **National Clearinghouse for Bilingual Education (NCBE)**
    http://www.ncbe.gwu.edu

36. **TESOL Online**
    http://www.tesol.edu/index.html

These sites are annotated on pages 4 and 5.

The articles selected for this section discuss current issues about language that are of concern not only to linguists and educators but also to the general public. While many of the issues are controversial, they also help to expand our perceptions of the dynamic nature of language within a society and the important cultural influences and biases that are at the core of our belief systems. Language reflects our world view. A language that is alive and well, like English, is changing constantly to reflect our experiences as a people and as a society.

Understanding how language is valued within a society by its native speakers may seem, at the outset, superfluous, but it is an integral part of language study. Knowledge and sensitivity about the controversies and complexities surrounding language issues are crucial to resolving educational as well as political policy issues that can be divisive and destructive to any society.

As relatively new tools for teaching English, advances in technology, such as CD-ROMs and ready access to the Internet, have revolutionized ideas about how to enhance the complex process of second-language acquisition. The fascinating world of cyberspace, which offers many possibilities for teaching English as a second language, can also be a wasteland when used ineffectively. As an inexpensive resource, many linguists and educators value sharing their ongoing progress as they search the Internet to find ways to make language learning interesting and meaningful for all language learners.

The perception of language as the glue that holds a society together has long been an accepted idea. Language transmits culture and values. In a country as large and as diverse as ours, the importance of teaching and maintaining English as the language of instruction in our schools is considered tantamount to preserving the nation. A more radical view considers any departure from this path as anti-American. In recognizing this rigid perspective, we can begin to understand why so many people feel emotionally opposed to bilingual education and other programs that are believed to threaten the American way of life. It is no wonder that interest groups like English Only are gaining support.

The English Only movements has been influential in opposing funding for a variety of government programs that affect minority language groups. In favoring a "sink or swim" approach to learning English, which ignores the minority language student altogether, these movements fail to recognize that the demands of the workplace in an information society are far more academically and linguistically rigorous than those of an industrial society. People who came to this country during the height of the industrial movement did not need language or literacy skills to function successfully in the workplace. Those who refuse to pay attention to linguistic cultural and dialectal differences now are ignoring the long-term benefits of a well-qualified workforce that can positively affect our nation in the future.

Another issue that has recently emerged deals with nonstandard American English dialects. The Ebonics debate has forced educators and policymakers to focus on issues about standard English instruction for African American students. Seen as limitations, nonstandard dialects are blamed for many of the problems that lead to academic failure. Recognizing AAVE (African American Vernacular English) and its value as a rich language system that has evolved over several hundred years deserves serious consideration. However, it is also important to recognize the need to provide all students, regardless of linguistic orientation, with the linguistic skills that are essential for academic success.

The focus on providing quality instruction to students from diverse language groups is foremost on the minds of many. At risk is the survival of our public educational system. Given the demands of a growing linguistic and culturally diverse student population, what are the strategies that can best serve the linguistic interests of all students? Such questions are complex and difficult to answer, especially when there are so many considerations and so many opinions on how to resolve the problems.

As school boards and community groups struggle with these issues, teachers working with minority language students must recognize their potential as leaders in working to resolve problems of prejudice and intolerance within their classrooms. Evidence points to misinformation, ignorance, economic threat, and the loss of our national identity and belief system as reasons for negative attitudes toward minority language groups. It is our hope that discussion of the many and complex issues related to language will enhance the teacher's understanding and provide ways to work toward amicable resolution of the problems inherent in this controversial subject.

CRUISING THE WEB WITH ENGLISH LANGUAGE LEARNERS

Laura Chris Green, Ph.D.

Dr. Laura Chris Green is an education associate in the IDRA Division of Professional Development. Comments and questions may be sent to her via E-mail at idra@idra.org.

Although creative teachers have always accomplished wonders with their students using such basic tools as paper, pencil and chalk, an abundance of high quality materials can enhance any educational program. For more than 20 years I have collected catalogs, books, textbooks and software; visited publishers' exhibits; attended conferences; read reviews in professional journals; exchanged materials with other teachers; and even created materials myself in an effort to find the very best instructional materials for bilingual and ESL classrooms. Most of the teachers I know who serve English language learners also constantly search for materials that will work for their students. The Internet might help us with this worthy quest if we know how to take advantage of its offerings effectively.

The good news is that we have seen a dramatic increase in both the quality and quantity of bilingual instructional materials. Of special note has been the explosive growth of children's literature in general, and of multicultural and books in Spanish in particular. Even basal readers in both languages have gotten better.

The bad news is that appropriate materials, especially in Spanish, are still a hundred times harder to come by than in English. In recent years I have monitored the development of instructional software in Spanish. Although there have been recent improvements, there are probably a thousand software programs developed in English for every program developed in Spanish, and most of these are translations of programs originally developed in English. Finding materials in other languages is even more problematic.

My latest passion has become "cruising" the Internet, especially the World Wide Web (web), looking for instructional resources that can be used by bilingual and ESL teachers. Every time I take such a journey, I find exciting new caches of information that did not even exist a month ago. And I dream about how I would use these rich resources if I were still a classroom teacher with access to the Internet. Come dream with me as I describe some hypothetical, but possible, scenarios.

Vignette One

The setting is a second grade self-contained bilingual classroom in South Texas. There are 20 Spanish dominant students, half at beginner level, half at intermediate level for English proficiency.

The technology is one computer, connected to a television monitor so all can see what is on-line.

We are working on a thematic unit called *Monstruos, dragones, y otras criaturas espantosas* ("Monsters, Dragons and Other Scary Creatures"). In addition to sharing books such as *Harry y el terrible Quiensabequé* (by Dick Grackenback), *Monster Mama* (by Liz Rosenburg) and *Scary Poems for Rotten Kids* (by Sean O'Huigin), we read aloud stories we have found on the web at such sites as "Monsters by Kirsten" (www.ankiewicz.com), and "Spooky Spots" (alexia.lis.uiuc.edu/~watts/spooky.html). I print these stories out so students can have their individual copies that they take home to read and reread with their families.

We also investigate sites that specialize in movie monsters like the "Destroyer Minipage," (www.ama.caltech.edu/users/mrm/godzilla/gallery/html/destroyer.html), "Welcome Monster Lovers!" (www.in.net/fmof/menu.html) and "Famous Monsters of Filmland" (www.in.net.fmof/menu.html). Each student chooses one movie monster about which to create a story. I provide a printout copy of the picture of the chosen monster to each child who then cuts it out and pastes it into a scene created with markers, crayons and/or tempera paint. We share our pictures, and, af-

 From *IDRA Newsletter*, May 1997, pp. 1, 10-13. © 1997 by the Intercultural Development Research Association. Reprinted by permission.

ter brainstorming adjectives that describe our monster scenes, we write our stories in Spanish. We also create a monster encyclopedia, listing alphabetically all our monsters and including a short description of each in English.

Vignette Two

The setting is a sixth grade English class at a rural middle school in West Texas. The students are three recent immigrants from Mexico (beginner level), 14 Spanish-speaking Mexican American students who are at intermediate and advanced levels of English proficiency, and seven English-speaking Anglo students. The technology includes three classroom computers with Internet access and biweekly access to a writing computer lab.

I have agreed to help the American history teacher on my academic team with the reading and writing components of a cross-disciplinary unit on World War II. We perform all of our work in teams of three people. When working with a computer, students take turns playing three roles: *keyboarder*, the person who handles the keyboard and the mouse; *recorder*, the person who keeps notes for the group longhand; and *navigator*, the person who decides which site to visit next or which task to perform.

We start the unit with a World Wide Web scavenger hunt in which teams of three students take turns finding the answers to factual questions such as "When did the United States enter World War II?" and "Which European and Asian nations were our allies?" Teams that are not on-line are engaged in reading a selected chapter from a book such as *The Diary of Anne Frank* or *Number the Stars* (by Lois Lowry). Our school follows a block schedule in which we meet for 90 minutes every other day. Daily the students read a chapter silently and write a literary letter for 30 minutes, engage in a group discussion of the chapter read, and cruise the Internet for their scavenger hunt answers (and later web assignments) for 30 minutes. Each team's Internet sessions are timed so that all teams have the same amount of time, keeping it equitable and competitive.

The sites that the students need to search are listed, along with the scavenger hunt questions, on an electronic mail (E-mail) message sent by me to the class. Using our *Netscape* mail program, students click

on the site addresses to be taken there immediately. The teams also use the mail program's "reply" function to record their answers to the questions. In addition to seeking the answers to specific questions, each team is on the lookout for a topic it wishes to research further, and then team members collect information about that topic.

After the scavenger hunt concludes, each team creates a short "what we know" report about their selected topic. They also come up with five questions they would like to have answered about their topic. These reports are written in the computer lab. I respond to the reports with a new list of sites that the teams investigate for their answers. The list includes the large World War II newsgroup (soc.history.war.world-war-ii) so that students can request direct, personal assistance from WWII veterans and history buffs of various kinds, and relevant museums such as the Holocaust Museum (www.ushmm.org) and the Smithsonian (www.si.edu), both rich resources for photographs and primary source documents.

The final reports are submitted to the students' history teacher for grading for content and to me for grading for form. For extra credit, individuals can select a political cartoon from the era (www.commonwealth.net) that they must explain, in writing, its historical significance.

Vignette Three

The setting is an inner-city high school newcomers class in North Texas. The students are eight students from Mexico, four from Central America, one from Thailand, two from Bosnia and one from Pakistan. All are at beginner levels of English proficiency and lack literacy skills in their primary languages. The technology is a teacher workstation with an LCD panel and Internet access along with three other computers with word processing and desktop publishing software.

We are comparing the customs and traditions of our countries of origin to those of our new country, the United States. Using the teacher workstation and LCD panel, I show the class web sites where they can view the maps of countries, artwork, recipe collections, song lyrics, folktales and proverbs (*dichos*). Each lesson centers on one of the types of sites we explore, focusing on identifying the drawings and photographs we find. I also read aloud portions of the texts we find, often simplifying the language

as I go and sometimes translating for the Spanish speakers. We follow up each whole group exploration session with individual writing assignments.

We begin by first visiting the "Guide to U.S. States" (galaxy.einet.galaxy/Community/US-States) and locate our state and city on the map as well as ports of entry or other U.S. places our students have been. Next we explore "The Virtual Tourist World Map" (wings.buffalo.ed), visiting the sites for Mexico, El Salvador, Guatemala, Thailand, Bosnia and Iran. I ask, "What country is this?", "Who came from this country?" and "When did you leave this country?" Each student also helps us locate their town or city of origin on their country's map. I print out copies of the six countries for the next activity. We follow up this whole group activity with individual writing assignments in which students tell where they are from, when they came to the United States, and one or two sentences about their experience of leaving. Students take turns entering their stories on the three student computers as I circulate among the rest, helping them develop their paragraphs. We create a bulletin board in which a U.S. map is surrounded by the other maps and the students' word-processed stories.

In the next activity we search for artwork from the United States and our countries of origin. We visit the Louvre ("WebMuseum Network," sunsite.unc.edu/louvre) and other art museums and return to "The Virtual Tourist World Map," going beyond the country maps in search of visual art images. This time I ask questions like, "Is this a painting or a pot, a statue or a mask?", "What country is it from?", "Is it beautiful or ugly, interesting or ordinary?" and "Have you seen anything like it before?" I share interesting tidbits about the pieces as we encounter them in the accompanying texts. Next, each student tells me which piece he or she wants a printout of. We use the "back" and "go" functions of our web browser to return quickly to the right places. Again we follow up our Internet cruising with individual writing assignments with each student describing his or her selected piece of artwork.

Over the next couple of weeks we repeat the process for recipes ("The Internet Kitchen," www.your-kitchen.com), popular songs (e.g., "Lyrics and Pictures," ftp.sunet.se), traditional folktales ("Aaron Shephard's Reader's Theater," www.aaronshep.com/rt) and proverbs ("Quotations," www.lexmark.com/data). In some cases we need to conduct library research or consult with parents or other knowledgeable informants. The recipes, songs, folktales and proverbs may be collected in the primary language but are translated into English with the help of the teacher, bilingual dictionaries, and parent or community interpreters, as needed. We also spend class time trying out our recipes, singing our songs, and retelling or role-playing our folktales.

We culminate our unit with a visit to the White House (www.whitehouse.gov) where we leave an E-mail message to the President, expressing our thanks for the opportunity to live in and learn about our new country. We also invite other classes to our classroom to view our work, listen to our songs and stories, and sample our delicious dishes on our Cultural Celebration Day.

Benefits and Barriers

This concludes my imaginary tour of the World Wide Web with my wonderful and talented English language learners. The Internet addresses listed are usually just one example of good starting points. Internet surfers find that web sites are often linked to similar sites via easily navigable hypertext links. If these links do not suffice, a search using the various search engines (such as Yahoo!, Lycos and InfoSeek) can be conducted by the teacher before the lesson so that he or she can preview the sites for content and student suitability.

I must also warn you that some may no longer be accessible because web sites tend to disappear without warning. On the other hand, two or three new similar sites usually spring up to take their place.

What have I discovered about the World Wide Web and its potential for helping bilingual/ESL teachers meet the instructional needs of their students? I found the following benefits.

- The World Wide Web is a rich source for visual images, text, and even audio and video clips on a wide variety of subjects. Some of the sponsoring organizations – for example, the Smithsonian, NASA, the Library of Congress – have impeccable credentials. **Students can conduct genuine research,** finding information that may not be available even through major public and university libraries.

EDUCATIONAL WEB SITES

Bilingual and Multicultural Education
Bilingual ESL Network www.redmundial.com/ben.htm
A.M. Data: Ethnic Studies Interactive www.libertynet.org:80/~amdata/
Center for Applied Linguistics www.cal.org
Center for the Study of Books in Spanish
  www.csusm.edu/cwis/campus_centers/csb/index.html
Culture Pages www.hut.fi/~rvilmi/Project/Culture/
CyberSpanglish Website www.actlab.utexas.edu/~seagull/spanglist.html
Elementary Spanish Curriculum www.veen.com/Veen/Leslie/Curriculum/
Eurocentres Home Page www.clark.net/pub/eurocent/
Intercultural E-Mail Classroom Connections www.stolaf.edu/network/iecc/
Multicultural Book Review Homepage
  www.isomedia.com/homes/jmele/homepage.html
Mundo Latino - Música Latina www.mundolatino.org/cultura/musica/
Mundo Latino - Rincón Literario www.mundolatino.org/litera.htm
NABE: Instructional Technology (ITSIG) www.redmundial.com/nabe/it.htm
National Clearinghouse for Bilingual Education (NCBE) www.ncbe.gwu.edu
The Rice School/La Escuela Rice riceinfo.rice.edu/armadillo/Rice/dev.html
Tesoros of the Web www.hisp.com/tesoros/index.html

English as a Second Language
Archive of CELIA (Computer Enhanced
  Language Instruction Archive)
  software www.latrobe.edu.au/www/
  education/celia/celia.html
Cutting Edge CALL Resources
  www.chorus.cycor.ca/Duber/m004d.html
Dave's ESL Café on the Web www.pacificnet.net/~sperling/
ESL Student Page www2.wgbh.org/mbcweis/ltc/telecom/esl.html
The ESL Virtual Catalog www.pvp.com/esl.htm
Heinemann World 195.224.76.130/index.htm
Impact! On-line journal www.ed.uiuc.edu/impact/
Intensive American Language Center www.ialc.wsu.edu/
Interactive Internet Language Learning babel.uoregon.edu/yamada/interact.html
Internet Resources for Language Teachers www.hull.ac.uk/cti/langsite.htm
Internet TESL Journal www.aitech.ac.jp/~iteslj/
The Language Teacher Journal On-line langue.hyper.chubu.ac.jp/jalt/pub/tlt/
Longman Dictionaries www.awl-elt.com/dictionaries/
Sarah and John's TEFL Pitstop www.classicweb.com/usr/jseng/jstefl.htm#free
TESL-EJ (Electronic Journal) violet.berkeley.edu/~cwp/TESL-EJ/index.html
The Virtual English Language Center www.comenius.com/
Welcome to TESOL On-line! www.tesol.edu/

English Language Arts
Children's Literature Web Guide www.ucalgary.ca/~dkbrown/index.html
Concertina - Books on the Internet www.iatech.com/books/
International Reading Association www.eden.com/~readthis/ira/about.htm
Internet Public Library ipl.sils.umich.edu
Literature Related Links elwing.otago.ac.nz:889/dsouth/links.html
Myths and Legends www.fireflies.com/myths.html
Project Gutenburg www.aligrafix.conk/oxford/guten.html
Quotations Home Page www.lexmark.com/data/quote.html
Reader's Theater Editions www.aaronshep.com/rt/RTE.html
Writing Around the World – Telecommunications and English
  www.nyu.edu/pages/hess/cities.html

– Compiled by Dr. Chris Green, IDRA. See also IDRA's site: www.idra.org

- The web provides **instantaneous access to sites in other countries**. This means that we can find resources written in other languages, including less common ones. It also provides us with access to the cultural riches of countries from which our students originated. E-mail exchanges between our students and students and adults overseas are an additional way to address instructional issues in multilingual and multicultural ways.

- **Resources abound for teachers** such as innovative lesson plans, free and low-cost instructional software, demonstrations of commercial software, electronic journals, the latest curriculum standards, reviews of tests and materials, and discussion groups. Universities, museums, state and federal education agencies, professional associations and educational publishers sponsor sites of a general nature and sites tailored to special interests such as math, science, bilingual, ESL, early childhood learning, etc.

- Once on-line, teachers find that the **web browsers are very user friendly** as well as either free or very inexpensive. The navigation features such as "bookmarks" that enables users to record addresses for sites they have visited, hypertext links that permanently change color once they are used, and the "go," "forward," "back" and "home" commands help keep track of where we have been. We can also "search" for key words and phrases within documents as well as use built-in search engines that help us find resources at sites with large data bases.

- Going from the screen to a printout copy of the web page requires merely clicking on the "print" button. **Web pages can then be reproduced**, cut up and inserted into student products, posted or read

---

THE MULTIMEDIA POSSIBILITIES OF THE WORLD WIDE WEB CONTRIBUTE ADDITIONAL INCENTIVES TO TEACHERS WHO WISH TO GIVE THEIR STUDENTS THE BEST EDUCATION POSSIBLE.

---

aloud. Computer-savvy teachers can learn how to "capture" texts, graphics and other media electronically for incorporation into their own lessons and student assignments. The usual copyright laws apply, so remember that you can never make a dime off something you got from the Internet, but the usual classroom uses are usually not a problem. The site will often have usage and copyright information listed, so look for it.

I have also found some potential barriers.

- The largest potential barrier is the **sheer size of the animal.** We have been told repeatedly that the growth of information has been exponential for years. The Internet graphically and dramatically demonstrates this phenomenon for us. Busy teachers are often unsure of where to begin.

- Because virtually anyone can set up a home page, the **quality of information varies greatly** on the Internet. Teachers require high degrees of historical and scientific accuracy in the information they present to students. Language teachers like to provide their students with well-written and edited texts as models for their own writing.

- **Students can be exposed to objectionable material** of a racist, sexist or pornographic nature. Many "netters" take pride in pushing the limits of our constitutional guarantees of freedom of expression, producing materials that could offend parents or shock children. Fortunately, a rare minority are reported to be dangerous individuals who like to psychologically and even physically harm others.

- **The texts on the Internet are largely authentic language**, written for learners who have mastered the oral and written components of the language. Students in the primary grades, poor readers and students who are at early levels of acquiring English may not be able to decode and comprehend much of the material they encounter on the web.

Solutions

Through this process of identifying benefits and barriers, I have some suggestions and solutions to offer.

Start with an area that interests you but for which you have had difficulty finding materials. Keep your focus relatively narrow, at least at first, until you become more experienced at locating and judging the resources you find.

Begin with a list of URLs (site addresses) developed by professional educators. Professional journals, especially those with an instructional technology focus, routinely publish such lists. My personal favorite is *Classroom Connect*, a monthly newsletter that lists new educational sites and suggestions for how to incorporate them into instruction. They also offer good teacher training materials. My own "top picks" list, focusing on bilingual and ESL sites, is located in the box on page 216.

Join a listserv or newsgroup that meets your professional interests. In most cases, all you need to do to join a listserv is send an E-mail message to the proper address with the message "Subscribe [your name]." Joining newsgroups is done on-line through your web browser. All you need is the newsgroup name. You use the "newsgroups" function to visit the newsgroup site where easy directions for joining are given.

In most cases you should **preview the sites you will include in the classroom lessons first.** Just as you would read the textbook or children's literature selection

---

before your students tackle it, you should also do so with Internet resources. If you stick to sites with obvious educational credentials such as U.S. Department of Education-sponsored sites, you will probably have few problems with misinformation or inaccuracies. Previewing sites can also help you identify places where the reading and language level of the texts is appropriate for your students.

Train your students to use a "beware of strangers" type of approach to the Internet. They should never share their phone numbers or home addresses without your permission. And be sure to monitor their usage by at least occasionally glancing at the screen when students are surfing. Explain that they may, by accident, encounter pictures of nude women, racist or sexist comments, or other objectionable material. If they report such incidents to you immediately, no disciplinary consequences will follow. If they do not inform you or if they seek such sites intentionally, they will be subject to your usual punishments for classroom infractions, which would probably include notifying their parents and/or the principal. You may also want to alert them to the fact that you can often retrace their explorations by following highlighted hypertext links and other navigation indicators. This will probably give your dishonest students pause for thought.

Teach your students to become discriminating consumers of information. Learning to deal with information overload by sifting efficiently through information, distinguishing between primary and secondary sources, establishing the credibility of the informant, and other strategies are lifelong skills that all students should acquire. The Internet can become your hands-on laboratory for helping your students do so.

English language learners deserve the opportunity to acquire computer literacy skills, engage in searches for information on topics of special interest, communicate with others around the world, and have access to more materials in their primary languages. The multimedia possibilities of the World Wide Web contribute additional incentives to teachers who wish to give their students the best education possible. If your principal needs even more reasons to get you a modem and an Internet account, explain that telecommunications dollars deliver a lot more for the money than dollars spent on electronic workbooks, laser disks and CD-ROMs. Good luck and happy surfing!

Technology and Language Minority Students

Column Editor: Dr. Dennis Sayers, University of California Educational Research Center

Confronting an Embarrassment of Riches: Internet Search Tools

by Dr. Dennis Sayers

In the year since Jim Cummins and I published *Brave New Schools: Challenging Cultural Illiteracy through Global Learning Networks* (New York: St. Martin's Press), much has changed on the Internet. Our initial goal with *Brave New Schools* was certainly ambitious. We sought to combine two distinct kinds of resources: first, a theoretical overview which offered educators a pedagogical rationale for involving their classes in global learning networks; and second, a practical, thoroughly annotated handbook detailing 800 of the best Internet resources available for parents, teachers, and students. Now, as the second edition is about to appear, we believe our framework remains sound — yet we are certain the Internet has grown so rapidly that no single volume could begin to capture the vast array of information resources that learners and teachers can find.

The key word here is *vast*. As a worldwide information resource, the Internet is best imagined as a very special library; yet unlike any library ever seen. Wherever you enter the Internet, there is an initial foyer containing numerous doors. One door usually leads to the reference room (the best place to start, I will suggest), and most of the other doors lead to the library's stacks and special collections. Open any of these doors and there are dozens of information resources there for the asking (and for downloading into a visitor's personal computer). But in each room there are also many other doors leading to other stacks and specialized collections. Indeed, some of these portals are "teleporting" doors; by opening them, a visitor to an Internet library in one country may be beamed, like a *Startrek* denizen, to another collection in a differ-ent nation, where other stacks, doors, and teleports await endless exploration.

If all this sounds dizzying and more than a little overwhelming, it is precisely because it is. If there were no way to search the Internet so as to quickly locate information resources — that is, if there were no automated reference tools — then using the Internet would be like being locked in the Library of Congress forever...but with no card catalog. (To continue with the analogies drawn from television series, this is where the theme for *Twilight Zone* would be playing).

In this brief article, I offer an overview of the various automated reference tools — most often called "search engines" — useful for mining the Internet's resources. Every Internet search engine consists of two essential elements: (a) a database of links, whether compiled by humans or by "robot" programs which have roamed the Internet, listing current addresses to information resources around the world, and (b) a searching component where a visitor may type a search term to discover "hits" within the search engine's database. For this article, I have relied extensively on the newly revised second edition of *Brave New Schools*, and have added specialized search tools for bilingual, ESL, and foreign language educators.

Building a Basic Internet Reference Shelf

In any library, the reference room has certain well-worn volumes that are much in demand since they explain how to use other essential reference tools available on shelves nearby. Similarly, some of the most helpful Internet reference tools are pages on the World Wide Web (often termed "WWW" or simply "The Web") which can lead you to other Internet search tools. These reference tools frequently offer invaluable guidance as to the most effective use of an abundant array or resource services. Any of these "search gateway" webpages provide such essential assistance that many Internet-savvy educators select a favorite gateway webpage and then set up their "information browser" programs (usually either *Netscape's Navigator* or *Microsoft's Explorer*) so that this is the first webpage (or "homepage") they see whenever they explore the Internet.

Perhaps the most complete search gateway webpage is "Internet Navigation" from Rice University, long a leader in networked resources for the academic community (To access this webpage, type "http://riceinfo.rice.edu/Internet/" [without the quotes] into your information browser program). The "Internet Navigation" webpage is organized into five general areas, with clickable links to numerous Internet search tools listed under each of these major headings:

- Find resources by subject
- Find resources by keyword
- Find resources by location
- Find resources by type
- Find forums, newsgroups, and mailing lists by Dr. Dennis Sayers
- Find people

Nearly all of the various search tools which I will discuss in the remainder of this article have links on the Rice University "Internet Navigation" webpage. In addition, "Internet Navigation" provides several links to helpful articles on advanced search strategies.

Another extremely useful general resource is the service provided by C\Net's Search.Com (http://www.search.com/) which allows visitors to search the Internet for all the major search engines appropriate to their topic of interest. Selecting "Education," "Health," or any of 25 different subject areas on this webpage will provide a computer user with a dozen or more subject-specific search engines to "test drive" in her or his quest for germane Internet information resources.

Finally, there are certain websites on the Internet which bilingual, ESL, and foreign language educators can count on to have searchable databases of resources for language learning and intercultural education. Chief among these are the websites of the *National Clearinghouse for Bilingual Education* (http://www.ncbe.gwu.edu/), the *ERIC Clearinghouse on Languages and Linguistics* of the Center for Applied Linguistics (http://www.cal.org/ericcll/), and the *Links to all ERIC Sites* webpage (http://www.aspensys.com/eric/barak.html) where all 16 federally-funded ERIC education clearinghouses, comprising the largest educational database in the world, can be accessed.

Subject-Oriented Internet Search Tools

In this category, we find the Internet search tools which are the most human labor intensive. *Yahoo!* is the oldest and most widely known among the subject-oriented search engines (http://www.yahoo.com/search.html). When a visitor types "bilingual education" in the search descriptor area of this webpage, these are four of the dozens of clickable links that will be provided within seconds.

1. *Business and Economy: Products and Services: Education: Languages: English as a Second Language*
   - *Bilingual Language-Speech-Hearing Association (BiLaSHA)* - foreign accent modification training to ESL professionals and speech therapists.
   - *Dynamic English* - course in English as a second language (ESL) on CD-ROM. Emphasis is on listening and a systematic presentation of language in context.

Teacher guide and bilingual support is available.

2. *Education: Languages: German*
   - *Association of Parents for Bilingual Education (NCBE)* - non-profit organization of parents who canvass for immersion methods in teaching German as a second language in South Tyrol. Links to related sites.

3. *Government: Executive Branch: Departments and Agencies: Department of Education*
   - *National Clearinghouse for Bilingual Education* - educating linguistically and culturally diverse students. Site includes all NCBE publications, plus databases, journal articles, and many links to related sites.

Each of these "hits" is indicated by a "button" which is filed on one of three specific subject-specific shelves; for example the NCBE button is filed under the shelf labeled *Government: Executive Branch: Departments and Agencies: Department of Education*. By clicking on the NCBE "button," the visitor will be teleported to the website indicated (which happens to be http://www.ncbe.gwu.edu/), but without the visitor's having to know the exact Internet address. But if she or he wishes, the visitor can choose to click on the shelf itself, and will then be taken to the *Yahoo!* area where the NCBE link is filed along with all the other links to Executive Branch agencies of the U.S. government. Many educators find *Yahoo!* an especially useful resource because its organization is so like that of the familiar library card catalogue.

This kind of superordinate and subordinate categorization is only possible through human intervention. *Yahoo!* employs hundreds of Internet reference librarians whose job it is to visit websites around the clock and to categorize them on *Yahoo!'s* shelves. To support their efforts, *Yahoo!* sells small advertising billboards, or "banners," which appear at the top of every page of *Yahoo!* search results. Indeed, every search engine described in this article supports its labor- or computer-intensive efforts through "banner" advertising.

Some labor-intensive search engines

provide not only categorizations but searchable reviews of websites; principal among these are *Magellan* (http://www.mckinley.com/) and *Excite's NetReviews* (http://www.excite.com/). Finally, other labor-intensive subject-oriented guides authored by experts are available at *The Argus Clearinghouse* (http://www.clearinghouse.net/) and at Ohio State University's *FAQ's* (Frequently Asked Questions) Search Engine (http://www.cis.ohio-state.edu/hypertext/faq/usenet/FAQ-List.html).

Full-Text Search Engines

If *Yahoo!*, *Magellan*, and *The Argus Clearinghouse* depend on intensive evaluation of websites by expert reference librarians, other Internet search tools rely on brute computer force to compile vast databases of searchable webpages. Digital Corporation's *Alta Vista* (http://altavista.digital.com/) has carved out a special niche in this category of Internet search tools, but *Infoseek* (http://www.infoseek.com/) and *Excite* (http://www.excite.com/) have a growing number of adherents. Day in and day out, *Alta Vista*, *Excite*, and *Infoseek* gather webpages automatically throughout the world. *Alta Vista*, for example, currently provides surprisingly rapid full-text searches of 11 billion words found in over 22 million webpages; typing in the phrase "bilingual education" yields no less than 5,000 clickable links to webpages on the Internet which use this phrase, all produced in no less than 3 seconds. The word "Hmong," to offer another telling example, reveals 2,000 different webpages which mention the language or culture of this Southeast Asian immigrant group with large communities in Fresno, California, throughout Minnesota, and in various other states.

"Meta-" Search Engines

The reader will recall that C\Net's Search.Com allows computer users to search the Internet for search engines with databases appropriate to a particular topic, which can then be searched one-by-one. It was only a matter of time until someone designed a *meta*search engine that would automatically search other search engines, report back the findings, eliminate duplicates, and collate the results, providing a report with clickable links to pertinent Internet resources. Two such search engines are *Metacrawler* at http://metacrawler.cs.washington.edu, a metasearch tool which searches eight of the major search engine databases (*Open Text, Lycos, WebCrawler, InfoSeek, Excite, Inktomi, Alta Vista, Yahoo!*, and *Galaxy*) and *Use It!* at http://www.he.net/~kamus/useen.htm which offers visitors the choice of searching all these databases as well as search engines in other languages.

Search Engines for Electronic Discussion Groups

Thus far I have concentrated on Internet search tools useful for locating a range of information resources. In the remainder of this article, I will focus on those search tools which can be helpful in discovering the myriad of human resources accessible over the Internet. There are two major classes of search tools in this arena, corresponding to the two technological means which are used to facilitate communication over the Internet among people with similar interests: (a) *electronic mail-based discussion groups*, and (b) *USENET newsgroup-based discussion groups*. In both cases, people with common interests share their concerns, questions, and expertise with one another.

Electronic mail-based discussion groups are made possible by a key characteristic of digital communication: one copy of an e-mail message can be instantly "broadcast" to any number of recipients who have listed themselves in an electronic mailing list, hosted by a network somewhere on the Internet. Electronic mail-based discussion groups are created and maintained by "robot" computer programs on this host computer (for example, Listserv, Listproc, and Majordomo) which automatically create and update mailing lists for discussion groups. These list manager programs receive and automatically process e-mail commands issued by subscribers and directed to the discussion group's *management address*. Aside from its management address, each discussion group has a *participation address* where subscribers direct their actual messages to the group. Any message sent to the participation address by one subscriber is duplicated and sent to every other subscriber, creating a worldwide

virtual forum in each subscriber's personal electronic mailbox.

Liszt.Com is the major search engine for electronic mail-based discussion groups. Its database is something like *Alta Vista's* in that *Liszt.Com* automatically queries Internet host computers around the world asking for the latest information on discussion group mailing lists maintained by each network. At present, the *Liszt.Com* offers a searchable database of more than 65,000 discussion groups on over 2,000 Internet hosts.

Like electronic mail-based discussion groups, *USENET newsgroups* facilitate conversations between people with common interests. However, newsgroups do not operate through e-mail; that is, newsgroups do not work by filling electronic mailboxes around the world with a copy of each message sent by any subscriber (thus saturating a great deal of Internet "bandwidth," the cyberspace equivalent of killing far too many trees for newsprint). In order to participate in one of the USENET educational newsgroups, a user's Internet Service Provider (AT&T, America Online, CompuServe, Prodigy, or a local service provider) must subscribe to a "newsfeed" for a particular newsgroup, rather than the user herself or himself, as is the case with electronic mail-based discussion groups. To participate in a newsgroup, a user must literally "go to the source" by logging into her or his Service Provider and visiting the newsgroup area there. While theoretically this is a more efficient system for conducting discussion, newsgroups are not as widely used for educational purposes as are electronic mail-based discussion groups.

DejaNews is the only widely used search engine designed exclusively for newsgroups (http://search.dejanews.com/); however, many of the most popular search engines for Internet information resources also have special settings permitting searches of USENET newsgroups, notably *Alta Vista* (http://altavista.digital.com/), *Infoseek* (http://www.infoseek.com/), and *Excite* (http://www.excite.com/).

Search Engines for Locating Individuals

Generally, the most efficient way to locate anyone's electronic mail address is

simply to give them a telephone call and ask. However, there are automated search engines that will locate electronic mail addresses as well as current phone numbers and street addresses if these are available through regular "Information" directory assistance services. Chief among these are *WhoWhere?* at (http://www.whowhere.com/) and *Yahoo!'s People Search* at (http://www.yahoo.com/search/people/). For example, a search of *Yahoo!* revealed the author's current e-mail addresses as

dmsayers@ucdavis.com
dennis_sayers@hotmail.com
dsayers@panix.com

and correctly identified his former and now obsolete e-mail address as sayers@acfcluster.nyu.edu

Privacy Issues

The ability of Internet search engines to find nearly any reference to an individual and his or her professional and casual communications over the Internet may be disturbing to some computer users now, and will become unsettling to many more in the future. Not everyone wants their home phone number available to anyone on the Internet. And what if a potential future employer searched for everything you've written or anything that's been written about you? If these issues are a concern — and they should be — a useful reference is the document prepared by Cl*Net* on privacy in the digital age which can be found at http://www.cnet.com/Content/Features/Dlife/Privacy2/ss02.html, which offers specific guidance on how to unlist, remove, and otherwise render unsearchable specific personal information.

Conclusion

We, as bilingual and second language educators, are uniquely positioned to assume leadership in the productive use of networked resources to encourage critical intercultural learning. Yet this historic opportunity can only be seized if we recognize the importance of mastering the many automated search tools at our fingertips for locating, sifting through, and evaluating Internet resources, separating the wheat from the chaff for our students and their families as they seek to bridge two worlds.

The Case for Bilingual Education

Stephen D. Krashen

Dr. Krashen is a Professor of Education at the University of Southern California.

Before presenting the case against bilingual education, it will be helpful to first present the case for bilingual education. Underlying successful bilingual education is the fundamental principle of language acquisition and literacy development: We acquire language by understanding messages, by obtaining comprehensible input (the "input hypothesis"; Krashen, 1994). Similarly, we develop literacy from reading (the reading hypothesis).

When we give children quality education in their primary language, we give them two things:

1. Knowledge, both general knowledge of the world and subject matter knowledge. The knowledge that children get through their first language helps make the English they hear and read more comprehensible. This results in more English language acquisition.

Consider the case of two limited English proficient children. One has had a good education in the primary language, and is well-prepared in math, while the other has not had a good foundation in math. They enter a fourth grade class in which math is taught only in English. Clearly, the child with a good background in math will understand more, and will thus learn more math, and acquire more English, because she is getting more comprehensible input. The child with a poor math background will learn less math and acquire less English.

2. Literacy, which transfers across languages.

Here is a simple, three step argument supporting the transfer of literacy from the first to the second language:
(1) As Frank Smith and Kenneth Goodman have argued, we learn to read by reading, by making sense of what we see on the page (see e.g. Goodman, 1982; Smith, 1994). This hypothesis is very similar to the input hypothesis.

(2) If we learn to read by reading, it will be much easier to learn to read in a language we already understand.
(3) Once you can read, you can read. The ability to read transfers across languages.

Another aspect of literacy transfers as well: The ability to use language to solve problems and thereby grow intellectually. Once, for example, someone can use writing to clarify ideas ("the composing process") in one language, it can be used in any other: Once we are educated, we are educated.

Rossell and Baker (1996) complain that "it is impossible to say why" native language development will help second language development: "there is no underlying psychological mechanism that accounts for the facilitation effect" (p. 31). According to my understanding, knowledge and literacy together make up what Cummins (1981) refers to as "academic language" (formerly CALP). This characterization helps us understand what the advantages are in providing first language support: Knowledge gained through the first language makes English input more comprehensible and literacy gained through the first language transfers to the second.

The Three Components

If the arguments given here are correct, they predict that good bilingual programs will have the following components:

1. Comprehensible input in English, provided directly in the form of ESL and sheltered subject matter classes.[1]
2. Subject matter teaching done in the first language, without translation. This indirect help provides background information that helps make the English that children read and hear

From *Under Attack: The Case against Bilingual Education*, 1996, pp. 3-7. © 1996 by Stephen D. Krashen. Published by Language Education Associates, Culver City, CA.

more comprehensible. Methods that use the first language for concurrent translation (the teacher speaking in one language, and thcn translating what was said into the second language) are not effective in helping children acquire English (Legaretta, 1979, Wong-Fillmore, 1985); when a translation is available, the children do not attend to the input in the second language and teachers do not have to try to make this input comprehensible.

3. Literacy development in the first language, which transfers to the second language.

A fourth very desirable component is the continuation of the development of the primary language. There are good practical reasons (e.g. international business), and cognitive reasons (bilinguals do better on certain linguistic tasks as well as measures of "divergent thinking") to do this. In addition, a high level of competence in the first language contributes to a healthy sense of biculturalism, an avoidance of the state of "bicultural ambivalence," shame of the first culture and rejection of the second culture (Cummins, 1981).

Explaining Bilingual Education: "The Paris Argument"

It is not easy to explain the theory underlying bilingual education to the public. I have had some success, however, with the following analogy. Pretend you have just received, and have accepted, an attractive job offer in Paris. Your French, however, is limited (you had two years of high school French a long time ago). You have also never been to France, and know very little about life in Paris.

Before your departure, the company that is hiring you will send you the following information, in English: What to do when you arrive in Paris, how to get to your hotel, where and how to find a place to live, where to shop, what kinds of schools are available for your children, how French companies function (how people dress in the office, what time work starts and ends, etc.) and specific information about the functioning of the company and your responsibilities.

It would be very useful to get this information right away in English, rather than getting it gradually, as you acquire French. If you get it right away, the world around you will be much more comprehensible, and you will acquire French more quickly.

Anyone who agrees with this, in my opinion, agrees with the philosophy underlying bilingual education.

Russian Language TV and Bilingual Education

A recent article in the Los Angeles Times (June 27, 1995) enthusiastically described a new television station, CRN-TV which broadcasts, in the Russian language, "a mix of news, political discussion, culture and kids' shows to help acclimatize immigrants to life in the U.S." (p. F-3). CRN-TV has won the support of West Hollywood Mayor John Heilman, who is quoted as saying "CRN has really helped us get the word out to our Russian residents, who make up such a large part of the community. They know about the services we have, and how to report crime, fires, and earthquakes. We're excited to have them in the city." One of the founders of CRN, Michael Kira, states that one of the jobs of CRN is "to bring America into the hearts of everyone who comes here."

It is gratifying that there is such support for an enterprise such as CRN. What is fascinating is that no one seems to object to the fact that the broadcasting is in Russian. Instead, people seem to understand that when immigrants are knowledgeable about the world around them, they adjust more easily, and that providing information in the first language is very efficient.

This is, as noted above, one of the major rationales underlying bilingual education: When we give children subject matter knowledge through the first language, we help them adjust more easily to their new situation, and it makes the instruction they get in English more comprehensible. Because we acquire language by understanding it, this speeds their acquisition of English.

CRN-TV is a very good idea. I am sure that it is a big help in helping Russian immigrants adjust. It can also help their English language development: Someone who is up-to-date on the news, because they have heard it discussed in Russian on CRN, will have an easier time reading English language newspapers and understanding the news on English language television and radio.

(I am not arguing that Russian-language TV is all immigrants need in order to acquire English. They also need comprehensible input in English. But having some background knowledge in Russian will help make this input more comprehensible. Similarly, students in bilingual programs should be, and are, getting comprehensible input in English in addition to subjects taught in the primary language.)

If Russian language television is a good idea, so is bilingual education.

Note

1. In sheltered subject matter classes, intermediate second language acquirers are given comprehensible subject matter instruction in the second language. The focus of the class is on subject matter learning, not language acquisition. Students in these classes typically acquire as much language as students in traditional intermediate classes, and often acquire more, and learn subject matter at the same time (Krashen, 1991).

References

Christon, L. 1995. Educational TV for Russian immigrants. Los Angeles Times, June 27, 1995, p. F-5.

Cummins, J. 1981. The role of primary language development in promoting educational success for language minority students. In Schooling and Language Minority Students. Sacramento, CA: California Department of Education. pp. 3–49.

Goodman, K. 1982. Language and Literacy. London: Routledge and Kegan Paul.

Krashen, S. 1991. Sheltered subject matter teaching. Cross Currents 18:183–189.

Krashen, S. and Biber, D. 1988. On Course: Bilingual Education's Success in California. Ontario, CA: California Association for Bilingual Education.

Legarreta, D. 1979. The effects of program models on language acquisition by Spanish-speaking children. TESOL Quarterly 8: 521–576.

Rossell, C. and Baker, K. 1996. The educational effectiveness of bilingual education. Research in the Teaching of English 30:7–74.

Smith, F. 1994. Understanding Reading. Fifth Edition. Hillsdale, NJ: Erlbaum.

Wong-Fillmore, L. 1985. When does teacher talk work as input? In S. Gass and C. Madden (Eds.) Input in Second Language Acquisition. New York: Newbury House. pp. 17–50.

WHAT'S NEW IN...

BOB REISING, *Column Editor*
The University of North Carolina at Pembroke
Pembroke, North Carolina

EBONICS

When Is Dialect Acceptable English?

JACQUELINE BRICE-FINCH

As a teacher who has taught students from diverse cultural and ethnic backgrounds, I have always told my classes that we are all bi-dialectal. We speak a dialect or vernacular that reflects a culture (Black English, for example). Or our English may reflect a region (Boston or Brooklyn) or a multicultural influence ("Spanglish," or Puerto Rican English). As an English professor, I must be able to teach language to the students, to communicate with them. If I can't understand what they say, it is my problem, not theirs. I have to learn what their words mean, to learn their vernacular, in order to get them to understand the necessity of their learning educated English, the lingua franca of the United States.

When I first heard reports that the Oakland Public School System was teaching children something called Ebonics, I, like many educators, was incensed that language that was community-based was being imported into the classroom, supplanting educated English, what is called standard English. Then, the media had to modify their inflammatory headlines once the Oakland superintendent publicized the correct information. It is my understanding that the program is designed to help teachers understand the local English spoken by many of their students. At that point, my opposition to the program ceased.

Much of the controversy is fueled by the frustration that educators experience when they try to find appropriate teaching methods to educate students who are deficient in their command of educated English. A similar discussion arose over bilingual education: whether students who were non-native speakers benefited more from total immersion in English-only classes or from bilingual classes. For the teacher who now has a mix of those students, how to teach is a daunting task.

Familiarity with the language of the students—and especially awareness of the features of their languages that make acquisition of educated English difficult—enables the teacher to use a variety of techniques. An affirmation of the student's orality is essential to ensure student cooperation. Denigrating a student's speech in the classroom can have adverse repercussions, especially if the student's attempt to practice the newly acquired language structures is also ridiculed or dismissed in the home environment. Sometimes, parents will view their children's use of educated English as pretentious or, more problematic, as an indirect criticism of their own speech and will forbid the children to use such language in the house. The same effect may occur on the playground or in other peer-related situations.

Students need to know that educated English is a norm for all speakers of English, developed as a means of ensuring effective communication. The rules of grammar and diction serve to minimize ambiguity. Language is fluid, however, constantly expanding and contracting as new words and new meanings are added while others become archaic. The words *rap, hip hop,* and *dissing* have been absorbed into the language of the nineties as part of our multicultural popular culture. (Even an American president

Jacqueline Brice-Finch is a professor of English at James Madison University, Harrisonburg, Virginia.

From *The Clearing House,* May/June 1997, pp. 228-232. Reprinted with permission of the Helen Dwight Reid Educational Foundation. © 1997 by Heldref Publications, 1319 Eighteenth St., N.W., Washington, D.C. 20036-1802.

has dared to use what some would label substandard speech: Former President George Bush once began a national speech with "Yo!") The teacher should also explain the importance of learning and using educated English in formal situations, such as the classroom, the workplace, and the business environment.

What about the plaint that many teachers voice, that they have not been trained in linguistics, which is a feature in innovative teaching in a diverse classroom? Well, think about how we approached the varieties of English we encountered in high school. We all read Shakespeare, right? Elizabethan English was spelled funny and sounded weird too. Yet our teachers assured us that the literature was worth reading and speaking about in order for us to learn certain truths about the human condition. By the time we got to Chaucer in twelfth grade, we were used to tackling different versions of the language. We tried saying, "Whan that Aprille with its shoures soote." The teacher coaxed us to pronounce the words correctly and to pay attention to rhyme. We suffered through repeated glances at footnotes to glean meaning about pilgrims of another age.

Our teachers acted as if they knew exactly how to pronounce words that had become archaic, whose definitions and spelling may have changed. Yet, to the best of my knowledge, there were no classes in Pronouncing Old English, Middle English, and Elizabethan English. Our teachers relied on their exposure to oral recordings or presentations of the material—and passed on the skill as they understood it.

The same can be said about the English spoken in the United States. Some teachers are reluctant to use multicultural readings in their classrooms because they do not know how to pronounce dialect. However, if we look at some standard "classics," we find ample inclusion of dialect. In spite of ongoing censorship challenges, *The Adventures of Huckleberry Finn* is still read and enjoyed in American classrooms. Yet, the dialect that was roundly criticized in

Mark Twain's time as being unsuitable for inclusion in a novel is still vibrant and essential in the Mississippi Valley. Another perennially popular text, Eugene O'Neill's *The Hairy Ape*, is a celebration of linguistically diverse voices emanating from the boiler room of an early-twentieth-century steamer.

On television, we view popular sitcoms in which variations of English are often quite marked. *All in the Family, Head of the Class, Good Times,* even the recent show *Pearl,* include characters who speak a vernacular that is not educated English. Likewise, the film industry has embraced dialects as a reflection of the varieties of English. The film *Secrets and Lies* recently garnered a Best Actress Award for an actress who spoke in a Cockney accent throughout the film. If we Americans initially had a little difficulty understanding her, our decision that she must be comprehensible or the producers would have given us subtitles was sufficient to get us to listen more intently to hear what language features we shared with the actress so that the undecipherable parts did not interfere with our understanding. We were willing to work hard to achieve success in the oral exercise. Likewise, for the recent film adaptation of *Romeo and Juliet,* which has a modern setting but maintains the original language of Elizabethan England, the producers expected the movie audience to make the effort to understand what the actors say.

English is no longer just the primary language of Americans and the British. Increasingly, it is a national language that is taught in conjunction with the primary tongue of countries as diverse and multilingual as South Africa, Japan, and India. The term *international English* is increasingly becoming a replacement for *standard English.* As CNN, the Internet, and multinational trade and political agreements bring us closer to the concept of a global village, tolerance and acceptance of a panoply of dialects is a must, not a choice.

A Case for Orality in the Classroom

A. DUKU ANOKYE

Language and culture are inextricably connected. Society's attitudes toward a particular language variety affect the users' perceptions of self and their performance in the classroom as well as the marketplace. African Amer-

A. Duku Anokye is an assistant professor of English at the University of Toledo, Toledo, Ohio.

icans historically have been recipients of negative language attitudes in education and society. Over the years they have been mislabeled as culturally deprived and culturally disadvantaged, based on their language use. However, African American Vernacular English (AAVE) is a valid language that is not the result of deprivation or disadvantage but instead is simply linguistically different, just as other dialects of a language differ from one another. That fact is yet to be accepted widely by educators. Be that as it may, it is important to understand that AAVE runs much deeper than grammatical, syntactic, and morphological differences; it personifies different cultural expectations and norms for performance as well. Teachers of African American students have an obligation to familiarize themselves with some of the important differences in their students' language and culture that affect their learning in the classroom.

A Rich Oral Tradition

African Americans come from a rich oral tradition. The ability of a person to use active and copious verbal performance to achieve recognition within his or her group is widespread in the African American community, having its roots in African verbal art. Among the Limba of Sierra Leone, for example, individuals are not identified as Limba unless they learn to speak Limba well. The ability to speak well, to "have mouth," is often equated with intelligence and success among the Igbo of southeastern Nigeria. In Central Africa, one of the most important personal qualities of the Barundi people is *ubgenge* (successful cleverness), which is demonstrated by "intellectual-verbal management of significant life-situations" (Albert 1964, 44). Among the Fang of Gabon, individuals achieve highly respected positions as a result of their oratorical powers.

Here in America one need only observe those who are most admired by African Americans. They are those who are known as skillful practitioners of language whatever the content—Martin Luther King, Jesse Jackson, Barbara Jordan, L L Cool J, Malcolm X, Mohammed Ali. Each of those speakers has in common the ability to manipulate language orally, to use the oral tradition to convey the message.

Aspects of the African American oral tradition are observable in African American student behavior. For instance, in story telling, African Americans render abstract observations about life, love, and people in the form of concrete narrative sequences that may seem to meander from the point and take on episodic frames. That is a linguistic style that causes problems with Anglo-American speakers who want to get to the point and be direct. In African American communication style we find the following: overt demonstration of sympathetic involvement through movement and sounds; a prescribed method for how the performer acts and how the audience reacts; total involvement of the participants; the tendency to personalize by incorporating personal pronouns and references to self (African American students tend to use first-person-singular pronouns more frequently than Anglo-American students to focus attention on themselves); and use of active verbs coupled with adjectives and adverbs with potential for intensification (which are called features of elongation and variable stress). Prosodic structure of speech often reflects the way information is organized for presentation. All of those observable aspects of the African American communication style provide leads for teaching innovations.

Where writing is concerned, African Americans make use of features associated with oral language. However they are often penalized because those features depend for their effect on interpersonal involvement or the sense of identification between the writer or the characters and the reader. For example, rhetorical devices found in oral language (such as figures of speech, repetition, and parallelism in the grammatical system) may be transferred in writing, but the paralinguistics, such as pacing and vocal inflection, that must be translated into paragraphing, punctuation, and other conventions are often lost. African American communication emphasizes shared knowledge and the interpersonal relationship between communicator and audience. According to Deborah Tannen (1986), people coming from an oral tradition elaborate the metacommunicative function where words are used to convey something about the relationship between communicator and audience. This shows up as a deficit in writing if not properly enhanced. Teachers who are aware of those features can help their students transfer from an oral modality to a literate one (in appropriate situations) by enhancing the oral rhetorical skills in which the students take pride.

A Group-Centered Ethos

Shirley Heath's 1983 study of the African American community of Trackton, North Carolina, provides us with more insights. She identified members of the community as literate who were able to read printed and written material and on occasion produce written messages. Using the literacy event as a conceptual tool, she found that in a majority of cases adults showed their knowledge of written materials only through oral means. Furthermore they used a group-centered ethos, where the written materials only came to have meaning when interpreted through the experiences of the group, which turned them into occasions for public discussion. This heavy influence of an expressive performance style incorporating orality and group cohesiveness takes its toll when the interaction with audience is distanced and the call-and-response nature of the African American discourse style is impeded. Stating and counterstating, acting and reacting, testing the performance as it progresses are habitual dynamics in African American communication that writing often does not permit and traditional class dynamics may hinder. Armed with this kind of fundamental understanding of how the African American community functions orally, a teacher can use creative methods to lead to deeper, more profound learning.

Michele Foster (1989) conducted ethnographic research in the classroom of a African American woman teacher in an urban community college. Her study revealed two distinct but culturally appropriate styles of speaking and evaluated the styles in terms of success in the classroom. She concluded that the African American sermonic style—following the preacher-as-teacher model—lessened the social distance and created an identification with indigenous African American cultural norms. That style tended to promote a group-centered ethos toward learning and achievement and thereby reinforced group-sanctioned norms. This research, along with Heath's, highlights the impact that a group-centered ethos has on literacy activities.

While I am not advocating that teachers adopt the black sermonic style, I do encourage educators to promote achievement among African American students by using a group-centered approach to learning. Even students coming from varying socioeconomic backgrounds have benefited from the collective ethos. According to Foster, "By adopting cooperative learning activities congruent with the group ethos of the African American community, institutions can and do actually build on its strength" (27). Those are the strategies educators can exploit in order to improve their teaching styles and maximize African American learning.

Language learning is complicated. When compounded by teachers' unfamiliarity and, sometimes, disdain, the fundamental tool through which the majority of us learn is lost to a large population of African American children. We owe it to ourselves as well as to our children to learn as much as we can about their methods of knowing and taking in information.

REFERENCES

Albert, E. 1964. "Rhetoric," "logic," and "poetics" in Burundi cultural patterning of speech behavior. *American Anthropology* 66(6) pt. 2: 35–54.

Foster, M. 1989. "It's cooking now": A performance analysis of the speech events of a black teacher in an urban community college. *Language in Society* 18: 1–29.

Heath, S. B. 1983. *Ways with words: Language, life and work in communities and classrooms.* Cambridge: Cambridge University Press.

Tannen, D. 1986. Introducing constructed dialogue in Greek and American conversational and literary narrative. In *Direct and indirect speech,* edited by F. Coulmas. Berlin: Mouton.

Do We Need a National Language Policy?

BOB REISING

Dr. William Cartwright, former chair of education at Duke University, was well known for his often-uttered and elaborately explained belief that "If one will stand still long enough in education, the world will catch up with him or her." The wisdom of the retired professor's contention is illustrated in the current "flap" over Ebonics, which is but a continuation or rekindling of the controversy accompanying "The Students' Right to Their Own Language," the resolution proclaimed in 1974 by the Conference on College Composition and Communication (CCCC), an institutional arm of the National Council of Teachers of English (NCTE). The storm of the moment features the Oakland, California, school system; that of the 1970s, the Ann Arbor, Michigan, school system. Within five years of the publication of "The Students' Right," the U.S. District Court validated its claim concerning the linguistic legitimacy of "Black English," roughly the equivalent of Ebonics. In July 1979, Judge Charles W. Joiner ruled against the school system and for the plaintiffs, the parents of eleven children at Martin Luther King Elementary School who were in command not of standard English but Black English. The ruling demanded that Ann Arbor educators cease stigmatizing the speech of the eleven, all

from a low-income housing project, and find ways to teach them to read. The ball, so to speak, was placed in the school system's court; after listening to expert witnesses for days on end, Joiner declared that the children should not be labeled educationally handicapped or learning disabled because they spoke Black English.

Identical issues have bubbled to the surface in Oakland and everywhere else the Oakland decision has been discussed in America. The legitimacy of Black English (however labeled), students' rights to their own speech, and success in reading remain the "hot buttons" that invariably get pushed when Ebonics enters a discussion or editorial. Every educated citizen, every legislator, and every columnist has an opinion. It might appear that this time a Supreme Court ruling, not simply one from a district court, is needed to allow the nation peace of mind, or at least resolution, concerning Ebonics.

But an alternative exists. On the eve of a new millennium, the nation may well want to entertain a National Language Policy, a supplement to the National Education Goals and to the national standards that have appeared in recent years. Such a policy would provide recommendations and suggestions helpful not merely to educators but to all citizens in the land—parents, industrialists, elected officials, school board members—everyone anxious to determine how languages and language-users can most constructively function in the twenty-first century.

Bob Reising is a professor of communicative arts at The University of North Carolina at Pembroke, Pembroke, North Carolina.

A position paper developed in 1988 by CCCC, entitled "National Language Policy," might well serve as a catalyst for or draft copy of that policy. Outlined and discussed most recently in the January 1995 issue of *English Journal*, a publication of NCTE, that paper suggested that a national language policy should commit every student to three languages: (1) the language of wider communication; (2) a student's mother tongue (i.e., his or her home language); and (3) "a totally foreign language" (Smitherman 1995, 26). The best-known advocate of the three-commitment policy, Geneva Smitherman, a Distinguished Professor of English at Michigan State University, would be ideally credentialed to serve on the policy-making body.

Convening the body, and no less ideally credentialed for the assignment, could be Bill Bradley, a Rhodes Scholar from Princeton University who later spent ten years in the National Basketball Association and eighteen in the United States Senate. It is Bradley's contention that the nation must "speak about race . . . with a lot more candor . . . and recognize that after we have the conversation . . . we can move to action" (Krueger 1977, 29A).

Experiences and expertise such as those that Bradley and Smitherman "bring to the table" can lead the nation to a national language policy that appeases, not antagonizes, enlightens, not irritates. The United States needs such a policy by the year 2000, unless it prefers that every generation of Americans angrily and unproductively debate minority dialects and languages ad infinitum.

REFERENCES

Conference on College Composition and Communication (CCCC). 1974. Students' right to their own language. *College Composition and Communication* 25(3): 1–32.

Krueger, B. 1997. Bradley urges nation to confront its ills: Former senator lists political, racial tensions. Raleigh, North Carolina, *News and Observer* (Feb. 16): 29A, 34A, 35A.

Smitherman, G. 1995. "Students' Right to Their Own Language": A retrospective. *English Journal 84(1): 21–27.*

Beyond Adversarial Discourse:
Searching for Common Ground
in the Education of Bilingual Students

Originally written for the California State Board of Education

February 1998

by Jim Cummins
University of Toronto

As someone whose research and theory has influenced policy on the education of bilingual students for more than 20 years, I have watched the growing acrimony surrounding this issue with some dismay. The crucially important debate regarding what types of educational interventions are likely to reverse the underachievement of many bilingual students has degenerated into the adversarial discourse of courtroom lawyers with each side trying to "spin" the interpretation of research to fit its strongly held beliefs.

From the time of my initial publications on this topic, I have argued that the research on bilingual education both in North America and from around the world is highly consistent in what it shows. I have also suggested that the research data can be largely accounted for by three theoretical principles that permit accurate predictions regarding student outcomes from any well-implemented bilingual program. I am therefore disturbed to see what I have written sometimes misunderstood and misapplied by advocates of bilingual education and almost invariably distorted beyond recognition by opponents of bilingual education.

I have also argued (e.g. Cummins, 1981a, 1986) that bilingual education by itself is no panacea. The reasons why some groups of culturally diverse students experience long-term persistent underachievement have much more to do with issues of status and power than with linguistic factors in isolation. Thus, educational interventions that challenge the low status that has been assigned to a linguistic or cultural group are much more likely to be successful than those that reinforce this low status. It follows that a major criterion for judging the likely efficacy of any form of bilingual education or all-English program is the extent to which it generates a sense of empowerment among culturally diverse students and communities by challenging the devaluation of students' identities in the wider society.

In principle, the incorporation of students' primary language into the instructional program should operate to challenge the devaluation of the community in the wider society, and thus contribute to students' academic engagement. Strong

Reprinted by permission of Jim Cummins. A revised version of this article will appear as a chapter in Carlos Ovando and Peter McLaren, eds., *The Politics of Multiculturalism: Students and Teachers in the Crossfire* (McGraw-Hill, 2000). Copyright © 1998 by Jim Cummings. All rights reserved.

promotion of students' primary language literacy skills not only develops a conceptual foundation for academic growth but also communicates clearly to students the value of the cultural and linguistic resources they bring to school. However, only a small proportion of bilingual programs (specifically two-way bilingual immersion and developmental [late-exit] programs) aspire to develop students' first language literacy skills and it is therefore primarily these programs that would be expected to succeed in reversing the underachievement of bilingual students.

In this paper I restate what my own empirical research and that of many others is clearly saying and also outline the theoretical principles that permit us to explain these findings and predict the outcomes of various types of programs for bilingual students. Then I attempt to move beyond the divisive discourse of courtroom lawyers to search for areas of agreement in the perspectives and interpretations of both opponents and advocates of bilingual education. I believe that there are many such areas of agreement and focusing on them might provide a starting point for reconstructing a viable research-based approach to reversing a legacy of school failure.

Research Findings on Language Learning and Bilingual Education

The research is unambiguous in relation to three issues: (a) the distinction between conversational and academic skills in a language; (b) the positive effects of bilingualism on children's awareness of language and cognitive functioning; and (c) the close relationship between bilingual students' academic development in their first and second languages (L1 and L2) in situations where students are encouraged to develop both languages. [1]

Conversational and Academic Proficiency
Research studies since the early 1980s have shown that immigrant students can quickly acquire considerable fluency in the target language when they are exposed to it in the environment and at school but despite this rapid growth in conversational fluency, it generally takes a minimum of about five years (and frequently much longer) for them to catch up to native-speakers in academic aspects of the language (Cummins, 1980, 1981b, 1984). [2] During this period, especially for younger students, conversational fluency in the home language tends to erode. This is frequently exacerbated by the temptation for teachers to encourage students to give up their first language and switch to English as their primary language of communication; however, the research evidence suggests that this retards rather than expedites academic progress in English (Cummins, 1991a; Dolson, 1985).

The major implication of these data is that we should be looking for interventions that will sustain bilingual students' long-term academic progress rather than expecting any short-term "quick-fix" solution to students' academic underachievement in English.

The Positive Effects of Additive Bilingualism
There are well over 100 empirical studies carried out during the past 30 or so

years that have reported a positive association between additive bilingualism and students' linguistic, cognitive, or academic growth. The term "additive bilingualism" refers to the form of bilingualism that results when students add a second language to their intellectual tool-kit while continuing to develop conceptually and academically in their first language. My own studies of this issue have involved French-English bilinguals, Irish-English bilinguals, and Ukrainian-English bilinguals (Cummins, 1978a, 1978b; Cummins & Gulutsan, 1974; Cummins & Mulcahy, 1978).

The educational implication of these research studies is that the development of literacy in two or more languages entails linguistic and academic benefits for individual students in addition to preparing them for a working environment in both domestic and international contexts that is increasingly characterized by diversity and where knowledge of additional languages represents a significant human resource.

Interdependence of First and Second Languages

The interdependence principle has been stated as follows (Cummins, 1981a):

> To the extent that instruction in Lx is effective in promoting proficiency in Lx, transfer of this proficiency to Ly will occur provided there is adequate exposure to Ly (either in school or environment) and adequate motivation to learn Ly.

The term **common underlying proficiency (CUP)** has also been used to refer to the cognitive/academic proficiency that underlies academic performance in both languages.

Consider the following research data that support this principle:

- In virtually every bilingual program that has ever been evaluated, whether intended for linguistic majority or minority students, spending instructional time teaching through the minority language entails no academic costs for students' academic development in the majority language. This is borne out in the review of research carried out by Rossell and Baker (1996) as well as by the 30 chapters describing an extremely large number of bilingual programs in countries around the globe in the volume edited by Cummins and Corson (1998). (See also: Cummins, 1977, 1978c; Cummins & Gulutsan, 1974; Lapkin & Cummins, 1981)
- Countless research studies have documented a moderately strong correlation between bilingual students' first and second language literacy skills in situations where students have the opportunity to develop literacy in both languages (for a detailed review of these studies see Cummins, 1991b). It is worth noting, as Genesee (1979) points out, that these findings also apply to the relationships among very dissimilar languages in addition to languages that are more closely related, although the strength of relationship is often reduced (e.g. Japanese/English, Chinese/English, Basque/Spanish – see Cummins et al., 1984; Cummins et al., 1990; Cummins, 1983; Gabina et al., 1986; Lasagabaster Herrerte, 1997, in press; Sierra & Olaziregi, 1989, 1991).

Fitzgerald's (1995) comprehensive review of U.S. research on cognitive reading processes among ESL learners concluded that this research consistently supported the common underlying proficiency model:

> ...considerable evidence emerged to support the CUP model. United States ESL readers used knowledge of their native language as they read in English. This supports a prominent current view that native-language development can enhance ESL reading. (p. 181)

The research data show clearly that within a bilingual program, instructional time can be focused on developing students' literacy skills in their primary language without adverse effects on the development of their literacy skills in English. Furthermore, the relationship between first and second language literacy skills suggests that effective development of primary language literacy skills can provide a conceptual foundation for long-term growth in English literacy skills.

Misconceptions and Distortions

The research data are very specific in what they are saying: to reiterate, superficial conversational fluency is not a good indicator of long-term academic growth in English. Thus, premature exit from a bilingual program into a typical mainstream program is likely to result in underachievement in both languages. Bilingual students will usually require most of the elementary school years to bridge the gap between themselves and native speakers of English; this is, in part, due to the obvious fact that native speakers are naturally also progressing in their command of academic English year by year. Bilingual students' prospects for long-term academic growth in English will not be reduced in any way as a result of spending part of the instructional day developing academic skills in the primary language. In fact, the research suggests that students may experience some linguistic and cognitive benefits as a result of developing literacy in both languages.

Misconceptions Among Some Bilingual Program Advocates

These psychoeducational data do not show, nor do they claim to show, that all forms of bilingual education are more effective than all forms of all-English instruction. In fact, I have argued for more then 20 years that quick-exit transitional bilingual education is an inferior model based on an inadequate theoretical assumption (what I have termed the **linguistic mismatch** assumption) (Cummins, 1978, 1979, 1981a). Any adequate bilingual program should strive to develop, to the extent possible, literacy in both languages; transitional bilingual programs, however, almost by definition, aspire to monolingualism rather than bilingualism. Such programs also generally do little to address the causes of bilingual students' underachievement which, as sketched above, are rooted in the subordination of the community in the wider society.

The psychoeducational data also say nothing about the language in which reading instruction should be introduced. A survey I conducted of bilingual programs in Ireland (which catered both to Irish L1 and English L1 students) showed that teachers were equally divided with respect to whether reading should be taught first in L1, L2 or both simultaneously (Cummins, 1978d, 1979) and I would agree that under different circumstances all three of these approaches are probably viable. For Spanish-speaking students, the much greater regularity of phoneme/grapheme correspondence in Spanish in comparison to English might suggest that this is a more logical language in which to introduce reading. Thus, I would expect those who strongly advocate direct instruction in phonics also to support initial reading instruction in the native language for these students. For my part, however, the promotion of literacy in bilingual students' two languages throughout elementary school is far more important than the specific language in which students are introduced to literacy.

A third misconception that may operate in a small number of bilingual programs is the notion that English academic instruction should be delayed for several grades until students' L1 literacy is well-established. This approach can work well for bilingual students, as the data from two-way bilingual immersion programs demonstrate (e.g. Dolson & Lindholm, 1995; Christian et al., 1998; Porter, 1990). However, in these cases, there is a coherent instructional program from kindergarten through grade 6 with L1 literacy instruction continued through elementary school as the proportion of English instruction increases. There is also direct contact with native speakers of English who are in the same classes. What is much less likely to work well is L1-only instruction (with some oral English) until grades 2 or 3 and then dropping students into all-English programs taught by mainstream teachers who may have had minimal professional development in strategies for supporting bilingual students' academic growth. I have argued that a bilingual program should be a genuine bilingual program with coherence across grade levels and a strong English language literacy development syllabus built in to the overall plan (Cummins, 1996). Ideally, teachers would work for two-way transfer across languages to amplify bilingual students' awareness of language (e.g. through drawing attention to cognate connections, student collaborative research projects focused on language, etc. [see Corson, 1998]).

The final misconception that sometimes characterizes the implementation of bilingual programs is the notion that bilingual education is a panacea that by itself will miraculously elevate student achievement levels. I have argued (Cummins, 1986, 1996) that no program will promote bilingual students' academic achievement effectively unless there is a genuine **school-wide** commitment (a) to promote, to the extent possible, an additive form of bilingualism, (b) to collaborate with culturally diverse parents and communities in order to involve them as partners in their children's education, and (c) to instruct in ways that build on bilingual students' personal and cultural experience (i.e. their cognitive schemata) and that promote critical literacy; such instruction would focus on providing students with opportunities to generate new knowledge, create literature and art, and act on social realities (see Cummins and Sayers, 1995, for a discussion of "transformative" pedagogy).

It is doubtless much easier to promote students' bilingualism, involve parents (who may speak little or no English), and build on students' background experience, in the context of a genuine bilingual program than in a monolingual program. A shared language between teachers, students, and parents clearly facilitates communication. However, I would have no hesitation in choosing a "monolingual" program where the entire school was striving to implement these forms of pedagogy over a so-called "bilingual" program where there was little commitment to these goals.

Distortions by Opponents of Bilingual Programs

A few examples from the Rossell and Baker (1996) paper will serve to illustrate the frequent distortions both of my work and that of others who have carried out research on immersion and bilingual programs.

Rossell and Baker characterize me (and virtually all others who have evaluated bilingual or immersion programs) as a supporter of transitional bilingual education despite the fact that I have argued strongly and consistently for 20 years **against** transitional bilingual education and its theoretical rationale.

They also attribute to me what they term "the facilitation theory" despite the fact that I have never used this term. As noted above, in attempting to account for the research on the relationship between L1 and L2, I have employed the term **interdependence** to signify the consistent positive relationship between L1 and L2 academic proficiency and the fact that instruction through a minority language for a considerable period of the day results in no adverse long-term effects on students' academic development in the majority language.

Rossell and Baker do acknowledge that I have advanced a "'developmental interdependence' hypothesis that states that the development of skills in a second language is facilitated by skills already developed in the first language" (p. 27). They go on to state that they are in agreement with this principle: "..even though **it is true that it is easier to teach a second language to individuals who are literate in their native tongue,** this tells us nothing about how non-literate individuals should be taught, nor the language in which they should be taught" (p. 30) [emphasis added]. As I have outlined above, I fully agree that neither the interdependence principle, nor the research data showing that students taught bilingually suffer no adverse academic consequences in English, demonstrate by themselves that bilingual instruction will lead to better long-term achievement. What the research data and theory do show and what Rossell and Baker apparently agree with is, to quote Rossell's commentary on the Ramirez report, "large deficits in English language instruction over several grades apparently make little or no difference in a student's achievement" (1992, p. 183). Expressed more positively, promoting literacy in students' primary language will provide a foundation for the development of literacy in English such that no deficits in English language development result as a consequence of spending less instructional time through English. [3]

A final, more general, set of distortions in the Baker and Rossell article can be noted. They cite ten research studies which they claim show structured immersion to be superior to transitional bilingual education (TBE). Seven of these studies were studies of French immersion programs in Canada. One (Malherbe, 1946) was an extremely large-scale study of Afrikaans-English bilingual education in South Africa involving 19,000 students. The other two were carried out in the United States (Gersten, 1985; Pena-Hughes & Solis, 1980).

The Pena-Hughes and Solis program (labelled "structured immersion" by Rossell and Baker) involved an hour of Spanish language arts per day and was viewed as a form of bilingual education by the director of the program (Willig, 1981/82). I would see the genuine promotion of L1 literacy in this program as indicating a much more adequate model of bilingual education than the quick-exit transitional bilingual program to which it was being compared. Gersten's study involved an extremely small number of Asian-origin students (12 immersion students in the first cohort and nine bilingual program students, and 16 and seven in the second cohort) and hardly constitutes an adequate sample upon which to base national policy.

Malherbe's study concluded that students instructed bilingually did at least as well in each language as students instructed monolingually despite much less time through each language. Malherbe argues strongly for the benefits of bilingual education and his data are clearly consistent with the interdependence principle.

So we come to the seven Canadian French immersion programs. First, it is important to note that these are all fully bilingual programs, taught by bilingual teachers, with the goal of promoting bilingualism and biliteracy. It seems incongruous that Rossell and Baker use the success of such bilingual programs to argue for monolingual immersion programs taught largely by monolingual teachers with the goal of developing monolingualism.

More bizarre, however, is the fact that their account of the outcomes of these programs is erroneous in the extreme. Consider the following quotation:

> Both the middle class and working class English-speaking students who were immersed in French in kindergarten and grade one were almost the equal of native French-speaking students until the curriculum became bilingual in grade two, at which point their French ability declined and continued to decline as English was increased. The 'time-on-task' principle--that is, the notion that the amount of time spent learning a subject is the greatest predictor of achievement in that subject--holds across classes in the Canadian programs. (p. 22)

Rossell and Baker seem oblivious of the fact that the "time-on-task" principle is refuted by every evaluation of French immersion programs (and there are hundreds) by virtue of the fact that there is no relationship between the development of students' English proficiency and the amount of time spent through English in the program. Consistent with the interdependence principle, French immersion students who spend about two-thirds of their instructional time in elementary school through French perform as well in English as students who have had all of their instruction through English.

Rossell and Baker also seem oblivious to the fact that by the end of grade one French immersion students are still at very early stages in their acquisition of

French. Despite good progress in learning French (particularly receptive skills) during the initial two years of the program, they are still far from native-like in virtually all aspects of proficiency – speaking, listening, reading, and writing. Most grade 1 and 2 French immersion students are still incapable of carrying on even an elementary conversation in French without major errors and insertions of English. [4] To claim that two years of immersion in French in kindergarten and grade 1 results in almost native-like proficiency in French in a context where there is virtually no French exposure in the environment or in school outside the classroom flies in the face of a massive amount of research data.

Similarly, it is ludicrous to claim, as Baker and Rossell do, that the French proficiency of grade 6 immersion students is more poorly developed than that of grade 1 students and to attribute this to the fact that L1 instruction has been incorporated in the program. Significantly, Rossell and Baker cite no specific study to back up these claims. The validity of the claims can be assessed from Swain and Lapkin's (1982) overview of the French immersion research conducted in Ontario:

> even by grade 1 or 2, the immersion students were scoring as well as
> about one-third of native French-speaking students in Montreal, and
> by grade 6 as well as one-half of the Montreal comparison group.
> (pp. 41-42)

These data refer to performance on a standardized achievement measure; Swain and Lapkin point out that there are major differences at all grade levels in the productive skills of speaking and writing (see also Swain, 1978).

Lambert & Tucker (1972) similarly report highly significant differences between grade 1 immersion and native French-speaking students on a variety of vocabulary, grammatical and expressive skills in French, despite the fact that no differences were found in some of the sub-skills of reading such as word discrimination. By the end of grade four, however, (after 3 years of English [L1] language arts instruction), the immersion students have caught up with the French controls in vocabulary knowledge and listening comprehension, although differences still remain in speaking ability.

In short, the French immersion data are the opposite of what Rossell and Baker claim. There are very significant differences between the immersion students and native French-speaking controls at the end of grade 1 (after two years of monolingual total immersion) but the immersion students catch up in French listening and reading in the later grades of elementary school after the program becomes bilingual (and obviously after they have had several more years of learning French!).

Rossell and Baker's discussion of the French immersion data is presumably meant to imply that two years of "structured immersion" in English should be sufficient for limited English proficient students to come close to grade norms in English. The fact that the one large-scale "methodologically acceptable" study that investigated this issue (Ramirez, 1992) found that early-grade students in "structured immersion" were very far from grade norms in English even after four years of immersion does not seem to disturb them.

The significance of these points is that the empirical basis of Rossell and Baker's entire argument rests, according to their own admission, on the performance in French of English-background students in the first two years of Canadian French immersion programs. Not only are a large majority of the programs they cite as evidence for "structured immersion" Canadian French immersion programs, but Rossell (in response to critiques from Kathy Escamilla and Susan Dicker) suggests that:

> In the first two years, the program is one of total immersion, and evaluations conducted at that point are considered to be evaluations of "structured immersion." It is really not important that, in later years, the program becomes bilingual if the evaluation is being conducted while it is still and always has been a structured immersion program. (1996, p. 383)

Rossell and Baker's argument thus rests on their claim that students in monolingual "structured immersion" programs (Canadian French immersion programs in kindergarten and grade 1) come close to grade norms while the program is monolingual in L2 but lose ground in comparison to native speakers when the program becomes bilingual in later grades. As we have seen, the data show exactly the opposite: there are major gaps between immersion students and native French speakers after the initial two years of monolingual L2 instruction but students catch up with native speakers after instruction in their L1 (English) is introduced and the program has become fully bilingual.

Based on their own premises and interpretation of the data, it is clear that Rossell and Baker should be arguing *for* bilingual instruction rather than against it. [5] [6]

Reconciling Differences: Investing in Quality Education

It seems clear that if only because of the shortage of bilingual teachers, at least 70% of limited English proficient students will continue to be taught in English-only programs. However, for the 30% who might continue to be in some form of bilingual program, the perspectives of those who ostensibly oppose bilingual education are instructive in highlighting directions for implementing quality bilingual programs.

I look briefly at some of the arguments made by four of the most prominent opponents of bilingual education (Keith Baker, Charles Glenn, Rosalie Pedalino Porter, and Christine Rossell) and suggest that both their interpretation of the research data and their stated educational philosophies in relation to bilingual students provide ample overlap with the positions I (and many others) have advocated. With the possible exception of Rossell, all have endorsed high quality "dual immersion" or "two-way bilingual immersion" programs as a highly effective way to promote both bilingualism and English academic achievement among bilingual students. This is exactly the type of optimal program that is implied by the theoretical principles I have outlined earlier.

According to Porter (1990), a two-way or dual immersion program is "particularly appealing because it not only enhances the prestige of the minority language but also offers a rich opportunity for expanding genuine bilingualism to the majority population" (p. 154). Such programs promise "mutual learning, enrichment, and respect" (p. 154) and "are also considered to be the best possible vehicles for integration of language minority students, since these students are grouped with English-speakers for natural and equal exchange of skills" (p. 154). She goes on to argue that two-way programs are "the best opportunity for families that are seriously committed to genuine bilingualism for their children" and these programs "do not cost any more than the average single-language classes to maintain" (p. 156). She points out, however, that probably the maximum proportion of language minority students such programs could serve would be about ten per cent (p. 157). Since only about 30 per cent of limited English proficient students are in any form of bilingual program at this point in time (University of California Minority Research Institute Education Policy Center, 1997), and a large proportion of those are in questionable forms of quick-exit transitional bilingual program, aspiring towards a ten per cent coverage for dual immersion programs would be a worthy goal that obviously Porter and I would strongly agree on. As is evident from the quotations above, Porter does not appear at all concerned that in dual immersion programs, generally between 50% and 90% of instructional time in the early grades is devoted to instruction through the minority language, and language arts instruction in this language is continued throughout schooling, despite the fact that this appears to contradict the "time-on-task" principle that she advocates elsewhere in her book.

Keith Baker (1992) has similarly endorsed dual immersion programs, ironically in an extremely critical review of Porter's book *Forked Tongue*. He repudiates Porter's interpretation of dual immersion program evaluations in El Paso and San Diego as representing support for English-only immersion:

> She summarizes a report from El Paso (1987) as finding that an all-English immersion program was superior to bilingual education programs. The El Paso report has no such finding. What Porter describes as an all-English immersion program in El Paso is, in fact, a Spanish-English dual immersion program. The El Paso study supports the claims of bilingual education advocates that most bilingual education programs do not use enough of the native language. It does not support Porter's claims that they should use less.

> Like El Paso, San Diego has an extensive two-language program. Like El Paso, there is evidence that the extensive bilingual education program worked better than the typical bilingual education program. Like El Paso, the results of the San Diego study argue for more bilingual education programs, not fewer as Porter maintains. (p. 6)

It is worth noting that the El Paso (1987, 1992) study is one of those considered methodologically acceptable by Rossell and Baker (1996), so presumably Rossell also would regard dual immersion programs as a promising model to implement. This is particularly so in view of the fact that another "methodologically acceptable" study, Legarretta (1979), also reported that a 50% L1, 50% L2 model resulted in more English language acquisition than models with less L1 instruction. Yet another "methodologically acceptable" study (Pena-Hughes & Solis, 1980) showed that a program with consistent L1 literacy instruction (for 25% of the school day) aimed at promoting students' Spanish literacy worked better than a program that did not aim to promote Spanish literacy.

It seems clear that Rossell and Baker could have constructed a far more convincing case for the efficacy of dual immersion or two-way bilingual immersion than the case they attempt to construct for English-only "structured immersion." Nine of the ten studies they cite as supporting monolingual "structured immersion" are in fact bilingual programs and almost all of these were conducted outside the United States with students very different from those who are currently underachieving in U.S. schools. On the basis of their own review of the literature and Baker's published statements endorsing the El Paso and San Diego models, they would surely have to agree with Porter and me that dual immersion is a model with demonstrated success in promoting bilingual students' academic achievement and that this model should be promoted as vigorously as possible.

Charles Glenn's review of the National Research Council (1997) report on schooling for language-minority children similarly appears highly critical of bilingual education, at least on the surface. Glenn views as "one of the central articles of faith of bilingual education" that children must be taught to read first in the language which they speak at home. As I noted above, I have argued for more than 20 years against this simplistic "linguistic mismatch" assumption underlying early bilingual programs in the United States. I fully agree with Glenn's concluding statement which demonstrates his personal support for bilingual education as a means of developing children's bilingualism:

> What cannot be justified, however, is to continue substituting a preoccupation with the language of instruction for the essential concern that instruction be effective. Bilingual education, it has become clear, is not of itself a solution to the under-achievement of any group of poor children. It is time that those of us who support bilingual education – in my case, by sending five of my children to an inner-city bilingual school – insist upon honesty about its goals and its limits. Bilingual education is a way to teach children to be bilingual, but it possesses no magic answer to the challenge of educating children at risk. Bilingualism is a very good thing indeed, but what language-minority children need most is schools that expect and enable them to succeed through providing a demanding academic program, taught very well and without compromise, schools which respect the ways in which children differ but insist that these differences must not be barriers to equal opportunity. (1997, p. 15)

Glenn concurs with the NRC report's recommendation of three components that should characterize any effective program:

- Some native-language instruction, especially initially
- For most students, a relatively early phasing in of English instruction
- Teachers specially trained in instructing English-language learners

To this list I would add the goal of genuinely promoting literacy in students' L1, where possible and to the extent possible, and continuation of L1 literacy development throughout elementary school. Glenn approvingly cites the common European (and Canadian) practice of providing immigrant students with the opportunity to continue to study the heritage language and culture as an elective, so presumably he would endorse the goal of L1 literacy development for bilingual students in the United States, at least for Spanish-speaking students where numbers and concentration make this goal administratively feasible.

Glenn, however, is clearly concerned that, in his view, many bilingual programs segregate students and retain them too long outside the mainstream, with newcomers "simply dumped into a bilingual class of the appropriate age level" (p. 7). In addition, he suggests that these programs may lack coherent, cognitively challenging opportunities for students to develop higher order English literacy skills.

As noted earlier, these concerns may certainly be justified in the case of a proportion of poorly-implemented bilingual programs; however, concerns about segregation, low teacher expectations, and cognitively undemanding "drill and practice" instruction equally characterize the English-only programs attended by about 70 per cent of limited English proficient students. Segregation in schools is primarily a function of housing and neighborhood ghettoization and will exist regardless of the language of instruction. A major advantage of two-way bilingual programs, as noted above, is that they overcome segregation in a planned program that aims to enrich the learning opportunities of both minority and majority language students. However, even in segregated, low-income, inner city contexts, the findings of Ramirez (1992) and Beykont (1994) show that well-implemented developmental (late-exit) bilingual programs can achieve remarkable success in promoting grade-level academic success for bilingual students.

A final point of agreement in relation to Glenn's analysis is his statement that "the under-achievement of Hispanics in the United States and of Turks and Moroccans in northwestern Europe, I suggested in my recent book, may have less to do with language differences than with their status in the society and how they come to terms with that status" (p. 10). I have elaborated on essentially the same point in many publications (Cummins, 1979, 1981, 1982, 1986, 1996) drawing on John Ogbu's (1978) initial distinction between "caste" and "immigrant" minorities and attempting to work out how status and power differentials in the wider society are played out in the interactions between educators and students in school.

The distinction that Glenn draws between "language differences" and "status in society" implies an "either-or" logic that suggests that if underachievement is related to status and power differentials then it has nothing to do with language. Clearly, this is absurd. As Glenn knows better than most, the subordinated status of colonized and stigmatized minority groups in countries around the world has been reinforced in the school by punishing students for speaking their home language and making them feel ashamed of their language, culture and religion. In other words, the interactions that subordinated group students experience in school have reinforced the inferior status that the minority community has experienced in the wider society.

It seems obvious that if one diagnoses that the roots of the problem of minority student underachievement are to be found in the low status of the subordinated group in the wider society (as Glenn appears to do), then surely one would acknowledge that a significant rationale for promoting students' primary language in school through bilingual education is to challenge this subordinated status and the coercive power relations that gave rise to it. The evidence is overwhelming that strong promotion of literacy in the primary language will result in no adverse consequences for literacy in English (provided there is also an equally strong program for literacy promotion in English which any well-implemented bilingual program will have). Promotion of literacy in the L1 for subordinated group students is obviously not by itself a total solution, but it can certainly make an important contribution to academic achievement for many bilingual students.

Conclusion

I have suggested that when the adversarial screen of courtroom discourse is lifted, there is actually much that advocates and opponents of bilingual education can agree on. Opponents consistently acknowledge the value of bilingualism and their endorsement of dual immersion or two-way bilingual programs ranges from implicit in the case of Rossell (through citing considerably more U.S. examples of successful dual immersion programs than successful structured immersion programs) to explicit and enthusiastic in the case of Porter and Baker. Glenn is also clearly a strong advocate of using bilingual education to develop students' bilingualism, although highly critical of the way in which many bilingual education programs in the United States have been implemented (as are virtually all academic advocates of bilingual education – see, for example, Krashen, 1996; Wong Fillmore, 1992).

The challenge for opponents and advocates is to create an ideological space to collaborate in planning quality programs for bilingual students in view of the fact that (a) there appears to be consensus on the desirability of promoting students' individual bilingualism (and the linguistic resources of the nation) and (b) as acknowledged by Rossell in her analysis of the Ramirez report, there is clear evidence in virtually all the research data (reviewed by Rossell and Baker and many others) that promotion of bilingual students' primary language, in itself, will not in any way impede the development of English academic proficiency.

Working together to disseminate information on the effectiveness of two-way bilingual immersion programs, as advocated by Porter, would be a good place to start. Another initiative would be to defuse the acrimony regarding the language of instruction issue by acknowledging that the deep structure of interactions between educators and students is a primary determinant of students' academic engagement or withdrawal; these interactions are much more likely to be effective in promoting student engagement when they challenge explicitly the low status that has been assigned to the subordinated group in the wider society (as implied by Glenn's analysis). Instructional models that explicitly challenge what Glenn terms the "demoralized underclass" status of the group are likely to vary with respect to the amount of L1 and L2 instruction depending on the context, parental wishes, and the availability of bilingual teachers; but all will have in common a deep structure that affirms the value of students' cultural and linguistic identity and offers students opportunities to develop powerful intellectual and linguistic tools to act on the social realities that affect their lives.

Footnotes

1. In support of these principles, I will cite primarily my own empirical research studies since the claim has been made by Christine Rossell that I have carried out virtually no research in support of the theoretical principles I have advanced. This claim was made in a presentation at the California State Department of Education, January 13, 1996. Her exact words are as follows:

> By the way, I often hear people talk about Jim Cummins' research. Jim Cummins doesn't do research on bilingual education. He has not done a single study of bilingual education. He has done one study of how long it takes kids to learn a second language. That's it. That study can tell you nothing about what language they should be taught in while they're learning the second language. So he doesn't do research.

> Nevertheless, he does do theories. And his theory that he came up with to try and reconcile these findings – that transitional bilingual education was not superior and often was inferior to doing nothing, not even getting any help at all - his theory was the facilitation theory. He came up with the facilitation theory. It has two parts, the threshold effect and the interdependence of skills.

> The threshold effect says – I've got it – the reason why some of these programs don't have kids who come out with superior achievement is they weren't taught long enough in their native tongue. It must be that you have to be taught for a long time in your native tongue and you have to reach a threshold in that native tongue before you can be transitioned to English. He did no research to support that. I've read all his research so I can say with full confidence there's not an ounce, and anyone who says "Jim Cummins' research" I simply say show it to me.

Rossell here totally misrepresents the "threshold hypothesis" which was advanced to account for apparently contradictory research data concerning the effects of **bilingualism** (not bilingual education) on cognition. It suggested that the levels of proficiency bilinguals attain in their two languages may act as an intervening variable in mediating the effects of bilingualism on their cognitive functioning. The threshold hypothesis says nothing directly about bilingual education - in fact the term "transitional bilingual education" had scarcely entered the lexicon of public debate when the threshold hypothesis was first advanced (Cummins, 1976). It is worth noting that in addition to my own research which is consistent with the notion of "threshold effects" (Cummins, 1974, 1978a, 1978b, Cummins & Mulcahy, 1978) several more recent studies have also supported the notion (e.g. Lasagabaster Herrarte, 1997, in press; Lee & Schallert, 1997; Mohanty, 1994; Ricciardelli, 1992). Particularly interesting is Beykont's (1994) analysis of Site E grades 3-6 longitudinal data from the Ramirez (1992) study which showed that academic progress in English reading was faster for those students whose initial (grade 3) Spanish reading scores were high and slower for those with low initial Spanish reading scores. Beykont also observed a strong relationship between English and Spanish reading at the grade 3 level, a finding predicted by the interdependence hypothesis.

In order to correct the claim that Jim Cummins "doesn't do research," I have asterisked papers in the bibliography that report original research that I have carried out related to bilingualism, bilingual education, and second language learning.

2. Collier's (1987) research among middle-class immigrant students taught exclusively through English in the Fairfax County district suggested that a period of 5-10 years was required for students to catch up. Recent data from the Santa Ana district in California suggest that even longer periods (average 10 years) are required. The Ramirez Report data illustrate the pattern (Ramirez, 1992): after four years of instruction, grade 3 students in both structured immersion (English-only) and early exit bilingual programs were still far from grade norms in English achievement. Grade 6 students in late-exit programs who had consistently received about 40% of their instruction through their primary language were beginning to approach grade norms (see also Beykont, 1994).

3. Rossell and Baker's use of the term "facilitation hypothesis" to describe my theoretical constructs is just one of many distortions in their paper. It permits them, however, to claim that the results of studies such as the large-scale evaluation of programs for minority francophones in Manitoba conducted by Hébert (1976) are contrary to the "facilitation hypothesis" (pp. 28-29). Hébert's study showed that French L1 students taught primarily through French throughout their schooling were doing just as well in English as similar students taught primarily in English. This study not only refutes Rossell and Baker's "time-on-task" principal (as do all of the other evaluations they cite) but it also provides direct support for the interdependence principle. Rossell and Baker, however, argue that it is inconsistent with the "facilitation hypothesis" because the minority students instructed through the minority language did not do **better** in English than those with less instruction through English. Thus, in their version of the "facilitation hypothesis" (which they inaccurately attribute to me) minority students taught through their L1 should always perform better in English than students taught exclusively through English regardless of the conditions or sociocultural context. This is a very different prediction than that which derives from the interdependence hypothesis which is that the transfer of conceptual and

linguistic knowledge across languages can compensate for the significantly reduced instructional time through the majority language. Rossell and Baker's version of the "facilitation hypothesis" makes linguistic and instructional factors independent variables, whose effects can be predicted in isolation, rather than intervening variables whose effects will be significantly influenced by sociocultural and sociopolitical conditions. I have consistently argued (e.g. Cummins, 1979) that linguistic factors cannot be considered in isolation from the social context and Rossell and Baker's inability or unwillingness to acknowledge this is extremely surprising. As articulated above, bilingual programs have considerably more potential to reverse historical patterns of underachievement than monolingual English programs, but whether or not any bilingual program will do so depends on the interaction of a variety of linguistic and non-linguistic factors.

4. The same pattern is reported by Christian et al. (1997) for English L1 students in U.S. two-way immersion programs. They report, for example, that in the River Glen program in San Jose, 60% of the English-L1 students were rated as fluent in Spanish by the end of grade 1 (compared to 100% of the Spanish L1 speakers) but students had bridged the gap by fifth grade where 100% of the English-L1 students were rated as fluent. Students had also caught up to grade norms in Spanish reading by this stage.

5. The lack of credibility of the claims in Rossell and Baker's review (e.g. in comparisons of reading performance in TBE versus Structured Immersion, no difference was found in 17% and TBE was worse in 83%) can be gauged from even a superficial examination of the programs that are being compared. They state that they had to "translate" the French immersion programs into United States terminology. This means labelling as "transitional bilingual education" programs for majority English native language speakers that were 100% minority language (French – students' L2) in kindergarten, and 50% French, 50% English from grades 1-6. "Structured immersion" programs were those that were 100% French (students' L2) from K-grade 1, with English (L1) being gradually increased to 50% between grades 2 and 6. In other words both programs are fully bilingual and are intended to develop bilingualism. Surely it stretches credibility to label as "transitional bilingual education" a program intended for majority rather than minority language speakers and in which there is no transition from one language to another.

If the foregoing appears confusing, consider the fact that two of the evaluations considered to demonstrate the superiority of monolingual English-only structured immersion programs were actually evaluations of **trilingual** programs (Hebrew, French, English) which demonstrated clearly that such programs were highly feasible (Genesee & Lambert, 1983; Genesee et al., 1977).

In reporting the superiority of "monolingual" (structured immersion) programs over "bilingual" (TBE) programs by a spread of 83% to 17%, research ethics might have dictated to many scholars that they inform their readers that 90% of these ten studies demonstrate the effectiveness of certain forms of either bilingual or trilingual education. Furthermore, all the authors of these studies are strong advocates of bilingual and trilingual education on the basis of the research they have carried out.

6. It is worth highlighting an additional point in relation to the Rossell and Baker review. In designating evaluations of many examples of apparently successful bilingual education programs as "methodologically unacceptable," Rossell and Baker rejected all studies that did not compare "students in bilingual education to similar students not in bilingual education" (p. 15) (although as noted above, this criterion was not observed in the comparisons between different forms of French immersion programs, all of which are fully bilingual or trilingual). The designation of only one type of research study as relevant to policy totally ignores the role of theory in understanding what works and what doesn't work. Prediction of the outcomes of any particular program is dependent on which theoretical principles have been supported by research and which have been refuted by research. I have suggested in many publications (e.g. Cummins, 1979, 1981a) that the research clearly refutes both the "time-on-task" hypothesis (what I have termed the "maximum exposure" assumption) and the "linguistic mismatch" hypothesis. The former (endorsed by most opponents of bilingual education) argues that the instructional time spent through English (the majority language) will be directly proportional to achievement in that language. As noted above, the research from all of the evaluations of bilingual education (including French immersion programs in Canada) totally refute this hypothesis. The "linguistic mismatch" hypothesis was invoked by some proponents of bilingual education in order to argue that instruction through a second language would invariably result in academic retardation on the grounds that students could not learn effectively through a language they did not understand. This is also clearly refuted by the research (e.g. the French immersion data). The interdependence hypothesis is, by contrast, supported by virtually all the research data from bilingual programs for both minority and majority language students from around the world.

Let us take a hypothetical example to illustrate the role of theory in policy making decisions. Suppose that dual language or two-way bilingual immersion programs (which usually have between 50% and 90% minority language instruction in the early grades) were to show consistently the pattern that most of those that have been evaluated to this date apparently do show: by grade 6 students from majority language backgrounds in these programs develop high levels of biliteracy skills at no cost to their English (L1) academic development; students from minority language backgrounds by grade 6 show above average Spanish (L1) literacy development and attain or come close to grade norms in English (L2) academic skills. Let us suppose, hypothetically, that we have 100 such programs demonstrating this pattern from around the United States and the few programs that do not demonstrate this pattern can be shown to have been poorly implemented or not to have followed the prescribed model in some important respects. However, none of these programs have acceptable control groups for comparison purposes, if only because they were freely chosen by parents (as is the case for all French immersion programs) whereas students in comparison programs just enrolled in their neighborhood school.

Do these 100 programs demonstrating a consistent pattern of achievement in relation to grade norms tell us anything that is policy relevant? Rossell and Baker say no - this pattern is totally irrelevant to policy decisions regarding the efficacy of any form of bilingual education because no control group is present.

I have argued, by contrast, that such a pattern would be directly relevant to policy because it permits us to test certain theoretical predictions against the research data. The fact that the research data may be from case studies and report students' achievement levels in relation to standard scores is not an impediment to examining the consistency of the data with theoretical predictions. Thus, the hypothetical pattern described for both minority and majority students would clearly refute the "time-on-task" hypothesis because students instructed through the minority language for significant parts of the school day (or as Rossell [1992] has expressed it, experiencing "large deficits" in amount of English language instruction) suffered no adverse effects in English language academic development. These data would also refute the linguistic mismatch hypothesis since majority language students instructed through Spanish experienced no long-term difficulty learning to read through their second language. The data, however, would be consistent with the interdependence hypothesis since transfer of conceptual and linguistic knowledge across languages is clearly implied by the fact that less instructional time through English (for both groups) resulted in no academic deficits in English academic development.

In short, Rossell and Baker's review of research on bilingual education is highly misleading. Not only are 90% of the studies they claim demonstrate the superiority of monolingual English education over bilingual education in fact fully bilingual or trilingual programs, but the premises underlying the review totally obscure the role of theory in policy-making.

References

Baker, K. (1992, Winter/Spring). Review of *Forked Tongue. Bilingual Basics*, pp. 6-7.

Beykont, Z.F. (1994). Academic progress of a nondominant group: A longitudinal study of Puerto Ricans in New York City's late-exit bilingual programs. Doctoral dissertation presented to the Graduate School of Education of Harvard University.

**Carey, S. & Cummins, J. (1984). Communication skills in immersion programs. *Alberta Journal of Educational Research, 30*, 270-283.

**Carey, S. & Cummins, J. (1983). Achievement, behavioral correlates and teachers' perceptions of Francophone and Anglophone immersion students. *Alberta Journal of Educational Research, 8*, 117-138.

Christian, D., Montone, C.L., Lindholm, K.J., & Carranza, I. (1997). *Profiles in two-way immersion education.* Washington, DC: Center for Applied Linguistics and Delta Systems.

Collier, V.P. (1987). Age and rate of acquisition of second language for academic purposes. *TESOL Quarterly, 21,* 617-641.

Corson, D. (1998). *Language policy across the curriculum. Mahwah, NJ: Lawrence Erlbaum Associates.*

**Cummins, J. (1977). A comparison of reading skills in Irish and English medium schools. In V. Greaney (Ed.) *Studies in reading.* (pp. 128-134). Dublin: Educational Co. of Ireland, 1977. Reprinted in *Oideas,* 1982, *26,* pp. 21-26.

**Cummins, J. (1978a). Bilingualism and the development of metalinguistic awareness. *Journal of Cross-Cultural Psychology, 9*, 131-149.

**Cummins, J. (1978b). Metalinguistic development of children in bilingual education programs: Data from Irish and Canadian (Ukrainian-English) programs. In M. Paradis (Ed.) *Aspects of bilingualism.* (pp. 127- 138). Columbia, S.C.: Hornbeam Press.

**Cummins, J. (1978c). Immersion programmes: The Irish experience. *International Review of Education, 24,* 273-282.

**Cummins, J. (1980). Psychological assessment of immigrant children: Logic or intuition*? Journal of Multilingual and Multicultural Development, 1,* 97-111.

Cummins, J. (1981a). The role of primary language development in promoting educational success for language minority students. In California State Department of Education (Ed.), *Schooling and language minority students: A theoretical framework.* (pp. 3-49). Los Angeles: National Dissemination and Assessment Center.

**Cummins, J. (1981b). Age on arrival and immigrant second language learning in Canada. A reassessment. *Applied Linguistics, 2,* 132-149.

**Cummins, J. (1983). *Policy report: Language and literacy learning in bilingual instruction.* Austin, Texas: Southwest Educational Development Laboratory.

Cummins, J. (1984). *Bilingualism and special education: Issues in assessment and pedagogy.* Clevedon England: Multilingual Matters.

Cummins, J. (1986). Empowering minority students: A framework for intervention. *Harvard Educational Review,* 56, 18-36.

**Cummins, J. (1991a). The development of bilingual proficiency from home to school: A longitudinal study of Portuguese-speaking children. *Journal of Education, 173,* 85-98.

Cummins, J. (1991b). Interdependence of first- and second-language proficiency in bilingual children. In E. Bialystok (Ed.) *Language processing in bilingual children.* (pp. 70-89). Cambridge: Cambridge University Press.

Cummins, J. (1996). *Negotiating identities: Education for empowerment in a diverse society.* Los Angeles: California Association for Bilingual Education.

Cummins, J. & Corson, D. (Eds.). (1998). *Bilingual education.* Dordrecht, The Netherlands: Kluwer Academic Publishers.

**Cummins, J. & Gulutsan, M. (1974). Bilingual education and cognition. *The Alberta Journal of Educational Research, 20,* 259-269.

**Cummins, J., Harley, B., Swain, M., Allen, P. (1990). Social and individual factors in the development of bilingual proficiency. In B. Harley, P. Allen, J. Cummins, & M. Swain (Eds.) *The development of second language proficiency.* (pp. 119-133). Cambridge: Cambridge University Press.

**Cummins, J. & Mulcahy, R. (1978). Orientation to language in Ukrainian-English bilinguals. *Child Development, 49,* 479-482.

Cummins, J. & Sayers, D. (1995). Brave new schools Challenging cultural illiteracy through global learning networks. New York: St. Martin's Press.

**Cummins, J., M. Swain, K. Nakajima, J. Handscombe, D. Green and C. Tran. (1984). Linguistic interdependence among Japanese immigrant students. In C. Rivera (Ed.)

Communicative competence approaches to language proficiency assessment: Research and application. (pp. 60-81). Clevedon, Avon: Multilingual Matters.

Dolson, D. (1985). The effects of Spanish home language use on the scholastic performance of Hispanic pupils. *Journal of Multilingual and Multicultural Development, 6,* 135-156.

Dolson, D. & Lindholm, K. (1995). World class education for children in California: A comparison of the two-way bilingual immersion and European Schools model. In T. Skutnabb-Kangas (Ed.) *Multilingualism for all.* (pp. 69-102). Lisse: Swets & Zeitlinger.

El Paso Independent School District (1987). *Interim report of the five-year bilingual education pilot 1986-87 school year.* El Paso, Tx: Office for Research and Evaluation.

El Paso Independent School District (1992). *Bilingual education evaluation.* El Paso, Tx: Office for Research and Evaluation.

Fitzgerald, J. (1995). English-as-a-second-language learners' cognitive reading processes: A review of research in the United States. *Review of Educational Research, 65,* 145-190.

Gabina, J.J. et al. (1986). EIFE. Influence of factors on the learning of Basque. Gasteiz: Central Publications Service of the Basque Country.

Genesee, F. (1979). Acquisition of reading skills in immersion programs. *Foreign Language Annals, 12,* 71-77.

Genesee, F., & Lambert, W. (1983). Trilingual education for majority-language children. *Child Development, 54,* 105-114.

Genesee, F., Lambert, W., & Tucker, G.

(1977). *An experiment in trilingual education.* Montreal: McGill University.

Gersten, R. (1985). Structured immersion for language minority students: Results of a longitudinal evaluation. *Educational Evaluation and Policy Analysis, 7,* 187-196.

Glenn, C.L. (1997). *What does the National Research Council study tell us about educating language minority children?* Washington, DC: The READ Institute.

Hébert, R. et al. (1976). *Academic achievement, language of instruction, and the Franco-Manitoban student.* Winnipeg: Centre de Recherches, Collège Universitaire de Saint Boniface.

Krashen, S.D. (1996). *Under attack: The case against bilingual education.* Culver City, CA: Language Education Associates.

Lambert, W.E. & Tucker, G.R. (1972). *Bilingual education of children: The St. Lambert Experiment.* Rowley, Mass.: Newbury House.

**Lapkin, S. & Cummins, J. (1981). Evaluation of the Frontenac-Lennox and Addington Roman Catholic Separate School Board grades five and six bilingual program, Year 2. Toronto: Research report, OISE.

Lasagabaster Herrarte, D. (1997). *Creatividad conciencia metalinguistica: Incidencia en el aprendizaje del Ingles como L3.* Doctoral dissertation. Universidad del Pais Vasco/Euskal Herriko Unibertsitatea.

Lasagabaster Herrarte, D. (in press). The threshold hypothesis applied to three languages in contact at school. *International Journal of Bilingual Education and Bilingualism, 1.*

Lee, J-W, & Schallert, D.L. (1997). The relative contribution of L2 language proficiency and L1 reading ability to L2 reading performance: A test of the threshold hypothesis in an EFL context. *TESOL Quarterly*, 31, 713-739.

Legaretta, D. (1979). The effects of program models on language acquisition by Spanish speaking children. *TESOL Quarterly, 13*, 521-534.

Mohanty, A.K. (1994). *Bilingualism in a multilingual society: Psychological and pedagogical implications*. Mysore: Central Institute of Indian Languages.

National Research Council. (1997). *Improving schooling for language minority children: A research agenda.* Washington, DC: National Academy Press.

Ogbu, J. (1978). *Minority education and caste*. New York: Academic Press.

Pena-Hughes, E. & Solis, J. (1980). *ABCs* (unpublished report). McAllen, TX: McAllen Independent School District.

Porter, R. P. (1990). *Forked tongue: The politics of bilingual education*. New York: Basic Books.

Ramirez, J.D. (1992). Executive summary. *Bilingual Research Journal*, 16, 1-62.

Ricciardelli, L. (1992). Bilingualism and cognitive development in relation to threshold theory. *Journal of Psycholinguistic Research*, 21, 301-316.

Rossell, C.H. (1996). Letters from readers (reply to critiques from Kathy Escamilla, & Susan Dicker). *Research in the Teaching of English, 30*, 376-385.

Sierra, J. & Olaziregi, I. (1989*). EIFE 2. Influence of factors on the learning of Basque*. Gasteiz: Central Publications Service of the Basque Country.

Sierra, J. & Olaziregi, I. (1991). *EIFE 3. Influence of factors on the learning of Basque. Study of the models A, B and D in second year Basic General Education.* Gasteiz: Central Publications Service of the Basque Country.

Swain, M. (1978). French immersion: Early, late, or partial? *Canadian Modern Language Review,* 34, 577-585.

Rossell, C.H. & Baker, K. (1996). The effectiveness of bilingual education. *Research in the Teaching of English, 30,* 7-74.

Swain, M. & Lapkin, S. (1982). *Evaluating bilingual education*. Clevedon, England: Multilingual Matters.

University of California Linguistic Minority Research Institute Education Policy Center. (1997). *Review of research on instruction of limited English proficient students*. Davis: University of California Davis.

Willig, A.C. (1981/82). The effectiveness of bilingual education: Review of a report. *NABE Journal, 6*, 1-19.

Wong Fillmore, L. (1992). Against our best interest: The attempt to sabotage bilingual education. In J. Crawford (Ed.), *Language loyalties: A sourcebook on the Official English controversy*. Chicago: University of Chicago Press.

A

Aardema, Verna, 85
academic achievement: low-income families and, 144–147; learning a second language and, 17, 18, 19
academic content, bilingual education and, 177–180
academic language proficiency, components of, 96
accountability, as purpose of assessment, 120
African-Americans, Ebonics and, 199–203
alternative assessment methods, 116–118, 119–124, 129–141
Americanization, of Hispanic children, 158–159
analysis, academic language proficiency and, 96
anecdotal records, as alternative assessment method, 134, 135, 138
application, as cognitive process, 96
artifacts, in portfolio assessment, 125, 127
assessment: alternative methods of, 116–118, 119–124, 129–141; of integrated language and content instruction, 129–141
assimilation forces, influence of, on language development, 35, 42
attestations, in portfolio assessment, 126, 127
attitudes, in integrated language and content assessment, 133–141
auditability, of assessment instruments, 117
authentic assessment, 116, 119–124, 130, 131
author-illustrator studies, multicultural children's literature and, 85

B

Baker, Keith, 212, 213, 216, 218, 219, 220–221
basic-interpersonal communication skills (BICS), 109
Bishop, Rudine Sims, 87
bodily/kinesthetic intelligence, 103–107
book publishing, teaching language arts and, 68–69
Bradley, Bill, 203
Browne, Vee, 85
Buchanan, Pat, 8
buddy journals, writing skills instruction and, 71–75
Bureau of Indian Affairs, 41
Bush, George, 45

C

Cambodian youth, as refugees, 48–52
Cameron, Anne, 85
caring classroom, bilingual education and, 33–34
Cartwright, William, 202
Chamot, Ana, 99

Chavez, Linda, 8, 156, 159
Chipewyan language, disappearance of, 41–42
Clinton, Bill, 154
Cognitive Academic and Language Learning Approach (CALLA), 99–102
cognitive academic linguistic proficiency (CALP), 109
cognitive development, learning a second language and, 17, 19
communication skills, in integrated language and content assessment, 133–141
comprehension, as cognitive process, 96
common underlying proficiency (CUP), bilingual education and, 206–207
concept comprehension, in integrated language and content assessment, 133–141
conceptual-linguistic knowledge, language proficiency and, 95
constructed response, in performance-based assessment, 121
content ESL, assessment of, 129–141
contextual support, language proficiency and, 97
contextualized assessment, 116
cooperation, as learning strategy, 100, 130, 178
counseling, of Vietnamese youth, 50
credibility, of assessment instruments, 117
Crews, Donald, 85
crime, youth gangs and, 49
Cucelogu, Dogan, 52
culture, classroom, language arts instruction and, 67–68
Culture and Power (Darder), 144
Curriculum and Evaluation Standards for School Mathematics (National Council of Teachers of Mathematics), 130–131

D

Darder, Antonia, 11, 144
Day, Frances Ann, 87
Delacre, Lulu, 84
demographics, Hispanic Americans and, 153–162
depth vs. breadth, in performance-based assessment, 122
Dewey, John, 76
dialect, Ebonics as, 199–203
dialogue journals, writing skills instruction and, 71–75
discourse, language acquisition and, 17
discovery learning, 19
discussion groups, Internet search engines for, 195
dual immersion, 212
dual language programs, 173–176

E

early childhood education, for linguistic and culturally diverse students, 22–29, 153–162
early exit approach, to bilingual education, 129, 172
Eastman plan, 182
Ebonics, 199–203
electronic mail-based discussion groups, Internet, 195
empowerment, of Mexican immigrants, 56–61
English as a Second Language (ESL), definition of, 172
English First, 153
English, teaching reading of, 34–35
English to Speakers of Other Languages (ESOL) Instruction, definition of, 172
English-only movement, 10, 18, 42
Ericksen, Robert, 52
evaluation, academic language proficiency and, 96
exhibition, assessment by, 116
exit, as purpose of assessment, 120

F

facilitation hypothesis, bilingual education and, 218–219
Forked Tongue (Porter), 213
Foster, Michele, 201–202
full-text Internet search tools, 194
functional meaning, academic language proficiency and, 96

G

gambling casinos, Native Americans and, 45
gangs, youth, 49
Gardner, Howard, 12, 103–107
Garza, Carmen Lomas, 85
genre approach, to multicultural children's literature, 84–85
Glenn, Charles, 212, 214–216
Goodman, Kenneth, 196
gradual exit model, for limited English proficient children, 181–185
Gramci, Antonio, 10
grammar, language acquisition and, 17, 18, 96
Grant, Ulysses S., 42
Greenfield, Eloise, 84
group behavior, in integrated language and content assessment, 133–141

H

Haitian students, use of learning strategies of, 99–102
Hamilton, Virginia, 85
Harris, Violet, 87

Hayes, Joe, 85
Head Start, 23
Heath, Shirley, 201
Heilman, John, 197
higher-order thinking skills, authentic assessment and, 119–124
Hispanic children, early childhood education and, 153–162
Hmong youth, as refugees, 48–52
hooks, bell, 13
hotseating, reading instruction and, 76–80
Hunger of Memory (Rodriguez), 156
Huron language, disappearance of, 41

I

identity, bilingual education and, 13–14
immersion method, of language learning, 81–83, 173–176, 208, 209, 210–212; definition of, 172
immigrants, 70, 71, 77, 81, 126; Mexican, resilience and empowerment of, 56–61
individual behavior, in integrated language and content assessment, 133–141
individuals, Internet search engines for locating, 195
informal assessment, 116
input hypothesis, 181
integrated language and content instruction, assessment of, 129–141
integrated language learning, 64–70
integrated schooling, 20
integrative, performance-based assessment as, 122
intelligence testing, of bilingual students, 14–15, 36
intelligences, multiple, Gardner's theory of, 12, 103–107
Intercultural Development Research Association (IDRA), 92
interdependence hypothesis, bilingual education and, 218–219
international English, 200
International Reading Association, 156, 160
Internet. *See* World Wide Web
interpersonal communication skills, components of, 96
interpersonal intelligence, 103–107
intrapersonal intelligence, 103–107
Isleta language, disappearance of, 43–44
issues approach, to multicultural children's literature, 86–87

J

Johnston, Tony, 86
Joiner, Charles W., 202
journals, buddy, writing skills instruction and, 71–75

K

Kellogg, Steven, 85
Kira, Michael, 197
knowledge, as cognitive process, 96
Krauss, Michael, 41

L

language arts: multicultural children's literature and, 85–89. *See also* oral language; reading; writing skills
language-sensitive content instruction, assessment of, 129–141
Laotian youth, as refugees, 48–52
late-exit approach, to bilingual education, 82, 172, 182–183, 218
Lau v. Nichols, 16, 172
learning disabilities, language-minority students and, 94
learning strategies, for ESL students, 19, 99–102
leveling, 159
linguistic mismatch assumption, 207, 214, 220
listening skills, as learning strategy, 99
Literature as Exploration (Rosenblatt), 79
literature, multicultural children's, 85–89
Lobel, Arnold, 85
logical/mathematical intelligence, 103–107
low-income families, academic achievement and, 144–147

M

maintenance bilingual programs, 172
Martinez, Alejandro Cruz, 85
mathematical intelligence, 103–107
mathematics, teaching of, 58–59, 92–93, 130–131, 137
maximum exposure hypothesis, bilingual education and, 220
McLeod, Beverly, 146
Menominee language, disappearance of, 42, 46
"meta" search engines, Internet, 194–195
Mexican-American children, preschool, 163–167
Mexico, resilience and empowerment of immigrants from, 56–61
middle schools, language minority students in, 177–180
monitoring student progress, as purpose of assessment, 120, 121
morphology, language acquisition and, 17, 18
multicultural education, 12, 163
multiple intelligences, Gardner's theory of, 12, 103–107
multiple-choice tests, 119, 121, 130
musical intelligence, 103–107

N

National Association for the Education of Young Children (NAEYC), 158, 160–161; position statement of, on early childhood education for linguistically and culturally diverse students, 22–29
National Council of Teachers of English, 156, 160
national language policy, 202–203
Native Americans: culture of, vs. American education system, 53–55; disappearances of languages of, 40–47
North American Free Trade Agreement (NAFTA), 60

O

objectivity, of alternative assessment procedure, 116–118
Ogwehowe:ka? language, preservation of, 44
O'Malley, J. Michael, 99
oral language, strategies to develop, 34, 64–70
Out of the Barrio (Chavez), 156

P

paralinguistics, language acquisition and, 17
paraprofessionals, use of, in bilingual education, 184
parents: and early childhood education, 25–26; involvement of, in bilingual education, 144–147, 148–152, 163–167, 178; learning strategy instruction and, 101–102
peer language models, immersion programs and, 175
performance-based assessment, 116, 121–122, 134–135
phonology, language acquisition and, 17, 18
placement, as purpose of assessment, 120
Pol Pot, 50–51
Polacco, Patricia, 85, 86
Porter, Rosalie Pedalino, 212, 213, 216
portfolio assessment, 116, 122, 125–128, 131, 132, 133–141
post-traumatic stress disorder, refugees and, 50–51
poverty, Hispanics and, 158
pragmatics, language acquisition and, 17, 18
privacy issues, Internet and, 195
problem solving, in integrated language and content assessment, 133–141
process and product, in performance-based assessment, 122
productions, in portfolio assessment, 126
program evaluation, as purpose of assessment, 120, 121

pull-out ESL, 183–184

qualitative research, alternative assessment and, 117–118
quick-exit approach, to bilingual education, 82

Ramirez, Gonzalo and Janet Lee, 87
reading and writing inventories, as alternative assessment method, 134
reading hypothesis, 181
reading instruction, in bilingual education, 34–35, 64–70, 76–80, 130. *See also* literature
Reagan, Ronald, 156
reclassification, as purpose of assessment, 120
refugees, education of East Asian, 48–52
reliability, of alternative assessment procedures, 116–118
reproductions, in portfolio assessment, 126
resilience, of Mexican immigrants, 56–61
resistance politics, 8
Riley, Richard, 154
Ringgold, Faith, 85, 86
Rodriguez, Richard, 144, 156
Rosenblatt, Louise, 79

San Souci, Robert, 85
Say, Allen, 85
science instruction, project approach to, 92–93
screening and identification, as purpose of assessment, 120
search tools Internet, 193–159
self-assessment, student, 122, 134, 136, 137
semantics, language acquisition and, 17, 18, 96
sheltered English, 129, 172, 181
situated assessment, 116
skill and concept checklist, as alternative assessment method, 134, 135–136
Smith, Frank, 196

Smitherman, Geneva, 203
Sneeve, Virginia Driving Hawk, 84, 86–87
social studies instruction, use of videos in, 108–113
sociocultural processes, in learning a second language, 16–17, 19
Spanish, teaching reading of, 34–35
Spanish as a Second Language (SSL), 31
spatial/visual intelligence, 103–107
speech and language disabilities, language-minority students and, 94
speech-print connection, 66
Spencer, Paula Underwood, 85
standard English, 200
standardized testing, 116, 119, 121, 130
structured immersion, definition of, 172, 219
subject-oriented Internet search tools, 194
submersion, definition of, 172, 183–184
Successful Texas Schoolwide Programs (Charles A. Dana Center), 144–147
summaries, as learning strategy, 100
surface fluency, language proficiency and, 95, 96
Swain, Melinda, 92
syntax, language acquisition and, 17, 18
synthesis, academic language proficiency and, 96

Tannen, Deborah, 201
technology: and project approach to math and science instruction, 92–93; and use of videos in social studies instruction, 108–113
testing: intelligence, of bilingual students, 14–15, 36; standardized, 116, 119, 121, 130. *See also* assessment
thematic approach, to learning, 19, 67, 85–86
thinking skills, higher-order, authentic assessment and, 119–124
Thompson, Vivian, 85
threshold hypothesis, 217
time-on-task principle, immersion programs and, 210, 218, 220
transitional bilingual programs, 172, 209

triangulation, alternative assessment and, 117–118
trilingual programs, 219
trustworthiness, of assessment instruments, 117
two-way developmental bilingual programs, 212; definition of, 172

USENET newsgroup–based discussion groups, 195

validity, of alternative assessment procedure, 116–118
Van Manen, Max, 163
variable threshold model, for limited English proficient children, 181–185
verbal/linguistic intelligence, 103–107
videos, use of, in social studies instruction, 108–113
Vietnamese youth: as refugees, 48–52; use of learning strategies by, 99–102
"Visit Home, The" (Leyson), use of, in reading instruction, 71–75
visual/spatial intelligence, 103–107
Vizenor, Erma, 45
vocabulary, language acquisition and, 17, 18, 67, 92, 96, 130, 137
Vygotsky, Lev, 76

Whitethorne, Baje, 85
World Wide Web, use of, as bilingual education resource, 188–192, 193–195
writing skills, teaching of, 64–70, 71–75, 130

Yupik language, preservation of, 46

Zuni language, preservation of, 44

AE Article Review Form

We encourage you to photocopy and use this page as a tool to assess how the articles in **Annual Editions** expand on the information in your textbook. By reflecting on the articles you will gain enhanced text information. You can also access this useful form on a product's book support Web site at **http://www.dushkin.com/online/.**

NAME: _____ DATE: _____

TITLE AND NUMBER OF ARTICLE:
_____

BRIEFLY STATE THE MAIN IDEA OF THIS ARTICLE:
_____

LIST THREE IMPORTANT FACTS THAT THE AUTHOR USES TO SUPPORT THE MAIN IDEA:

_____

WHAT INFORMATION OR IDEAS DISCUSSED IN THIS ARTICLE ARE ALSO DISCUSSED IN YOUR TEXTBOOK OR OTHER READINGS THAT YOU HAVE DONE? LIST THE TEXTBOOK CHAPTERS AND PAGE NUMBERS:

_____

LIST ANY EXAMPLES OF BIAS OR FAULTY REASONING THAT YOU FOUND IN THE ARTICLE:

_____

LIST ANY NEW TERMS/CONCEPTS THAT WERE DISCUSSED IN THE ARTICLE, AND WRITE A SHORT DEFINITION:

_____

ANNUAL EDITIONS revisions depend on two major opinion sources: one is our Advisory Board, listed in the front of this volume, which works with us in scanning the thousands of articles published in the public press each year; the other is you—the person actually using the book. Please help us and the users of the next edition by completing the prepaid article rating form on this page and returning it to us. Thank you for your help!

ANNUAL EDITIONS: Teaching English as a Second Language 99/00

ARTICLE RATING FORM

Here is an opportunity for you to have direct input into the next revision of this volume. We would like you to rate each of the 35 articles listed below, using the following scale:

1. Excellent: should definitely be retained
2. Above average: should probably be retained
3. Below average: should probably be deleted
4. Poor: should definitely be deleted

Your ratings will play a vital part in the next revision. So please mail this prepaid form to us just as soon as you complete it. Thanks for your help!

We Want Your Advice

RATING

ARTICLE

1. Bilingual Education and the Politics of Teacher Preparation
2. Acquiring a Second Language for School
3. NAEYC Position Statement: Responding to Linguistic and Cultural Diversity—Recommendations for Effective Early Childhood Education
4. Factors Affecting Language Development from the Perspectives of Four Bilingual Teachers
5. The Disappearance of American Indian Languages
6. Between Two Worlds: Refugee Youth
7. An Indian Father's Plea
8. Mexican Immigrants from El Rincón: A Case Study of Resilience and Empowerment
9. Reading and Writing Pathways to Conversation in the ESL Classroom
10. Buddy Journals for ESL and Native-English-Speaking Students
11. Entering the Fictive World: Enhancing the Reading Experience
12. Literacy Instruction for Students Acquiring English: Moving beyond the Immersion Debate
13. Multicultural Children's Literature: Canon of the Future
14. Effective Math and Science Instruction—The Project Approach for LEP Students
15. Below the Tip of the Iceberg: Teaching Language-Minority Students
16. Learning Strategy Instruction in the Bilingual/ESL Classroom
17. Teaching and Learning Languages through Multiple Intelligences

RATING

ARTICLE

18. The Social Studies Video Project: A Holistic Approach for Teaching Linguistically and Culturally Diverse Students
19. Alternative Assessment: Responses to Commonly Asked Questions
20. Moving toward Authentic Assessment
21. Portfolio Assessment in Second Language Teacher Education
22. Assessing Integrated Language and Content Instruction
23. Low Income Does Not Cause Low School Achievement: Creating a Sense of Family and Respect in the School Environment
24. Parents as First Teachers: Creating an Enriched Home Learning Environment
25. The Education of Hispanics in Early Childhood: Of Roots and Wings
26. Attending to New Voices
27. Language-Minority Student Achievement and Program Effectiveness
28. Two Languages Are Better than One
29. School Reform and Student Diversity
30. A Gradual Exit, Variable Threshold Model for Limited English Proficient Children
31. Cruising the Web with English Language Learners
32. Confronting an Embarrassment of Riches: Internet Search Tools
33. The Case for Bilingual Education
34. What's New in Ebonics?
35. Beyond Adversarial Discourse: Searching for Common Ground in the Education of Bilingual Students

(Continued on next page)

ABOUT YOU

Name   Date

Are you a teacher? ☐   A student? ☐
Your school's name

Department

Address   City   State   Zip

School telephone #

YOUR COMMENTS ARE IMPORTANT TO US !

Please fill in the following information:
For which course did you use this book?

Did you use a text with this *ANNUAL EDITION*? ☐ yes ☐ no
What was the title of the text?

What are your general reactions to the *Annual Editions* concept?

Have you read any particular articles recently that you think should be included in the next edition?

Are there any articles you feel should be replaced in the next edition? Why?

Are there any World Wide Web sites you feel should be included in the next edition? Please annotate.

May we contact you for editorial input? ☐ yes ☐ no
May we quote your comments? ☐ yes ☐ no